The Best of

HAWAII

Editor
Jim Burns

Contributing Editors
Colleen Dunn Bates, Jeanette Foster,
Rick Gaffney, Wayne Harada, Sandra Rosenberg,
Merrill Shindler, Stuart Silverman, Deborah Sroloff

Associate Editor
Catherine Jordan

Additional editorial assistance
Lynn Chang, Nicky J. Leach, Jan Trojan

Prentice Hall Press Editor
Amit Shah

Operations
Alain Gayot

Directed by
André Gayot

**PRENTICE
HALL
PRESS**

New York ■ London ■ Toronto ■ Sydney ■ Tokyo ■ Singapore

*Other Gault Millau Guides Available
from Prentice Hall Press*

The Best of Chicago
The Best of France
The Best of Hong Kong
The Best of Italy
The Best of London
The Best of Los Angeles
The Best of New England
The Best of New Orleans
The Best of New York
The Best of Paris
The Best of San Francisco
The Best of Washington, D.C.

PRENTICE HALL PRESS and colophons
are registered trademarks of Simon & Schuster Inc.

 Published by Prentice Hall Press
A division of Simon & Schuster Inc.
15 Columbus Circle
New York, NY 10023

Please address all comments regarding
The Best of Hawaii to:
Gault Millau, Inc.
P.O. Box 361144
Los Angeles, CA 90036
(213) 965-3529

Please address all advertising queries to:
Mr. Geoffrey Gropp, Vice President
Welsh Publishing Group, Inc.
300 Madison Avenue
New York, NY 10017
(212) 687-0680

Library of Congress Cataloging-in-Publication Data
The Best of Hawaii / [editor, Jim Burns ; contributing editors,
Colleen Dunn Bates . . . et. al.].
  p.   c.m.
  ISBN 0-13-084062-9 : $16.95
  1. Hawaii—Description and travel —1981- —Guide-books.
I. Burns, Jim, 1952- . II. Bates, Colleen Dunn.
DU622.B47 1990
919.6904'4—dc20   90-7097

Special thanks to the staff of Prentice Hall Press for
their invaluable aid in producing these Gault Millau guides.
Manufactured in the United States of America

CONTENTS

A DISCLAIMER

Readers are advised that prices and conditions change over the course of time. The restaurants, hotels, shops and other establishments reviewed in this book have been reviewed over a period of time, and the reviews reflect the personal experiences of the reviewers. The reviewers and publishers cannot be held responsible for the experiences of the reader related to the establishments reviewed. Readers are invited to write the publisher with ideas, comments and suggestions for future editions.

INTRODUCTION

A PLUGGED-IN PARADISE

If Elvis were still around, he'd be singing about "New Hawaii" instead of "Blue Hawaii." It can be argued that the beginning of what we call "New Hawaii" can be traced to one man, who drove around Honolulu's ritzy Makaha area in a white limousine, buying up residential properties with the point of a finger—not unlike a financial Merlin. The man was Japanese financier Genshiro Kawamoto, his magic wand was the all-powerful yen and the year was 1988. The fact that Kawamoto was there at all shows the incredible magnetism of the Islands, a lure that is worth millions in tourist dollars each year. The yen has settled down since then, but the surging Hawaiian economy hasn't. What you'll find in this book is our first critical look at the evolving bric-a-brac of a trans-Island culture.

When envisioning "New Hawaii," it helps to remember that just 31 years ago, when Hawaii became a state, its economy was based on agriculture. Plodding ships brought in tourists by the dozens until the year 1959, when the first Boeing 707s crossed the Pacific to Honolulu. That banner year 243,000 people visited the Hawaiian Islands; today, of course, thousands arrive by the planeload daily. Twenty years ago, television broadcasts from the mainland were delayed for anywhere from 24 hours to an entire week, which was great for betting on sports but not much else. Now everything is simultaneous, and so much the better. Even surrounded by all of that water, Hawaii is connected, and has connections.

What kind of a place is this "New Hawaii"? Is it really the cloudless utopia that travel posters would have us believe? Well, yes and no. If you leave Chicago on Christmas week for a vacation on the Big Island, the answer will be a resounding "yes." The weather is perhaps the best in the world. But if you're thinking of buying a vacation villa in Honolulu, be ready to pay the highest median price in the United States: $238,000 at the time of this writing. This means that many of those who live in paradise can feel materially estranged from it as well. Not everyone can "buy a house to keep a change of clothes in," which was the reason Kawamoto gave for his purchase (he actually bought 120 homes, including a beachfront estate that, alone, cost $40 million). If you plan to spend a majority of your time "power-lounging" on the beach or engaging in water sports, the answer, again, is a resounding "yes." There are 280 beaches in the state, abounding with pristine spots for scuba-diving, snorkeling, deep-sea fishing, windsurfing, parasailing, waterskiing and, of course, the favored Island sport, surfing. If you rent a car, however, the traffic jams might seem something less than paradisiacal.

What we like to do on vacation is eat well, nosh, stay in marvelous hotels, do some dancing, buy a few dozen presents for Mom and see the sights. Part of the newness of Hawaii is the upturn in its cooking. For years, many Island restaurants and hotels seemed to function according to the "captive audience" theory: why improve, because where else are guests going to go for a meal? The result was high prices for poorly prepared, uninspired fare. Although you can still pay a small fortune for a mediocre dining experience in Hawaii, there are many examples of innovative, technically well prepared meals, created with fresh, local ingredients. There's also the chance to drink your fill of America's only native coffee (from Kona), eat some expensive macadamia nuts (which, for years, were unshellable), delight in consuming a fresh pineapple (what a difference!), and learn that mahimahi has other equally delectable finned friends with equally lilting appelations. As for noshing, don't forget to try saimin (a noodle dish with vegetables, pork and fish cakes) for lunch. The luau can be your first experience of kalua pig roasted in a classic *imu* pit. But choose wisely: some luaus are nothing more than a degrading commercialization of Hawaii's indigenous culture.

On the hotel front, we only wish that we could keep up with the new construction. For example, by fall 1992, 7,000 more rooms will be ready in the Ko Olina resort area on Oahu's leeward side. As we go to press, the luxe Prince is about to open in Waikiki; ditto for the Four Seasons in Maui and the Ritz-Carlton on the Big Island. Waikiki itself, along with many of the hotel operators there, recently spent millions to spiff up its tired Las Vegas/Pacifica image, and you'll notice the difference, right down to the police substation near the beach. The Hilton Hawaiian Village was renovated to the tune of $100 million, while the Hyatt Regency Waikiki spent $35 million. If you want to disco all night on Maui, you can; or if you dream of isolating yourself in luxury on Lanai, that's possible, too. There are fantasy resorts, condominiums, weekly hotels, bed-and-breakfasts, even remote outposts in the mountains of Kauai or in the Big Island's Waipio Valley—any sort of accommodation you can imagine is available somewhere on the Islands.

Nor has it escaped those in charge of truly high-end fashion that Honolulu is ripe for their wares. Consider the figures: the typical westbound visitor (read American or Canadian) spends $200 to $300 a day, while the average eastbound visitor (read Japanese) visitor shells out $700 to $750 a day. So who can't afford a new ensemble? A few dozen alligator handbags? An Imelda Marcos–size shoe collection? The second level of the Ala Moana Shopping Center is beginning to resemble a Park Avenue or a Rodeo Drive. If you thought that shopping in Hawaii meant picking up a few puka shells—which, incidentally, you still can get at Woolworth's—look out for the likes of Chanel, Vuitton and Versace.

New Hawaii's greatest resource is its diversity—of cultures, of lifestyles, of languages and of ideas. And it's that exciting blend of potpourri that our team of French, mainland and local critics has enjoyed exploring and mapping out for you. You might not always agree with us. But know that every effort has been put into this guidebook to make it useful, fair, accurate and honorable. You deserve no less. Neither does budding "New Hawaii," a paradise with connections.

AN ISLANDER'S GUIDE TO HAWAIIAN & PIDGIN

Although everyone in Hawaii speaks some form of English, it helps to know how to pronounce a few of the more common Hawaiian words, since they are generously sprinkled in the vocabulary. The Hawaiian alphabet consists of only twelve letters: five vowels: a, e, i, o, u, and seven consonants: h, k, l, m, n, p, w. Every syllable ends in a vowel and every vowel is pronounced. Pronunciation of vowels is similar to Spanish, and the accent often occurs on the next-to-last syllable.

Traditional Hawaiian orthography would require that the hundreds upon hundreds of place names in this book be written with the proper diacritics to indicate pronunciation: a reverse apostrophe for the glottal stop (such as Hawai'i), a macron over vowels that are long and stressed (such as Pua-kō or Nēnē-hānau-pō) and hyphens or spaces separating individual words that make up many names (such as Makuahine-me-ke-kaikamahine, which translates literally as "mother and the daughter." However, to go with the traditional pronunciations would have created visual and mental havoc for most non-Hawaiian-speaking readers, so we've left all place names simply written, without diacritics. Visitors are just lucky that most Hawaiians speak English, or they'd spend most of their vacation time in rabid frustration, trying to determine the real meaning of

A PRIMER ON PIDGIN

Pidgin originated when people from many different ethnic groups (Chinese, Japanese, Filipino, Portuguese) arrived in Hawaii to work the sugarcane. The most common phrase is "da kine" (the "i" is a long vowel), which can mean almost anything. Other key pidgin phrases:

"Broke da mouf" - Delicious!
"Fo' real" - Really?; You can say that again!; I mean it
"Fo' what?" - Why?
"Hey brah" - Hello, brother
"Howzit?" - How is it?
"Stink eye" - Dirty look
"Talk story" - Talk, gossip
"Whatyouwanknow da kine for?" - What do you want to know about it?

Also, make sure you know the shaka sign: a common local greeting, it consists of sticking out your thumb and little finger and twisting your wrist back and forth, as you say "howzit."

words such as *aa*, which could be *a'a* (a small root, vein, nerve or tendon), *'a'a* (to challenge; or the fiber from a coconut husk), *'a'ā* (to burn; or rough lava), or *ā'ā* (to stutter; or a dwarf; or panic-stricken; or a male *'o'o* bird). Feeling faint yet? There's no need to learn much more Hawaiian than the few common terms we've listed on the following page; just take the book and memorize them while you watch the *Napo'o 'ana o ka lā*, or sunset.

ai (*eye*) - eat
ala (*ah-lah*) - road (as in Ala Moana)
alii (*ah-lee-ee*) - old royalty of Hawaii
aloha (*ah-low-hah*) - hello, goodbye, love
aole (*ah-o-lay*) - no
auwe (*ow-way*) - woe, alas
hale (*hah-lay*) - house
haole (*how-lay*) - Caucasian, foreigner
hapa (*hah-pah*) - part, half (as in hapa
haole: "half white")
heiau (*hey-ee-ow*) - temple
honi (*ho-nee*) - kiss
hui (*hoo-ee*) - corporation, union
hukilau (*hoo-kee-lau*) - community fishing using a net
hula (*hoo-lah*) - the native dance
imu (*ee-moo*) - underground oven
kai (*kye*) - ocean
kamaaina (*kah-mah-eye-nah*) - oldtimer, native, local
kane (*kah-nay*) - man
kapu (*kah-poo*) - keep out, taboo
kaukau (*kow-kow*) - food (slang)
keiki (*kay-kee*) - child
kokua (*ko-koo-ah*) - help
lanai (*lah-nah-ee*) - porch
lei (*lay*) - necklace of flowers
lua (*loo-ah*) - bathroom
luau (*loo-ow*) - feast
mahalo (*mah-hah-low*) - thank you
malihini (*mah-lee-hee-nee*) - stranger, newcomer
mele (*may-lay*) - song
muumuu (*moo-oo-moo-oo*) - long, loose dress
nui (*noo-ee*) - big
ohana (*oh-hah-nah*) - family
ono (*oh-no*) - the best
pali (*pah-lee*) - cliff
paniolo (*pah-nee-oh-low*) - Hawaiian cowboy
pau (*pow*) - finished
pilikia (*pee-lee-kee-ah*) - trouble
poi (*poy*) - pounded taro root, a food staple
puka (*poo-kah*) - hole
pupu (*poo-poo*) - hors d'oeuvre
wahine (*wah-hee-nay*) - woman
wikiwiki (*wee-kee-wee-kee*) - quickly

IT'S THATTA WAY

Island geography is not suited to traditional ways of giving directions. Instead of north, south, east and west, you are likely to hear *mauka* (toward the mountain) and *makai* (toward the sea). In Honolulu, you may also hear Ewa (toward the city of Ewa) and Diamond Head (toward Diamond Head Crater).

TIPS ON WEATHER & WHAT TO WEAR

Hawaii's semitropical weather changes very little from season to season, although it is slightly warmer from May to October, and cooler from November to April. The median temperature is about 75 degrees year-round, and can range from the high 60s at night to the high 80s on a summer day. Ninety degrees is considered hot in Honolulu. Remember, though, that the Islands, especially the Big Island, experience all but the most extreme weather, depending on elevation. Rain storms are likely to occur during winter, and snow is very common on Haleakala (Maui's highest mountain), Mauna Loa and Mauna Kea (on the Big Island). But if it rains, or you are chilly, you can just head to another part of the island! On any island, you can generally head south or west for warm, sunny weather, or up to the mountains for cooler temperatures.

Travel light, because Hawaiian dress is casual. Bring a jacket for rain and cool elevations. "Aloha-wear" (loud, brightly colored Hawaiian sport shirt, baggy shorts, sandals) is the norm in even the best restaurants. Bring comfortable shoes for hiking and appropriate beachwear. Don't forget sunscreen, sunglasses, snorkeling gear and a camera—but if you do leave an item behind, you can buy or rent just about anything on all of the islands.

ABOUT THE RESTAURANTS

A COMING OF CULINARY AGE

It's only too easy to poke fun at Island gastronomy, so we will save you the usual cracks, such as the advice given us by a reputed cook (and compassionate friend): "Take some olive oil and vinegar with you. That way, at least you'll be able to pick some wild watercress and have a decent meal." Not to mention the well-worn complaint, "When you're in Hawaii, you'll think you're still on board the plane; the food is about the same."

Well, having a tendency to doubt the clichés that are inevitably attached to places, we decided to send an exploratory mission across the archipelago to find out how bad it really was. Surprisingly, not only did our missionaries survive the expedition, they also discovered the emergence of a new culture in cooking. We're not talking about the traditional Hawaiian (Polynesian) cuisine that we applaud for its authenticity and freshness, but rather a cooking style that is being created for the increasing flood of tourists and the growing population of Island denizens.

Once considered an easy captive audience, incoming tourists (known in pidgin as JOJs, "Just Off the Jet") were treated to nothing better than mediocre cooking for ghastly prices; the closest three-toque restaurant was 5,000 miles away in New York. In the past few years, however, the passive flock of visitors has begun to show signs of impatience. Those coming from California in particular, and from progressive cities around the world—cities where nouvelle, California-nouvelle and nouvelle-nouvelle cuisine have flourished for more than a decade—bring with them a sophisticated taste, a prejudice for the best.

But the point about the watercress is well taken: what discerning visitors don't need to bring are the ingredients required to satisfy their taste: a cornucopia of marvelous ingredients has been growing on the Islands all along, waiting for the local chefs to treat them with a little more sophistication and finesse. Nothing in the world matches the sweetness of GRANO 1015Y, which, before you're scared off by the sound of it, is just the scientific name of the onion that grows on the slopes of Maui's Mount Haleakala. And who could forget the Islands' three varieties of papaya (Pona, Sunrise Solo and the Waimanalo); the buttery delicacy of macadamia nuts; the just-picked Big Island tomatoes; the succulent Nihau lamb; America's only native coffee, Kona; the golden grapes; the superb potatoes and, of course, the fabulous seafood—all the more fabulous with exotic appellations such as mahimahi, opakapaka and ahi.

Hawaii's chefs are now well aware of the prodigious nature of the Islands' bounty, and the innovative ways in which they're using it shows that a good bit of thinking—and rethinking—is being done in Hawaii's kitchens. Also, money is flowing rapidly into Hawaii—mostly in the form of Japan's yen—which can help to encourage new culinary talent. (Quality usually costs.)

Of course, this isn't to say that Hawaii has become a gastronomic paradise overnight—but it would be an injustice to overlook its chefs' efforts to restore the kitchen to its rightful place of honor. What follows, in the restaurant section for each island, is our preliminary mapping of Hawaii's head-spinning coming of culinary age. We applaud you, Hawaii, and we will be watching hopefully. Appropriately, so will the legions of JOJs who are mighty hungry when they deplane.

André Gayot
Gault Millau, Inc.
5900 Wilshire Blvd.,
29th Floor
Los Angeles, CA 90036

RANKINGS & REVIEWS

R estaurants are listed by island, and each restaurant section also includes a cuisine index for that island. Restaurants are ranked in the same manner that French students are graded, on a scale of one to twenty. The rankings reflect *only* the quality of the food; the decor, service, wine list and atmosphere are explicitly commented on within each review. Restaurants that are ranked 13/20 and above are distinguished with toques (chef's hats), according to the table below:

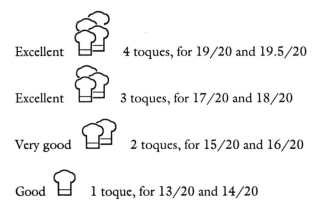

Excellent   4 toques, for 19/20 and 19.5/20

Excellent   3 toques, for 17/20 and 18/20

Very good   2 toques, for 15/20 and 16/20

Good   1 toque, for 13/20 and 14/20

Keep in mind that we are comparing Hawaii's restaurants to the best in the world, and that these ranks are *relative*. A 13/20 (one toque) is not a very good ranking for a highly reputed (and very expensive) restaurant, but it is quite complimentary for a small place without much culinary pretension.

Unless otherwise noted, the price given at the end of each review is for a complete dinner for two, including an appetizer and a main course and dessert per person, along with tax, tip and a bottle of wine. It is, naturally, hard to estimate the cost of wine; for our purposes we assume a modest bottle at a modest restaurant and a good California wine (usually $20 to $30 a bottle) at a more serious place. Lovers of the great Burgundies, Bordeaux or Champagnes will find their tabs higher than our estimates; conversely, those who like to eat lightly, sharing appetizers and desserts, will spend less. However, prices continue to creep up, so forgive us if a restaurant has raised its prices by the time you visit it.

Credit cards are abbreviated as follows:

AE: American Express and/or Optima
D: Discover
DC: Diners Club and/or Carte Blanche
JCB: Japan Credit Bureau
MC: MasterCard
V: VISA

A WORD ABOUT FOOD

For those with more adventurous palates, look for restaurants that offer New American or Pacific Rim cuisines. Both cooking styles are evolutionary, and are interpreted uniquely by every chef who employs them, so we'll define them broadly: New American, a derivative of nouvelle cuisine, uses American ingredients in new, innovative dishes; classic French techniques are employed, but with a lighter, fresher touch. Pacific Rim cuisine is any creative melding of Japanese, Chinese, Thai, Korean, Filipino, Vietnamese, Mexican and so on, added to fresh local ingredients; it might be anything from the subtle addition of shiitake-mushroom sauce to a plate of fettuccine, to such fabulous creations as Peking Duck salad with hot kim chee or sautéed foie gras in plum-wine sauce with fresh pineapple.

WHAT'S IN A NAME?

Ordering fish in a Hawaiian restaurant can be akin to sailing into uncharted waters. All those strange names can have a numbing effect on the brain, so we've produced this simple guide to make sure that your palate doesn't suffer. We're only including the most popular, so don't look for the likes of hapuu or oio, please. All are saltwater fish.

AHI - Here's one Hawaiian fish that has made it onto mainland restaurant menus, along with mahimahi. Usually served grilled, a yellowtail tuna can weigh up to 300 pounds. The white, firm flesh is also delicious as sushi.

AKU - This is another type of tuna. Much smaller than the yellowtail, it averages around twenty pounds.

AKULE - In Hawaii, the bigeye scad has to be over seven inches to be called "akule." Those in the five-to-seven-inch range are known as "maau," while those that are up to five inches are referred to as "halalu."

MAHIMAHI - You might just remember this as the world's most delicious fish, or be horrified by the translation as "dolphin." No, it's not the same dolphin that we all know and love, and, yes, it is the tastiest fish in the world, thank you.

ONAGA - Occasionally seen on Island menus, the onaga is none other than the ubiquitous red snapper. The average size is about four pounds.

ONO - Some folks love the flavor of the six-foot-long wahoo, but all others can say is "watch out for the numerous bones." It's a great fish for display cooking.

OPAKAPAKA - Did you realize that besides the red snapper, there is also a blue snapper? This delicious fish is usually served in filets.

ULUA - You probably know him best as jack crevalle, but in Hawaii this tasty jack goes by a different name. The young fish is called "papio."

TOQUE TALLY

16/20

Roy's Restaurant (*Oahu*)

15/20

Golden Dragon Restaurant (*Oahu*)
Merriman's (*Big Island*)
Plantation Veranda (*Maui*)
Prince Court (*Maui*)
Sound Of The Falls (*Maui*)

14/20

Bagwells 2424 (*Oahu*)
Bali-by-the-Sea (*Oahu*)
East-West Dining Room (*Maui*)
Gallery Restaurant (*Big Island*)
Imperial Teppanyaki Dinner (*Maui*)
La Mer (*Oahu*)
The Maile Room (*Oahu*)
Orchids (*Oahu*)
Pagoda Floating Restaurant (*Oahu*)
Restaurant Suntory (*Oahu*)
Ruth's Chris Steak House (*Oahu*)
Tempura Garden (*Kauai*)

13/20

Avalon Restaurant & Bar (*Maui*)
Café Kiowa (*Maui*)
Canoe House (*Big Island*)

Gerard's Restaurant (*Maui*)
Hakone (*Maui*)
Inn on the Cliffs (*Kauai*)
Kama'aina Suite at The Willows (*Oahu*)
Kapalua Bay Club Restaurant (*Maui*)
Keo's Thai Cuisine (*Oahu*)
The Masters (*Kauai*)
Plantation Gardens (*Kauai*)
Raffles (*Maui*)
The Woodlands (*Oahu*)

12/20

The Aloha Café (*Big Island*)
Baci (*Oahu*)
Black Orchid Restaurant (*Oahu*)
Bree Garden Restaurant (*Big Island*)
Brennecke's Beach Broiler (*Kauai*)
Dynasty II Restaurant (*Oahu*)
Hanamaulu Restaurant/Tea House/Sushi Bar and Robata (*Kauai*)
Hard Rock Café (*Oahu*)
Hee Hing Restaurant (*Oahu*)
House Without a Key
Hy's Steak House (*Oahu*)
Kilauea House and Restaurant (*Big Island*)
King And I (*Kauai*)
Kyo-Ya (*Oahu*)
Lahaina Treehouse (*Maui*)
Maui Outrigger (*Maui*)
Michel's at the Colony Surf (*Oahu*)
Chez Paul (*Maui*)
Poo Ping Thai Cuisine (*Big Island*)
Rainbow Lanai (*Oahu*)
Roussels (*Big Island*)
Siam Thai (*Maui*)
Sunset Grill (*Oahu*)
Tasca (*Maui*)

Trattoria Manzo (*Oahu*)
The Willows (*Oahu*)

11/20

Andrew's Restaurant (*Oahu*)
Aurelio's Restaurant (*Maui*)
California Pizza Kitchen (*Oahu*)
Compadres (*Oahu*)
Duke's Canoe Club (*Kauai*)
Flamingo Cantina (*Kauai*)
Il Fresco (*Oahu*)
Greek Island Taverna (*Oahu*)
The Grill & Bar (*Maui*)
Helena's Hawaiian Food (*Oahu*)
Horatio's (*Oahu*)
Koloa Broiler (*Kauai*)
Longhi's (*Maui*)
Mama's Fish House (*Maui*)
Maple Garden (*Oahu*)
Mekong I Restaurant (*Oahu*)
Musashi (*Oahu*)
Naniwa (*Kauai*)
Norberto's El Café (*Kauai*)
La Perouse (*Maui*)
Quinn's Almost By The Sea (*Big Island*)
Saigon Café (*Oahu*)
The Secret (*Oahu*)
The Shell House (*Kauai*)
The Terrace Restaurant (*Big Island*)

10/20

La Bretagne Restaurant (*Maui*)
Chez Michel French Restaurant (*Oahu*)
Edelweiss (*Big Island*)
Fisherman's Landing (*Big Island*)
Gaylord's Restaurant (*Kauai*)
Hanalei Dolphin (*Kauai*)
Harrington's (*Big Island*)
Huggo's (*Big Island*)

Island Fish House (*Maui*)
Kanazawa-tei (*Big Island*)
Kapa'a Fish Chowder House (*Kauai*)
Kimo's Restaurant (*Maui*)
Kona Hilton Beach and Tennis Resort (*Big Island*)
Kona Provision Co. (*Big Island*)
Leilani's On The Beach (*Maui*)
Nick's Fishmarket (*Oahu*)
Phillip Paolo's (*Big Island*)
Restaurant Benkei (*Oahu*)

9/20

Alex's Hole In The Wall (*Maui*)
The Beach Club (*Big Island*)
Casa Italiana (*Kauai*)
Dillon's Restaurant (*Maui*)
The Fishmonger's Wife Restaurant & Bar (*Oahu*)
Jameson's by the Sea (*Big Island*)
John Dominis (*Oahu*)
Kobe (*Oahu*)
Kona Inn Restaurant (*Big Island*)
Kona Ranch House (*Big Island*)
Mangos Tropical Restaurant & Bar (*Kauai*)
Matteo's (*Oahu*)
Monterey Bay Canners (*Oahu*)
Poki's Pasta (*Big Island*)
Rose City Diner (*Oahu*)
Sergio's (*Oahu*)
Tahiti Nui (*Kauai*)

8/20

Batik Room (*Big Island*)
Beamreach Restaurant (*Kauai*)
La Bourgogne (*Big Island*)
Eclipse (*Big Island*)
Fisherman's Landing (*Big Island*)
Hartwell's At Hale Kea (*Big Island*)

House of Seafood (*Kauai*)
Ono Family Restaurant (*Kauai*)
Orson's (*Oahu*)
Swan Court (*Maui*)

Lanai Terrace (*Maui*)
The Old Spaghetti Factory (*Oahu*)

NO RANKING

The Lodge at Koele Dining Room
(*Lanai*)
Sirena del Lago (*Kauai*)

7/20

Charo's (*Kauai*)

ABOUT THE HOTELS

Every sort of accommodation you can imagine can be found on the Islands: there are fantasy resorts, condominiums, weekly hotels, bed-and-breakfasts, even remote outposts in the mountains of Kauai or in the Big Island's Waipio Valley. No matter what your idea of heaven, just read on—it's all here.

Note that some hoteliers put as high a price on charm or modern facilities as others do on pure luxury. In other words, don't assume that "charming" means "cheap." Conversely, don't assume that hotels falling under the "Luxury" heading are truly luxurious: the place may position and price itself as a luxury hotel, but that doesn't mean it delivers the goods. Lodgings are listed in five categories: Bed & Breakfasts, Condominiums, Luxury, First Class and Practical. Our opinion of the comfort level and appeal of each hotel is expressed in the following ranking system:

Very luxurious

Luxurious

Very comfortable

Comfortable

Credit Cards are abbreviated as follows:
    AE: American Express and/or Optima
    D: Discover
    DC: Diners Club and/or Carte Blanche
    JCB: Japan Credit Bureau
    MC: MasterCard
    V: VISA

OAHU

RESTAURANTS

All the restaurants we have listed below are located in the city of Honolulu, and we've also noted the ones located on the Waikiki strip (see map of Waikiki, page 332). For more information on how our rating system works, how we estimate meal prices and so on, turn to About the Restaurants, page 6. Also in that section is the Toque Tally, page 10, which lists all the restaurants in this book by rating.

BY CUISINE

AMERICAN

Hard Rock Café
Hy's Steak House (*Waikiki*)
Pagoda Family Restaurant
Rainbow Lainai (*Waikiki*)
Rose City Diner
Ruth's Chris Steak House

CALIFORNIAN

California Pizza Kitchen

CHINESE

Dynasty II Restaurant
Golden Dragon Restaurant
(*Waikiki*)
Hee Hing Restaurant
Maple Garden
The Woodlands

CONTINENTAL

Bali-by-the-Sea (*Waikiki*)
Black Orchid Restaurant
House Without a Key (*Waikiki*)
Kama'aina Suite at the Willows
(*Waikiki*)
Maile Room
Michel's at the Colony Surf
(*Waikiki*)
The Secret

FRENCH

Bagwell's 2424 (*Waikiki*)
Chez Michel French Restaurant
(*Waikiki*)
La Mer (*Waikiki*)

GREEK

Greek Island Taverna

HAWAIIAN

Helena's Hawaiian Food
Rainbow Lanai (*Waikiki*)
The Willows (*Waikiki*)

ITALIAN

Andrew's Restaurant
Baci (*Waikiki*)
California Pizza Kitchen
Il Fresco
Matteo's (*Waikiki*)
The Old Spaghetti Factory
Sergio's (*Waikiki*)
Trattoria Manzo
Trattoria Restaurant (*Waikiki*)

JAPANESE

Kobe (*Waikiki*)
Kyo-Ya (*Waikiki*)
Musashi (*Waikiki*)
Pagoda Floating Restaurant
Restaurant Bankei
Restaurant Suntory (*Waikiki*)

MEXICAN

Compadres

NEW AMERICAN

Sunset Grill

PACIFIC RIM

Bagwells 2424
Black Orchid Restaurant

Orchids (*Waikiki*)
Roy's Restaurant
The Willows (*Waikiki*)

SEAFOOD

The Fishmonger's Wife Restaurant
& Bar
Horatio's
John Dominis
Monterey Bay Canners (*Waikiki*)
Nick's Fishmarket (*Waikiki*)
Orson's

STEAKHOUSE

Hy's Steak House (*Waikiki*)
Ruth's Chris Steak House

THAI

Keo's Thai Cuisine (*Waikiki*)
Mekong I

VIETNAMESE

Saigon Café

*We're always interested to hear
about your discoveries, and to
receive your comments on ours.
Please feel free to write to us, and
do state clearly exactly what you
liked or disliked.*

Andrew's Restaurant
Ward Centre,
1200 Ala Moana Blvd.,
Honolulu
• 523-8677
ITALIAN

11/20

Andrew's is a decent enough traditional Italian eatery that happens to feature some very good live jazz in the evenings. Service is good, and if you're looking for an intimate evening, reserve one of the booths and unspool a plate of pasta. The restaurant puts together a nice antipasto, a pretty credible fettuccine Alfredo, and a very good chicken cacciatore, but don't expect too much from the veal Marsala or frogs' legs Provençale, should you be compelled to order such things. For the most part, the pastas taste good, and there's also a nice Sunday brunch here. Don't miss the baked Alaska for dessert! Dinner for two, with wine, is about $75.
Open Mon.-Thurs. 11 a.m.-10 p.m., Fri.-Sat. 11 a.m.-11 p.m., Sun. 10 a.m.-10 p.m. All major cards.

Baci
Waikiki Trade Center,
2255 Kuhio St.,
Waikiki
• 924-2533
ITALIAN

12/20

One of Honolulu's newer, trendier Italian eateries, Baci offers traditional food served in a fairly hip decor. The interior shimmers in slick gray, black and white, and the atmosphere is lively and casual. The *cucina* produces some tasty fare, with an emphasis placed on fresh ingredients and homemade pastas. Try the smoked salmon or carpaccio as an appetizer; also, the sausage rigatoni tempts the palate, with its fat-ribbed macaroni and spicy meat flavors. Pizzas are good, and there's a decent selection of grilled fresh-daily fish. The extensive wine list also includes some gentle prices. Two can dine, with wine, for about $50.
Open Mon.-Fri. 11:30 a.m.-11 p.m., Sat.-Sun. 5 p.m.-11 p.m. Cards: AE, MC, V.

Bagwells 2424
Hyatt Regency Waikiki,
2424 Kalakaua Ave.,
Waikiki
• 923-1234
FRENCH/PACIFIC RIM

Eating at Honolulu's "finer" restaurants can be disheartening at times, an exercise in taste frustration that leaves you very much the poorer. As is the case at so many of its competitors, Bagwells will wreak havoc on your wallet (at least $150 for two, probably more), but for once you'll dine on food that's worthy of the tab. For this, we have a modest young woman named On-Jin Kim to thank. This talented chef, born and raised in Korea, not only received excellent formal training in French cuisine, but she also earned a master's degree in voice from the American Conservatory of Music. It isn't surprising that her refined French cooking (with Hawaiian and Asian overtones) does more than just display technical mastery—it positively sings.

Hyatt has given Kim a properly plush setting for her elegant dishes: deep, high-backed banquettes, crystal chandeliers, blond wood, a floor-to-ceiling glass fountain, a baby grand piano, and such opulent touches as an eighteenth-century Chinese screen. And On-Jon Kim's cooking is matched by an excellent (though costly) wine list, particularly strong on the great French châteaus of Bordeaux, along with an admirable by-the-glass selection.

The menu offers a selection of tiny "grazing portions," along with the expected range of appetizers and entrées, but we prefer to order one of the three fixed-price dinners: the four-course Menu from the Ocean for $58 and the four-course Gourmet Menu for $56, each comprised of dishes from the à la carte menu, and the six-course Chef's Menu Surprise for $68. The Menu from the Ocean is simple yet full of flavor. It starts with sumptuously rich Hawaiian lobster chowder, much like a classic lobster bisque, then moves on to a lovely salad of local Manoa lettuce, endive, walnuts and sun-dried tomatoes, topped with a perfect piece of seared salmon. The entrée is Pacific Rim cuisine at its best: a fat piece of juicy Hawaiian opakapaka, marinated deftly in a Chinese-style, soy-based concoction, steamed, then served with a vibrantly fresh julienne of vegetables. Then comes your choice of the rich French desserts (try the passion-fruit soufflé with mint-chocolate-chip ice cream, a better marriage than you might think) and a fine cup of coffee. If that meal doesn't set your appetite humming, you can be sure that whatever you order will be prepared with a light touch and will be bursting with flavor. The hotel setting and general formality may prevent Bagwells from having the vibrancy and spirit of a place such as Roy's, but the food is first-rate—not just for Hawaii, but for anywhere. Dinner for two, with a good bottle of wine, can run as high as $200.

Open nightly 6 p.m.-10 p.m. All major cards.

Bali-by-the-Sea
Hilton Hawaiian
Village,
2005 Kalia,
Waikiki
• 941-2254
CONTINENTAL

After all the revolutions the culinary world has seen in the past fifteen or so years, perhaps it's time for a revival of Continental cuisine. If so, Bali-by-the-Sea is a good place to start. The restaurant itself is quite lovely, its chic, elegant pastel decor allows the fabulous ocean views to predominate. Service is exemplary—attentive and even anticipatory without being obsequious or intrusive. And the food is as fabulous as the view. The oysters on the half-shell are fresh and briny; for those who prefer that mollusk in a more elaborate preparation, try the gratin of oysters with a julienne of duck. The Pacific salmon and ahi, served with pumpernickel bread and all the appropriate garnishes, are rightly smoked. The coquille of shrimp and scallops in a light ginger sauce breathes some new life into that tired old war-horse. Salads follow suit. We were particularly fond of the Belgian endive and watercress topped with tender, warm slices of pheasant in a tarragon dressing, and the chicory-and-radicchio salad with hot goat cheese in a walnut vinaigrette. The red-snapper soup served en croûte is a success.

Seafood is perfectly prepared here (a feat that is disappointingly rare in Hawaii), especially the opakapaka in a fresh basil sauce and the simply grilled tuna in a mint-and-tomato vinaigrette. For the more carnivorous diner, the butter-tender medallions of veal with sautéed apples and Calvados sauce are wonderful, as is the fat veal chop with morels. The roast duck Lawrence, with papaya purée and macadamia-nut liqueur doesn't work well, but the elegant roast rack of lamb in a shallot-and-rosemary sauce certainly compensated for it.

Bali-by-the-Sea is one of the few restaurants in Hawaii (or in the entire country, for that matter) that offers a cheese course for dessert, which we appreciate. But if you prefer a sweet ending (and we're not immune to those charms, by any means), the hot soufflés are fabulous, as are the fresh tropical-fruit sorbets served tableside from a unique cart. The wine list is cleverly constructed, and although the pleasure of dining here doesn't come cheaply (about $120 for two, with wine), you'll have one of the best all-around dining experiences in all of Hawaii. *Open nightly 6 p.m.-10 p.m. All major cards.*

Black Orchid Restaurant

500 Ala Moana Blvd.
(Restaurant Row,
Building 6D),
Honolulu
• 521-3111
CONTINENTAL/
PACIFIC RIM

12/20

One of Honolulu's latest and toniest joints has a show-biz connection, so let's get that out of the way first. Yes, the Black Orchid is partially owned by Tom Selleck, who was a local during his "Magnum, P.I." days, and his former TV sidekick, Larry Manetti. But that's just window dressing; the real juice behind Black Orchid is provided by majority owners Randy Schoch and Pat Bowlen, who also own Nick's Fishmarket. Well, a little glamour never hurts.

Selleck (or rather, his aura, as well as a sort of photographic shrine to him that lines one of the walls) isn't the only draw here, however. Though, like other celebrity restaurant owners (such as Sonny Bono, Clint Eastwood, Charo), he actually does show up here when he's in town, you shouldn't expect ol' Tom to bring you a margarita or bus your table. We are told, however, that's he's only too happy to sign autographs. He wasn't in the restaurant the night we dropped by, but his spirit was definitely in the air, and on the menu.

This is the sort of solid food that Magnum would have enjoyed in between nailing baddies. The kitchen serves forth a very good Cajun-style ahi, crisply seared on the outside and tenderly rare within. The chefs also make a a fine appetizer of plump Pacific prawns in a reasonably hot chipotle-chile sauce—a sauce that curiously reappears on the filet mignon. Go for the grilled opakapaka or rack of lamb. You can even go for the overly ornate, art-deco setting, making the Black Orchid look like a latter-day Waikiki saloon—albeit a classy one. But don't go for the Maine lobster; it's a long way from Maine to Ala Moana.

Another plus here is the live music. The Black Orchid offers good live jazz in the lounge, featuring such local talent as Azure McCall. It is open until 3 a.m. and serves appetizers into the wee hours. Dinner for two, with wine, will run about $100. *Open daily 11 a.m.-2 p.m. & 5 p.m.-11 p.m.; Live entertainment nightly 4 p.m.-3 a.m. All major cards.*

California Pizza Kitchen

Kahala Mall,
4211 Waialae Ave.,
Honolulu
• 737-9446

1910 Ala Moana Blvd.,
Ste. 5,
Honolulu
• 955-5161
CALIFORNIAN/ITALIAN

11/20

In Honolulu, they make some of the worst pizza we've ever tasted. Pizza so bad, you keep looking around to see if some old college buddies are back in the kitchen, cracking up as they watch you try to eat the soggy lump of cardboard they've whipped up especially for you. It's not just that they put things like pineapple on their pizzas, which is sacrilegious enough. It's that virtually few are those cooks in Hawaii who seem to have any notion of what a pizza is supposed to look or taste like. It's as if they're making pizza by rumor, knowing only that it involves some sort of dough topped with ingredients that may or may not include poi.

The California Pizza Kitchen people, part of a growing Southern California chain, have brought what's probably the very first good pizza to Hawaii. In fact, it's surprisingly good pizza, proving that although New York–style pizza may not travel well, California-style pizzas (like Californians) are always ready to go. The pies, cooked in wood-burning ovens, come with a wide array of toppings, both ordinary and odd. Probably the best CPK pizza is topped with barbecued chicken, red onions, cilantro and smoked gouda cheese; sounds odd, we know, but it works. There are others made variously with duck sausage, Thai chicken, Peking duck, shrimp and pesto, and even a Cajun model, all of which work, more or less. And in honor of Hawaii, there's a Lanai model, topped with pineapple, Canadian bacon, and tomato sauce. It's as good as pineapple pizza gets; and it's still not very good.

Don't neglect the salads or pastas here, either: CPK's mixed-leaf version of a Caesar is generous, fresh and very good, as is the Greek-style salad. The chicken-tequila fettuccine, with red onion, cilantro and multicolored peppers, is pleasant, and so is the Asian-influenced black-bean sauce with angel-hair pasta. There are also some grilled items (chicken breast and duck or chicken sausage) available, as well as a most respectable old-fashioned hot-fudge sundae. And the price is certainly right, especially for overinflated Waikiki.

We wish that the atmosphere of the Kahala Mall were a bit less desultory and dated (and that the lighting weren't so dreadful). Dinner for two, with beverages, costs about $35. *Open daily 11 a.m.-11 p.m. Cards: AE, MC, V.*

Chez Michel French Restaurant

444 Hobron Ln.,
Waikiki
• 955-7867
FRENCH

10/20

We've seldom had so slapdash a meal at a purportedly fine restaurant as on our last venture here. Food ran the gamut from wretched to excellent; service limped through four courses indifferently and then shifted to apologetic kowtowing during coffee; smokers and nonsmokers were intermingled. All this does not come cheap, of course. The interior walks a difficult line between Island kitsch and French provincial. Except for packed-in tables, the main room and terrace adjunct project a comfortable, low-key chic. Latticework divides the room into several areas and gives the ceiling definition. It also complements pink table linen and rattan seats. Subdued track lighting in a rose hue flatters guests.

Strangely, the lavosh (cracker bread) proved crisp, unusual in the Islands. Cream of asparagus left a distinct metallic residue on the palate, and the vegetable dissolved into slimy tendrils, suspiciously reminiscent of canned vegetables. While one of us pondered these deficiencies, the other waited for strange crème Sénégalaise (we had never heard of this African fantasy before), which arrived ten minutes later flaunting an unpleasant and uncharacteristic dried-pea flavor and texture overlaid by generic curry. A shared, generously apportioned duck pâté, with moderately coarse, tartly gamey meat, made some amends, despite an overly salty aspic in improperly large cubes. What was inexplicable was a five-minute wait to receive a second plate when we had clearly stated that the pâté would be shared. A medley of three meats would have been all right, despite being overdone, had it not been blanketed by variations on cream sauce that had to be removed to distinguish beef from lamb from veal. Grilled squash and carrots made pleasant accompaniments. Lobster Provençale with another creamy sauce suggested an herby Newburg rather than Mediterranean cookery.

To our surprise, desserts went past acceptable to downright good. A Grand Marnier soufflé, that most daunting of concoctions, arrived high, wide, and handsome, tasting of eggy custard and the liqueur-imbued crème anglaise served tableside. Bûche de Noel sported a smooth buttercream. Fine, cinnamon-stippled cappuccino and intense, pungent espresso would have done a better meal proud. Were all dishes on the level of the conclusion, our rating would jump four points and we'd be less rancorous about the $140 to $175 a couple must shell out for dinner with wine.

Open Mon.-Thurs. 11:30 a.m.-2 p.m. & 6 p.m.-9 p.m., Fri.-Sat. 11:30 a.m.-2 p.m. & 5:30 p.m.-10:30 p.m., Sun. 5:30 p.m.-10 p.m. All major cards.

Compadres
Ward Centre,
1200 Ala Moana Blvd.,
Honolulu
• 523-1307
MEXICAN

11/20

Compadres is part of a restaurant chain that has branches in such far-flung outposts as Australia and San Francisco; it's brought to you by the same folks who cooked up the Victoria Station concept. But don't let that put you off—Compadres is an upbeat, fun cantina of sorts, serving up some pretty good Mexican food. The restaurant is very attractive—bright, airy, and dotted with ceiling fans, Mexican and Hawaiian geegaws and exotic birds. The bar area is the scene of much revelry (Compadres does a land-office business in margaritas and tequila shooters); if you prefer a little privacy, there's a patio seating area.

The guacamole here is decent; the potato nachos, made with Maui potato chips instead of the usual tortilla chips, are a good concept, but don't work too well. The quesadilla platter, however, grilled fajita sticks and queso fundido are better appetizer bets. Also, burritos and chimichangas are tasty, as are the mahimahi Vera Cruz and the enchiladas poblanas. But the food is almost secondary here—Compadres is essentially a hangout for all ages. Prices are very reasonable; two can dine, with beverages, for about $30.

Open Mon.-Fri. 11 a.m.-1 a.m., Sat.-Sun. 9 a.m.-1 a.m. Cards: AE, MC, V.

Dynasty II Restaurant
Ward Warehouse,
1050 Ala Moana Blvd.,
Honolulu
• 531-0208
CHINESE

12/20

Dynasty II is an elegant Chinese restaurant with service and food to match. Plush Oriental rugs cushion glistening black marble floors; gorgeous antiques are artfully displayed on rosewood pedestals and in glass cases; the lighting is subdued and flattering. The entire effect is rather stunning.

Dynasty II is almost more of a temple devoted to food than a restaurant, but in the best sense—one feels awfully comfortable here. The menu is a creative one, featuring dishes such as stuffed taro with scallops, and banana-shrimp tempura as appetizers, as well as a roast-meat platter with duck, honey-glazed pork, chicken and jellyfish. The creamed corn with crabmeat soup is a savory treat, and the seafood dishes are wonderful, especially the oyster fritters, king prawns sautéed with honey-glazed walnuts, and the braised abalone. The deep-fried pork chops would give nightmares to a cardiologist, but a chop-lover would dream of them, and the Peking duck is well worth ordering (and you don't have to do it in advance). For dessert, try the deep-fried water-chestnut sticks. Dinner for two, with beverages, is about $60.

Open daily 11 a.m.-2 p.m. & 5:30 p.m.-10:30 p.m. All major cards.

Fishmonger's Wife Restaurant & Bar

Ala Moana Center,
1450 Ala Moana Blvd.,
Honolulu
• 941-3377
SEAFOOD

9/20

The Fishmonger's Wife is one cut above your average, generic fish house. It's not a place you'd single out as a destination, but if you're shopping in the Center here, it'll do just fine. The restaurant is low-key, done in a sort of upscale Holiday Inn dining room mode, with soft greens and mauves. If you stick to the simpler, broiled preparations of the mahimahi and other local fish, you'll do okay; just avoid the veal scallopine and crabcakes. Also there are some wok-cooked stir-fry dishes that are decent, including shrimp, vegetables, or scallops prepared in a black-bean or garlic sauce, and there are lots of salads as well. Bypass the clam chowder. A meal for two, with beverages, runs about $50.
Open Sun.-Thurs. 10:30 a.m.-10 p.m., Fri.-Sat. 10:30 a.m.-11 p.m. All major cards .

Il Fresco

Ward Centre,
1200 Ala Moana Blvd.,
Honolulu
• 523-5191
ITALIAN

11/20

For proof that contemporary Italian food has found its way to the Islands, head over to Il Fresco, a charming trattoria in the handsome Pavilion wing of the Ward Centre. From your café-style table, you can watch your meal being prepared in the exhibition kitchen, home to the obligatory brick pizza oven. From the short, appealing menu you can choose a fresh garden salad; a generous, cheesy Caesar salad; a starter of blackened ahi in a hot mustard sauce (superb fish but a heavy-handed sauce); California-style pizzas (meaning no tomato sauce), big enough for two to split, with such toppings as mozzarella, shrimp and pesto; a few pastas; and a handful of daily specials. For dessert, chocolate fiends will be pleased with the rich chocolate torte. All in all, Il Fresco combines an inviting, unpretentious setting with friendly service and good, fresh food prepared with care and intelligence. Lunch for two will run about $25; a three-course pizza dinner, with wine, is $50.
Open Mon.-Thurs. 11:30 a.m.-2 p.m. & 6 p.m.-10 p.m., Fri.-Sat. 11:30 a.m.-2 p.m. & 6 p.m.-11 p.m., Sun. 6 p.m.-9 p.m. All major cards.

Golden Dragon Restaurant

Hilton Hawaiian
Village Hotel,
2005 Kalia Rd.,
Waikiki
• 946-5336
CHINESE

The Golden Dragon is quite a surprise on any number of levels. It's a truly first-rate Chinese restaurant in, of all places, the awesomely huge (and awesomely well-run) Hilton Hawaiian Village. Despite the fact that it offers a remarkable view of the ocean and the setting sun, the food is still marvelous, a wholly unexpected happenstance. In terms of food, this plushly elegant room, with its silver and jade place settings, serves some very good Cantonese dishes—most notably the Beggar's Chicken (one of the best we've ever had), a dish of herbed chicken wrapped in lotus leaves, then encased in clay and baked, a dish that (like the Peking duck) needs 24 hours' advance notice. They smoke their own baby back ribs, chicken, pork and duck in a glass-fronted "Smoke Pavillion." They make a wonderfully crispy lemon chicken, and an oddly refreshing chocolate-mint crème brulée for dessert. And for those who have an adventurous streak when it comes to obscure liqueurs, the Golden Dragon is quite a find; you can drink things here not often found east of Hong Kong. Savor (if that's the term) Hugu Mugua Jiu (made with tiger bones), Hakai Da Bu Chiew (barrel-fermented with live lizards), and Lu Wei Ba By Jiu (made with dried female deer tail). Their tea selection is only a little less exotic.

Chef Dai Hoy Chang, who was born in Honolulu and raised in Canton, opened the Golden Dragon in 1958 and has remained ever since. He deserves special plaudits, and so do the Hilton folks for making this one of Honolulu's best dining experiences—or was that the Hugu Mugua Jiu talking? Dinner for two, with wine, will cost about $80.

Open nightly 6 p.m.-10 p.m. All major cards.

Greek Island Taverna

2570 S. Beretania St., Honolulu
• 943-0052
GREEK

11/20

Fun and cheap—what more do you want? The setting, looking out over a copy store and parking lot, is less than glamorous, but if you're looking for a lively, inexpensive family restaurant, and you've got a hankering for Greek food, Greek Island Taverna should do the trick.

The usual Hellenic (and Turkish posing as Hellenic) favorites are on the menu here: Greek salad, moussaka, calamari, dolmas, spanakopita and, of course, baklava. There are also various kebabs and gyros as well as a very tasty fish stew. It's great for lunch, but the real action takes place at dinnertime, when patrons heed the call of the bouzouki, and take to the postage-stamp-sized dance floor. Dinner for two, with retsina, is $45.

Open Tues.-Fri. 11:30 a.m.-2 p.m. & 5 p.m.-10 p.m., Sat-Sun. from 5 p.m.-10 p.m. Cards: AE, MC, V.

Hard Rock Café

1837 Kapiolani Blvd., Honolulu
• 955-7383
AMERICAN

12/20

A Hard Rock is a Hard Rock is a Hard Rock (with apologies to Gertrude Stein)—except in Honolulu, where it's a culinary truce. Not that the Hard Rock's all-American fare isn't up to snuff in its other locations—given the phenomenal popularity of this chain, the food is far, far better than it has to be. This particular Hard Rock is quite handsome. Housed in a large, white rotunda-shaped building, in the colonial Hawaiian mode, the high-ceilinged room is airy, with every available inch of wall space hung with rock-and-roll memorabilia. The inevitable concession stand, hawking all manner of Hard Rock T-shirts and sweatshirts, drinking glasses, caps, and other logoed goodies, is conveniently located next to the parking lot entrance, making it quite easy to forklift your booty into your rental car. We weren't surprised to find out that Hard Rock–related merchandise accounts for about one-third of the chain's revenues.

Along with making a fashion statement, the hip and slick owner, Peter Morton, also has something to say about the sorry state of our Earth and how he is taking pains to remedy it. We applaud his efforts to "Save the Planet" (a Hard Rock catchphrase—you can wear it, too!), by using only biodegradable and recyclable paper goods, as well as his generous donations to many local and international charitable organizations. His efforts with the menu succeed with us, too. The Hard Rock makes a great burger, and a good lime-grilled chicken served with crispy, skinny fries. The fresh fish is just fine. Miraculously, the apple pie actually tastes as though a real human being baked it; and other desserts, such as the brown-black devil's food cake, the hot fudge sundae, and the fudge brownie oozing hot fudge and vanilla ice cream are gooey, messy, American dream desserts. The Hard Rock may be preprogrammed fun, but it is fun—and with good food to boot. Dinner for two, with nutty cocktails, runs about $35.
Open daily 11 a.m.-midnight. All major cards.

Hee Hing Restaurant
Diamond Head Center,
449 Kapahulu Ave.,
Honolulu
• 735-5544
CHINESE

12/20

Hee Hing, with its encyclopedic menu, hyperbolic space and comically brusque service is about as close as any Honolulu restaurant comes to the Hong Kong–style of mass feeding. Though parts of the menu have a distinct Americanized edge to them (you know—almond chicken, crisp wontons—buzz words like those), with a little patience, you can put together quite an authentic meal. Come lunchtime, Hee Hing serves some five-dozen types of dim sum, an admirable selection. At dinnertime, the dishes grow more serious, with the sound of platters of sizzling seafood filling the air, and the smells of drunken prawns, lobster and crab in black-bean sauce, whole fish in sweet-and-sour sauce, crackling chicken, and a multitude of fried rice and panfried noodle dishes filling the room. Go with a large group if you can—the more the merrier and the heartier the feast. Dinner for two, with beverages, is about $25.
Open Sun.-Thurs. 10:30 a.m.-9:30 p.m., Fri.-Sat. 10:30 a.m.-11 p.m. Cards: AE, MC, V.

Helena's Hawaiian Food
1364 N. King St.,
Honolulu
• 845-8044
HAWAIIAN

11/20

Since 1946, through three post–World War II generations, Helena Chock has been serving the real deal at her legendary restaurant—honest-to-God Hawaiian cuisine that's a favorite with locals. The restaurant isn't exactly gorgeous (it used to be Helena's father's general store), with its turquoise formica tables and wooden stools, but Helena and her longtime employees make everyone feel at home, and the food is a good introduction to Hawaiian cuisine, as everything is absolutely fresh and made on the premises.

Good bets are the plate dinners (the Hawaiian version of the blue plate special), laulau, lomi salmon, Kalua pork (baked in an underground oven by the same cook who's been doing it for 40 years), chicken long rice and, naturally, poi (which is definitely an acquired taste). Also good is the poke, Island-style sushi seasoned with the juices of local limpets, and to end your meal, haupia (coconut-cream pudding). This place is a real gem and should be a required stop for anyone who wants to scratch the local surface. A meal for two will run about $25. *Open Tues.-Fri. 10:30 a.m.-7:30 p.m. No cards.*

Horatio's

Ward Warehouse,
1050 Ala Moana Blvd.,
Honolulu
• 521-5002
SEAFOOD

11/20

If you're looking for good, simply prepared fresh fish, you could do a lot worse than Horatio's. Located in the Ward Warehouse, Horatio's is a very handsome restaurant, done in a spare, New England–style, schooner-intensive decor. It's also a very popular restaurant, so be sure to make reservations unless you are prepared for up to an hour's wait (however, you can get appetizers at the bar).

There's a great selection of fresh fish that changes daily, depending on what's available at market. Horatio's does an especially good job with ono, ahi and moonfish, all of which you can order in a variety of preparations and sauces (for example, ginger cream, Vera Cruz–style, Szechuan chili, or just plain mesquite-grilled with herbs). Also good are the oven-roasted prawns brushed with Key-lime butter and fresh garlic and the sautéed scallops in black-bean sauce. There's a better-than-decent charcoal-grilled lamb in a crispy herb crust and a good prime rib that's slowly roasted in rock salt. Even the clam chowder is good.

Horatio's prides itself on its commitment to healthy food preparations and is very accommodating to most dietary restrictions. But for those who look the other way at such things, make sure to order the zingy Key-lime pie for dessert—with a side order of Lappert's obscenely rich and delicious ice cream. Dinner for two, with beverages, will run about $55. *Mon.-Thurs. 11 a.m.-10 p.m., Fri.-Sat. 11 a.m.-10:30 p.m., Sun. 5 p.m.-10 p.m. (Bar menu served until midnight). Cards: AE, MC, V.*

House Without a Key

Halekulani Hotel,
2194 Kalia,
Waikiki
• 923-2311
CONTINENTAL

12/20

What images "House Without a Key" conjures up! Anyone familiar with the Charlie Chan mysteries will recognize that title. Novelist Earl Derr Biggers conceived the series while staying in a Halekulani cottage in 1925. This first book was called "House Without a Key," supposedly based on a real-life murder and its solution. In any case, it's a wonderful story, and it's easy to see how a writer could be inspired by these surroundings. Located in one of Honolulu's most beautiful hotels, House Without a Key is the Halekulani's casual eatery. A giant kiawe tree shelters

the restaurant, and the room is open and airy (don't feed the bold, friendly birds!). There are lots of good salads and sandwiches on the menu (try the spinach-and-goat-cheese salad), as well as a Hawaiian fish chowder. In the early evening, you will behold a good selection of appetizers, known as *pupus*. The pork dumplings and seared ahi will please your taste buds, and there is some nicely grilled mahimahi with a tasty eggplant relish. One sweet "key" to this house is the unbeatable coconut cake. A meal for two, with beverages, is about $50.
Open daily 7 a.m.-10 p.m. All major cards.

Hy's Steak House

Waikiki Park Heights Hotel,
2440 Kuhio Ave.,
Waikiki
• 922-5555
AMERICAN/STEAKHOUSE

12/20

Hy's is as diametrically opposed to its environment as could possibly be imagined. Dark, upholstered and Wasp-clubby, Hy's absolutely denies any relationship to where it is. But then, that seems to be a fairly common resort-town syndrome—look at Palm Springs, for instance. All that apart, Hy's does mostly steaks, and it does them (and other menu items) very well. The Caesar salad is good, and the smoked salmon is smooth and mellow. Though there are fish, chicken, veal, pasta and even, heaven help us, beef Wellington, not ordering a steak here is akin to traveling to Egypt and bypassing the pyramids. There are several different cuts, including the Only (a thirteen-ounce slab of New York steak basted with a secret sauce) as well as a Delmonico, peppercorn and sirloin.

Hy's is mainly a tourist mecca, but the service is friendly and accommodating, and for restaurants of this genre, the food is certainly above par. Dinner for two, with wine, is about $90.
Open nightly 6 p.m.-12:30 a.m. All major cards.

John Dominis

43 Ahui St.,
Honolulu
• 523-0955
SEAFOOD

9/20

If, for some masochistic reason, you're compelled to recycle great quantities of money for very mediocre food, you'll have no trouble doing so at John Dominis. As is the case with many of Honolulu's hotly hyped, big-deal restaurants, you'll find the setting excessive, the food disappointing, and the bill ludicrous. You have been warned. Caveat *haole* (yes, that's a foreigner)!

The best part about dining at John Dominis is getting there; you have to negotiate your way through a dark, scary alleyway. Once you get inside, you wind your way through forests of hanging plants and indoor streams running with rather sluggish-looking lobsters and various finned critters, as well as some rather stunning displays of fresh-looking fish on ice. Remember those faces, as they'll haunt you after you've eaten your meal, when you realize that they died in vain.

Lest you think we're mean-spirited curmudgeons, let's start off with John Dominis's good points: the room is a lively one; it has a great view of the water; the sourdough bread is good; and service is friendly and solicitous. Yet, somehow that doesn't make up for the fact that an entrée of mushy tiger prawns clocked in at around $30, that a vegetarian platter consisting of an artichoke, asparagus, potatoes, tomato, squash and rice is $14.95, and that side dishes of vegetables cost an average of $3.75. A dish of overcooked pasta primavera or a once-beautiful piece of ahi that had been cooked unto grayness were not cheap, either. The view and the service just can't take enough of the sting out of the dining experience here. Dinner for two, with wine, will run about $110.

Open Sun.-Thurs. 6 p.m.-10 p.m., Fri.-Sat. 6 p.m.-midnight. All major cards.

Kama'aina Suite at The Willows,
901 Hausten St.,
Waikiki
• 946-4808
CONTINENTAL

13

Tucked away on the second floor of the well-known restaurant Willows is the Kama'aina Suite. Kamaaina means "native born" in Hawaiian. It does not apply to the chef, but it will help you to feel like a native son (or daughter) in this lovely, open room overlooking the thatched roofs of Willows below. The mood is very subdued and casually elegant here. Windows reach from floor to ceiling; well-worn antique pieces tastefully furnish the room; and the crisp, white napery and tropical plants lend the room the atmosphere of a thirties movie shot in the tropics.

Chef Kusuma Cooray hails from Sri Lanka and melds many of her native flavors and spices with local ingredients in classic Continental preparations. The menu, which changes monthly, is a prix-fixe selection, which can be accommodated to vegetarian or particular tastes. All meals begin with aromatic, freshly baked brioche with Brie, and continue with such dishes as an ethereal spinach timbale, papadums (wafer breads) served with homemade chutney, roast quail with foie gras in a frizz of mountain yams, or medallions of lamb with candied lemon and sunchoke mousse. The sorbets that serve as palate cleansers (especially the mint) taste refreshing and light, and the desserts are mostly of the rich, sophisticated haute variety. Considering the quality of the food and the peaceful gestalt of dinner here, prices are indeed reasonable: six courses for $42.50 per person, without wine. Reservations 24 hours in advance are recommended.

Open nightly from 5 p.m.-10:30 p.m. All major cards.

THE *POI*-FECT STAPLE

China has its rice, India has its breads, Mexico its tortillas, Italy its pasta; in Hawaii, the ubiquitous carbohydrate staple is poi. It's made from the starchy taro root, which is boiled and then mashed or pounded into a gray, glutinous substance reminiscent of baby mash, and is served with almost anything. Taro root is also used to make chips, biscuits, turnovers and so on, and its greens are eaten as a vegetable, boiled and seasoned with coconut milk.

Not even the snails that live in taro fields escape the cook's pot: these small creatures (called—you guessed it—taro snails) are prepared like escargots, or stir-fried with ginger and garlic. Taro snails must be soaked overnight in water before cooking, however, or they taste, literally, like mud.

Keo's Thai Cuisine

625 Kapahulu Ave.,
Waikiki
• 737-9250
THAI

If we dared utter a negative word about Keo's, surely the wrath of Pele would immediately drown us in molten lava, so beloved is Hawaii's best and best-known Thai restaurant. Fortunately, we can't say bad things about the place. But we do have one caveat for those accustomed to eating first-rate Thai food in London, Los Angeles or, for that matter, Bangkok: Keo's serves fresh, creative and thoroughly delicious Thai food, but it may not be the all-consuming religious experience for Thai-cuisine gourmands that it is for those whose experience with Thai food has been more limited. Keo's fans are legion and fanatical. Those used to the run-of-the-mill Thai standards—your basic mee krob/pad Thai/barbecued chicken assortment—will marvel at the menu, full of all sorts of unusual and appealing creations. Perhaps the most famous Keo's dish is the Evil Jungle Prince, an addictive blend of chicken or shrimp with fresh basil, coconut milk and fresh chilis, set on a bed of chopped cabbage. The ginger chicken soup is fabulous, rich and smoothly spicy; the green papaya salad is sweetly refreshing; the noodle dishes are warmly satisfying; and the curries are uniformly excellent. Swell exotic fruit-juice cocktails (or Thai beer) pair well with this spicy cooking, and the prompt service and very comfortable setting will add to your hot-food-induced feeling of well-being. And by Hawaiian standards, the prices are moderate: about $55 for a feast for two, with drinks. This location is the best, but there are two branches, at 1485 S. King Street in Honolulu (947-9988) and in Ward Centre between Waikiki and downtown (533-0533).
Open daily 5:30 p.m.-10:30 p.m. All major cards.

Kobe

1841 Ala Moana Blvd.,
Waikiki
• 941-4444
JAPANESE

9/20

Kobe bills itself as "Honolulu's most beautiful sushi bar." Come on, guys. It may be Honolulu's most singles-intensive sushi bar, and is quite popular with the fraternity and tourist crowds, but "most beautiful"?

The food isn't so beautiful, either. Part of a chain, Kobe behaves as if we've learned nothing about Japanese food since 1970—this stuff is strictly for *gaijin* who still think that raw fish is scary. Sitting at the sushi bar is a pretty depressing experience—on our visit, the sushi chef seemed supremely bored by his work, but then, who could blame him after tasting the sub-par fish he had to work with? Everything just tasted pallid, and the sluggishness with which each order was delivered had nothing to do with meticulous craft. One understands why a whole lot of drinking is going on here. The rest of the menu runs to surf-'n'-turf, teriyaki chicken, and teppan dishes, none of which are terribly good. And fraternity boys have a field day

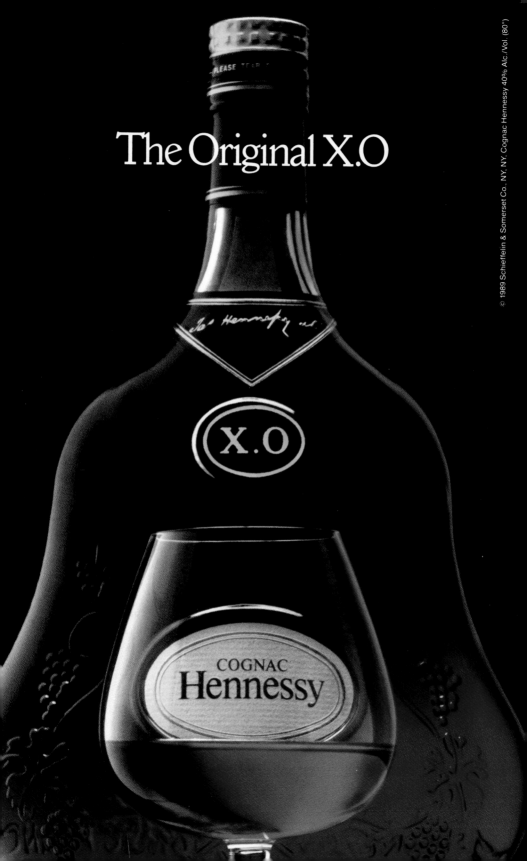

The Original X.O

CHAMPAGNE

Veuve Clicquot Ponsardin

MAISON FONDÉE EN 1772

REIMS
FRANCE

*"Une seule qualité:
la toute première"*

*"One quality...
the very finest"*

Madame Veuve Clicquot Ponsardin

with Kobe's "knife-wielding samurai chefs"—give us a break. Dinner for two, with saké, is about $60.
Open nightly 5:30 p.m.-2 a.m. Cards: AE, JCB, V..

Kyo-Ya
2057 Kalakaua Ave.,
Waikiki
• 947-3911, 946-1121
JAPANESE

12/20

Kyo-Ya (pronounced kee oh 'yah) displays a kind of simple beauty. The single-room teahouse has walls covered by off-white paper festooned with flower-budding branches, rice-paper globes as ceiling fixtures, and the plainest jet-black tables project a comfortable austerity. Service by kimono-clad women—not those peach-cheeked youngsters favored else-where—may lurch from hustle to hiatus, yet these inconsisten-cies seldom grate on our sensibilities. The food is reliably good rather than excellent, except for occasional peerless sashimi, tearose hamachi, robust maguro, and pale onaga, for example. Even these would have gained from the contrast of pickled ginger, lacking for some reason. Instead, chewy tendrils of dark-fuschia seaweed, tasting a bit like lemon-dressed raw clams, add an odd, not altogether appealing note. Seven inexpensive dishes grace the luncheon menu only, but several upscale rela-tives, notably shabu-shabu and sukiyaki, show up for dinner. Both menus offer yosenabe, a bourgeois Japanese hot pot, whose aromatic and zesty stock conceals yeoman portions of cord-thick rice noodles, clams in the shell, scallops, tofu, and chunks of fish—the seafood, alas, was not up to the vegetables and bean curd components. Skip the unagi kabayaki—the eel is a frozen import. Share ton-katsu, deep-fried, sliced pork loin, which makes a heavy and fatty burden for one person. To enjoy Kyo-Ya most, we suggest ordering a sashimi-and-sushi assort-ment along with tempura and plenty of saké. The latter, at a modest $3 per miniature decanter, makes getting a glow on fairly inexpensive. It shouldn't take more than $50 for two to dine à la carte with saké; for an additional $7 to $10, you can enjoy a seven-course meal, all inclusive.
Open Mon.-Sat. 11 a.m.-2 p.m. & 6 p.m.-midnight. All major cards.

Maile Room
Kahala Hilton Hotel,
5000 Kahala Ave.,
Honolulu
• 734-2211
CONTINENTAL

If you simply must eat Continental cuisine, you might as well eat it here. The Maile (pronounced "miley") Room is the crown jewel of the Kahala Hilton, which, in turn, is one of the crown jewels of the Honolulu hotel scene.
The decor runs to classy Island kitsch, with orchids climbing over the lava rock entryway. Tropical horticulturists will likely go mad here, what with all the feverish bromeliads, orchids, and proteas massed in profusion throughout. You can order either à la carte or from the prix-fixe menu (at $38, it's the restaurant's best full-course bargain), a four-course meal that changes weekly. Among the best dishes are the opakapaka soup, a light,

crystalline brew swimming with fish and matchstick veggies. In fact, fish is what the kitchen does best. Try a sashimi appetizer, or the seafood potpourri, or the smoked salmon medallions. Although some dishes run to the precious, like the salmon parfait with salmon roe, or the collar(!) of sole filets, not everything is quite so fussy. The roast rack of lamb is very good, as is the duckling Waialae. And the ragoût of wild mushrooms is a lovely accompaniment, as are the delicately sautéed fiddle-head ferns. Desserts are a real treat, especially the Maile's take on that classic dish of Hawaiian coconut pudding, haiupia, served with a refreshing lime sauce and strawberry ice cream. Also wonderful is the chocolate-mint soufflé.

This is one of the few restaurants in the land of Bermuda shorts and zori in which gentlemen are required to wear jackets—yes, it's that kind of place. It also boasts one of the best wine lists in the Islands. Dinner for two, with wine, is about $110.

Open Mon.-Sat. 6:30 p.m.-9:30 p.m., Sun. 10 a.m.-1 p.m. & 6:30 p.m.-9:30 p.m. All major cards.

Maple Garden
909 Isenberg St.,
Honolulu
• 941-6641
CHINESE

11/20

Maple Garden is a terrific, no-frills Szechuan restaurant—and practically everything on the menu is worth ordering. The most popular dishes in this very popular restaurant are the delicious tea-smoked duck, the spicy eggplant, hot-and-sour soup, and the seafood with black-bean sauce. The price is right, too: a meal for two, with beverages, is about $30.

Open Mon.-Sat. 11:30 a.m.-2:30 p.m. & 5:30 p.m.-10 p.m. All major cards.

Matteo's
Marine Surf Hotel,
364 Seaside,
Waikiki
• 922-5551
ITALIAN

9/20

Far from being the best Italian restaurant in Oahu, Matteo's nonetheless has a huge, loyal following. We're talking old-fashioned southern Italian here—dimly lit, with comfortable, oversize leather booths. Matteo's boasts that semi-ornate elegance peculiar to Italian eateries of this type.

The menu is just what you'd expect it to be, with dishes like stuffed mushrooms, classic antipasti, calamari Fra Diavolo, saltimbocca, chicken cacciatore, and eggplant Parmigiana. The seafood dishes are pretty good, especially if you stick to critters from local waters, or the cioppino. And the Caesar salad is darned tasty, too. If you're in the mood for pasta, stick to the simpler preparations, such as the pomodoro. The wine list is extensive and well chosen. For dinner for two, with wine, you'll spend about $100.

Open nightly 6 p.m.-2 a.m. All major cards.

Mekong I Restaurant

1295 S. Beretania St.,
Honolulu
• 531-2025
THAI

11/20

Though Evil Jungle Prince is the signature dish of this popular restaurant, the opening shot in what appears to be a Thai dynasty, there's little that's evil and not much to suggest a prince here. That leaves the jungle, and Mekong tries to evoke one in its minuscule interior. Vanda orchids burst from the tips of saplings on and between tables, while palm silhouettes parade across the front edge of a dropped ceiling that juts a third of the way into the storefront from the rear. What else? Well, very little. The usual tourist posters dress up the walls and oiled-silk parasols from Chiang Mai in northern Thailand sway overhead under a simulated hut roof. Keo Sananikone, who started it all, now owns three other Thai restaurants—including our favorite, Keo's (see page 28). Locals still swear by Mekong I for food while visitors frequent the others to gawk at the likes of Tina Turner and Tom Selleck. In any case, the hullabaloo is unwarranted. Mekong dishes up fair-to-good Thai food in generous portions at reasonable prices but the place is hardly a dining mecca. Chiang Mai tofu salad, a northern specialty, makes a pleasant alternative to satay or spring rolls for appetizers. Fresh tofu, diced and then heated without oil, is eaten with mint and Thai parsley wrapped in lettuce or cabbage leaves. The ulua (which are various species of jack crevalle, important game and food fishes) in spicy fish soup had toughened a bit, and the stock, though long on straw mushrooms, came up short on lemon grass and green onion. Evil Jungle Prince may be ordered with meat or seafood. Rich, oily gravy and your choice of fish or meat cover a bed of shredded cabbage. Our pork version improved markedly when we added hot chili paste from a cruet on the table. Ong Choi (Asian watercress) with shrimp proved a mild disappointment: the shellfish were small and bland, the watercress tough. Thai green curry with eggplant (not the globular Thai variety but stubby sections of "long" eggplant), the sauce savory sweet thanks to lots of coconut and fresh basil, better reflected Bangkok's rich cuisine. The soapy sweet Pad Thai let us down seriously, however. Tapioca pudding and homemade coconut ice cream may be combined for dessert, or a sweet and simple Thai iced coffee. Though liquor isn't served, diners may bring their own beer or wine for a modest $1 corkage charge. Two people can leave sated for $35.
Open Mon.-Fri. 11 a.m.-1:30 p.m. & 5 p.m.-9 p.m., Sat.-Sun. 5 p.m.-9 p.m. All major cards.

I SELL SEA SHELLS

Among the many exotic local ingredients that are beginning to find their way into Hawaii's restaurant kitchens are *opihi*: small mollusks that come in black, red or yellow. Their chewy, briny-tasting meat is similar to that of the abalone, and even more expensive: a gallon sells for about $160. Hawaiians traditionally have eaten them raw or in salads, and chefs are now mixing them into dishes of fettuccine or angel-hair pasta.

La Mer

Halekulani Hotel,
2199 Kalia Rd.,
Waikiki
• 923-2311
FRENCH

Along with the Kahala Hilton's Maile Room, La Mer is considered the sine qua non of Honolulu's "fancy" restaurants (read: gentlemen must wear jackets). But unlike most haute restaurants elsewhere, haute in Hawaii does not mean snooty service and an entombed atmosphere. Rather, at La Mer, the friendly Island spirit prevails, and the room, while elegant, also is very comfortable. The restaurant, open and airy, takes full advantage of its view of the Pacific; the balmy breezes seem to blow the cobwebs out of any preconceptions we had of French food.

The chefs at La Mer are authentically French (the executive chef George "Marvel" Mavrothalassitis trained at La Pyramide), and the resulting cuisine is a fine blend of classic French technique using local ingredients. Diners receive a complimentary glass of champagne and an *amuse-gueule* (appetizer) at the start of the meal; the dishes that follow are beautiful versions of great classics such as foie gras, frogs' legs, veal medallions and tournedos of beef. More modern creations are escargot ravioli, Molokai venison, roasted squab with lentils and Maui onions.

La Mer also offers a prix-fixe menu and has a marvelous cheese cart as a dessert option (a rarity these days), as well as such achingly good sweets as passion-fruit soufflé. The wine list is quite comprehensive—and quite expensive—but then, in the case of La Mer, if you have to ask, you can't afford it. Dinner for two, with wine, will run about $140.
Open nightly 6 p.m.-9:30 p.m. All major cards.

Michel's at the Colony Surf

Colony Surf Hotel,
2895 Kalakaua Ave.,
Waikiki
• 923-6552
CONTINENTAL

12/20

In all the years we've been making the obligatory pilgrimage to Oahu's culinary éminence grise, the lavosh bread rising in ragged bundles from white linen has been a bit soggy. That's the price one pays for eating on the edge of the ocean, all continental elegance—crystal chandeliers, darkwood panels, plush banquettes—improbably serenaded by surf foundering on jagged rocks 40 feet from the seaside tables. The menu panders to an earlier time and taste. Cheesy seafood crêpes and Madeira-laved meats recall a time when nouvelle cuisine had not shocked the culinary world out of what, in another context, David Hume called a "dogmatic slumber." Amid the likes of vichyssoise, veal Oscar and crab-stuffed avocado, a few fish preparations (steamed onaga, mahimahi meunière) offer concessions to the 29 years that have elapsed since Michel's won its first *Holiday Travel* award. Still, the fact that onaga, a superb fish, has been coupled with a dismal black-bean sauce and rice that would not seem out of place in a TV dinner is disappointing. The seafood crêpe confirmed our worst fears: its cheese top was baked to a Bakelite consistency and taste; crab and shrimp appeared minimally. Liver pâté, listed as "duck and goose," beats out the better canned varieties but only by a nose.

Best bets seem to be the meats. Beef Lucullus consists of two almost fork-tender medallions, grainy and blood-tangy. A smooth ginger-enhanced cream sauce and two good shrimp add grace. Thick and juicy lamb chops, that hoariest of gastronomic chestnuts, steak au poivre, and similar meats do better than dishes that depend on saucing. Prices in all cases spiral up from high to inaccessible. Chateaubriand, served only for twosomes, runs $35 per person. A half dozen baked oysters will set the diner back $14, and Michel's version of surf 'n' turf, filet cardinal, deflates the wallet by $44.

Desserts include a very bizarre chocolate cheesecake surmounted by inch-long chunks of banana. The wine list holds a few good and affordable bottles, such as Clos du Bois Merlot 1987 for $27. Called the most romantic restaurant on the island, Michel's has little more than its setting, natural and artificial, going for it, though that's hardly likely to deter the misty-eyed and muddleheaded, who continue, in their dream, to flock to the place—probably unconscious of what they will eat. Each duet will have to pay for its supper to the tune of $145, including wine.

Open Mon.-Sat. 11:30 a.m.-3 p.m. & 5:30 p.m.-10 p.m.; Sun. 11 a.m.-3 p.m. & 5:30 p.m.-10 p.m. All major cards.

Monterey Bay Canners

Ward Centre,
1200 Ala Moana Blvd.,
Honolulu
• 536-6197

Outrigger Waikiki
Hotel,
2335 Kalakaua Ave.,
Waikiki
• 922-5761
SEAFOOD

9/20

Though the Waikiki branch of Monterey Bay Canners has the better view, the Ward Centre clone is the nicer-looking of the two, so take your pick. This is a good family place—at Ward Centre, the room looks like an authentic Monterey, California, tourist attraction, with all the mandatory fishery paraphernalia throughout. But it's done quite well, making for a pleasant atmosphere.

The food is all right, running that familiar gamut of salads, seafood and steaks. The seafood Cobb salad is pretty good (portions are quite generous here), and the fried bacon-and-oyster sandwich is better than it sounds, although you may want to have your cholesterol level checked after eating it. Play it safe with the fresh local fish, broiled on kiawe wood, and skip the pastas and the fussier appetizers, like the crab-stuffed mushroom caps and oysters Rockefeller (get the raw ones instead). Watermelon sorbet is a nice, refreshing finish. Prices are fairly reasonable, making Monterey Bay Canners a good place to take the kids (there is a children's menu). Two can dine, with wine, for $60 or so.

Open Mon.-Sat. 7 a.m.-midnight. All major cards.

Musashi

Hyatt Regency Hotel,
2424 Kalahana Ave.,
Waikiki
• 323-1234
JAPANESE

11/20

Named after a legendary samurai warrior who, as the back cover of the menu tells us, represented and represents still the qualities the Japanese admire, Musashi generates a sense of expectation that the reality of it fails to satisfy. The short walk past a sushi bar, lit in a suitably indirect and subtle manner, leads to a room in which two teppanyaki grills share space huggermugger with western-style tables and blond bentwood chairs press. Smoke from the grills drifts across the room. Overall, the effect leans more toward an institutional eat-and-run than an exemplar of Japanese ethos and style. Service, however, proceeds smoothly and is generally informed, and we can't complain about the food except to wish that it rose above "quite good" more often, given prices that rise above most of the competition. The Imperial Selection for Two clearly displays Musashi's eagerness to milk the customer. It offers chawan mushi, a subtle egg custard with shellfish and chicken, as a starter, goes to such sashimi as beeflike minislabs of yellowfin tuna, pale and succulent hamachi (yellowtail), and resilient strips of red snapper, all commendably fresh; continues with shrimp tempura, sunomono salad, and either shabu-shabu or sukiyaki; and ends with fruit and sorbet. It's a nice array, but at $95 exceeds by half the same assortment in any number of rival houses. Simpler shabu-shabu or sukiyaki dinners run $35 per person and are served for a minimum of two. The best deal is the Shakudo Dinner. A lacquered six-compartment box holds sashimi, deep-fried shrimp, a handsome grilled filet sliced into blood-rare strips, a trio of daily specials such as freshwater prawn garnished with stuffed chicken, purple sweet potato, fish pudding, salty grilled salmon, and excellent green-tea sorbet. It's a satisfying $31 repast, sort of a bento box with ambition. A meager allotment of sashimi eked out by rice, tea, miso soup, and munchkin-sized pickled veggies commands $27 as the Sashimi Teisoku dinner, which seems more suited to nibbling than dining. A couple, by choosing carefully, may be able to keep the bill down to $75 with saké, but it can easily run the tab up to $125.
Open daily 5:30 a.m.-10:30 a.m. & 6 p.m.-10:30 p.m. All major cards.

Nick's Fishmarket

Gateway Hotel,
2070 Kalakaua Ave.,
Waikiki
• 955-6333
SEAFOOD

10/20

Nick's Fishmarket is one of Honolulu's old (well, twenty years old, anyway) favorites—although many would say that it's seen its day, especially since the eponymous Nick is no longer around (he also garnered a certain measure of infamy for kicking out any restaurant critic that dared enter his portals). The food here is good, but that's all it is. And for the prices, one hopes to eat better than just good food. The fresh Island fish is the best bet here; get it pan-seared. Also good are the steamed clams, the calamari fritti, and Caesar salad, but we wished that the clam chowder had been more convincing. There are also creations such as veal Oscar, flambéed peppercorn filet mignon (yes, it's that kind of place) and lobster thermidor, but don't bother with them. However, there is live music and dancing in the lounge, which also makes you feel as though you've almost gotten your money's worth. Dinner for two, with wine, is about $100. *Open nightly 5:30 p.m.-1:30 a.m. All major cards.*

The Old Spaghetti Factory

Ward Warehouse,
1050 Ala Moana Blvd.,
Honolulu
• 531-1513
ITALIAN

7/20

At the Old Spaghetti Factory, what you see isn't necessarily what you get. The place is great-looking, reminding us in a way of Main Street in Disneyland, done in all manner of ornate Victoriana. The interior is complete with leaded glass windows, authentic Tiffany lamps (Louis Comfort T. is probably rolling over in his grave), dark woods, plush area rugs and lots of polished brass. There's even a streetcar parked in the main room in which diners who long for the old days can chow down. The atmosphere is quite lively, and there is nearly always a line to get in—this place is a very popular family restaurant.

The bad news is the food. The Old Spaghetti Factory is part of a chain that is notable mainly for very big portions of fairly poor food at low prices, which obviously makes a lot of people happy. And the cost is incredibly low—you can get a salad, sourdough bread, a plate of pasta, dessert and a beverage for less than $8 per person. Unfortunately, none of it is very good—but kids love it.
Open Mon.-Thurs. 11:30 a.m.-2 p.m. & 5 p.m.-10 p.m., Fri.-Sat. 11:30 a.m.-2 p.m. & 5 p.m.-11 p.m., Sun. 4 p.m.-10 p.m. All major cards.

Orchids

Halekulani Hotel,
2199 Kalia Rd.,
Waikiki
• 923-2311
PACIFIC RIM

Orchids is one of the most beautiful restaurants in all Hawaii, what with its gorgeous, open-air look dressed in crisp, white linen and the stunning ocean views. It's exactly the kind of restaurant you'd expect at the Island-elegant Halekulani, and, fortunately, the food equals the beauty here.

For dinner, you can order either à la carte or from the prix-fixe menu (a very reasonable $34 per person), and if you're lucky, your visit will coincide with one of the special menus prepared here, including ones from the various regions of the mainland. But you can eat splendidly with the regular menu, too. The appetizer of pork dumplings with a wasabe mustard-and-garlic sauce are marvelous and habit-forming; the sautéed squid with a red curry and fresh mint sauce is so tender, you may think you're eating cream. The Peking-duck salad with hot kim chee is slyly spicy, and the ahi sashimi with sliced avocado and matchsticks of daikon radish is a very tasty jewel, indeed. There are some wonderful soups, too: the Peking-duck soup with wonton looks simple, yet it's woven with a complexity of flavors;

and the Thai chicken soup with coconut and galangal will cure any cold. Entrées don't disappoint. We loved the udon noodles with chicken in a black-bean sauce, as well as the broiled red shrimp with a tangy-sweet mango relish. The Peking duck is perfectly done, as is the roasted veal chop with a chili tomato mustard sauce.

Orchids offers some swoony desserts, as well. The cream-of-coconut rice with mango salad is refreshing, and a fabulous mix of flavors; so is the tapioca with raisins, papaya, banana and coconut cream. But the two we really flip over are the coconut cake with a raspberry coulis (purée) and the soufflé flavored with iced vanilla, macadamia nuts and Kona coffee, topped with candied ginger. Dinner for two, with wine, is about $110.
Open daily 7 a.m.-10:30 p.m. All major cards.

Orson's

Ward Warehouse,
1050 Ala Moana Blvd.,
Honolulu
• 521-5681
SEAFOOD

8/20

This rather bland-looking, bland-tasting, generic fish house smacks of a chain operation. The decor is bare-bones phony New England, and the food is just plain average. If you stick to items such as raw clams or oysters, or simply prepared local fish, you'll sup decently, but why bother, when there are so many other, better places in Ward Warehouse alone? Although they don't rip you off too badly here, the price is still too high for such a drab eating experience. Dinner for two, with beverages, is about $60.
Open Sun.-Thurs. 11 a.m.-10 p.m., Fri.-Sat. 11 a.m.-11 p.m. Cards: AE, JCB, MC, V.

Pagoda Floating Restaurant

Pagoda Hotel,
1525 Rycroft St.,
Honolulu
• 941-6611
JAPANESE/AMERICAN

If the night screams for "sushi, sashimi and saké," this plantation-style restaurant dressed up in pink and white might be just right. Meanwhile, for less adventurous souls, there's also a western (sort of) menu. Amiable, though only moderately well-informed, service will ease any anxiety about eating the delicacies of Japan. Besides which, the food is absolutely first-rate, too.

Both sashimi and sushi retain a scrumptious luster, whether sea bass resembling translucent ivory, gray-white snapper, or beef-red maguro tuna. The rest of the assortment similarly is accomplished: boiled shrimp butterflied and folded around a thumb-sized mound of vinegared rice, Japanese omelet on rice secured by a band of aromatic nori, and so on. Tempura (its batter a frizzled, fat-free halo around shrimps, sweet potatoes, shiitake mushrooms) vies with the catch of the day, mahimahi, which on our visit, was sliced into twin medallions. The sukiyaki, either beef or chicken, at $12.95, which includes soup, rice and various accoutrements, must be one of Honolulu's best buys. Both yakitori (skewered chicken and vegetables) and miso-marinated broiled butterfish, prepared and presented with considerable panache, rival the ubiquitous plate lunch.

The "Western" LaSalle room flexes its culinary muscles with blackened ahi or opakapaka, and a surprisingly good seafood fettuccine, one whose cream sauce goes native with the addition of coconut milk, kaffir-lime leaves from Thailand, ginger and Chardonnay. Best in our book is an herb-bussed calamari steak, though kiawe-smoked salmon teased by a sauce of passion fruit and pink peppercorns makes a close contender. Elvis Presley pie, pastrified homage to the King's favorite food—a fried-banana-and-peanut-butter sandwich—tastes better than it sounds. Seating opposite the waterfall gets snapped up quickly, but it generally will be held for those who make reservations. Visitors who find watching the carp (goldfish) an amusing pastime should show up at 8 a.m., noon or 6 p.m. A couple will spend around $55 for a Japanese meal with beer or saké, and about $75 for a Western meal in LaSalle with wine.

Open Mon.-Sat. 6:30 a.m.-10:30 a.m. & 11 a.m.-2 p.m. & 4:30 p.m.-9 p.m., Sun. 6 p.m.-9:30 p.m. All major cards.

Rainbow Lanai

Hilton Hawaiian Village,
2005 Kalia Rd.,
Waikiki
• 949-4321
HAWAIIAN/AMERICAN

12/20

The Rainbow Lanai is the Hilton's "casual" restaurant, and a very satisfying al fresco dining experience. After all, if you can't eat outdoors in Hawaii, what's the point? The Lanai offers a breathtaking view of the beach and the Pacific, and recently, a concerted effort has been made here to incorporate modern Hawaiian and Pacific dishes into the menu, an effort that has been, for the most part, quite successful.

The trio of satays is delicious: beef with wasabe mustard and macadamia essence (whatever that is), chicken with hot sesame and local fish with spicy lemon grass. So are the soups, including the baked Maui onion, the cream of taro with smoked ahi and the Portuguese bean. A fresh, locally grown salad is tasty: lotus root, sautéed scallops, endive, and watercress on a bed of Waimea spinach dressed with a tangy kumquat-ginger sauce and fresh mint. There are some missteps, such as the oat-bran pasta with oyster, shiitake and chanterelle mushrooms, and Maui tomatoes; why ruin all those lovely vegetables with that awful pasta? But the fresh, roast Hawaiian chicken with shallots and mushrooms, garnished with some intriguing burnt pineapple, is tasty, and so is the Kona yearling steak, with sautéed local fiddlehead ferns and zucchini.

All-American sandwiches abound—burgers, Philly steak, Reuben, and even a dreadful marinated-tofu sandwich on oat-bran bread, which is enough to turn any sane person into a saturated-fats abuser—the Pacific dishes are the ones to go with. Desserts are sinfully yummy—mile-high banana-cream pie, guava chiffon pie, and a riot of ice creams and sauces called the Diamond Head Crater. Every evening from 5 p.m. to 9:30 p.m., the

Rainbow Lanai lays out a very reasonably priced ($16.95 for adults, $7.95 for children under 12) buffet, piled with fresh local fruit, huge joints of roast beef, local fish, curries, a salad bar, and lots of desserts. Another nice touch is that the Lanai will happily halve the portions and the prices of most menu items for kids, too. Dinner for two, with beverages, will run about $40. *Open daily 6 a.m.-11:30 p.m. All major cards.*

Restaurant Benkei

Ward Warehouse,
1050 Ala Moana Blvd.,
Honolulu
• 523-8713
JAPANESE

10/20

Restaurant Benkei sparkles as a very attractive, mid-range Japanese restaurant that features a fine salad bar, of all things, as well as a Japanese buffet with a choice of dishes that changes every night. Some of the buffet items include various sushi, vegetables and fish in tempura, and crab legs. The food quality is pretty good. And the whole set-up is well tended. There is also a regular menu, with the usual teriyaki grilled items, as well as some Western dishes. And you can arrange to dine in the upstairs tatami room, where a kaiseki dinner, very reasonably priced at between $20 and $30 per person, is offered. Benkei is a good choice for a large group, or families with children, since there's basically something for everyone here. And the service is unfailingly polite and friendly. Dinner for two, with beverages, is about $50.
Open Tues.-Sat. 10 a.m.-2 p.m. & 5:30 p.m.-9:30 p.m., Sun. 10 a.m.-2 p.m. & 5 p.m.-9 p.m. Cards: MC, V.

Restaurant Suntory

Royal Hawaiian Center,
3rd Fl.,
2233 Kalakaua Ave.,
Waikiki
• 922-5511
JAPANESE

In a setting reminiscent of upscale Osaka, the local branch of Suntory's restaurant empire purveys seafood lustrously fresh and deftly prepared, whether by the Japanese kitchen staff and teppanyaki chefs or the group of enthusiastic Hawaiians on their own in the Shabu-Shabu room. The teppanyaki room strikes us as particularly handsome, decked out in rust-shot silver fabric on which hang powerful ink-blot prints by the modern master Tanaka, but each room has its own character, and the movement from one to another along restrained passageways suggests the seductive elegance of Japanese culture. Portions seem at first Lilliputian, but intense and varied flavors prove surprisingly satisfying. Tempura dishes survive three vital criteria: light, crisp, dry batter outside; steamy-moist fish or veggies inside; clean aftertaste. When onaga, deep-water red snapper and Kuaui prawns share the sashimi plate with the likes of mirugai (giant clam) and yellowfin tuna, go for it. The onaga is pearlescent and faintly acrid-pungent under a cloak of sweetness; the prawns, sweetly gamey. Shabu-shabu (roughly "swish it, swish it) constitutes a do-it-yourself potluck dinner. The waitress starts things going and explains the cellophane noodles, mushrooms and the rest. The fresh lobster we've had rivaled Maine's, a confession we don't often feel compelled to make. Steamed

Kona crab arrives and departs with the seasons, but it's worth looking for. One dessert surprises: mashed red beans with sweetened cubes of gelatin topped by Häagen-Dazs ice cream, an exotic concession to Americans' sweet tooth. A couple will have to dip into their kimonos to the tune of $115 for a shabu-shabu dinner with all the trimmings and saké, but half that amount will provide them with an ample selection of à la carte dishes.
Open Mon.-Sat. 11:30 a.m.-2 p.m. & 6 p.m.-10 p.m., Sun. 6 p.m.-10 p.m. All major cards.

Rose City Diner

500 Ala Moana Blvd.
(Restaurant Row),
Honolulu
• 524-7673
AMERICAN

9/20

The Rose City Diner is mostly style with very little substance, but in this case, that's okay. It looks great, it's fun and the prices are dirt cheap—which makes it a perfect place to take kids and teenagers. A clone of the Rose City Diner in Pasadena, California, the Honolulu version is even better-looking than the original. A hyper-idealistic version of a fifties diner (you know, the kind in which Ozzie Nelson's progeny hung out), the jukebox spins platters by Elvis, Chuck Berry, Bill Haley and other rock-and-roll dinosaurs. The walls are lined with memorabilia and bowling balls. One major difference: in the fifties, you couldn't fax your orders in from your office.

The usual diner suspects are on the menu here: pancake sandwiches for breakfast, blue-plate specials, chicken-fried steak, burgers and sandwiches, as well as meatloaf with lumpy mashed potatoes, egg creams, and vanilla cokes. There are even a couple of concessions to local tastes—we seriously doubt that Buddy Holly ever ate saimin. Two will escape for under $20.
Open Mon.-Fri. 7 a.m.-midnight, Sat. 8 a.m.-2 a.m., Sun. 8 a.m.-midnight. No cards.

Roy's Restaurant

Hawaii Kai Corporate
Plaza,
6600 Kalanianaole
Hwy.,
Honolulu
• 396-7697
PACIFIC RIM

Before Roy Yamaguchi headed back to his hometown, Honolulu, to open Roy's, he was the toast of the Hollywood foodie set, thanks to his wildly innovative cooking at a restaurant called 385 North, which competed with Wolfgang Puck's Chinois on Main for the title of top Euro-Asian eatery. Two years ago, Yamaguchi grew tired of the fickle loyalties of Lotusland diners, and turning into the prodigal chef, returned home to show his family and friends what he had learned. He opened Roy's on the far side of Hawaii Kai, some distance from the moiling mobs of Waikiki, in a space that's airy, lush and comfortable. Then he got down to work, blending French, Italian, Thai, Japanese and Chinese foods and techniques into what's far and away the best cooking to be found in Honolulu, or Hawaii, for that matter. Roy's is the only restaurant in the Islands that's worth a special journey. One of the youthful (he's in his early 30s, but looks to be in his late teens) Yamaguchi's fortes is his ability to create unexpected combinations that taste as if they've always been meant to be served together—locally caught spiny lobster in a macadamia-nut butter; Louisiana crabcakes in a spicy sesame butter; crunchy thin-crusted pizza topped with marinated Chinese-style chicken, shiitake mushrooms, pickled ginger and spiced sprouts; mesquite-smoked, Peking-style duck with candied pecans and a passion-fruit-ginger sauce. What Yamaguchi has done is to create foods that you can't stop eating, mixing sweet with sour, spicy with crunchy. You'll be tempted to eat here every meal. At Roy's surprisingly reasonable prices, you could easily do worse.

A kind of tropical Spago, Roy's attracts a real show-biz crowd; the room is crammed with executives involved with locally shot network-TV series, wearing their best Montana and Armani, talking deals and "syndie" rights—it's so L.A., you may actually feel a little geographically displaced. But the goodies coming out of Roy's kitchen truly add to the festivities. Dinner for two, with wine, is about $75.

Open Sun.-Thurs. 5:30 p.m.-10 p.m., Fri.-Sat. 5:30 p.m.-11 p.m. All major cards.

Ruth's Chris Steak House

500 Ala Moana Blvd.
(Restaurant Row),
Honolulu
• 599-3860
AMERICAN/
STEAKHOUSE

Honolulu's attractively glitzy Restaurant Row is a burgeoning hotbed of happening eateries—the Black Orchid, Rose City Diner, Sunset Grill, to name but a few—and one of the best of the bunch is Ruth's Chris Steak House. A part of the New Orleans–based chain that operates 23 branches from coast to coast, Ruth's Chris serves some of the best steaks around. It uses only corn-fed U.S. prime beef, bred in the Midwest and dry-aged. The individual steaks are cut to order at the restaurant and are cooked in special broilers at 1,800 degrees to sear the juices in. For those curious about the origin of the rather idiosyncratic name, the chain was founded in 1965 by a single mom in New Orleans, Ruth Fertel, who gave up her career as a lab technician to become a restaurateur with no prior experience in that field. She bought Chris Steak House, taught herself how to butcher meat, tacked her first name onto the existing sign, and was an immediate success.

The quality of the food—not only the beef—served at Ruth's Chris is excellent. Salads are fresh, the garlic cheese bread is addictive, the onion rings crispy and crumbly, and the creamed spinach nutmeggy and plate-lickin' good. All the potato preparations are winners, too—especially the Lyonnaise, sautéed with onions, and the fries, which you can get either as skinny French-style frites or fat steak-cut logs, are fabulous. And though they're almost a meal in themselves, the au gratin potatoes, a pretty mess of spuds, cream sauce, and scads of Cheddar cheese, are wonderful. No matter which steak you choose—New York strip, ribeye, porterhouse or filet—it will be cooked perfectly, to buttery tenderness. But don't neglect the veal chop or lamb chops here, as they're first-class. But those who eschew red meat, don't despair: Ruth's Chris also serves chicken and seafood. The dessert of choice is the bread pudding with 86-proof whiskey sauce, although the pecan pie à la mode runs a close second. Play it safe and wear dinner clothes with elastic waistbands. Dinner for two, with wine, will run about $100.

Open Mon.-Thurs. 11 a.m.-3 p.m. & 5 p.m.-10 p.m., Fri. 11 a.m.-3 p.m. & 5 p.m.-11 p.m., Sat. 5 p.m.-11 p.m., Sun. 5 p.m.-10 p.m. All major cards.

Saigon Café
1831 Ala Moana Blvd., Waikiki
• 955-4009
VIETNAMESE

11/20

A stone's throw away from the Hilton Hawaiian Village, Saigon Café is a real find. It's sinfully inexpensive, is open continuously from the crack of dawn through the dinner hour, and offers a very good selection of tasty, authentic Vietnamese dishes. This sweet, bright little restaurant—neat as a pin, pristine white and airy as an aerie—also offers a nice respite from the rigors of busy Ala Moana, and it serves some very good food, to boot. Among the best, discover the spicy lemon-grass chicken, the tangy garlic shrimp, and the yummy barbecued chicken. The soups here are comforting—despite the fact that Hawaii doesn't offer the optimum in desirable soup weather, but then neither does Vietnam. Best bets are the hu tieu, composed of rice-stick noodles, sliced pork and shrimp or chicken in a delicate pork-and-chicken broth, and the dried noodle soup. There's a terrific green papaya salad (goi du du), a heady pile of shredded green papaya with lean, flavorful pork slices, and shrimp tossed with fresh basil and peanuts in a spicy vinegar sauce. And don't miss the spring and summer rolls or the barbecued pork and rice paper (banh trang thit nuong)—thin slices of barbecued pork served with gossamer rice paper and noodles, lettuce, mint, cucumber and peanut sauce.

Noodle dishes are also a must here, most notably the fresh rice noodles with barbecued beef, chopped cucumber, mint and peanut sauce (we're fools for that sauce!), and the various saimin preparations. For breakfast, the macadamia-nut pancakes are the thing to order. A meal for two will run about $18.

Open daily 6:30 a.m.-10 p.m. Cards: MC, V.

The Secret

The Hawaiian Regent
Hotel,
2552 Kalakaua Ave.,
Honolulu
• 922-6611
CONTINENTAL

11/20

There's nothing particularly wrong with The Secret—it's a handsome restaurant (although elements look a bit dated), with nice, private seating, attentive service, and good food—but there is nothing very exciting, either—there are better places in town for this type of fare.

You won't find many surprises on the menu—scampi Provençale, steak Diane, prime rib, roast venison—but you will notice strolling musicians, which we found a tad annoying. Desserts are of the Black Forest cake/French pastry frou-frou variety, but in The Secret's favor, it does have a very comprehensive wine list. Also keep in mind that dining here is an expensive proposition: dinner for two, with wine, is about $100.

Open nightly 6:30 p.m.-10:30 p.m. All major cards.

PARTY-SIZE PARADISE

Ready for a shock? Waikiki Beach is only two-thirds the size of New York's Central Park. Unhindered, the 75,000 daily visitors can enjoy 1,000 retail shops, 440 restaurants, 350 bars and nightclubs, 34,000 hotel rooms, six beaches and a golf course.

Sergio's

Ilima Hotel,
445 Nohonani St.,
Waikiki
• 926-3388
ITALIAN

9/20

This old-world Italian restaurant must belong to Hawaiian mythology, and many routinely evoke its name when they think of famous places in the islands. So off we went, ready for the deeply satisfying tastes of northern Italy after a steady (albeit satisfying) diet of ahi and opakapaka. We sensed trouble the minute we entered, as our eyes adjusted to the gloom and our waiter, reminiscent of Zero Mostel in *The Producers*, swooped down upon us with great flourishes. We settled into our standard-issue, oversize booth and studied the menu, which also set us to worrying—how can any kitchen turn out 32 starters, 16 pastas and 27 main courses with consistency and skill? The answer is, it can't—at least this kitchen can't. The risotto, though filled with shellfish, was gummy and insipid. We also tried the homemade tortellini, which were set in a pool of Gorgonzola cream sauce that would have weighed down even a weightless astronaut. Entrées were no better: the saltimbocca alla romana combined overcooked, ridiculously tiny veal slices with an overdose of tough, salty prosciutto (and we adore prosciutto), and the chicken breast stuffed with cheese and prosciutto brought back memories of all those hotel banquet dinners we've suffered through over the years. Only the superbly rich and chocolatey gianduia (Italian bitter chocolate) ice cream saved the meal from total disaster. With one of the less expensive bottles of Italian wine, a three-course dinner for two will set you back $125.

Open Mon.-Wed. & Sat.-Sun. 5:30 p.m.-11:30 p.m., Thurs.-Fri. 11 a.m.-2:30 p.m. All major cards.

Sunset Grill

500 Ala Moana Blvd.
(Restaurant Row),
Honolulu
• 521-4409
NEW AMERICAN

12/20

The Sunset Grill is another notch in the belts of restaurant entrepreneurs Richard Bradley and Richard Enos (of Compadres fame), and it's quite an impressive one. This contemporary, California-style eatery has their personal stamp: good food in a wonderful, convivial setting.

This airy room is full of lots of hustle and bustle, both in the open kitchen and the dining area. Everyone working here is so friendly, and looks so happy to be where they are, that you just can't help but be infected with their spirit, unless you're a hopeless curmudgeon.

The food furthers that good will. The menu wisely keeps things simple, while giving you a nice selection of dishes from which to choose; nothing is too gimmicky or tricky. The Maui onion soup tastes freshly made and is very good; the grilled radicchio brushed with olive oil and balsamic vinegar is also a winner. Try the grilled Pacific oysters with garlic butter and barbecue sauce and the absolutely delicious fried calamari with black-bean sauce. A positive must-order is the crunchy Maui onion strings. On the grill: local fish, chicken, steak, rack of lamb with a rosemary aïoli and white beans, skewers of seafood, and baby back ribs. There are also a few pastas and some yummy sandwiches, especially one containing hot Italian sausage. The desserts run to the All-American variety (apple pie, cobblers, chocolate cake), and the wine list (mainly good Californians) is well chosen and priced. In fact, the tariff here is pretty reasonable: dinner for two, with wine, is about $60.
Open Mon.-Thurs. 11 a.m.-11 p.m., Fri.-Sat. 11 a.m.-1 a.m. Cards: AE, MC, V.

Trattoria Manzo

500 Ala Moana Blvd.
(Restaurant Row),
Honolulu
• 522-1711
ITALIAN

12/20

This bright new addition to Restaurant Row is a pretty, open café serving some very good Italian food. Trattoria Manzo is chicly casual, a nice place in which to while away an afternoon or an evening, sipping a cappuccino and spooning up some gelato. But it's also, along with Il Fresco, one of the best casual Italian restaurants in Oahu.

You can easily make a meal of the appetizers here: the calamari fritti and malfatti (lightly fried veal dumplings in pepper sauce) are as tasty as the steamed clams and mussels, served in your choice of a white-wine or red sauce. The roasted bell peppers with anchovies also wake up your palate. The mozzarella caprera, basically a caprese, with buffalo mozzarella, tomatoes, basil and a drizzle of olive oil, is flavorful and fresh. There's a wide selection of mix-and-match pastas—eight different ones that you can have with a choice of about twenty sauces and/or preparations. Among the best, you can enjoy the simple pomodoro with fresh tomato and basil; the frutti di mare; the Paesano with Italian sausage and marinara sauce; and the

arrabiata, nicely spicy. Pizzas come in individual pies and taste quite good. So do the grilled chicken, the various veal dishes, and the gnocchi and tortellini. Prices remain mercifully reasonable here, especially for such good food in a comfortable setting. A meal for two, with beverages, costs about $40.
Open daily 11 a.m.-11 p.m. All major cards.

Trattoria Restaurant
Edgewater Hotel, 2168 Kalia Rd., Waikiki
• 923-8415
ITALIAN

10/20

Intended, it would seem, to suggest a rustic inn, a castello in Abruzzi, a middle-class ristorante in turn-of-the-century Venice, this whimsical creation does each by turns. It's Italia as Disney might have—probably did—conceive it. We try to enjoy the imitation Renaissance frescoes, the overhead wooden beams in a modern hotel, the ceilings painted with clouds and mythological figures, the *faux*-stained glass, mirrored pillars, and so on. Why not? Everyone else is having a ball, and it serves to divert our attention from food that teeters on the edge of abysmal and occasionally falls over the edge.

Like Venice during the rainy season, everything comes inundated. Order salmon, and a custardy glaze films the pink flesh. Choose any of several veal-and-cheese productions, and the cheese will coat the meat like a layer of wall enamel. Mushy gnocchi sit awash in pesto sauce that should merely tease the potato pasta. Fegato (liver) alla Veneziana arrives on a plate whose gravy literally sloshes rafts of onions precariously from edge to edge. Calamari Possillipo narrowly escapes complete censure, as does steak; the former because a spicy tomato sauce enhances the cephalopod, the latter thanks to the chef's reining in his saucy pretensions, at least this once. Zuccotto, sponge cake enclosing a medley of ice creams and drenched in liqueur, an exuberantly vulgar conflation of effects, is the dessert of choice. Espresso and mocha, a chocolate-laced cappuccino, make some amends for what has gone before. The tripartite wine list gives equal time to Italian, French, and Ameri-

MACADAMIA MANIA

As well as being the most expensive nut in the world, the macadamia nut must be one of the richest, sweetest, most buttery nuts in the universe. The nut is popping up on menus all over the world, as more and more chefs experiment with it, in salads, as a hidden thickening agent in sweet-hot sauces, as a "breading" for chicken or fish filets, in tarts, waffles and pancakes, and so on.

More than 65 percent of the world's supply of macadamia nuts comes from the Islands. It seems as if these heavenly morsels must just shower down from Hawaii's blessed skies, but in reality the crops are cultivated at great expense. The trees take about five years to bear fruit, and then another ten to reach the peak of productivity. Moreover, the nuts' shells are so tough that it's a difficult and delicate process to break them open without damaging the meat; to do this, the nuts are dried, until the meat separates slightly from the inside of the shell, and then subjected to 300 cubic pounds of pressure. Macadamia nuts are a rare commodity, and Hawaii has a virtual monopoly on their world production, so there isn't exactly price competition. But we say they're worth every penny!

can vintages. A "Sommelier Special Selection" adds about 50 more, with such elegant bottlings as Macarini Barolo Reserva Brunate 1982 ($60). Waiters vary from showman-pushy to businesslike. For two with modest taste in wine, a meal will come to about $85.
Open nightly 5:30 p.m.-10 p.m. All major cards.

The Willows

901 Hausten St.,
Waikiki
• 946-4808
HAWAIIAN/PACIFIC RIM

12/20

Just outside Waikiki, in a residential district, The Willows offers versions of native tastes in various guises. Like its sister restaurant upstairs, the Kama'aina Suite, Willows is nonchalantly elegant, in a beautiful garden setting complete with ponds and streams swimming with colorful koi.

The Willows has been an institution for about 40 years, and it's easy to see why: service is gracious and inviting; the surroundings are calming and comfortable; and the food is quite good. Try the mahimahi chowder and the lomi salmon with poi as appetizers, along with a side order of the Johnny mushrooms. Main courses tend to be more mainland, but with a Hawaiian twist, such as the garlic steak and Polynesian shrimp. For a real treat, though, come to The Willows on Thursday for the Hawaiian lunch, or for the Sunday brunch, when a full panoply of native dishes is served. Poi Thursday, as it's called, features a very popular group of local musicians, along with fare such as lau lau, poi, curries and glazed oysters. And don't forget to order the sky-high coconut-cream pie, which is the apotheosis of this confection. A meal for two, with beverages, costs about $65.
Open Mon.-Sat. 11:30 a.m.-1:30 p.m. & 5 p.m.-9 p.m., Sun. 10 a.m.-1 p.m. & 5 p.m.-9 p.m. All major cards.

The Woodlands

1289 S. King St.,
Honolulu
• 526-2239
CHINESE

The Woodlands is one of those great local secrets. Tourists generally don't wander in off the street here. And if they don't, they are ignoring a real treasure—what you eat at The Woodlands are the best dumplings and dim sum on the Islands. Don't let the pretty-in-pink interior intimidate you—this is down-home, authentic Chinese food (in fact, most of the customers are Chinese).

You'll find yourself asking for new orders of dumplings long after your hunger has been sated. The succulent chicken-and-chive dumplings with their crisp crust are heavenly, and so are the fish and chives gau gee, steamed in an almost translucent skin of dough. Other treats could be the black-bean fried noodles and the five-alarm hot-and-sour soup. In fact, there's not a dud on the menu, and how many restaurants can claim that? A meal for two, with beverages, is a breathtakingly inexpensive $20.
Open Tues. & Thurs.-Sun. 11 a.m.-2 p.m. & 5 p.m.-9 p.m. Cards: MC, V.

QUICK BITES

BAKERIES

Cinnabon
Kahala Mall
4211 Waialae Ave.,
Honolulu
• 737-6454

As self-professed experts on cinnamon rolls, we have scoured the Earth for the perfect specimen—and we truly believe that we have found it at Cinnabon. These are the biggest, freshest, gooeyest cinnamon rolls we've ever eaten, and they're fabulous for a number of reasons. First off, the dough is yeasty and buttery (even though it's made with margarine) and so pillowy you could sleep on it. Secondly, the dough is rolled around a wonderful cinnamon-caramel mixture instead of the usual dry streusel. And last but not least, each roll is thickly slathered with a not-too-sweet (is there such a thing when you're talking about cinnamon rolls?) cream-cheese frosting that is simply divine. Even the coffee's good here, and the folks working behind the counter are unfailingly friendly, offering free drink refills and extra containers of icing for a few cents extra. We have subsequently found out that Cinnabon is part of a growing nationwide chain; we wish that there were one close to home, but we're secretly relieved that there isn't. Close proximity to a Cinnabon would doom us to a life of elastic waistbands. A snack for two is about $5.
Open daily 9 a.m.-9 p.m. No cards.

King's Bakery & Coffee Shop
1936 S. King St.,
Honolulu
• 941-5211

This Portuguese coffee shop/bakery is the birthplace (actually, the original site in Hilo was, but that's a minor detail) of that nationally famous confection, King's Hawaiian Sweet Bread. Owner Bob Taira's wonderful treat is available here at the bakery part of the shop; good sandwiches and soups (especially the Portuguese bean) are up for grabs in the coffee shop section. A meal for two is about $15, with beverage.
Open daily 24 hours. No cards.

Paradise Bakery & Café
Ala Moana Center
(Makai Market),
1450 Ala Moana Blvd.,
Honolulu
• 946-0205

Paradise Bakery is part of a chain based in the western United States, and it does a terrific job with pastries, croissants, muffins, cookies and cakes. The setting is charming and cheerful, with tables at which you can enjoy coffee and a sweet, or a variety of soups, sandwiches and salads. Breezy and inexpensive, with absolutely fresh food, this is a good bet for a quick meal or snack. Two can dine for about $15, with beverage.
Open daily 7 a.m.-9:30 p.m. Cards: AE, MC, V.

The Pâtisserie
Kahala Mall
4211 Waialae Ave.,
Honolulu
• 735-4402

This clean, cheery, cafeteria-style bakery serves above-average baked goods and soups, salads and sandwiches. Not quite as good as some of the others in town, such as Heidi's, but it does the trick for a bite on the run. Two can eat for about $12, with beverage.
Open Mon.-Fri. 7 a.m.-9 p.m., Sat. 7 a.m.-7 p.m., Sun. 7 a.m.-5 p.m. Cards: MC, V.

BARBECUE

Kiawe Q Hawaiian Barbecue
Ala Moana Center
(Makai Market),
1450 Ala Moana Blvd.,
Honolulu
• 955-1177

Another Ala Moana winner. Kiawe Q specializes in very good Hawaiian barbecue dishes, smoked on the premises. Chicken, ribs, beef and ham are served in a variety of permutations: as sandwiches, combination plates or salads. They also sell their own barbecue sauce, which is finger-licking good, and prices are very low. Lunch for two is about $10, with beverage.
Open Mon.-Fri. 9:30 a.m.-9 p.m., Sat. 9 a.m.-6 p.m., Sun. 10 a.m.-5:30 p.m. No cards.

Rainbow Drive-in
3308 Panina Ave.,
Honolulu
• 737-0177

If you have only $2 for lunch and you want to get away from the tourists and practice your comprehension of pidgin, head for the Rainbow Drive-in. We can't in all honesty recommend the food at this beloved locals' hangout, but we will admit that it's dirt cheap (85 cents for a burger, $1.35 for a barbecued pork sandwich) and authentically Hawaiian. The locals order the

barbecue plate lunch, which combines thin, chewy pieces of beef in barbecue sauce, two scoops of white rice (gravy 10 cents extra), and that curious Island staple, macaroni salad. Avoid the underdone fries. Two can fill up for less than $5.
Open daily 8 a.m.-10 a.m. No cards.

Yummy Korean Bar-B-Q
Ala Moana Center
(Makai Market),
1450 Ala Moana Blvd.,
Honolulu
• 946-9188

Yummy Korean lives up to its name. For very little dough, you get lots of good food, including noodles and soup and various platters featuring a choice of barbecued short ribs, bulgogie, miso stew and barbecued chicken. Combination plates are also available, and all the plates come with a choice of four vegetables and two large scoops of rice. There's also a children's plate for $3.25 with a skewer of barbecued chicken, macaroni salad and rice, as well as fried chicken wings, another fun food for kids. Lunch for two is about $10, with beverage.
Open Mon.-Fri. 9:30 a.m.-9 p.m., Sat. 9:30 a.m.-6 p.m., Sun. 10 a.m.-5 p.m. No cards.

CAFES

Chiang Mai
2239 S. King St.,
Honolulu
• 941-1151

Beloved by locals, Chiang Mai (featuring northern Thai cuisine, as the name implies) is a spotless, straightforward-looking café that serves very good food. The seafood casserole and calamari with fresh lemon grass are terrific, as are the Cornish game hens and assorted curries. This place is quick, cheap and good. Two can dine for about $25, with beverage.
Open Mon.-Sat. 11:30 a.m.-10 p.m., Sun. 5:30 p.m.-10 p.m. Cards: AE, MC, V.

Heidi's
Ala Moana Building,
1441 Kapiolani Blvd.,
3rd Fl.,
Honolulu
• 949-2768

Heidi's is a real local favorite, and it's easy to see why. The folks in this minuscule bakery/café are incredibly friendly and nice, and the food is quite good. The croissants, breads and muffins are wonderful, and so are the sandwiches, especially the good old BLT. Fine chili, too—and if you happen by on a Tuesday, be sure to get the creamy corn chowder. Heidi's is quite a treat, and is just across the way from the Ala Moana Center. Lunch for two is about $10, with beverage.
Open Mon.-Fri. 6:30 a.m.-3:30 p.m., Sat. 7 a.m.-2 p.m. No cards.

Little Café Siam
Ala Moana Center
(Makai Market),
1450 Ala Moana Blvd.,
Honolulu
• 943-8424

Makai Market is the Ala Moana Center's version of Restaurant Row—a real hotbed of good little cafés that straddle the line between fast food and more leisurely dining. Little Café Siam offers tasty, fresh Thai dishes such as pad Thai noodles, curries, ginger chicken, hot chili-garlic chicken and Evil Jungle Prince (chicken simmered in red-curry-peanut sauce with basil, bell

pepper, bamboo shoots and lime leaves), as well as very inexpensive plate lunches. Fun food in a cheery atmosphere. Two can eat for about $10, with beverage.
Open Mon.-Fri. 9:30 a.m.-9 p.m., Sat. 9:30 a.m.-6 p.m., Sun. 10 a.m.-5 p.m. No cards.

Mocha Java/Crêpe Fever
Ward Centre,
1200 Ala Moana Blvd.,
Honolulu
• 521-9023

These little "sidewalk cafés" are operated by the same owners and sit cheek-by-jowl in the Ward Centre. Both have a friendly, hip, cosmopolitan feel—almost like a San Francisco café. Crêpe Fever, naturally, specializes in crêpes stuffed with various entrée and dessert fillings, and offers good sandwiches and salads as well. But we prefer the espresso/cappuccino bar section of Mocha Java and its variety of coffee drinks, milkshakes (try the divine chocolate/espresso one), and yummy assortment of cheesecakes, cardamom cake and peanut-butter cookies. Both are terrific refueling spots and are quite gentle on the pocketbook. Two can eat for about $10, with beverage.
Open Mon.-Sat. 9 a.m.-9 a.m., Sun. 9 a.m.-4 p.m. Cards: AE, MC, V.

Panda Express
Ala Moana Center
(Makai Market),
1450 Ala Moana Blvd.,
Honolulu
• 941-8686

Part of the ubiquitous Panda chain (they're in malls throughout the country), Panda Express does a pretty good job with its Chinese fast food. Especially good are the shrimp with garlic sauce, the mu shu pork, barbecue pork, and roast duck, and there are even old war-horses such as chow mein and fried rice. Kids love this place, and you'll love the prices. Lunch for two is about $15, with beverage.
Open Mon.-Fri. 9:30 a.m.-9 p.m., Sat. 9:30 a.m.-6 p.m., Sun. 10 a.m.-5 p.m. No cards.

Tapa Café
Hilton Hawaiian Village,
2005 Kalia Rd.,
Waikiki
• 949-4321

This is the Hawaiian Village's al fresco coffee shop. The food is quite good for this type of fare—burgers, salads, fried chicken and even some more elaborate dishes, such as teriyaki steak and fettuccine al pesto. Stick to the simple stuff, though, or come for coffee and dessert. Lunch for two is about $25.
Open daily 5:30 a.m.-10 p.m. All major cards.

DELIS

Bernard's New York Deli
Kahala Mall
4211 Waialae Ave.,
Honolulu
• 732-3354

A sweet little New York–style deli, Bernard's features kosher goodies (the smoked fish is flown in from Brooklyn), and just the garlicky aroma of the place evokes Proustian memories of delis past. You'll find good corned beef, pastrami, and turkey sandwiches, as well as decent potato pancakes, stuffed cabbage, blintzes and even herring. Bernard's satisfies homesickness

more than it does one's taste buds, but the folks here are so nice, it's a pleasure just to come and schmooze. A meal for two is about $15, with beverage.
Open Mon.-Thurs. 7 a.m.-9 p.m., Fri.-Sat. 7 a.m.-10 p.m., Sun. 7 a.m.-8 p.m. All major cards.

Hawaiian Bagel Co.
753-B Halekauwila St., Honolulu
• 523-8638

This very popular, unassuming little deli, tucked away on a side street, is, unfortunately, not quite as good as one would wish. Everything looks good—the bagels, cream cheese and lox, the muffins and cinnamon rolls, the assorted sandwiches—but the bagels taste as if they were the pre-packaged, supermarket variety. But this is a fun little neighborhood hangout; there are several tables, and the folks who run the place are extremely friendly. About $10 for two, with beverage.
Open daily 6 a.m.-5 p.m. No cards.

HAMBURGERS

Aloha Grill
Ala Moana Center (Makai Market), 1450 Ala Moana Blvd., Honolulu
• 945-2687

This flashy, fun fifties-style diner is a hoot—and the food's pretty good, too. Run by a real character, Tony "The Tiger" Hernandez, the Aloha serves up fat burgers, fries and fountain specialties (vanilla and cherry Cokes, root beer freezes), along with vintage rock-and-roll. This is a great place for cranky, sunburned kids, and you can't go wrong at these prices: lunch for two is about $10, with a beverage.
Open Mon.-Fri. 9:30 a.m.-9:30 p.m., Sat. 9:30 a.m.-6 p.m., Sun. 10 a.m.-5 p.m. No cards.

Hamburger Mary's Organic Grill
2109 Kuhio Ave., Waikiki
• 922-6722

Like its counterpart in San Francisco, the Honolulu branch of Hamburger Mary's is located in the city's gay neighborhood, an area chock-full of lively boutiques and cafés. Like the original, the decor is eclectic and wacky: if Cecil Beaton at his campiest married Hilo Hattie, this would be the result. The burgers here are great—fat and juicy—as are all the sandwiches and salads. There is a good selection of vegetarian dishes (including a meatless version of eggs Benedict), and portions are fairly sizable. A meal for two is about $20, with a beverage.
Open daily 10 a.m.-2 a.m. All major cards..

Zippy's
7102 Kalanianaole Hwy., Honolulu
• 396-6977

Zippy's is a local fast-food chain, all bright plastic and molded seats, featuring Japanese-American food. Saimin and sushi nestle on the menu alongside bacon and eggs, burgers and chili. It's pleasant enough for a fast-food outlet. Two can eat for about $10, with an iced tea each.
Open 7 a.m.-10 p.m. No cards.

ICE CREAM

Lappert's

Hilton Hawaiian
Village,
2005 Kalia Rd.,
Waikiki
• 943-0256

No exaggeration—aside from Vivoli in Florence, Lappert's may just have the best ice cream in the world. Created by Walter Lappert in 1983, the ice cream is "super premium," meaning that it contains up to 20 percent butterfat, the highest designation for ice cream. Lappert's makes use of the island's native resources—papaya, passion fruit, coconut, macadamias and lychee—for his flavors, and the result is some of the most sinfully rich, smooth and unforgettable ice cream you're ever likely to savor. For instance, the Reese's Cup features entire Reese's peanut butter cups, not just chopped-up pieces. The coconut-macadamia-caramel is a riot of giant macadamias, thick rivers of caramel and plentiful tangles of coconut. Lappert's also serves terrific cookies and cinnamon buns, along with its own excellent house-brand coffee, which you can buy by the pound. Too bad you can't take the ice cream home, as well. About $6 for two, with coffee.
Open daily 10 a.m.-10 p.m. Cards: MC, V.

PIZZA

Zorro's New York Pizza

2310 Kuhio Ave.,
Honolulu
• 926-8730

2139 Kuhio Ave.,
Honolulu
• 926-5555

2320 S. King St.,
Honolulu
• 944-5555

The pizza joints of Waikiki have names that sound like an unholy alliance of the Marx Brothers and the Seven Dwarfs: Hippo's, Harpo's, Magoo's, Zorro's—who could take them seriously? And while most of them are pretty lousy, a couple are pretty good. One of those is Zorro's, which offers pizza by the slice or the pie. The sauce is homemade, the ingredients quite fresh, the crust is good and the cheese is real. This may not be Original Ray's (which is New York's best), but it'll do the trick. A meal for two is about $15, with beverage.
Open daily 11 a.m.-4 a.m. No cards.

SEAFOOD

Amorient Aquefarm, Inc.

56669 Kamehameha
Hwy.,
Kahuku
• 293-8661

Past the Dole pineapple plantation, just about at the apex of Oahu's northwest shore, is an aquaculture farm, where shrimp and prawns are commercially bred. It's also the site of a little hut that is one of the island's great finds, Home of Royal Hawaiian Shrimp & Prawns. Quite a grandiose name for what is basically a shotgun shack, you might say, but carloads of folks aren't lined up here for nothing. Shrimp and prawns of all shapes

and sizes are done in various preparations: in tempura, grilled on a stick and in cocktail sauce. All are unbelievably fresh and delicious; the long drive (which is a very scenic one) and the wait in line are well worth the trouble. Bring your own beverages, however: due to a bizarre zoning regulation, no drinks are sold here. This is one of the greats in the annals of roadside dining—don't miss it. Lunch for two is about $18.
Open daily 10 a.m.-5:30 p.m. No cards.

Orson's Chowderette
Ala Moana Center
(Makai Market),
1450 Ala Moana Blvd.,
Honolulu
• 946-5548

This very cute, spic-and-span stand is related to Orson's fish house and offers a truncated version of its big sibling's menu. You'll find decent clam chowder, grilled and broiled fish, and a host of seafood and nonseafood salads here, at very reasonable prices. Lunch for two is about $15, with beverage.
Open Mon.-Fri. 9:30 a.m.-9 p.m., Sat. 9:30 a.m.-6 p.m., Sun. 10 a.m.-5 p.m. No cards.

HOTELS & CONDOMINIUMS

CONDOMINIUMS

Colony Surf Hotel
2895 Kalakaua Ave.,
Waikiki 96815
• 923-5751,
(800) 252-7873
Fax 922-8433

This is probably one of the worst-kept secrets in Waikiki, thanks to the high profile of Michel's, the hotel's exceedingly trendy, high-fashion French restaurant (see Oahu Restaurants, page 32). Dating back to the early sixties, the Colony Surf is actually a condominium facility consisting of a 21-story beachfront building and the adjoining thirteen-story Colony East. The main building is the one to stay in, with its oversize studio-apartment-style accommodations, and wonderful views of Diamond Head, which is just a short jog down the road from the Colony Surf. The staff has a strong reputation for remembering you from trip to trip, in the style of most great hotels; they'll even store away beach stuff for regulars, so you don't have to trouble

yourself to pack and unpack your aloha shirts year after year. There are only 120 condos, making this a small hotel in Waikiki terms.
1-bedroom & 2-bedrooms: $100-$1,000.

Waikiki Banyan
201 Ohua Ave.
• 922-0555
Fax 922-0906

The Waikiki Banyan can be a welcome sight after that long plane ride over from the mainland. It's not on the beach, but close enough. Some 300 of the 800-plus condominiums are for rent. There's a full kitchen and dining room, which, along with the bedroom, adds up to around 500 square feet. Parking at this high-rise condo will cost you an extra $3 per day.
1-bedroom suites only: $147-$177.

LUXURY

Aston Waikiki Beach Tower
2470 Kalakaua Ave.,
Waikiki 96815
• 926-6400,
(800) 92-ASTON
Fax 926-7380

Ever so slightly off the beaten path, this all-suite hotel is one of the leaders in the move away from the single-room rabbit warren style of beach hotel, toward a more luxurious alternative for a week by the shore. In this case, there are only four suites per floor, with a modest total of 140 suites in the whole, exceedingly tall (39-story) structure. The Tower offers a remarkable view of the beach, stretching from one end of creation to another; some swear on a clear day you can see Japan. As with most suite hotels, there's a kitchen (convenient when you're tired of battling the crowds in front of the Hard Rock), along with the usual spa, sauna, and paddle tennis amenities.
Suites: $199-$600.

Halekulani
2199 Kalia Rd.,
Waikiki 96815
• 923-2311,
(800) 367-2343
Fax 926-8004

Like many of Waikiki's first wave of hotels, after half a century of facing the sea, the Halekulani (which translates as "House Befitting Heaven") had turned genteelly shabby by the beginning of the eighties, just in time for a multimillion-dollar remodeling job. What's interesting about the remodeling is the way in which the hotel maintains the elegance of age, while still looking as new as can be. This is actually a community of hotels, with five buildings scattered over several acres stretching along a prime bit of Waikiki beachfront. Along with the remodeling came an avalanche of amenities—fresh flowers in the rooms, fluffy bathrobes, exotic soaps, marble baths and so forth. Like many of the big-deal hotels, the Halekulani also offers a number of major restaurants, most notably Orchids and La Mer (a third restaurant, oddly called House Without a Key, appeared in a 1925 Charlie Chan novel). But mostly it offers the sand, the sea and the surf, and lots of both.
Doubles: $175-$300; suites: $350-$2,300.

Hilton Hawaiian Village

2005 Kalia Rd.,
Waikiki 96815
• 949-4321,
(800) HILTONS
Fax 947-7898

The Hilton Hawaiian Village is to Waikiki resorts what Steven Spielberg is to moviemakers—bigger than life, entertaining beyond all expectations, so slick you find yourself being swept along despite all misgivings. With a staggering 2,520 rooms spread out over four buildings, in what's been called a separate suburb within the city limits of Waikiki proper, the Hawaiian Village is, by far, the biggest hotel complex on Oahu. It's also, despite its awesome statistics, a very good, even an excellent, hotel. It's so good you'll be tempted not to leave the grounds, which would be a pity, for the Hawaiian Village also sits in the midst of one of the busiest, most exciting sections of Waikiki. In this case, you can be as isolated as you want and still be in the middle of the action—no small trick.

There are four towers that make up the Village—the Tapa, the Rainbow, the Diamond Head, and the exceedingly elegant Alii, which is the tower of choice. The Alii, which was the original Hilton, was gutted and remodeled in 1988 and turned into what amounts to a luxury hotel within a hotel, where the Hilton concentrates the most attentive service and finest amenities. The Hilton is also home to two very good restaurants, Bali-by-the-Sea and the Golden Dragon. And this is where Don Ho performs in the Hilton Dome. The downside is that the Hilton is popular with groups, lots of groups, huge groups. And tour groups are tour groups, with all the herding problems that term implies.

Doubles: $135-$310; suites: $375-$2,000.

Kahala Hilton

5000 Kahala Ave.,
Honolulu 96816
• 734-2211,
(800) 367-2525
Fax 737-2478

Far from the madding crowds of Waikiki, the Kahala is subdued, understated and remarkably plain in a land where brightly colored shirts and screamingly bright flowers are ubiquitous. It's no surprise that, since the hotel opened in 1964, just about everyone who's anyone has chosen to stay here, from American presidents through a wide assortment of royalty (King Juan Carlos of Spain stayed here on his honeymoon), to a vast array of celebrities, who shuttle between the Kahala and the Hana-Maui in search of that elusive amenity known as privacy.

In a land where the hotels stretch to the sky, the 370-room Kahala is strikingly low key and almost low rise (the main building is a modest ten stories tall). It's built around a lagoon that flows throughout the property, filled with a wide assortment of local creatures (plus some not-so-local ones—penguins are definitely not native to the Islands). As with most great hotels, the quality is found in the details—the complimentary pineapple that greets you on your arrival, the light Japanese yukata robes, the "his and hers" bathrooms. Oddly, not much else is convenient—the beach is only average; tennis courts are

down the road; the nearby golf course isn't part of the hotel. And yet, those who know the great hotels of the world rave about the Kahala. It's a haven, a sanctuary, and it's as luxurious as things get in these parts. It's also home to the Maile Room Restaurant, one of Oahu's best (See Oahu Restaurants, page 29).
Doubles: $165-$400; suites: $450-$1,510.

Royal Hawaiian Hotel

2259 Kalakaua Ave.,
Waikiki 96815
• 923-7311,
(800) 325-3535
Fax 924-7098

When you step through the portico at the Royal Hawaiian, you're stepping into a grand and marvelous bit of Island history, dating back to 1927, when the structure was built by the Matson cruise line as a destination for its first class passengers. Long before the Polynesian modernity of the Hilton Hawaiian Village, the stylish choice was the Spanish Revival design so popular in Southern California; indeed, like the Beverly Hills Hotel, the Royal Hawaiian is often referred to as the Pink Palace. It looks, for all the world, like a Spanish castle dropped onto a private beach at Waikiki. And in its heyday the Royal Hawaiian lived up to its name, attracting both European and Hollywood royalty (along with Hawaiian royalty—the first guest was Princess Kawananakoa). Though the hotel was significantly updated in 1969, this 576-room, Sheraton-run structure remains a haven for Hawaiian nostalgia; there's even a weekly tea dance in the Monarch Room. The best dining here is in the Surf Room; the beach is private and the gardens have that lushness that comes with more than a half century of Hawaiian growth.
Doubles: $135-$255; suites: $270-$2,700.

Sheraton Moana Surfrider

2365 Kalakaua Ave.,
Waikiki 96815
• 922-3111,
(800) 325-2525
Fax 923-0308

As with the Royal Hawaiian, we are unabashedly nostalgic when it comes to the Moana Surfrider. Moana is Hawaiian for "wide sea," and from this 1901 Victorian pile, that's exactly what you have—one of the best views of the broad Pacific found along Waikiki. The Moana is a piece of Hawaiian history that transcends all others, and deserves its title as the First Lady of Waikiki. It also, up until just a few years ago, was one of the saddest-looking hotels around, the result of nearly a century of the rigors of surf, sand and sun. The place, in short, had become a dump. But in 1987, it was acquired by a Japanese company, who made a mega-million-dollar commitment not just to restore the old Moana, but to bring it back to its turn-of-the-century glory. The job is remarkable, thanks to an abundance of old photographs and still-extant plans that allowed the builders to restore the hotel to perfection. Each floor features a different type of wood from mahogany to teak. Some things have been modernized (bathroom technology has improved significantly

in the twentieth century). But the feeling of Hawaiian Victoriana is still there. At the Moana, you can feel like Robert Louis Stevenson writing his tales under the banyan tree, or the Prince of Wales happily dancing the night away.
Doubles: $135-$275; suites: $335-$360.

FIRST CLASS

Hyatt Regency Waikiki
2424 Kalakaua Ave.,
Waikiki 96815
• 923-1234,
(800) 233-1234
Fax 926-3415

The Hyatt, situated at the Hemmeter Center, may offer the single best lobby in all of the Hawaiian Islands. It's a relatively awesome ten-story atrium (in the trademark Hyatt style) with a waterfall that spews out 30,000 gallons of recycled water a day. There are moments when, standing in the lobby of the Hyatt after an evening spent battling the crowds of Waikiki, you get the feeling that this might be the Hawaii you traveled all those miles to see. What the Hyatt people have managed to create is a sort of "Dream Hawaii" that's half Disney and half Magnum PI. On either side of the Great Hall (an oddly Maoist name) are a matched set of twin 40-story towers, filled with 1,230 rooms appointed with all the usual Hyatt amenities; in other words, you can be comfortable here, though a bit chilled by the place. The Hyatt also offers one of the best (though stuffiest) restaurants in Waikiki, Bagwells 2424, for those who feel the need to travel thousands of miles to eat French food in the tropics.
Doubles: $105-$235; suites: $350-$1,500.

Ilikai Hotel
1777 Ala Moana Blvd.,
Waikiki 96815
• 949-3811,
(800) 367-8434
Fax 947-4523

This 800-unit, combination twin-tower hotel and condominium complex stands right next to the lovely Ala Wai Yacht Harbor, where boating aficionados can while away a fine afternoon strolling (heck, ogling) some of the most beautiful ships ever set afloat on the blue Pacific. Even those of us who get seasick on the Staten Island Ferry find the polished teak and burnished brass of the Yacht Harbor quite a marvel. The best nearby dining, in fact, is found at the Club in the Yacht Harbor. Beyond that, the Ilikai is notable largely for its good-sized rooms, its fine views (though what hotel worth its salt in Waikiki doesn't offer a view?), and its spacious second-floor terrace featuring twin swimming pools.
Doubles: $100-$180; suites: $220-$360.

Turtle Bay Hilton and Country Club

Kahuku 96731
• 293-8811,
(800) HILTONS
Fax 293-9147

If a *nene* (the endangered Hawaiian goose that is Hawaii's state bird) were to fly directly north from Waikiki, it would wind up at the Turtle Bay Hilton, which at Kahuku is on exactly the opposite side of Oahu. Kahuku also is situated very near what are supposed to be the best surfing beaches in the world, including Sunset Beach, Ehukai Beach and the legendary Banzai Pipeline; in the winter, the waves here frighten with their ferocity. The Turtle Bay sits on a peninsula that juts out into the Pacific, making it one of the most dramatically posed hotels in the Islands. And one can spend a good deal of time sitting on the lanais, watching the surf crash below—a strangely soothing experience, especially at night. Beyond that, the hotel is ordinary and in need of a bit of renovation. The elements have taken their toll on the Turtle Bay. But, if you can overlook that, there are many excellent, lighted tennis courts, an 18-hole golf course and absolute isolation from everything but the surf.
Doubles: $120-$220; suites: $270-$895.

PRACTICAL

Aston Waikikian on the Beach

1811 Ala Moana Blvd.,
Waikiki 96815
• 949-5331,
(800) 92-ASTON
No fax

For the truly nostalgic among us, this spot offers a fine taste of what life used to be like along Waikiki, before the Big Boys came with their mondo-condo monster hotel complexes and 186th-floor religious-experience views. This is pure James Michener, just a low-rise structure (with an attached high-rise Tiki Tower) and a decor that's right out of "Hawaii Five-O." The Trader-Vic-meets-Don-Ho style is refreshingly sweet, with rates to match: one has the sense of being in on a pleasant local secret. By the way, it's the Duke Kahanamoku Lagoon and not the Pacific that forms the beach of the place's name.
Singles & doubles: $84-$180.

Diamond Head Beach Hotel

2947 Kalakaua Ave.,
Waikiki 96815
• 922-1928,
(800) 367-6046
Fax 924-8980

When it comes to planning a trip to Waikiki, one important strategy is to decide whether you're willing to sacrifice the ebb and flow of the crowds for the quietude of the sand and surf. Those who'd rather watch the tide come in than the bikinis go by choose the Diamond Head end of Waikiki, where things can be almost serenely peaceful. In the case of the Diamond Head Beach Hotel—a 56-room,14-story facility—what you get are carefully designed rooms, with views of either the mountains or the sea, and access to nearby Kapiolani Park. There are complimentary continental breakfasts (a rarity in Waikiki) and free bikes for touring the streets. The leitmotif here is peace and quiet, though if your mood changes, the heart of Waikiki is just within walking distance.
Doubles: $90-$130; suites: $150-$400.

Hawaiian Regent Hotel

2552 Kalakaua Ave.,
Waikiki 96815
• 922-6611,
(800) 367-5370
Fax 921-5255

The almost-twin towers (one 24 stories tall, the other 33) of the Regent can be seen from just about anywhere along Waikiki, making the hotel one of the landmarks used to figure out just how far you've meandered down the beach. Curiously, this is a grand hotel that seems obsessed with pretending that it's not in the midst of one of the greatest conglomerations of hotels in the world. Or perhaps, the Regent stays grand because it keeps itself above the surrounding fleshpots. In either case, despite the fact that this 1,346-room complex is the third-largest hotel in Waikiki, there's an undeniable sense of intimacy found at the Regent. You enter not on manic Kalakaua Avenue, but on Ohua Street. And instead of stepping into a hotel fraught with modernity, you'll find that the style of the house leans more toward teak and rattan. Service is swift and effortless, as it would be in a far smaller hotel. Restaurants abound, most notably The Secret and The Summery. This is one of the few hotels where you can find solace in the midst of the excitement of Waikiki. *Doubles: $99–$185; suites: $320–$700.*

Moana Valley Inn

2001 Vancouver Dr.,
Honolulu 96822
• 947-6019,
(800) 634-5115
Fax 946-6168

Despite the relentless rush to modernism in Waikiki, there is history here, and quite a bit of it. Once named the John Guild, this inn dates back to 1915, which in Hawaiian terms is prehistoric. A bit of Island Victoriana, it was originally built as a home for the businessman of its former name. But in the half century that followed, this fine old structure fell upon hard times. The place was on the verge of being turned into a minimall, when it was saved in the late seventies by, of all people, the owner of Crazy Shirts, who had the building lovingly restored to its Victorian elegance. Now under the ownership of a Japanese company, the Moana Valley Inn has seven guest rooms, infinitesimal compared to the big hotels along the beach. Like the inns of New England, the rooms are decorated with period wallpaper and furniture, and guests sleep in squeaky four-poster beds. Meals are served on the lanai overlooking the lush lawn. *Doubles: $80–$145.*

New Otani Kaimana Beach Hotel

2863 Kalakaua Ave.,
Waikiki 96815
• 923-1555,
(800) 252-0197
Fax 922-9404

The New Otani Chain runs one of the best hotels in Tokyo and one of the most Japanese hotels in Los Angeles. Not surprisingly, there are many very Japanese touches to be found at the Hawaiian property, one of which is a curious smallness to the rooms. On the other hand, in exchange for a lack of space, you get a view of Kapiolani Park across the street, and the generally less crowded (though never uncrowded) Sans Souci Beach, one of Waikiki's most discovered secrets. This is one of the better smaller hotels in Waikiki, with a mere 124 rooms, many of them occupied by tour groups from Tokyo, which flock to the hotel's

Miyako Restaurant for a nostalgic taste of home after a week of trying to eat poi and lomi-lomi salmon. *Doubles: $71-$150; suites: $135-$305.*

Outrigger Prince Kuhio Hotel

2500 Kuhio Ave.,
Honolulu 96815
• 922-0811,
(800) 367-5170
Fax 923-0330

Things are so fiercely competitive in the hotel trade in Waikiki, that even though the Outrigger Prince was opened in 1980, it underwent a sizable renovation just seven years later, to improve it even more. This 37-story, 626-room tower is as close to the middle of Waikiki as one physically can get. Things, we've found, can get rather noisy here, as conventioneers stagger and hobble back to their rooms in the small hours of the morning, after a night of too many mai tais and chi chis. As with a number of Waikiki hotels, there's a hotel within the hotel (the Kuhio Club), offering a bit more in exchange for slightly higher rates. All things considered, even with its club, this is a decent though certainly not special place to stay. *Doubles: $90-$140; suites: $195-$375.*

Sheraton Makaha Resort and Country Club

84-626 Makaha
Valley Rd.,
Waianae 96792
• 695-9511,
(800) 325-3535
Fax 695-5806

Makaha sits on the west side of the Waianae Mountains of Oahu. To get there, you drive northwest from the airport, through small towns with scenic names like Ewa, Nanakuli, and Maili. Drive a little farther past the hotel, and you get to Kaena Point, from which you can see Kauai. The resort is about as far from Waikiki as you can be and still remain on the island of Oahu. It offers all the amusements you'd expect at a Hawaiian country resort—golf, tennis, horseback riding (a thrill along the nearby beach), an oversize swimming pool. There are 200 rooms here, more cottages than anything else, where you can play on a beach that hasn't seen a random tourist in years. Expect to remain here for most of the trip; Honolulu is a long drive for dinner. *Doubles: $95-$165.*

Sheraton-Waikiki

2255 Kalakaua Ave.,
Waikiki 96815
• 922-4422,
(800) 525-3535
Fax 923-8785

The towering 30-story Sheraton-Waikiki is the second-largest hotel in the state (losing out to the Hilton Hawaiian Village), with 1,852 rooms smack in the center of Waikiki. Indeed, one of the best views in Honolulu is to be found from the rooftop Hanohano Room, from which you can almost see everything from Alaska to Australia—if the weather is clear. Aside from that, this is basically a functional hotel with a good location, period. The rooms are pleasant enough; the restaurants are a bit on the hokey side—the ersatz Polynesian-themed Kon Tiki, the bad Italian Ciao, the buffet-intensive Ocean Terrace. Once again, the Sheraton is very popular with large groups of tourists who seem to crowd themselves into the elevators all at one time. *Doubles: $95-$220; suites: $290-$355.*

Waikiki Parc Hotel

2233 Helumoa Rd.,
Waikiki 96715
• 921-7272,
(800) 422-0450
Fax 923-1336

Basically a more affordable clone of the Halekulani (both are owned by the same company), offering what the hotel calls "affordable luxury." And the Waikiki Parc succeeds fairly well at that. There are 298 spacious rooms in this 22-story tower (compared with 1,852 rooms in the 30-story Sheraton Waikiki), with the possibility of either an ocean or a mountain view, and a lanai on the upper stories. Beyond that, the Waikiki Parc, which opened in 1987, is relentlessly modern, centrally located, functionally comfortable. It's for the traveler who plans to spend the bare minimum of time in his or her hotel room. *Doubles: $90-$165.*

NIGHTLIFE

BARS	61
CABARET	63
COMEDY	63
DANCING	64
DINNER SHOWS	67
JAZZ	69
LUAUS	70
MUSIC CLUBS	70

When the Hawaiian sun sets, the fun begins in the Islands. Honolulu in particular reflects the pulse of a metropolis—though the beat, as well as the lifestyle, is indeed tropical. The Waikiki strip is where you'll find most of the action. Admittedly, there is a severe shortage of authentic Hawaiian entertainment (hula, slack-key, ukulele), but the rewards are there for those who are willing to put up with a modest search. In ample quantity, however, are bars, clubs and showrooms offering Las Vegas–style productions, as well as comedy and conventional lounge entertainment. And yes, there are music videos in the discos. Here's a tip: many of the larger showrooms gear traffic to tour-bus patrons, and crowds are commonplace. Smaller venues off the tour-bus track often can give you a far better time.

Those who love to pull out that little black dress will be disappointed. Casual couture rules the day (and consequently the night) in the Islands; only a few rooms insist on jackets for the gents. After all, you came to Hawaii to escape the rituals of big-city life.

For specific weekly and monthly listings, consult "The Great Index to Fun" in the *Honolulu Advertiser* (at the end of the month as well as in the Friday editions), *Honolulu* magazine, and visitor-oriented publications such as *This Week* and *Spotlight on Oahu* as well as the *Neighbor Islands*.

BARS

Columbia Inn
645 Kapiolani Blvd.,
Honolulu
• 531-3747

The Columbia Inn is a bastion for journalists (it adjoins the News Building), as well as media, sports and show-biz types. Here you'll find The Roundtable, a place of honor and tradition in the city, where folks hoist draft beers and share the day's stories. Around the cluttered bar, where two TV sets are permanently tuned to either sports or cable-news shows, one might find Bill Conrad, Tom Selleck, Sid Fernandez, the mayor or even the governor.
Open Mon.-Sat. 6 a.m.-12:30 a.m., Sun. 6 a.m.-midnight. All major cards.

Compadres Mexican Bar and Grill
Ward Centre,
Building 3,
1200 Ala Moana Blvd.,
Honolulu
• 523-1307

This is the bar that had the dubious distinction of introducing Corona Beer to Hawaii. *Caramba!* Every night is fiesta time on the patio, where young and old alike congregate for fellowship, margaritas *grandes*, and free taco chips. The under-the-umbrella tables are handy, but even without seats, the elbow-to-elbow revelers seem perfectly content. Annual rituals abound: big Cinco de Mayo to-do on May 5; big Mexican Independence Day party September 15. Don't forget the manager's party every Wednesday, when complimentary quesadillas are served, and the Friday night *pau hana* (after work) merriment from 6 p.m. to 10 p.m. with music by Frank Leto. It's a perfect time to meet the locals. Daring imbibers should try an upside-down margarita.
Open Mon.-Fri. 11 a.m.-1 a.m., Sat.-Sun. 9 a.m.-1 a.m. Cards: AE, MC, V.

Cupid's Lounge
Outrigger Prince
Kuhio Hotel,
2500 Kuhio Ave.,
Honolulu
• 922-0811

The Pat Sylva Trio provides a ticket to yesteryear on Friday and Saturday nights in this off-the-lobby bar. A singer, pianist and stand-up bassist caress myriad songs from the fifties with all the fun of a lost Hawaiian era. Sylva solos Tuesday through Thursday, and singer-guitarist Leon Siu entertains Sunday and Monday evenings.
Shows 6 p.m.-10 p.m. All major cards.

Hard Rock Café

1837 Kapiolani Blvd.
(at the gateway to
Waikiki),
Waikiki
• 955-7383

If this is Monday, it must be Honolulu, or London, or maybe Los Angeles. Peter Morton has cloned so many Hard Rocks it's hard to keep track. The long lines are often deceptive—T-shirt buyers by the dozens, queueing in the parking lot. A "woodie" (that's wood-paneled station wagon to you) suspended over the central bar is the focal point of this local rendezvous point. "Pray for Surf" never seemed more appropriate. Another Hard Rock opened in August of 1990 in Lahaina, Maui (900 Front Street; 667-7400).
Open daily 11 a.m.-midnight. Cards: AE, DC, MC, V.

House Without a Key

Halekulani Hotel,
2199 Kalia Rd.,
Waikiki
• 923-2311

If ever there were the perfect place to watch the sun go down, this is it. An outdoor oasis beneath a landmark tree, The House is home to two resident acts: The Islanders (Sunday, Monday, Tuesday, and Thursday) and the Hiram Olsen Trio (Wednesday, Friday, and Saturday), which opens up its musical scrapbook to create sweet visions of bygone days. Kanoelehua Miller provides beauty and hula daily except Sunday; Debbie Nakanelua does the honors on Sunday. Both are former Miss Hawaiis, so bring your camera.
Open nightly 5 p.m.-10 p.m. All major cards.

Hula's Bar & Lei Stand

2103 Kuhio Ave.,
Honolulu
• 923-0669

For sixteen years, Hula's has been a hangout for gays and straights alike, who gather under a banyan tree that is festooned with bright white lights. There's dancing for both inclinations. On a summery night, the patio atmosphere is especially chic. The last Sunday of every month, Hula's Backyard Bash (5 p.m. to 7 p.m.) is possibly the most Hawaiian and hearty party of its kind, often with inspired performances by local guest stars. Another plus: this place actually sells flower leis.
Open daily 2 p.m.-2 a.m. No cards.

Lewers Lounge

Halekulani Hotel,
2199 Kalia Rd.,
Waikiki
• 923-2311

Ginai and Take Three enliven the evenings with a pop and light-jazz format in a clubby atmosphere of elegance, except Sunday and Monday, when Con Brio, featuring Connie Kissinger, takes over.
Open nightly 9 p.m.-1 a.m. All major cards.

Sunset Grill

500 Ala Moana Blvd.
(Restaurant Row),
Honolulu
• 521-4409

The Grill features a San Francisco–style stand-up bar and an extensive list of California wines by the glass. Check out the airy, cheerful decor; doodle with the crayons on the blank place mats covering the oak tables. Standard-issue bar drinks—such as strained Bloody Marys—are a little-known specialty. A late-night menu, from 11 p.m. to 1 a.m., draws after-show throngs.
Open Mon.-Fri. 11 a.m.-1 a.m., Sat.-Sun. 9 a.m.-1 a.m. Cards: AE, MC, V.

CABARET

Trappers
Hyatt Regency Waikiki,
2424 Kalakaua Ave.,
Waikiki
• 923-1234

The chic, clubby environs draw a dressy, local-celebrity-studded crowd, thanks largely to Mai Tai Sing, the room's manager. Honolulu, a young band with an impressive repertoire of oldies, show tunes and pop favorites, entertains Tuesdays through Saturdays. Jan Brenner and Big Daddy take over Sundays and Mondays, with a *karaoke* (singing to taped music) format by L.A. Sound Machine from 1 to 3 in the morning.
Shows nightly 9 p.m.-3 a.m. No cover for members; nonmembers $5 . All major cards.

COMEDY

Ferdinand's Coffee House
2299 Kuhio Ave.,
Honolulu
• 923-5581

Freddie Morris and Moku Kahana—the former is a singer-ventriloquist-comic, the latter is his dummy—are a Waikiki rarity. Seldom has a blockhead so endeared an audience—let's face it, folks come to talk to Freddie's better half. You might even spot a celeb: Linda Blair (*The Exorcist*), Bill Conrad (*Jake and the Fatman*) and Jeannie Cooper (*The Young and the Restless*) have all been here. The unpretentious show is easy to take and as intoxicating as a mai tai.
Shows Tues.-Sat. 10 p.m.-midnight. No cover, two-drink minimum. All major cards.

Honolulu Comedy Club
Ilikai Hotel,
1777 Ala Moana Blvd.,
Honolulu
• 922-5998

Charlotte and Eddie Sax, who operate the club, have succeeded where others have failed: to keep the laughs and cash flowing. The room is as funny as the stream of mainland acts that parade through it weekly: there's a makeshift stage, from which most stand-ups can reach the ceiling. A glass-elevator ride takes you to the top of the hotel, where the view of the city depends on where you're seated. Now in its second year, the Honolulu Comedy Club also has outposts on Maui, Kauai and the Big Island.
Shows Tues.-Wed. & Thurs. 9 p.m.; Fri. 8 p.m. & 10 p.m.; Sat. 7 p.m., 9 p.m. & 11 p.m.; Sun. 8 p.m. (nonsmoking performance). Cover $10 weeknights, $12 Fri.-Sat. plus a one-drink minimum. Cards: AE, MC, V.

The Peacock Room
Queen Kapiolani Hotel,
150 Kapahulu Ave.,
Honolulu
• 922-1941

Frank DeLima, Hawaii's best-known musical parodist, is at home in a new venue, The Peacock Room, on the second floor of the hotel across from the Honolulu Zoo. DeLima pokes fun at the framed portraits of Hawaiian royalty on the walls, as well as the scents from the zoo animals. His calling card, however, is ethnic comedy, and the usual suspects include Filipinos,

Chinese, Japanese, Koreans, blacks . . . you name them. Thank goodness it's all in the spirit of fun. DeLima and his backup group, Na Kolohe, offer a terrific primer to pidgin English. *Shows Wed.-Sun. 9:30 p.m., Fri.-Sat. 9:30 p.m. & 11 p.m. Cover $7 plus a two-drink minimum. Cards: AE, MC, V.*

DANCING

The Black Orchid Restaurant
500 Ala Moana Blvd.
(Restaurant Row,
Building 6D),
Honolulu
• 521-3111

Art-deco elegance and the prospect of catching a glimpse of co-owner Tom Selleck make The Black Orchid a natural gathering place for its trendy clientele. Coats are not required, but it's wiser to dress up rather than down. On a busy night it's tough to find a seat in the lounge, which features a central bar and a fish tank in the middle; the brass-and-glass motif lends a contemporary feeling. If Selleck isn't there in the flesh, there's a whole wall of photographs to peruse. Tropical drinks on the menu include a prize-winning concoction called the Chocolate Volcano, created by the bartender. Azure McCall sings jazz up to 9 p.m. (Stephen Charles dispenses jazz on Sundays), after which there's dancing to pop sounds by No Excuse.
Open Mon.-Thurs. 11 a.m.-2 a.m., Fri. 11 a.m.-4 a.m., Sat. 6 p.m.-4 a.m., Sun. 6 p.m.-2 a.m. No cover. All major cards.

Bobby McGee's Conglomeration
Colony Surf Hotel,
2885 Kalakaua Ave.,
Waikiki
• 922-1282

This is Honolulu's hottest disco club for all ages, both resident and visiting. The mood is casual and relaxed during dinner hours, when an older clientele enjoys standard hits (Frank Sinatra) and mellow pop (Barry Manilow). As the evening wears on, the younger folks dominate—and the volume and the thumping increase. A great spot, nonetheless, for hobnobbing, if you don't mind crowds.
Open nightly 5:30 p.m.-2 a.m. Cover $2 Sun.-Thurs. after 10 p.m., $4 Fri.-Sat. & holidays after 8 p.m. (Dinner Mon.-Thurs. 5:30 p.m.-10:30 p.m., Fri.-Sat. 5 p.m.-11 p.m., Sun. 5 p.m.-10 p.m.) All major cards.

Captain's Table Lounge
Holiday Inn Waikiki
Beach,
2570 Kalakaua Ave.,
Waikiki
• 922-2511

The bar is noisy but in step with the buoyant, joyous salsa sounds of Rolando Sanchez and Salsa Hawaii on weekends. The musical mood is decidedly Latin, with flourishes of jazz and reggae. Worry less about getting a table than squeezing on to the dance floor in front of the stage. André Branche provides dinner music from 7 p.m. to 9 p.m. and then mans the synthesizer from 9 p.m. to 11 p.m.
Open nightly 6:30 p.m.-1:30 a.m. No cover. All major cards.

Esprit Lounge

Sheraton Waikiki Hotel,
2255 Kalakaua Ave.,
Waikiki
• 922-4422

Esprit has a split personality: it looks like a casual bar, with open windows that welcome the tradewinds, yet patrons are led to seats and tables in showroom fashion. Bernadette & the Sunshine Company, a dance band evolving into a show band, plays lounge-style Tuesday through Saturday; the Love Notes, a bebop combo, maintains the mood Sunday and Monday.
Open daily 10:30 a.m.-2 a.m. Dancing & shows 9 p.m.-1 a.m. Cover charge $3 for Love Notes only. All major cards.

Hot Rod Dinin' & Dancin' Discovery Bay

1778 Ala Moana Blvd.,
Waikiki
• 955-1956

Hot Rod Dinin' & Dancin' (yes, without g's) is Hawaii's latest blast from the past, a 24-hour restaurant and dance club, with *vroom* to spare. Co-owner Fred Piluso, a hot-rod buff, has transformed an avocation into a place dedicated to good times, good food and good memories. Hot rod touches are everywhere: a '32 Ford roadster hangs upside down over the Pit Stop Gift Shop; a jukebox is shaped like a Ford Thunderbird; a replica of driver Al Nosse's '57 Chrysler anchors a drive-in movie set; there's even the front end of James Dean's '49 Mercury. "Licensed to Party" is the motto here, and one can party heartily.
Open daily 24 hours. Dancing daily 4 p.m.-2 a.m. Cards: AE, MC.

Maharaja

Waikiki Trade Center,
2255 Kuhio Ave.,
Waikiki
• 922-3030

The newest of the Waikiki hot spots and easily one of the most luxurious (chrome, glass, and tony appointments run top to bottom), this dinner-and-dance club, created by Japanese investors, draws a cosmopolitan, international crowd. Enter through a first-floor check-in; a world of nocturnal fantasies awaits on the second level. Pricey, but precious.
Open nightly 6 p.m.-2 a.m. Cover $5 weeknights, $8 weekends & holidays. All major cards.

Maile Lounge

Kahala Hilton,
5000 Kahala Ave.,
Honolulu
• 734-2211

For the last seventeen years, it's been the same old thing—Kit Samson's Sound Advice combo—and thank goodness. The Maile Lounge remains one of the nicest places to go either before or after dinner. The attractions are limitless: a splendid blend of vocals (by singer Bonet) and instrumentals (Samson's on keyboards), from Big Band to Broadway, from the 1940s to the 1960s. Dancing water fountains frolic to the tempo, and the place often is buzzing with celebs.
Open Mon.-Sat. 8 p.m.-1 a.m. No cover, two-drink minimum Fri.-Sat. All major cards.

Masquerade

224 McCully St.,
Honolulu
• 949-6337

The rank and file is young and trendy; the sounds swing from videos of Top-40 favorites to occasional "name" shows (Paula Abdul has played twice since the club opened). Oodles of video

screens, fluorescent pinks and blues, flickering strobes, shadowy images and two dance floors all add up to an "in" spot for teeny-boppers. This is one of the few places that approves of very casual attire, including shorts and tank tops.
Open nightly 9 p.m.-2 a.m. Cover $5 after 10 p.m.; admission varies for pop concerts. No cards.

Monarch Room

Royal Hawaiian Hotel, 2259 Kalakaua Ave., Honolulu
• 923-7311

Del Courtney's matchless tea-dance orchestra, a one-of-a-kind tradition that the maestro originated and still maintains at the Hyatt Regency Embarcadero in San Francisco, attracts an older audience that has lived through and still worships the big-band movement. On the beachfront setting with a panorama of Waikiki Beach and Diamond Head, it's a postcard-pretty image of another time, another place.
Open Sun. 4:30 p.m.-8 p.m. Cover $6. All major cards.

Nicholas Nickolas

Ramada Renaissance Ala Moana Hotel, 410 Atkinson Dr., Waikiki
• 955-4466

Dance at this 36th-floor club and you'll feel like you're frolicking in the clouds. Let us count the ways: first, there's a spectacular view of the Ala Wai, Ala Moana, and Waikiki skylines; then there's the romance (soft lighting, cozy booths for snuggling); finally, late-night *pupus* are served till 2:30 a.m. Live music performed by Aura, Tuesday through Saturday; by Augie Rey on Sunday and Monday.
Open nightly 5 p.m.-2:30 a.m. Dancing Sun.-Thurs. 9:30 p.m.-2:30 a.m., Fri.-Sat. 10 p.m.-2:30 a.m. No cover, no minimum. Cards: AE, D, DC, MC, V.

Nick's Fishmarket

Waikiki Gateway Hotel, 2070 Kalakaua Ave., Waikiki
• 955-6333

Here you can dress to kill, play it casual or strike a balance somewhere in-between. The lounge is sensibly middle-of-the-road, ideal for first dates, honeymooners, anniversary celebrations, or après-show socializing. It's lively enough for rock fans, but romantic enough for the oldsters. A late-night *pupu* menu is available till 11:30 p.m. LeRoy Kahaku plays Sunday through Wednesday, Night Moods plays Thursday through Saturday.
Open nightly 5:30 p.m.-2 a.m.; dancing 9 p.m.-1:30 a.m. No cover, 2-drink minimum. All major cards.

The Point After

Hawaiian Regent Hotel, 2552 Kalakaua Ave. Waikiki
• 922-6611

Two ample dance floors, a convivial bar, and periodic renovations have earned points for The Point After, one of Waikiki's true pioneer dance clubs. While live music has been replaced by recorded sounds and videos, the Point's chic chrome-and-black motif (replacing football-inspired visuals) remains voguish. The Japanese have discovered this venue, and they seem to flock here straight from the tour buses.
Open nightly 7 p.m.-4 a.m. Cover $5 after 9 p.m. for minors, $3 after 9 p.m. for adults (over 21). Cards: AE, MC, V.

Rumours

Ramada Renaissance
Ala Moana Hotel,
410 Atkinson Dr.,
Waikiki
• 955-4811

Rumours has it all: a glitzy decor, a cordial staff, alcoves for quiet interludes, dance floors for exhibitionists, video screens galore and state-of-the-art sound and lights. For those unwilling to spring for dinner, there are free *pupu*s until 9 p.m. The big thrill continues to be "The Big Chill," a musical stroll down memory lane Thursday and Friday nights. If you want to mix with the locals, this is the right spot.
Open Sun.-Thurs. 5 p.m.-2 a.m., Fri. 5 p.m.-4 a.m., Sat. 8 p.m.-4 a.m. Cover $3 after 8 p.m. Sun.-Thurs., $5 Fri.-Sat. All major cards.

Studebaker's

500 Ala Moana Blvd.
(Restaurant Row),
Honolulu
• 531-8444

It looks like a diner—and there's even a vintage Studebaker just inside the front entrance. But Studebaker or no, on crowded evenings the lines to enter are long and the wait is tedious. We hate to wait, even if the eavesdropping is excellent. Deejays are hip, a sunken dance floor beckons, and you can bop till you drop. An all-you-can-eat buffet, served from 4 p.m. to 8 p.m. weekdays, is a bargain. Minimum age for admission is a self-imposed 23—two years higher than the law.
Open Mon.-Fri. 11 a.m.-2 a.m., Sat.-Sun. noon-2 a.m. Dancing nightly 8:30 p.m.-2 a.m. Cover $1-$3. Cards: AE, MC, V.

DINNER SHOWS

Ainahau Ballroom

Sheraton Princess
Kaiulani Hotel,
120 Kaiulani Ave.,
Honolulu
• 922-5811

"Sheraton's Polynesian Revue" is the flagship company of Tihati Productions, Inc., the state's largest producers of Polynesian spectacles. Short of traveling through the Polynesian islands or attending the extravaganza at the Polynesian Cultural Center, a show of such size and authenticity would be hard to find. Trademark specialties include Rarotonga and Fijian songs and dances. Costuming is vibrant. For twenty years, the devoted leadership of Jack and Cha Thompson, the original producers-directors, has made this show a Waikiki treasure.
Shows nightly 6:30 p.m.-9 p.m. Dinner seatings 5:15 p.m. ($44.50) & 7:45 p.m. ($39.50); cocktail seatings 6 p.m. & 8:30 p.m. ($20.50). Cards: AE, MC, V, JCB.

Hala Terrace

Kahala Hilton,
5000 Kahala Ave.,
Honolulu
• 734-2211

Danny Kaleikini has been performing in this room for nearly 25 years—the longest anyone has been in the same room on Oahu. He mixes Hawaiian and Polynesian numbers with a few Japanese tunes, with the aplomb of a gourmet chef whipping together ingredients from exotic cultures. The Terrace looks like a large canopied *lanai*. A few numbers are actually staged on the lawn just yards away from the lapping sea.
Shows Mon.-Sat. 9 p.m. Cover $8. Dinner seatings 7 p.m. & 7:30 p.m. ($42). All major cards.

Hilton Hawaiian Village Dome
2005 Kalia Rd.,
Waikiki
• 949-4321

Visitors always put Don Ho on their list of must-sees, along with Waikiki Beach, Diamond Head and the Arizona Memorial. No wonder: Mr. Waikiki delivers such standards as "Tiny Bubbles" and "I'll Remember You" with his trademark laid-back cool. A perennial supporter of up-and-coming talent, Ho also shares his stage with a family of real finds. Diners get the better seats, but the joy is in the entertainment, not the eating. *Shows Mon.-Fri. & Sun. 8:30 p.m. Dinner seating 6:30 p.m. ($41.50); cocktail seating 7:30 p.m. ($24). All major cards.*

Hula Hut Theater Restaurant
286 Beach Walk,
Honolulu
• 923-8411

As Elvis Presley impersonators go, Jonathon Von Brana, starring in "Flashback," is one of the best. He left "Legends" and the Presley role in a Las Vegas show to find true-Blue Hawaiian roots. Besides Presley, the evening includes tributes to Buddy Holly and Diana Ross. The showroom is Vegas-inspired, with main floor seating as well as ramped banquettes. *Shows Mon.-Sat. 9 p.m. Dinner seating 8 p.m. ($37), cocktail seating 8:15 p.m. ($19.50). Cards: AE, DC, MC, V.*

Monarch Room
Royal Hawaiian Hotel,
2259 Kalakaua Ave.,
Honolulu
• 923-7311

The Brothers Cazimero are Hawaii's premiere singing duo. Their repertoire reflects strong Island roots and history, but their music is also innovative and experimental. Known for a hybrid contemporary Hawaiian sound, Robert (on stand-up bass fiddle) and Roland (on guitar) often sound like a whole band, garnishing their music with exquisite harmonies, including falsetto tones; dancers stretch from traditional hula to balletic variations. The Monarch Room, in the famed Pink Palace that is the Royal Hawaiian, is the undisputed jewel of Waikiki showrooms and The Caz, as the brothers are called, are the perfect diamonds for this precious beachfront setting. *Shows Tues.-Thurs 8:30 p.m., Fri.-Sat. 8:30 p.m. &10:30 p.m. Dinner seating 6:30 p.m. ($57). Cocktail seating 8 p.m. ($20.50) & 10 p.m. Fri.-Sat. only ($15). All major cards.*

Outrigger Main Showroom
Outrigger Waikiki Hotel,
2335 Kalakaua Ave.,
Waikiki
• 923-0711, 922-6408

The Society of Seven, ensconced in this club for 21 years, offers a luxurious ride down music's memory lane with pauses on Broadway and in Hollywood. SOS also throws in some comedy and impressions to boot. A favorite among locals and visitors, SOS is known for its show-stopping costumed finales: recent productions have focused on *Les Misérables, The Phantom of the Opera,* and *Jerome Robbins' Broadway,* a montage of great hits from the Great White Way. Lead singers Gary Bautista and Albert Maligmat also unveil myriad familiar personalities via vocal impressions: Elvis, Julio Iglesias, Dean Martin, Liberace, Ray Charles, Stevie Wonder. The shoebox-shaped room is very crowded, and the two video screens don't really do the job of giving the audience a better look at the show.

Shows Mon.-Tues. & Thurs.-Sat. 8:30 p.m. & 10:30 p.m., Wed. 8:30 p.m. Dinner seatings 6 p.m. & 8 p.m. ($41), cocktail seatings 8 p.m. & 10 p.m. ($22.50). Cards: AE, D, DC, MC, V.

Polynesian Palace

Outrigger Reef Towers Hotel,
227 Lewers St.,
Honolulu
• 923-9861

"Book 'em, Danno." Al Harrington used to play Ben Kokua on "Hawaii Five-O." In his humbler days he was a schoolteacher. Harrington draws from both experiences in his Polynesian revue, in a partly Island-, partly Las Vegas–inspired package. He plays stand-up comic, crooner and raconteur, with mixed results. But audiences—largely out-of-towners—idolize him. Shows Mon.-Thurs. & Sun. 6 p.m. & 9:15 p.m.; dinner seatings 5 p.m. & 8 p.m. ($48), cocktail seatings 5:45 p.m. & 9 p.m. ($26). Cards: AE, MC, V.

Tropics Surf Club

Hilton Hawaiian Village,
2005 Kalia Rd.,
Honolulu
• 949-4321

Like a firecracker, she popped into Waikiki one January . . . and now Charo is in her second season at the Tropics, challenging skeptics who never thought salsa and flamenco would find a niche in Waikiki. Charo is all energy, all charisma, all motion, all hair, whether dancing, singing, strumming guitar, or just plain talking. She is totally Charo—no Hawaiian hula nonsense—and consequently the show works. The buffet has improved. One complaint: the showroom fails to mirror the tropics theme. Shows Mon.-Thurs. & Sat. 8 p.m.; dinner from 6:30 p.m. ($44.50), cocktails from 7:30 p.m. ($26.50). All major cards.

JAZZ

New Orleans Bistro

2139 Kuhio Ave.,
Honolulu
• 926-4444

It's not Bourbon Street, but you won't find more jazz, more often, on the Islands than at this cozy bistro. Word of mouth keeps the place hopping with late-night jamming de rigueur. Local jazz kingpins reign, often in a Mardi Gras spirit: Betty Loo Taylor and Joy Woode on Sunday; Sweet Mary Brown and Sir Charles Williamson on Monday; Miles Jackson and Danny Ironstone on Tuesday, Thursday and Friday; and Raga and Larry Huggins on Wednesday and Saturday. Man, oh, man. Open nightly 5 p.m.-1 a.m. Music nightly 10 p.m.-1 a.m.. No cover. Cards: AE, DC, MC, V.

Paradise Lounge

Hilton Hawaiian Village,
2005 Kalia Rd.
Waikiki
• 949-4321

Jimmy Borges, a life-long jazz buff, plays to his devotees as if he's singing in his living room. Indeed, the sofa-and-tables environment, with a usually crowded, tiny dance floor, is very much like a party for friends, with patrons often knowing each other and Borges's repertoire as well as they know the palms of their hands. Cozy and informal fun. Open nightly 5:30 p.m.-11:30 p.m. Music Fri.-Sat. 8:30 p.m.-12:30 a.m. All major cards.

LUAUS

Many visitors to the Islands want to sample that greatest of all picnics, the luau. While you'll see many advertised in magazines, in newspapers and even in your hotel, it pays to know exactly what you're getting into before you lay down your hard-earned cash. Many luaus emphasize fun over tradition, and present Hawaiian culture in extremely thin slices with polyester packaging. The luau audience—that's you—will usually be in the hundreds. For something authentic, try the Hanohano Family Luau, which takes place on Oahu's north shore in Punaluu. You participate in preparing the luau, which includes traditional foods, such as sticky poi and delicious kalua pig roasted in a covered pit. The only rub is that there must be 25 paying customers to make the event happen. For information, call (808) 949-5559. The cost for adults is $39, $30 for children ages 12 to 16, $20 for children 5 to 11.

GOING WHOLE HOG

Almost every luau features what must be one of the most memorable of Hawaiian feasts: kalua pig. Kalua ("baked" or "to bake in a ground oven") pig is prepared in a lengthy, festive procedure outdoors, not unlike a New England clambake. The ceremony begins with the digging of an *imu*, a pit six feet wide and four feet deep, which is lined with wood and lava rocks. When the wood has burned down to coals, the pig (usually about 60 pounds) is sliced open, salted and stuffed with some of the sizzling rocks. The pit is lined with banana leaves and the moist pieces of a banana-tree stump, which create steam for cooking. The pig is then wrapped in leaves and wire, hoisted into the pit and covered with tea leaves, banana leaves and hot stones (and sometimes dirt, burlap or canvas). It's left to cook for about four hours, to smoky succulence.

MUSIC CLUBS

Andrews Restaurant
Ward Centre,
1200 Ala Moana Blvd.,
Honolulu
• 523-8677

Mahi Beamer mans the piano bar; he's one of the Islands' authorities on Hawaiian music. He musically shares a catalogue of culture and history. It is not uncommon for spectators, often fellow entertainers, to burst into impromptu hula or song. *Open daily 11 a.m.-10 p.m. Shows Wed.-Fri. 8 p.m.-11 p.m. No cover. All major cards.*

The Colony Steakhouse

Hyatt Regency Waikiki
2424 Kalakaua Ave.,
Waikiki
• 923-1234

The bar is nondescript: a few tiny tables, angled in such a manner that you can't see the live entertainer, who is hidden in the shadows in the far corner. But make no mistake, the ukulele stylings are not canned but come from the agile fingers of Herb "Ohta-san" Ohta, known for his precision and grace. Ohta's instrumentals (remember "Song for Anna"?) are legendary, and certainly worthy of a larger showcase. For some reason he's content, if almost incidental to the trail of steak-and-seafood diners heading next door to the main dining room.
Open nightly 6 p.m.-11 p.m. Shows Tues.-Sat. 7 p.m.-11 p.m. No cover. All major cards.

Great Hall

Hyatt Regency Waikiki,
2424 Kalakaua Ave.,
Waikiki
• 923-1234

In the heart of the Hyatt's waterfall-accented atrium, the open-air Great Hall is comfortable, airy and pure joy, as long as the weather cooperates. Cecilio and Friends, a contemporary Island group, hold communion from 7 p.m. to 10 p.m., with Glenn Goto and Rachel Gonzales and their jazz format taking over Friday and Saturday. After a day on the beach, this is a wonderful retreat.
Open daily 7:30 a.m.-11 p.m. Music nightly 7 p.m.-10 p.m. No cover. All major cards.

Hy's Steak House Lounge

Waikiki Park Heights
Hotel,
2440 Kuhio Ave.,
Waikiki
• 922-5555

A self-styled singer-composer who looks more like an accountant, Audy Kimura performs in true troubadour fashion, sharing originals that have landed him several Hoku Awards (the Hawaii music industry's equivalent of the Grammys). The living room decor turns the entertainment into a mellow home-style party, but seats are limited and usually occupied by Kimura fans.
Open nightly 5:30 p.m.-1:30 a.m. Music Tues.-Sat. 9 p.m.-12:30 a.m. No cover. All major cards.

Jubilee

1007 Dillingham Blvd.,
Honolulu
• 845-1568

This jubilant outback outpost, populated by beer-drinking locals, is home to an array of top-notch Island recording groups, including Kapena, Ledward Kaapana and Ikona, the Peter Moon Band, the Makaha Sons of Niihau, and Kaleo-O-Kalani. An unmistakable "joint," this one jumps whenever a hot act's cooking. Better to journey with a resident guide; ya gotta know the territory to separate the land mines from the blanks.
Open nightly 7 p.m.-4 a.m. Music Fri.-Sat. 9 p.m. Cover varies (free to $3). Cards: MC, V.

Malia's Cantina

311 Lewers St.,
Honolulu
• 922-7808

Malia's frosty margaritas are hailed as Waikiki's best-kept secret libation. The crowd is young, dominated by surfer-types, but homogenized into a pleasant blend of locals and visitors alike. Live music at night (Henry "Kapono" Kaaihue on Sunday and Monday, Tony Conjugacion Tuesday through Saturday) augments the daytime music videos.
Open daily 11 a.m.-2 a.m. Music nightly 9:30 p.m.-1:30 a.m. No cover. Cards: AE, MC, V.

Sea Lion Café

Kalanianaole Hwy. at
Makapuu Pt. (Sea Life Park),
Honolulu
• 259-9911

Imagine bringing together the Beach Boys, the New Kids on the Block and Lionel Richie, and planting them in Sea World. Now add the trade winds, and you have the Sea Lion Café (formerly the Galley Restaurant), perhaps the most intriguing venue in the Islands. It's located on the grounds of Sea Life Park, and every Friday night there's another spectacle. A thick canopy of stars with an occasional moon augments live performances by some of the finer Island acts including Kapena, Olomana, Ledward Kaapana and Ikona and Genoa Keawe. All that sound is just a stone's throw away from the lava-lined shores of the Pacific.
Show Fri. 8:30 p.m. Cover $4. No cards.

PARTY-SIZE PARADISE

Ready for a shock? Waikiki Beach is only two-thirds the size of New York's Central Park. Unhindered, the 75,000 daily visitors can enjoy 1,000 retail shops, 440 restaurants, 350 bars and nightclubs, 34,000 hotel rooms, six beaches and a golf course.

Shell Bar

Hilton Hawaiian Village,
2005 Kalia Rd.,
Waikiki
• 949-4321

Located in Hawaii's largest convention hotel, this is easily Honolulu's most popular meeting spot: an open-air, sofa-dominated lounge/bar right next to the lobby. There's also a hubbub of musical sounds, with Sydette & Nightwatch in the earlier slot from 5:30 p.m. to 7:30 p.m. and dueling pianos featuring Ginny Tiu (yes, the former pigtailed wunderkind from "The Ed Sullivan Show") matching ivory power with Noly Paa from 8:30 p.m. to 12:30 a.m.
Open daily 11 a.m.-1 a.m. Music nightly 5:30 p.m.-7:30 p.m. & 8:30 p.m.-12:30 a.m. No cover. All major cards.

Wave Waikiki

1877 Kalakaua Ave.,
Waikiki
• 941-0424

Hawaii's best rock-and-roll club, where the hip and the hot assemble, also is a periodic "showcase" for visiting mainland talent; Grace Jones and Oingo Boingo have appeared in the past. It appeals to a younger trendoid clientele that wants to dance the night away.
Open nightly 9 p.m.-4 a.m. Music nightly 9 p.m.-1:30 a.m. Cover $5. No cards.

SHOPS

ANTIQUES

Aloha Antiques & Collectibles
926 Maunakea St., Honolulu
• 536-6187, 599-7721

Anything that anyone ever owned and threw away is likely to show up in this stuffed-to-overflowing shop in Chinatown. You'll find bric-a-brac of every size, color and persuasion. There are those who swear that dedicated hunting here pays off. You may just find that perfect gizmo—carnival glass, polyresin fighting staves, an acupuncture chart, maybe a shell lei . . . well, you get the picture. Prices are highly negotiable.
Open Mon.-Sat. 9:30 a.m.-4 p.m., Sun. 10 a.m.-2:30 p.m. & by appointment.

Antique Alley
1347 Kapiolani Blvd., Honolulu
• 941-8551

Recently we noticed a tall U.S. Mail chute for sale here, complete with instructions and penalty for misuse, that had been scavenged from an office building—a conversation piece if nothing else. A collection of old decorated tin boxes, an abacus, pistols, a stereopticon complete with pictures, old beads, bottles and jewelry that runs the gamut from intriguing to plain fill

every corner. Beaded bags, aloha shirts—just envision it and you'll probably find it here. Pillows of every size and shape, carnival and depression glass . . . we could go on and on. Six different dealers share this huge space, which will provide for dedicated junk junkies a few happy hours pawing through time's leavings.
Open Tues.-Sat. 10:30 a.m.-5 p.m.

Bushido Antiques
936 Maunakea St.,
Honolulu
• 536-5693

Bushido, so named because it specializes in Japanese swords and sword fittings from the eleventh century to the present day, caters to people from all over Japan and the mainland as well as local collectors. Mr. Benson, the owner and proprietor, who studied Japanese sword polishing, restoration and appraisal in the early sixties, also purveys fine Korean antiques. This shop is for serious collectors. Catalogues available by mail.
Open Mon.-Sat. 10 a.m.-5 p.m. & by appointment.

Caravan
1300 Makaloa St.,
Honolulu
• 942-2097

Virginia Randolph designs necklaces of antique amber, coral and jade beads. She also offers a fine collection of nineteenth-century European prints, Orientalia, African sculpture and Tibetan masks. The quality is high, often with commensurate prices. A number of upscale furniture items are also available, including a seventeenth- or eighteenth-century ice bucket, two feet square and one-and-a-half-feet high, and lined with tin. If you're looking for a Dan mask, an Oriental rug or a Wilson Evan nineteenth-century, hand-painted bird print, this is the place to go. Caravan Antiques has recently expanded into the adjacent shop that formerly housed Ailana. Ms. Randolph happily supplies information and prices on all of her stock.
Open Tues.-Sat. 10 a.m.-4 p.m.

Gallery Mikado
Eaton Square,
444 Hobron Ln.,
Honolulu
• 942-3999

Original Japanese woodcuts, Sukothai pottery from Thailand, Neolithic water jars and Sung Bowls from China, along with modern Japanese art are among the goodies Gallery Mikado displays. There are also excellent reprints of Hiroshige that look a lot better than late-run originals and sell at considerably less than one-tenth of the price. Some fair-to-middling Han and Tang dynasty court figures stand out among the collectibles arranged in glass cases.
Open Mon.-Sat. 10 a.m.-6 p.m., Sun. noon-6 p.m.

Garakuta-Do
Eaton Square,
444 Hobron Ln.,
Honolulu
• 955-2099

Deeply patinated, turn-of-the-century woven bamboo baskets and antique lacquered chests may be the most interesting items in this shop, though we must confess to a fascination for several cast-iron medicine grinders with wooden-handled rolling grinders for $260 and massive iron teapots perfect as door stops

or flower stands. But the best bargains may be the haori, women's jackets and full-length kimonos—100-percent silk, and authentically used, as the sweat patches on the inside prove—that go for $20 to $90.
Open Mon.-Sat. 10 a.m.-8 p.m., Sun. 11 a.m.-6 p.m.

I Remember When
930 Maunakea St.,
Honolulu
• 528-4722

Right next door to Aloha Antiques, another potpourri of silverplate candle snuffers, quilts, Chinese amber and Bohemian glass occupies much less cluttered quarters. Prices are equally negotiable.
Open Mon. noon-6 p.m., Tues. & Thurs.-Sat 10 a.m.-8 p.m., Wed. by appointment.

ARTS & CRAFTS

Academy Shop Honolulu Academy of Arts
900 S. Beretania St.,
Honolulu
• 523-1493

Hand-blown and etched glass, ceramic animals, hand-turned woods and tie-dyed silks, mostly by Hawaiian artists, are featured in this tiny gem of a shop inside the Honolulu Academy of Fine Arts. You'll find handmade papers, heavily crazed milk-blue raku pottery and a respectable sampling of fabrics from other parts of the world, such as Thailand and India, along with a fairly comprehensive selection of art books. Prices here strike us as better than reasonable—in fact, some are downright cheap.
Open Tues.-Sat. 10 a.m.-4 p.m., Sun. 1-5 p.m.

Arts of Paradise Gallery
International Market Place,
2330 Kalakaua Ave.,
2nd Fl.,
Honolulu
• 924-ARTS

If you can tear yourself away from the carver making coconuts, or the psychic readers that dot the market, or the all-Elvis Shop at the foot of the stairs, you'll find a gallery that purveys considerably better than run-of-the-mill watercolors, gouaches, hand-dyed papers, collages, pottery, small wood items, hand-painted silk blouses, caftans and *pareus.* Look especially for watercolor still-lifes by Misao Hashi, Jeanne Robertson's misty emerald and azure landscapes, and Leslie Tomamatsu's wave-form ceramics that hover halfway between craft and sculpture. There's even a small, comfortable, air-conditioned theater in which to rest your shopping-weary bones while taking in a lush travelogue about Hawaii for free.
Open daily 9 a.m.-11 p.m.

Gallery EAS
Makaloa Square,
1426 Makaloa St.,
Honolulu
• 947-1426

In an out-of-the-way location in Makaloa Square, this Hawaiian upstairs/downstairs devoted entirely to arts and crafts makes a worthwhile detour. Simple ceramic bowl and vase forms by Higa glow in lush enamel-like cinnabar reds and rose purples. Jason's predominantly yellow and ochre hand-blown glass sells for around $50. Batiks, baskets, wonderful pots with splashed-

on, vaguely floral patterns, carved wooden bowls and well-executed graphics, primarily photos and prints, fill out the corners. You can even get a whole 30-piece dinner set in hand-fired ceramics for $320. Call to check hours, which are, to use an Island euphemism, flexible.
Open Tues.-Sat. 11 a.m.-5 p.m.

Gateway Gallery
1050 Nuuanu Ave.,
Honolulu
• 521-6863

Shirley Reo Beene, one of the gallery owners, gives art lessons in the mornings and displays her portraits in the shop. The gallery features about sixteen Oahu artists, evenly divided between painters and sculptors. Esther Shimazu's chubby little figures reminiscent of the Venus of Willendorf, B. Mac's lava-and-coral sculptures, Timothy Ojile's brightly colored screens, and Roy Venters's abstract silhouettes cut out of canvas are all worth a look-see. Exhibits change frequently.
Open Mon.-Sat. 11 a.m.-5:30 p.m.

Pegge Hopper Gallery
1164 Nuuanu Ave.,
Honolulu
• 524-1160

There's an upstairs and a downstairs to the Pegge Hopper Gallery, but both are devoted exclusively to the work of Hawaii's best-known living painter. We're always astonished at the diversity of Hopper's work, a diversity that does not appear in published prints or on the walls of the high-priced galleries that normally handle her work. For example, a woman striding forward, cradling a cat in her arms, her expression reminiscent of Andrew Wyeth's Helga, is light years away from, but no less powerful than, the more familiar Polynesian *wahine* lying or sitting against pastel backgrounds. Pegge's nudes are fluid studies totally unlike the highly stylized portraits. There's even a lighter, tongue-in-cheek side to this artist, but go see for yourself.
Open Mon.-Fri. 11 a.m.-5 p.m., Sat. 11 a.m.-3 p.m.

Shop Pacifica
1525 Bernice St.,
Honolulu
• 848-4158

The Bishop Museum gift shop carries a large selection of books on Hawaiiana, as well as some wooden bowls, kukui-nut necklaces, feather leis, Niihau jewelry and a selection of Island jams, honeys and preserves, which visitors may sample. Though somewhat limited in comparison with other museum shops we've visited, there are enough calabashes, T-shirts and the like to satisfy most souvenir hunters. Instead of bringing your favorite *keiki* (youngster) the usual T-shirt, why not give him or her a copy of *The Eight Rainbows of 'Umi*, a charmingly illustrated myth that sells for $2.95, autographed?
Open daily 9 a.m.-5 p.m.

BOOKS

Honolulu Book Shop

Ala Moana Center,
1450 Ala Moana Blvd.,
Honolulu
• 941-2274

Those who can't do without knowing that the phrase *mai haule ke keiki* means "the child almost fell" or who want the inside dope on that archetypal Hawaiian form of terpsichore, the hula, or the dirt on *humuhumunukunukuapuaa* and his fishy relations, or almost anything else Hawaiian, should check in at this bookstore. Five separate stands groan under piles of such books as *Plants and Flowers of Hawaii*, *The Kahuna* (witch doctor), *Niihau* (the forbidden island), and *Whale Song*, including a whole section devoted to children's books. The usual guidebooks and several thousand non-Hawaiian titles fill every available bit of wall space and floor space not given over to narrow aisles jammed with shoppers. We particularly recommend *Olelo No'eau* by Mary Kawena Pukui, a gloriously illustrated book of "Hawaiian proverbs and poetical sayings," published by Bishop Museum Press.
Open Mon.-Fri. 9 a.m.-9 p.m., Sat. 9 a.m.-5 p.m., Sun. 9:30 a.m.-5 p.m.

CLOTHES

If you just plain have too much money with you and are looking for a convenient way to unload some of it, take the escalator to the second level of the **Ala Moana Center** (1450 Ala Moana Blvd., Honolulu). Such *très*-chic and ultrachic shops as **George Jensen** (for silver), **Bruno Magli** for high-fashion footwear, **Gucci, Chanel, Dior, Giorgio Armani** and a handful of others will gladly sell you all the European fashions that you presumably came here to get away from. It turns us off pronto, but locals and tourists flock here in numbers that would rival the pigeons in the Piazza San Marco. If you do decide to shop in any of these establishments, be prepared to take your place behind a gaggle of fellow visitors with credit cards that just won't quit.

Crazy Shirts

2201 Kalakaua Ave.,
Honolulu
• 924-6646

Garfield is right at home at Crazy Shirts, which can provide better than 40 heat-transfer appliqués of the great cat to T-shirts from plain white to Day-Glo pink or green and all shades between. Ailurophobes may choose from an assortment of nonfeline designs, and, name notwithstanding, Crazy Shirts sells shorts, caps and similar casual wear.
Open daily 9 a.m.-11 p.m.

Faubourg St. Honoré

Royal Hawaiian
Shopping Center,
2201 Kalakaua Ave.,
Honolulu
• 922-5755

If you want Paris originals *de vrai*—though why you should come to Oahu for them is beyond us—stop in here. You'll find, for example, an absolutely smashing woman's jacket of alternating squares and strips of leather and suede by Thierphil of Paris, for $810. Designs by Mary B., Pucci, Jean Pecarel's conservative business suits, Zary's playwear and casual leather are all sold here; original stylings otherwise all but unobtainable before landfall in Los Angeles or San Francisco.
Open daily 9 a.m.-10 p.m.

Kula Bay Tropical Clothing Co.

Royal Hawaiian Hotel,
2259 Kalakaua Ave.,
Honolulu
• 923-0042

Kula Bay, ensconced in the imposing Royal Hawaiian Hotel (alas, its pink presence no longer visible from the street, a shopping center having erupted like a concrete fungus between it and Kalakaua Avenue), sells those incredible Panama hats, flexible as linen, called *finos*, and actually woven in Ecuador. The hats, one continuous thread woven in concentric circles and spiral patterns, are as translucent as eggshells. Prices begin at $100 and go into the low thousands—they've sold hats here for $4,500. Kula Bay also carries a nice line of tropical wear—patterns from collector's archives of the thirties to the fifties, originally in polyester or rayon, which are printed on cotton at prices to match their obvious quality.
Open daily 8:30 a.m.-10 p.m.

Shirt-Stop

2236 Kalakaua Ave.,
Honolulu
• 922-3223

Francis Frost and five other artists will airbrush designs onto your T-shirts—in either set patterns or your own originals. Her masterpiece is Sean Connery, copied from a photo in *People* magazine, as macho as but considerably more hairy than the original. Textile dye colors stay fast, if the purchaser follows directions, for up to five years. Prices begin at $3 for a simple name and go up to $125 for a complex scene.
Open daily 8 a.m.-midnight.

Swim Suit Warehouse

Royal Hawaiian
Shopping Center,
3rd Fl.,
2201 Kalakaua Ave.,
Honolulu
• 922-8100

With more than 6,000 women's bathing suits to choose from and sizes that go up to 22, almost everyone should find something for the beach here. Bikinis are all $23.95, while one-piece suits go for $26.95 and $34.95. Name designers like Gottex turn up every once in a while, some at higher prices, and the variety isn't bad. Three other locations.
Open Mon.-Sat. 9 a.m.-10 p.m., Sun. 9 a.m.-9 p.m.

Very Classic

1512 Kona St.,
Honolulu
• 946-0088

For the traditional Hawaiian *muumuu*, rather like the ones pictured in nineteenth-century photographs of matrons presiding over the luau, take a peek at Very Classic, *mauka* (toward the mountain) from the Ala Moana Center. A typical garment by Tiare, a Hawaiian clothier, features crewel work florals and

lace trim, admittedly machine-made, on a long blue-and-white design overlaid with a rose trellis pattern. Prices range from $55 to $120. Nalei Brooks designs the dresses. She also designed much of the clothing worn by former Governor Arioshi's wife, as well as the inflight uniforms for United Airlines. Jade Dobashi designs the elegant costume jewelry in the front of the shop and will make things to order to your specifications.
Open Mon.-Fri. 10 a.m.-6 p.m.

FLOWERS

Aloha Leis and Flowers Shop
1145 Maunakea St., Honolulu
• 599-7725

Walking through Chinatown, we always like to stop off at one of the many small lei shops. You can see the family stringing them inside most of the storefronts, but on the corner of Maunakea and N. Pauahi streets, at the Aloha Leis and Flowers Shop, the whole family sits outside eating laulau or lomi lomi while stringing some of the nicest lantern ilima, carnation, and tuberose leis. These cost $2 to $20, depending on the flower and the pattern.
Open Mon.-Sat. 7 a.m.-9 p.m., Sun. 7 a.m.-6 p.m.

Cindy's Lei and Flower Shoppe
115 N. Hotel St., Honolulu
• 536-2169

Just down Maunakea Street toward the harbor, beneath the legendary Wo Fat Chop Suey Restaurant, which served its first plate just a touch over a century ago, you'll find Cindy's Flower Shop, specializing in anthuriums, orchids, and protea. If you're lucky enough to be invited to a local luau or other special occasion, here's the place for elaborate centerpieces. We particularly like an arrangement of a dozen blood-red roses rising out of a sea of baby's breath and Island ferns. It sells for around $35 during the summer and a little more around the holidays.
Open Mon.-Sat. 7 a.m.-7 p.m., Sun. 8 a.m.-5 p.m.

Exotics Hawaii
Royal Hawaiian Shopping Center, 2301 Kalakaua Ave., Honolulu
• 922-2205

For flowers to dress up your hotel or condo while on the Islands, or have shipped back to a favorite aunt on the mainland (not to mention yourself), pop in here. Among the most attractive centerpieces is one composed of three kinds of protea against red anthuriums and deep green ti leaves. Exotics Hawaii owns orchid nurseries on the Big Island and Oahu, so their displays of potted lime-green or bifoliate fuchsia cattleyas as well as a range of dendrobiums are always dewy-fresh. Prices per plant start at $15.
Open Mon.-Sat. 9:30 a.m.-10 p.m., Sun. 9 a.m.-8:30 p.m.

Lita's Leis & Flower Shoppe

59 N. Beretania St.,
Honolulu
• 521-9065

One of the few shops that accepts credit cards for its floral arrangements and leis, Lita's has been a Beretania Street institution for some time. Though Lita Caneso supplies a whole range of leis, some her own work, others purchased elsewhere, Islanders make the trek to Chinatown for her puakenikeni leis. This unusual exotic, in addition to its beguiling fragrance, has flowers that change gradually from ivory to a light golden beige, ending their brief life the honey-rust of a tawny Brazilian topaz. *Open daily 7 a.m.-9 p.m.*

Maunakea Leis and Flowers

1189 Maunakea St.,
Honolulu
• 538-7871

Sharon makes the leis here, and a particularly lovely set they are. Our favorites are the flat Mauna Loa (after the volcano on the Big Island), which sells for $16, and a half Mauna Loa, which runs about $17 or $18. Both involve a complex interweaving of vanda orchids.
Open daily 6:30 a.m.-9 p.m.

FOOD

Crack Seed Center

Ala Moana Center,
1450 Ala Moana Blvd.,
Honolulu
• 949-7200

Such treats as Chinese passion, crack seed, which is preserved fruit, and dried, salted shellfish may be sampled by the ounce or pound in the Ala Moana Crack Seed Center. Sweet-and-sour or salty plums, apricots preserved with sugar, vinegar and licorice, candied pineapple and pickled mango gives you an idea. Prices range from about $7 to $20 a pound, with a quarter-pound minimum.
Open Mon.-Fri 9 a.m.-9 p.m., Sat. 9 a.m.-5:30 p.m., Sun. 9 a.m.-5 p.m.

Kyotaru's Take Out Sushi

2160 Kalakaua Ave.,
Honolulu
• 924-3663

When hunger pangs strike us on the way to the beach and we don't feel like taking the time to stop off at a restaurant, we avail ourselves of Kyotaru's Take Out Sushi. Pick up prepacked Bento boxes from the display case on the right. They run from the nine-piece Rindo for $7.75 to Tsuru for $4.95 and, for quick snacks, various niguri-wrapped sushi rolls from $1.75 to $3.25. There's also a nice fruit pack for $2.95.
Open daily 10 a.m.-2 p.m. & 5 p.m.-9:30 p.m.

Lappert's Ice Cream

Ala Moana Center,
1450 Ala Moana Blvd.,
Honolulu
• 942-0320

Does this trigger your salivary glands? An astronomical butterfat content and Belgian waffle cones made fresh daily. Then make a beeline for one of the Lappert's ice-cream shops! You'll find such flavors as Cookies 'n' Cream, truffle-studded Grand Marnier, and a host of tropical fruit sorbets, including a daily fat-free flavor. The Ala Moana shop also offers a discount for senior citizens. If ice cream doesn't tempt you, have one of the homemade cookies with Kauai coffee (regular or decaf) or Hawaii's answer to Jamaica Blue Mountain, Kona coffee. *Open Mon.-Fri. 10 a.m.-9 p.m., Sat.-Sun. 9 a.m.-6 p.m.*

Oahu Market
King & Kekaulike Sts., Honolulu
• No phone

The Oahu Market hosts that jumble of shops typical of Asian markets. If you're not too fastidious, you can get chunks of cinnabar-red roast pork or glossy, mahogany-colored duck to nibble on while ogling fresh parrot fish and uku or considering whether the breadfruit at Young Yung's can be cooked in the coffee maker in your hotel room. Those with a condo or kitchen facilities will want to stock up on this produce, which is invariably fresher and mostly cheaper than in supermarkets around town. Right across the street, King Market handles a more westernized line of comestibles in a more traditional supermarket setting.
Open daily. Hours vary.

The Royal Deli
Royal Hawaiian Shopping Center, 2233 Kalakaua Ave., Honolulu
• No phone

On the ground floor of the Royal Hawaiian Shopping Center, just off Kalakaua Avenue, a snack shop dispenses superior hot dogs with a variety of toppings for $1.85 to $2.35. Irish-style corned-beef and turkey-breast sandwiches each go for $3.50, while $3.95 buys a well-filled sandwich of roast beef. Hot apple pie à la mode ($2.25) makes a satisfying dessert.
Open Mon.-Sat. 9 a.m.-10 p.m., Sun. 9 a.m.-9 p.m.

Shung Chong Yuein, Ltd. Chinese Cake Shop
1027 Maunakea St., Honolulu
• 531-1983

Should a spur-of-the-moment marriage bowl you over under the balmy tropic skies, this local Chinese pâtisserie will be happy to accommodate you with a wedding cake, Chinese style. Otherwise, do as the locals do, stop in for sesame-coated chunks of peanut candy, sugary preserved water chestnuts, lotus root, and less exotic fruits and vegetables, or pick up some steamed buns and coconut-almond cookies for streetside snacking.
Open Mon.-Sat. 6 a.m.-5 p.m., Sun. 6 a.m.-2 p.m.

GIFTS

Accessory Tree
Royal Hawaiian Shopping Center, A309, 2201 Kalakaua Ave., Honolulu
• 922-6595

Among the usual scarves, belts, and purses, a small selection of frogskin bags and shoes along with combination frogskin and snakeskin items stand out. Made especially for this shop and not available elsewhere on the island so far as we can tell, these unique accessories glow in almost-neon rainbow colors. Malachite-green and azure make especially striking statements.
Open Mon.-Sat. 9 a.m.-10 p.m., Sun. 10 a.m.-9 p.m.

Artlines

Ala Moana Center,
1450 Ala Moana Blvd.,
Honolulu
• 941-1445

If you come across a passable imitation of a limestone grotto in the Ala Moana Center, you're in Artlines. The collection is eclectic with a vengeance. Airport art—which is African sculpture we wouldn't be seen dead with—stands beside tolerable New Guinea yam masks. Yesterday's tourist-quality Indonesian puppets alternate with attractive crystal jewelry, silk scarves from India and an occasional Polynesian or new-world artifact.
Open Mon.-Fri 9 a.m.-9 p.m., Sat. 9 a.m.-5 p.m., Sun 10 a.m.-5 p.m.

China Treasures

Hilton Hawaiian Village,
2005 Kalio Rd.,
Honolulu
• 946-5752

To fill up any gaping holes on your knickknack shelves, take a gander at the cloisonné and soapstone, the porcelain Quan Yins and gilt bodhisattvas that dot this square shop in the middle of the Hilton Hawaiian Village. It's all last year's Hong Kong and Taiwan production, including rather flamboyant screens and cocktail tables, but it's just the sort of thing to provoke gasps of admiration without costing an arm and a leg.
Open daily 9 a.m.-10 p.m.

Coral Grotto

Hilton Hawaiian Village,
2005 Kalio Rd.
Honolulu
• 941-1122

Natural pink and black coral fans display, in the raw, the material that Hawaiians love to carve into rings and necklaces and pendants. Coral is so beguiling that even standard designs retain a considerable charm. We particularly like a half dozen strands of blush coral beads twisted into a rope necklace and cabachon oxblood-red Mediterranean coral in men's and women's rings. Rounding out the offerings are the newest variety of coral (gold-hued, and found in extremely deep waters) and a few noncoral minerals such as malachite .
Open daily 9 a.m.-10 p.m.

Iida S.M. Ltd.

Ala Moana Center,
1450 Ala Moana Blvd.,
Honolulu
• 973-0320

A somewhat classier grab-bag shop than most, Iida sells an unimaginable variety of Orientalia, from lacquerware candy bowls to rectangular pottery fish platters emblazoned with blue and pink carp to cotton kimonos, knickknacks, chopsticks, teacups and Japanese kites. Prices are low, quality is good, and service is helpful.
Open Mon.-Fri. 9 a.m.-9 p.m., Sat.-Sun. 9 a.m.-5 p.m.

Island Shells

Ala Moana Center,
1450 Ala Moana Blvd.,
Honolulu
• 947-3313

Island Shells carries the usual assortment of the more common shells, heavy on cowries, cones and New Zealand pauas. They also do a roaring trade in kitsch animals constructed from the cheaper shells. Of greater interest to us are the hand-painted wooden fish imported from Indonesia that go for as low as $2.50 and as high as $20. Also worth a look are wind chimes

constructed of the fish alternating with strips of driftwood and shells but unfortunately threaded on plastic.
Open Mon.-Fri. 9 a.m.-9 p.m., Sat.-Sun. 9 a.m.-5 p.m.

K. S. Eel Skin
2170 Kalakaua Ave.,
Honolulu
• 923-3499

This is one of the largest and most varied collections of eelskin items we've come across, and prices are lower here than on the mainland and the other islands. Pigskin-lined briefcases go for $69.95 and $139, attaché cases for $35.95; purses start at $19.95 and go up to $64. You can buy jackets and belts along with the usual wallets, key-holders and the like. Although you may find an occasional item slightly lower in the flea market or at one of the stands in the International Market Place, K. S. offers one of the widest selections in town.
Open daily 8:30 a.m.-11 p.m.

Moon's Stand
International Market Place,
2330 Kalakauua Ave.,
Honolulu
• No phone

Mr. Moon offers expertly hand-carved and hand-dipped candles that start at three for $5 and go up to $50 or $60. You'll find blue-and-white swans, bottle-nosed dolphins, and an emerald-and-lime-green frog looking as though he just swallowed a particularly delectable bluebottle fly. There are also pineapples in all stages of ripeness, from pale yellow to green-and-yellow tinged with mauve. You'll find this particular stand near the Kalakaua entrance to the International Market Place.
Open daily 10 a.m.-10 p.m.

Nautilus of the Pacific
Hilton Hawaiian Village,
2005 Kalia Rd.,
Honolulu
• 947-4755

Don't expect the unusual and you won't be disappointed. This hotel shop caters to a clientele that's satisfied with shell wind chimes, lacquered Australian trumpet shells for proud display on suburban coffee tables and bleached coral fronds supported by wooden tripods. For a kind of ultimate kitsch, a gallimaufry of *faux* bouquets put together from a combination of shells and minerals can't be beaten. These are without question the gifts for Aunt Amelia in Tallahassee.
Open daily 9 a.m.-10 p.m.

The Rainbow Collection
Ala Moana Center,
1450 Ala Moana Blvd.,
Honolulu
• 947-9092

Should a fossil ammonite dating from the Jurassic period (about 160 million years back) take your fancy, either as a gift or to add to your own private stash, drop in at The Rainbow Collection. Slabs of limestone bearing the imprint of ancient fish or leaves, handmade jewelry with an emphasis on coral and pearl, and a nice range of crystalized minerals round out the modest but high-quality collection. Serious collectors may also want to consider Dennis Deluz's unique tikis, hooks and poi pounders done in such semiprecious stones as lapis lazuli and turquoise.
Open Mon.-Fri. 9:30 a.m.-9 p.m., Sat. 9:30 a.m.-5 p.m., Sun. 10 a.m.-5 p.m.

The Royal Peddler

Hyatt Regency Waikiki,
2424 Kalakaua Ave.,
Waikiki
• 923-0136

For a fairly wide selection of modern scrimshaw, fine ink etchings on walrus or fossil ivory, both black-and-white and color, try the Royal Peddler at the Hyatt Regency Waikiki. Though the selection pales before what you'll find on Maui, it's reasonably good, and a few of the artists have achieved some local standing. If scrimshaw doesn't turn you on, there's a wild assortment of costume jewelry, wood veneer pictures, kitsch dolls, glassware and masks.
Open daily 8:30 a.m.-11 p.m.

Silk Flower & Plant Co., Inc.

1300 Makaloa St.,
Honolulu
• 947-7455

At Christmas you'll find a tree decorated with a flock of bright-red birds, the ensemble created out of feathers. Year-round, this shop stocks exquisitely fashioned silk replicas of red ginger, birds of paradise and anthurium, both in natural colors and strikingly unrealistic, satiny black. Alas, if you want to ship to the mainland, you'll have to do it yourself, packing as well as mailing. Prices range from about $25 for a bridesmaid's bouquet to several hundred dollars for a complete plant in a porcelain vase or bowl. Scented artificial flower cleaner sells for $7.50.
Open Mon.-Fri. 10 a.m.-6 p.m., Sat. 10 a.m.-5 p.m.

Woolworth's Candles

2224 Kalakaua Ave.,
Honolulu
• 923-2331

Mr. Chow dips and carves elaborately decorated, multicolored candles all year round in Woolworth's on Kalakaua. The hand-dipped and hand-carved candles range from toucans to Mickey Mouse and Minnie Mouse in a grass hut. Prices begin at three for $10 and go up to $40.
Open daily 8 a.m.-11 p.m.

MAJOR SHOPPING MALLS

Ala Moana Center

1450 Ala Moana Blvd.,
Honolulu

Billed as the world's largest open-air shopping center, with more than 200 stores and restaurants, Ala Moana has everything. Liberty House (941-2345), J.C. Penny (946-8068) and Sears Roebuck (listed in the phone book under specific departments) are the department-store anchors; Liberty House is the Macy's of the Pacific. For assorted souvenirs, there's Woolworth's (941-3005); for Japanese merchandise, Shirokiya's (941-9111); for sundries, Long's Drugs (941-4433).

But the magnet for discriminating visitors is a new two-level Palm Boulevard section, which is not complete as we go to press. Here, a veritable who's who in fashion wear and accessories reigns with tenants such as Adrienne Vittadini, Polo/Ralph Lauren, Lancel, Waterford, Wedgwood, the first Christian Dior boutique in the U.S., Cartier, Celine, the first fine-jewelry Chanel Boutique in the world, the second but largest Emporio Armani outlet, Fendi and Fila, among others. Also, a mammoth

Makai Market Food Court offers snacks and meals to fuel your shopping escapades. On Sundays, Young People's Hula Show, which has been performing for 23 years, is presented on Centerstage, offering excellent photo opportunities for visitors. *Open Mon.-Fri. 9 a.m.-5 p.m., Sat. 10 a.m.-5 p.m., Sun. during Christmas season 9 a.m.-9 p.m.*

Kahala Mall
4211 Waialae Ave., Honolulu

If you forgot your evening wear, you're likely to find what you need at Alion (735-7878), Atillo's European Menswear (734-3000), Carol & Mary (926-1264) or Liberty House (941-2345). Something Special (734-8504) boasts ceramic *musubi* (rice balls) and *manapua* (Chinese dim sum), plus a grand selection of Island-themed T-shirts; Paradizzio (737-6300) has a wonderful selection of glassware and party needs; Bebe Sport (734-6444) offers funky and trendy casual finds. If you get the hungrys, try Bernard's New York Deli (732-3354) for generous deli sandwiches and cheesecake; Spindrifter (737-7944) for hearty soups, sandwiches and grilled favorites; Yen King (732-5505) for Northern Chinese specials. *Open Mon.-Fri. 10 a.m.-9 p.m., Sat.-Sun. 10 a.m.-5 p.m.*

Pearlridge Center
Off Kamehameha Hwy. & Moanalua Rd., Honolulu

Overlooking a watercress farm, this two-phase air-conditioned shopping complex is one of Oahu's best suburban malls. Liberty House (941-2345) and J.C. Penny (488-0961) are the department store anchors in Phase I, Sears (487-4211) will be the big store in Phase II. The mix of merchants is wide and varied, from swimwear to books, from stationary to jewelry. Phase II also will take you to the movies with two movie-theater complexes—The Pearlridge Four-Plex and The Pearlridge West Twelve-Plex—showing first-run movies. Restaurants include Monterey Bay Canners (487-0048), which offers seafood specialties; and Bravo (487-5544), which has gourmet pizzas and Italian dishes. *Open Mon.-Sat. 10 a.m.-9 p.m., Sun. 10 a.m.-6 p.m.*

Windward Mall
46-056 Kamehameha Hwy., Windward Oahu

An air-conditioned mall on the windward side of Oahu, this one offers a convenient mix of gift shops and clothiers, anchored by Liberty House (941-2345), JC Penney (235-0011) and Sears (247-8360). Among the merchants: Crazy Shirts (235-6070), an emporium of logo shirts and whimsical cartoons; and Please Read To Me (247-1455), a children's bookstore. Eateries include Marie Callender's (235-6655) and a food court that offers Chinese and Korean plate lunches, pizza, ice cream and bakery goodies. *Open Mon.-Sat. 9:30 a.m.-9 p.m., Sun. 10 a.m.-5 p.m.*

MISCELLANEOUS

Aloha Stadium Flea Market
Aloha Stadium,
99-500 Salt Lake Ave.,
Honolulu

More than 20,000 Island shoppers flock to the 1,500 local merchants who assemble every Wednesday, Saturday and Sunday to buy bargains you can wear (T-shirts, muumuus, slippers) or eat (dried fruit, fresh produce, macadamia nuts). A flea-market shuttle departs from major hotels at about 7:30 a.m. the days of the event. The cost is $6 round-trip per person. Call 955-4050 or 486-1529 for information.
Open daily 6 a.m.-3 p.m.

China Sea Tattoo Co.
1033 Smith St.,
Honolulu
• 533-1603

Here's the place to change your image . . . permanently. Draw from the collection of rampant dragons, skulls and skeletons, demons and witches (each individually designed by owner Mike Malone) to just about any fantasy that can be dot-printed on the human epidermis. All instruments are routinely autoclave sterilized. Architectural motifs and machinery pose no problems for Mike. Prices begin at $20 and obviously spiral up quickly as designs become larger and more complex. Though human and animal motifs predominate, Mike is perfectly happy to tackle modern subjects such as skyscrapers twisting around the torso, tractors, missiles, or entire space stations.
Open Mon.-Sat. 11 a.m.-11 p.m., Sun. 11 a.m.-7 p.m.

Creative Fibers
450 Piikoi St.,
Honolulu
• 537-3674

Need a swatch of fabric illustrated with eighteenth- and nineteenth-century Hawaiian prints, or a bolt of handwoven Guatemalan *ikat* cloth, or a few yards of Indian Batik? Head right over to Creative Fibers. What about tie-dye cloth from Nigeria or mud cloth from Mali? You've come to the right place. Somewhere in the shop, ribbon edging, buttons and patterns and the rest will also be found. Some ready-to-wear blouses, dresses and T-shirts are also for sale, along with a few gorgeous hand silk-screened *pareos* that run about $30.
Open Mon.-Sat. 10 a.m.- 5:30 p.m.

Dilip's Nail Art
2330 Kalakaua St.,
International Market Place,
Honolulu
• 923-7122

Dilip Jadhav, a Honolulu artist, paints horses, palm trees, faces and even the Statue of Liberty on fingernails. She's in the Guinness Book of Records for having painted a five-foot high fabricated fingernail, working for 40 consecutive hours. Prices begin at $5 for simple flowers and palm trees, run $14 to $20 for more elaborately detailed animals, and top out at $50 for a portrait. If you can't wrap your significant other around your little finger you can, at least, have him or her perch thereon, with Ms. Jadhav's help. She also guarantees free touch-ups should wear and tear take their toll.
Open daily 9 a.m.-10 p.m.

Dole Cannery Square
650 Iwilei Rd.,
Honolulu

Honolulu's newest visitor complex is home to the Dole pineapple. A two-level promenade offers Island souvenirs; the Children's Museum also is located on the premises. There's a cafeteria-style food court, but what could possibly top this? Have your picture taken with Kenny Rogers, the droll Dole spokesman, who stands tall in cardboard glory.
Open daily 9 a.m.-5 p.m.

Downtown Honolulu/ Chinatown

This area falls within the streets bordered by Alakea, Merchant, Beretania and River. It includes Fort Street Mall, where Liberty House and Woolworth are the key stores, and Union Mall, which is still under renovation. The pulse beat of the city's Chinatown merchants are in a corridor of restored turn-of-the-century stores along King, Maunakea, Pauahi, Nuuanu and Smith streets—all a stone's throw from the Honolulu waterfront. Be sure to visit the Chinatown fish and produce markets, where looking at and smelling the wares are part of the fun.
Open daily. Hours vary.

F.C. Chee, Chinese Acupuncture
1159 Maunakea St.,
Honolulu
• 533-2498

F. C. Chee also sells Chinese herbs. The pleasantly plump might want to try Shi Szu, a "special selection of Chinese tea together with eight other species of Chinese herbs particularly for reducing weight." Beyond Shi Szu and ginseng, the Westerner must proceed with caution if not trepidation. Three charts of "the newest illustrations of acupuncture points" and a rather cavalierly displayed set of glass and steel instruments on two rolling carts provide a bare-bones sense of sawbones *materia medica*, sort of a reassurance that the doctor—any doctor—is in.
Open Mon.-Sat. 1 a.m.-noon

Hawaii Polynesian Cultural Supply
55-510 Kam Hwy.,
Laie
• 293-1560, 293-9463

Not far from the Polynesian Cultural Center, admire and acquire those magnificent feathered gourds and drums you saw accompanying the hula, as well as fire knives, Tahitian skirts, and the ceremonial paraphernalia indigenous to the islands southwest of Hawaii.
Open Mon.-Fri. 10 a.m.-5 p.m., Sat. 9:30 a.m.-noon.

Hi-Kong Gems/Martial Arts Supply
1041 Maunakea St.,
Honolulu
• 521-1581

An uneasy alliance of gold and steel makes its home at the Hi-Kong Hawaii Martial Arts Supply. Spears, nunchaku sticks, and *shuriken* provide martial arts aficionados with everything they need to follow in the steps of Bruce Lee. Over 200 books on everything from aikido to Japanese knife fighting are also stocked. Up front, however, gold chains cater to a more pacifistic side of the human animal.
Open Mon.-Fri. 8:30 a.m.-4 p.m., Sat. 9:30 a.m.-noon.

SCHOOL & CHURCH RESALE SHOPS

K*amaainas*—native Hawaiians—do a thriving business with the dozen or so resale shops that cluster in Honolulu, buying and selling classic aloha shirts, garden furniture and tools, books, dishes, kitchen appliances, and innumerable other flotsam and jetsam. The hours at these shops change frequently; it's always a good idea to check the yellow pages before trundling off on a treasure hunt.

Assistance League of Hawaii Thrift Shop
404 Piikoi St.,
Honolulu
• 531-6666

The Symphony Thrift Shop
1023 Pensacola St.,
Honolulu
• 524-7157

St. Andrews Economy Shop
Queen Emma Square,
Honolulu
• 536-5939

Waikiki Community Center
310 Paoakalani Ave.,
Honolulu
• 923-1802

SPECIALTY CENTERS

Ward Centre
1200 Ala Moana Blvd.,
Honolulu

This is an upscale minimall, with a savvy blend of restaurants (including Compadres Mexican Bar & Grill, Il Fresco and Keo's Thai Cuisine; see Oahu Restaurants), designer shops, such as Pappagallo (536-6443), Susan Marie (536-3811) and Peony Arts (536-0266). Leave temptation behind and try the sweets from Honolulu Chocolate Co. (531-2997); the chocolate-dipped Oreos are legendary.
Open Mon.-Fri. 10 a.m.-9 p.m., Sat. 10 a.m.-5 p.m., Sun. 11 a.m.-4 p.m.

The Ward Warehouse
1050 Ala Moana Blvd.,
Honolulu

This convivial two-story warehouse complex offers anything from heirlooms to arty gifts: Pomegranates In The Sun (531-1108), with casual women's wear; In Bloom (523-3742), with trendy items for the expectant mom and newborn babe; Blue Ginger Designs (526-0398), with simple and elegant Polynesian wear; and Mama Howell Inc. (522-0616), with designer *muumuus* and aloha shirts. You won't go hungry, either. Horatio's (521-5002) offers seafood and steaks; Orson's (521-5681) has seafood; Stuart Anderson's Cattle Co. (523-9692) grills steaks and chops.
Open Mon.-Fri. 10 a.m.-9 p.m., Sat. 10 a.m.-5 p.m., Sun. 11 a.m.-4 p.m.

Royal Hawaiian Shopping Center
2201 Kalakawa Ave., Honolulu

This center is larger than it looks and is still growing. The place is designed for visitors: you can get your money exchanged, buy travelers' checks and airline tickets, plus make travel arrangements here. In the new Galleria, a plush upscale section in the three-building promenade, check out the Chanel Boutique (923-9025), Hermès of Paris (922-5780), or Gianni Versace Boutique (922-5337). McInery (926-1351) with its designer-wear nooks offers everything from Perry Ellis to Polo/Ralph Lauren, from Ocean Pacific to Newport Beach. Louis Vuitton (926-0621) is a mecca for Japanese visitors, who have a yen for signature goods. Hungry? Good bets are the Seafood Emporium (922-5547), Restauranty Suntory (922-5511; see Oahu Restaurants, page 38) or the Bavarian Beer Garden (922-6535). The center is part of the legacy of a Hawaiian princess, Bernice Pauahi Bishop, who mandated that her estate help maintain the Kamehameha Schools. Thus, revenues generated from the shop and restaurant lease agreements go directly to the schools.
Open Mon.-Sat. 9 a.m.-10 p.m., Sun. 9 a.m.-9 p.m.

WAIKIKI TRADING POSTS

International Market Place
2330 Kalakaua Ave., Waikiki

In the heart of Waikiki, this tropical gathering of 200 shops, kiosks and restaurants in a food court has the flavor of an open-air bazaar. Sure, it's a tad rundown, but what a location! It's the top pick for the state's proposed convention center.
Open daily 9 a.m.-11 p.m.

Kuhio Mall
Kuhio Ave., behind the International Market Place, Waikiki

Look for an abundance of tropical offerings, much like the International Market Place.
Open daily 9 a.m.-11 p.m.

Rainbow Bazaar
Hilton Hawaiian Village, 2005 Kalia Rd., Waikiki

This exotic plaza includes a Liberty House, the Benihana of Tokyo flagship restaurant in Hawaii, plus merchants offering jade from Hong Kong, Mickey Mouse T-shirts, and all manner of towels and bathing suits.
Open daily 8 a.m.-10 p.m.

Waikiki Shopping Plaza
Kalakaua & Seaside Aves., Waikiki

This is a five-level vertical mall, anchored around a towering waterfall sculpture. You'll find apparel and jewelry shops, as well as restaurants. There's a free hula show at 6:30 p.m. and 8 p.m. daily.
Open daily 9 a.m.-11 p.m.

SIGHTS

AMUSEMENTS

Honolulu Zoo
151 Kapahulu Ave.,
Honolulu
• 971-7174,
971-7171 (recording)

The Honolulu Zoo, which has never achieved a zoological standard of excellence, has fallen into a state of disrepair. Located at the Diamond Head end of Waikiki, on the edge of the vast verdant plain that is Queen Kapiolani Park, Hawaii's largest animal collection is unfortunately little more than the usual lions and tigers and bears. The collection does include a few of the most prolific giraffes in captivity but regrettably, there are few good displays unique to the Pacific or the Hawaiian Islands. One plus, which makes any visit worthwhile, is that the spacious grounds are punctuated with some of the most exceptional banyan trees in Hawaii. Petting zoo for kids and regular elephant demonstrations. Gift shop with unusual T-shirts.
Open daily 8:30 a.m.-4 p.m. Petting zoo open Tues.-Sun. 9 a.m.-2 p.m. Adults $3, children under 12 free (when accompanied by an adult); $5 yearly pass good for Honolulu Zoo and Foster Botanical Garden.

Paradise Park
3737 Manoa Rd.,
Honolulu
• 988-2141
988-6686 (recording)

If performing tropical birds interest you, you won't find a better setting or a more comedic staff of avian actors. Great for kids. The facility, located in a rain forest, also includes lush tropical gardens, streams, ponds and waterfalls, as well as a "Dancing Waters" show with lights and music. Restaurant and snack bar. Free shuttle from major Waikiki hotels.
Open daily 10 a.m.-5 p.m. Adults $7.50, juniors 13-17 $6.50, children 4-12 $3.75.

Polynesian Cultural Center

Brigham Young University, Laie
• 293-3333

Here's your chance to take in not only the dances, songs and culture of the Hawaiians, but of other Pacific Islanders as well. The cultures of the entire Pacific basin come together at the Polynesian Cultural Center, which is located on Oahu's scenic North Shore, next to the Mormon university, Brigham Young. Seven accurately reproduced mini-villages, built by traditional artisans, are connected by a series of waterways and winding pathways. Visitors stroll or boat through the different island "villages," learning hands-on about the culture of each from native Polynesians. There are also two theaters: the immense (2,800-seat), very well-designed Pacific Pavilion features a 90-minute evening show, "This is Polynesia" (always packed), which brings to life the real songs, dances and legends of the Pacific (no flaming hula skirts or Day-Glo war clubs here); the smaller Hale Aloha Theatre, with its unusual water staging area, presents an afternoon show about the myths and legends of the seven islands. Many of the performers are Brigham Young University students from the Pacific areas represented, who work at the center to fund their schooling.

Plan to spend at least a half day, morning or afternoon, to really see and experience the villages, then stay for one of the shows. Transportation to Laie is available with a variety of carriers including the city bus.

Open Mon.-Sat. 12:30 p.m.- 9 p.m. Park: adults $24.95, children 5-11 $9.95; park & dinner show: adults $34.95, children 5-11 $14.95.

Sea Life Park

Makapuu Point, Waimanalo
• 259-7933

This exquisitely sited oceanarium at Makapuu features a number of unique displays, including a 300,000-gallon glass-walled Reef Tank. Visitors can walk around a Hawaiian "reef" and closely observe a wide array of Hawaiian ocean critters, ranging from endemic species of iridescent-hued butterfly fish to menacing sharks and rays, to the Hawaiian state fish, *humuhumunukunukuapuaa*, all of which are hand-fed on a regular schedule. A second glass-walled tank offers a unique perspective on marine mammal behavior and porpoise-training techniques. Finally, a huge open-air theater/pool features regular performances by dolphins and whales, with a Hawaiian twist. Additional displays in this truly exceptional facility include the endangered Hawaiian monk seal, various marine turtles, penguins, and Pacific sea birds. Plan to spend at least two hours; a half-day would provide more time to thoroughly enjoy the opportunity. Restaurant and gift shop on the premises.

Open Sat.-Thurs. 9:30 a.m.-5 p.m., Fri. 9:30 a.m.- 10 p.m. Adults $12.95, children 7-12 $8.50, children 4-6 $4.50.

Waikiki Aquarium
2777 Kalakaua Ave., Honolulu
• 923-9741

Located adjacent to Kapiolani Park and the Waikiki Natatorium at the foot of Diamond Head, this small but valuable aquarium, founded in 1904, is the third-oldest in the United States. The collections and exhibits here include some unique specimens from the Hawaiian Islands and various South Pacific reef flora and fauna. One of our favorite exhibits is the marine version of a petting zoo (Edge of the Reef exhibit). Kids and kids-at-heart will love it. Another special exhibit is the Hawaiian monk seal, one of Hawaii's only two endemic mammals. This well-managed aquarium introduces visitors to a cross-section of unique marine ecosystems and ocean life in a short period of time. Ask about their special programs and lectures. The exhibits and displays change constantly, making it a "must-stop" every time you visit Oahu. Don't miss the Natural Selection Gift Shop. *Open daily 9 a.m.-5 p.m. Optional donation ($2.50 suggested), children under 15 free.*

BEACHES

The beaches of Oahu range from what is probably the most famous in the world—Waikiki—to little-known, out-of-the-way spots that require some driving to get to and a bit of good sense to enjoy safely. Surf conditions generally dictate avoiding North Shore beaches in winter when north Pacific storms generate the big waves for which Hawaii is world famous. Similarly, summer swells out of the south can turn otherwise delightful beaches on the southern and eastern shores into extremely hazardous places for all but the most knowledgeable and well-conditioned ocean recreationalist. As a good rule of thumb, avoid any ocean area that appears at all rough, especially if there is no lifeguard present, and ask the advice of lifeguards if you are uncertain of the conditions at any time.

THE SHARKMAN OF MAKUA

This Oahu tale comes attached with a warning: Do not read past this point if you might be inclined to swim in Oahu's leeward or western waters. North of Makaha and just south of Makua lies Kaneana, the Cave of Kane, popularly known as the Makua Cave. The cave measures about 100 feet high and 450 feet deep, and was carved by ocean waves some 150,000 years ago. Ancient Hawaiians believed that the cave was home to Kamahoalii, a super being who could become a shark or a human at will. As a human, Kamahoalii was a gentle soul, but as a shark he would capture unsuspecting swimmers and carry them off to his lair in the cave for a feast—sort of like an aquatic Lon Chaney, Jr. Eventually Kamahoalii's dual disguises were discovered, and the villagers forced him back into the sea, where he still waits, hungrily.

Kailua Beach Park
450 Kawailoa Rd., Honolulu

This long lazy stretch of white sand is protected from rough water virtually all year long and, except for the hazard of high-speed wind surfers skimming along on the dependable breezes, it is a relatively safe place with substantially smaller crowds than any of the more urban beaches on Oahu. Crowded on weekends and on holidays.

Keawaula Beach
end of Farmington Hwy., Makaha

This wonderfully isloated beach is known to locals as Yokohama Bay, because it was once a favorite stomping ground for Japanese fisherman.

Makaha Beach
89-369 Farrington Hwy., Makaha

The most famous and beautiful beach on Oahu's leeward side, Makaha is the original home of Hawaii's big-wave surfing championships. It's well worth the drive whether the surf is up or "flat," when swimming and snorkeling replace one of the favored sports of Hawaii's kings. This beach has clean, white sand and more local residents than visitors, and is worth seeing particularly when it is being surfed (winter months). But beware of the rip current if any waves exist.

Makapuu Beach Park
41-095 Kalanianaole Hwy., Waimanalo

Set at the base of the sheer Koolau mountains is Makapuu Beach Park, a stark beauty that some will remember from the passionate love scene in the movie classic *From Here to Eternity*. A massive white-sand dune pours into a turquoise bay bounded by the cliffs of Makapuu Point. The bay is punctuated by the *lapin* silhouette appropriately named Rabbit Island, and a coastline view stretching forever. This is truly one of Hawaii's most majestic beaches. Treacherous when surf is breaking (despite all those happy little nebbishes frolicking in the white water—they know what they are doing). Go for the sun and the view. If there is any surf at all, stay out of the water unless you are a skilled bodysurfer. You can travel on down the coast to Bellows Beach Park if it is too rough to swim at Makapuu.

Malaekahana Bay
Kamehameha Hwy., between Makahoa & Kalanai Pts., Malaekahana
• 548-7455

Long the private domain of Hawaii's elite *kamaaina* families, this long stretch of creamy-white sand can be far more reminiscent of the beaches of the northeastern seaboard than one might expect of a Hawaiian beach, but this stretch of serenity is rarely found by visitors (though there is easy public access through the State Recreational Area at one end of the bay). Malaekahana offers a literal breath of fresh (salt) air and a real escape from the crowds. Great walking beach, safe swimming year-round, though beware of coral on bare feet. No lifeguards.

Sandy Beach

8800 Kalanianaole
Hwy.,
Koko Head
Regional Park
• 395-3407

Just minutes from Waikiki, this stretch of gorgeous white sand at the edge of the Kaiwi Channel can prove treacherous for all but the best bodysurfers when conditions are right, but it is a great place for closely observing Hawaii's best wave riders working this world-famous shorebreak with no equipment of any kind, or on body boards, boogie boards or sand skimmers. Best bikini-watching in Hawaii on most weekends. Generally uncrowded on weekdays, except during holiday periods. Surf can be treacherous, and necks are snapped in the tight beach break every year—only for experts if there is any surf at all.

Waikiki Beach

Kalakaua Ave.,
from the Outrigger
Canoe Club–Ala Wai
Yacht Harbor, Waikiki

The most famous of Hawaiian beaches is a crescent of dirty-white, imported sand stretching from the Ala Wai Canal (dug to drain the swamp that was once Waikiki) to the foot of famed Diamond Head. This beach sports more bodies per square foot than any stretch of sand in the state (in the Pacific, for that matter), particularly during the summer months or any school holiday. It is also the base for an incredible array of ocean recreation activities. Waikiki is the best place in Hawaii to learn board surfing (for the adventuresome and reasonably athletic), or to try canoe or catamaran surfing. It is also one of the safest places to swim in the ocean anywhere on Oahu. The famous beach at Waikiki may disappoint more than it enchants, but it will always be a "must see."

FALSE DIAMONDS

Most off-Islanders will have seen a photo of Oahu's Diamond Head long before they arrive. But how did this famous piece of rock get its name? Apparently, in 1825, some British sailors mistook worthless calcite crystals to be diamonds. They ran through the streets shouting that they had found the stones at the headlands. Thus the prominent point at the end of Waikiki Beach became known as Diamond Head.

The history of Diamond Head, or Leahi, as the Hawaiians called it, is much older. *Leahi*, meaning brow (*lae*) of a tuna (*ahi*), was named by the Hawaiian goddess Hiiaka during her struggle to return the volcano goddess Pele's husband, Lohiau, to her.

Leahi was also one of Hawaii's major religious sites, the Papaenaena Heiau. The *heiau* (temple) was the site of some of the last human sacrifices performed in the Islands. King Kamehameha the Great ordered them carried out to please the gods after his victory in the decisive unification battle of Nuuanu Valley in 1795. On very still nights, it is said that the spirits of the sacrificed victims can be seen just below the jutting brow of Diamond Head, musing the place of their fiery death.

Waimea Bay
61-031 Kamehameha
Hwy.,
Waimea

The Beach Boys crooned an incorrect pronunciation of the name of this exquisite, world-famous Oahu Beach into the collective consciousness of beach lovers the world around (they sang "why a MEE ah"—it should be "Wa e may ah"). In the winter, the largest rideable waves in the world, some exceeding 30 feet in height, pour into the bay, and top surfers perform. In the summer, the placid glass-clear waters offer great swimming and snorkeling opportunities. It can be treacherous to the unwary or uninitiated. When any surf is present, it is likely that dangerous undertows are present as well; check with lifeguards.

THE LEGEND OF THE CROUCHING LION

On Oahu's windward side, in Kahana Bay, there's a rock formation dubbed the Crouching Lion. Legend claims that the geological formation is called Kauhi, after a demigod from Tahiti. The fire goddess Pele took a liking to Kauhi and imprisoned him in the hills above Kahana Bay. One day, Kauhi saw Pele's younger sister, Hiiaka, and was immediately smitten. Crouching down to break out of the prison, Kauhi was caught by Pele, who instantly turned him into stone, freezing him forever in his crouched position. Kauhi became a prisoner of his passion forever, and a warning from Pele to all.

EXCURSIONS

Chinatown
Chinese Chamber of
Commerce,
42 N. King St.,
Honolulu
• 533-3181

Every major city has a Chinatown, but we find Honolulu's unique. Honolulu's 200-year-old Chinatown features colorful markets selling herbs, Chinese produce and imports. Shopkeepers banter in clipped tongues out of open-air stalls. Visit the streets where Charlie Chan got his start; learn about one of the most important cultural influences in Hawaii's history. Pick up a copy of "Chinatown," by Francis Carter, for a self-guided tour, or take the Chinese Chamber of Commerce's weekly tour, which leaves every Tuesday at 9 a.m. from the office. It lasts several hours, plus a stop for lunch. A $4 donation is suggested.

Hanauma Bay
7455 Kalanianaole
Hwy.,
Koko Head
Regional Park
• 395-3407

This volcanic crater, now open to the sea, is one of the most oversold destinations for snorkelers and beach lovers in the Pacific. Hanauma Bay, an underwater preserve that should be a tribute to Hawaii's exceptional underwater world, instead mirrors the overcrowding of a too-quickly urbanized island—wall-to-wall people, obnoxiously friendly fish with a passion for handouts, dirty sand, questionable water quality, a packed parking lot—and offers little reason for a stop, except perhaps to admire the vista, if you can even get into the parking lot.

Kahuku Sugar Mill
**56-700 Kamehameha Hwy.,
Kahuku**
• 293-2444

This recently retired sugar processing facility is a historical landmark, and it offers a unique perspective on Hawaii's largest agricultural enterprise. Displays of sugar-milling equipment, explanations of the process, museum displays detailing the industry and an array of shops and concessionaires. *Open daily 9 a.m.-5 p.m. Free admission.*

North Shore
**Mokuleia,
Laie**

Old Hawaii is still evident on Oahu's North Shore where sleepy, ex-plantation towns like Haleiwa and Kahuku reflect an earlier, slower way of life. Oahu's northern coastline is also home to some of her most beautiful beaches, some of her most famous waves (winter months—Sunset Beach, Waimea Beach and the Banzai Pipeline at Ehukai Beach Park), and some of her most extraordinary vistas. Start in Honolulu and head east through Wahiawa toward Haleiwa or north over the steep Pali Highway through Kaneohe, and then drive all the way around in one leisurely day, stopping as the whim or various attractions move you. You can really push and see it all in about three hours, but don't.

Nuuanu Pali Lookout
Pali Hwy.

In 1795, Kamehameha the Great forced the last defenders of the chief of Oahu off this precipice in the Battle of Nuuanu Pali on the last stop of his drive to unify the Hawaiian Islands for the first time under one leader. Today, the view from this geologic gap between urban Oahu and the bedroom communities of the windward side is as awe inspiring as it must have been to those warriors nearly two centuries ago. The sheer cliffs of the weathered side of the Koolau mountains, the expansive magnificence of Kaneohe Bay, the oddity of Chinaman's Hat island in the distance all evoke the majesty of the nature of these islands. It can be very windy: due caution with hats and hair pieces is advised.

Punchbowl Crater National Memorial Cemetery of the Pacific
**2177 Puowaina Dr.,
Honolulu**
• 541-1430

Punchbowl Crater is a national cemetery and shrine honoring America's war dead. The elliptical crater is the final resting place of over 34,000 GI's and their dependents. From the rim of the crater one can do a turnabout from the somber to the sublime and enjoy the grandeur of most of Honolulu and Waikiki in one of the most spectacular views on the island.
Fall, spring & winter: open daily 8 a.m.-5:30 p.m. Summer: open 8 a.m.-6:30 p.m.

Tantalus/Round Top Drive

Tantalus & Round Top Drives, Makiki

This circuitous yet short excursion into the lush rain forest of the Koolau Mountain range above Honolulu takes you through choking tropical jungle, past posh private homes, then onto a razorback ridge that offers views into two major valleys, before skirting down through more of the same, past a couple of lovely public park facilities (great for picnics), back into the bustle of metropolitan Honolulu. Aside from being a great diversion and offering superlative views, this tour ties in nicely with a trip to Punchbowl Crater.

Urasenke Tea House

245 Saratoga Rd., Honolulu
• 923-3059, 923-1057

This branch facility of the international Urasenke Foundation is dedicated to instruction in Chado, the way of Tea, the timeless Japanese tea ceremony that is more zen and tranquillity than it is the act of preparing a beverage. The master of the Urasenke Tea House is fifteenth in an unbroken line of tea masters dating back to the sixteenth century. Call for reservations.
Open Mon.-Fri. 9 a.m.-5 p.m.

MUSEUMS

Bishop Museum

1525 Bernice St., Honolulu
• 847-3511

The Bishop Museum was founded in 1889 by Charles Bishop, an American businessman living in Hawaii. The museum was erected as a tribute to his wife, Princess Bernice Pauahi Bishop, a member of Hawaii's royal family, who worked until her death to educate and improve native Hawaiians. This superb facility, containing the largest collection of Pacific natural history in the world, also includes unmatched collections of Hawaiian and Indo-Pacific archaeology and anthropology, and the royal artifacts of Princess Bernice's family. The ever-changing displays of ancient Hawaiian crafts, such as the feather capes of the *alii* (Hawaiian royalty) are both educational and exquisite; collections of animals, birds and insects are world-renowned. The grounds contain a planetarium as well as a twelve-acre campus of Hawaiian and Pacific plants.
Open daily 9 a.m.-5 p.m. Admission $5.95 adults, $4.95 children 6-17, children under 6 free (includes admission to both the museum and planetarium).

The Damien Museum

130 Ohua Ave., Honolulu
• 923-2690

The Father Damien Museum presents photos, film, and memorabilia of Father Joseph de Vesuter Damien, the Belgian Catholic priest who eased the suffering and championed the rights of the patients at the Kalaupapa leper colony on Molokai. It's scheduled for demolition within a couple of years, so this is your last chance to view this tribute to one of Hawaii's most famous citizens.
Open Mon.-Fri. 9 a.m.-3 p.m., Sat. 9 a.m.-noon. Free admission.

**Fort deRussy
Museum**
Kalia Rd.,
Honolulu
• 438-2821

Weapons, weapons and more weapons are on display here.
Check out the ancient Hawaiian clubs, made from sharks' teeth.
Open Tues.-Sun. 10 a.m.-4:30 p.m. Free admission.

**Hawaii Maritime
Center**
Honolulu Harbor,
Pier 7,
Honolulu
• 536-6373

This newly opened museum of Hawaii's maritime past, present
and future, located in Honolulu Harbor, is a monument to the
marine community and offers displays ranging from Polynesian
voyaging to commercial fishing. With a superb reproduction of
King David Kalakaua's original boat house, the Maritime Center also includes the schooner Falls of Clyde, the voyaging
outrigger canoe Hokule'a, and many other fascinating displays.
*Open daily 9 a.m.-8 p.m. Cost $6, children 6-17 $3, children
under 6 free.*

**Honolulu
Academy of
Arts**
900 S. Beretania St.,
Honolulu
• 538-3693

Hawaii's oldest (founded in 1927) and largest art museum
features an outstanding permanent collection of Pacific, Asian,
European, African, and American art treasures. It is well known
for James A. Michener's collection of *ukiyo-e* (Japanese woodblock prints). Over 30 galleries and six surrounding garden
courts. Delightful gourmet lunches, Sunday brunches and
Thursday dinners. It has constantly changing shows and is the
center for fine art in Hawaii.
*Open Tues.-Sat. 10 a.m.-4:30 p.m., Sun. 1 p.m.-5 p.m. Free
admission.*

Iolani Palace
Honolulu
• 522-0832,
538-1471 (recording)

The only royal palace in the United States, the Iolani Palace,
which was completed in 1882, was the official residence of King
David Kalakaua and his sister, Queen Liliuokalani, who be-
longed to the ruling family until the overthrow of the Hawaiian
monarchy in 1893. In the sad ending to royal rule in Hawaii,
the palace also served in 1895 as a prison for Queen Liliuokalani,
who had succeeded King Kalakaua as ruler. It later became the
seat of government for the Republic and the territorial and state
governments until 1969, when the present state capitol was
completed. At that time, the fabulous native materials, such as
koa wood, from which the Iolani Palace was constructed, were
painstakingly restored, and today it continues to be beautifully
maintained—a gem amid the architectural mishmash of downtown Honolulu.
*Open Wed.-Sat. 9 a.m.-2:15 p.m. Adults $4, children 5-12 $1 (no
children under 5 allowed).*

Kuan Yin Temple
170 Vineyard St.,
Honolulu
• 533-6361

A working Taoist temple in the heart of Honolulu, the Kuan Yin Temple was endowed by prominent local Chinese businessmen and is a masterpiece of Chinese architecture, containing the typically eclectic collection of images, art pieces and shrines found in traditional Chinese temples. Adjacent to Foster Botanical Garden, close to the foot of Punchbowl Crater.
Open daily 8:30 a.m.-2 p.m. Free admission (donations accepted).

Mission Houses Museum
553 S. King St.,
Honolulu
• 531-0481

An important part of Hawaii's history, these restored mission houses and work spaces on the site of the first Christian mission in Hawaii, near historic Kawaiahao Church, reveal the hard-working lifestyle of Hawaii's early missionary families from New England, who came here intent upon converting the heathens. The work of these missionaries changed forever the lifestyle of the native Hawaiians. The Christian influence is marked today by the large number of churches that dot the Hawaiian Islands. A history program on Saturdays transports the visitor back to 1831.
Open Tues.-Sat. 9 a.m.-4 p.m., Sun. noon-4 p.m. Adults $3.50, children 6-15 $1.

Queen Emma Summer Palace
2913 Pali Hwy.,
Honolulu
• 595-3167

This edifice is perhaps best described as the Hawaiian equivalent of the mansion in the movie *Gone With the Wind*. Set in the heart of the cool and verdant Nuuanu Valley, the lofty columns, white clapboard exterior and old-world carpentry of this summer home of one of Hawaii's most revered monarchs is a monument to the days of Hawaii's royalty. Wander through the palatial home, with the original furniture of Queen Emma and King Kamehameha IV and their vast landscaped gardens.
Open daily 9 a.m.-4 p.m. Adults $4, children 12-18 $1, children under 12 50 cents.

PARKS & GARDENS

Foster Botanical Garden
180 N. Vineyard Blvd.,
Honolulu
• 533-3214

One of the most magnificent collections of trees and tropical flora in the Pacific, Foster Botanical Garden, which has garnered national design awards, dates back to the 1850s. Centrally located at the edge of downtown Honolulu in the mouth of Nuuanu Valley and easily toured in a self-directed manner (although guided tours are available), this public garden is the centerpiece of an expanding network of horticultural displays and preservation centers known collectively as the Honolulu Botanical Gardens.
Open daily 9 a.m.-4 p.m. Admission $1, children under 12 free.
Best deal: $5 yearly pass good for both Foster Botanic Gardens and Honolulu Zoo.

Kawamoto Orchid Nursery

2630 Waiomao Rd.,
Honolulu
• 732-5808

A commercial enterprise dedicated to the furtherance of unique and exotic orchid culture, the Kawamoto Nursery is an excellent place to view the latest hybrids in greenhouses full of blooming orchids, to learn from the experts, and to shop for truly special gifts. The nursery is certified for overseas shipment.
Open Mon.-Sat. 8 a.m.-3:30 p.m. Free admission.

Lyon Arboretum

3860 Manoa Rd.,
Honolulu
• 988-3177

Set deep in the recesses of Manoa Valley, this 124-acre tropical botanical garden specializing in ginger, heliconia and ornamental ti plants promises to delight the senses with a panoply of colors and smells. Blessed by dependable moisture and afternoon cloud cover, Lyon Arboretum is always invitingly lush.
Open Mon.-Fri. 9 a.m.-3 p.m., Sat. 9 a.m.-noon. Donation suggested ($1).

Senator Fong's Plantation and Gardens

47-285 Pulama Rd.,
Kaneohe
• 239-6775

Hiram Fong was one of the first two senators elected to represent the people of the new State of Hawaii in the U.S. Senate. His beloved family plantation is home to over 75 kinds of fruits and flowers and is sited such that it commands an awe-inspiring view, sweeping from Kaneohe Bay to Coconut Island.
Open daily 10 a.m.-4 p.m. Admission: $6.50, children 5-12 $3.

Waimea Falls Park

59-864 Kamehameha Hwy.,
Haleiwa
• 638-8511

Ever wonder what Hawaii looked like in ancient times? Waimea Falls Park is the answer. This 1,800-acre park was the home of Oahu's *kahunas* (priests) from around 1092. The most powerful of these priests was Paao, who ruled in the thirteenth century and introduced the customs of human sacrifices and the *kapu* (taboo) system of death to a law breaker. This valley has been preserved and features the ancient culture, plants and animals of Hawaii. We suggest that before you go to this large (and overwhelming) park, you first send for the guidebook to become familiar with the myriad displays. Another way to see this wonderland is to take the guided tour to get the bearings of the exhibits then ride the open-air tram to the top of the valley and leisurely walk down, stopping to examine the exhibits that interest you (such as the ancient Hawaiian games of bowling or spear throwing; the lei garden, blooming with flowers that are used to make leis, in their natural state; or watching the wild boar being fed). In addition, the park has a gift shop, an education center, a restaurant with live entertainment, and the very popular moon walks during the full moon to watch the nocturnal plants.
Open daily 10 a.m.-5:30 p.m. Adults $11.95, children 7-12 $6.50, children 4-6 $2.25, children under 4 free.

TOURS

Action Hawaii
P.O. Box 75548,
Honolulu
• 732-4453

Personalized hiking-water tour to Oahu's secret places, specializing in beginners. Tours include a one-and-a-half-mile hike, boogie-boarding, snorkeling and underwater photography. Hotel pick-up.
Tours daily 8 a.m.-3:30 p.m. Adults $79, children under 18 $69 (lunch not included).

Atlantis Submarines Hawaii
560 N. Nimitz,
Ste. 201 C,
Honolulu
• 522-1710

Descend into the depths, in one of the few passenger submarines in the world, as part of a remarkable adventure. Broad portholes and professional crew promise superb views, a complete learning and pleasurable experience, especially for those who have never enjoyed the world underwater. The entire trip takes two hours, 45 minutes of which are underwater in the submarine. The boat departs from Hilton Hawaiian Village in Waikiki.
Boat departs daily 7 a.m. & 4 p.m. Adults $67, children under 12 $33.50 (height requirement is 36 inches), or $6 for the boat ride to the sub and back.

Pacific Quest
59-496 Pupukea Rd.,
Haleiwa
• 638-8338

A fourteen-day hiking-camping tour of four islands, led by expert guides. They take care of everything: meals, interisland transportation, camping gear, permits and lodging fees. Small groups, no more than sixteen people. The trips are for anyone fairly active: you don't have to be in shape for the Olympics, but couch potatoes might pale under the daily regime. It is a true fitness vacation in paradise.
Trips arranged on request. Cost $1,495. Minimum age 9.

Papillon Hawaiian Helicopters
1778 Ala Moana Blvd.,
Honolulu
• 836-1566

Everyone who has ever taken a helicopter tour raves about the experience, and for good reason. The perspective is impossible to duplicate in any other vehicle. Oahu is surprisingly beautiful from the air, and tours of several of the more remote areas, complete with spectacular waterfalls, hidden valleys and virtually inaccessible beaches, are the forte of Papillon. Sample tours: Honolulu tour includes Diamond Head, Waikiki Beach, Kahala Coast, Manoa Valley, Punchbowl National Cemetery and Iolani Palace in ten to twelve minutes; Oahu Experience includes all of the Honolulu tour plus Hanauma Bay, Makapuu Point, Windward Coast, Koolau Mountains, Pali Pass and Nuuanu Valley in 30 minutes; Oahu Epic includes the rugged eastern coastline to windward Oahu, Chinaman's Hat, Koolau Mountains, Sacred Falls, Polynesian Cultural Center, North Shore, sugarcane fields, pineapple fields and Pearl Harbor, 60 minutes; and Oahu and Molokai Quest includes highlights of Oahu, plus the North Shore of Molokai with its sea cliffs, valleys, waterfalls,

Father Damien's Church at Kalaupapa, lunch at Kaluakoi Resort on Molokai, 90 minutes in the air plus an hour for lunch. Helicopters leave from Ala Wai Heliport, Waikiki.
Tours daily. Cost $49 for Honolulu tour, $99 for Oahu Experience, $187 for Oahu Epic & $275 for Oahu & Molokai Quest.

Stories of Honolulu Adventures

Office of Community Services, Kapiolani Community College, 4303 Diamond Head Rd., Honolulu
• 734-9211

Experts from Kapiolani Community College (some of whom also teach commercial tour guides) offer a delightful way to see Honolulu—with a storyteller. Each of their numerous adventures is to a specific place with a specific theme. For example, stroll the palatial grounds of the Iolani Palace as the storyteller describes life under the Hawaiian monarchs, or visit old graveyards as the storyteller spins tales of yesterday, or walk Waikiki Beach and see it through the eyes of someone visiting in 1920. Each tour is two to three hours and limited to twenty people. *Call or send for program schedule for times and dates. Cost $5 & $2 children 5-16. Reservations taken four weeks in advance.*

USS *Arizona* Memorial

Pearl Harbor, Honolulu
• 422-0561

There are a number of charter-boat tours into Pearl Harbor, but the cheapest tour is the one offered by the USS *Arizona* Memorial Visitor Center, which is administered by the National Park Service and the U.S. Navy. This tour is free, and although reservations are not accepted, there are certain times of day and days of the week that are less crowded. One phone call will allow you to plan a tour to meet your time schedule. This is one of Oahu's most visited places and is really a must for every visitor. The memorial marks the spot where 1,177 servicemen lost their lives during the attack on the U.S. Navy at Pearl Harbor by the Japanese on Sunday, December 7, 1941. Within nine minutes the USS *Arizona* had sunk, drowning all of the 1,177 crew members aboard. By the end of the day, eight ships had sunk, thirteen were damaged and 347 aircraft were destroyed; a total of 2,403 Americans were killed.

Tours of the memorial are operated at regular intervals throughout the day. Visitors first watch a moving twenty-minute film about the events of that "Day of Infamy." A National Park Service historian then gives a talk on the subject, then you take a short shuttle-boat ride to the USS *Arizona* Memorial, which straddles the sunken USS *Arizona* in Pearl Harbor. A small museum exhibits memorabilia associated with the USS *Arizona* and the Pearl Harbor attack. Moored alongside the USS *Arizona* Memorial is the USS *Bowfin*, a renovated World War II submarine, where visitors can experience firsthand what it was like to live in such cramped quarters during wartime.
Open daily 7:30 a.m.-5 p.m.

MOST VISITED

Punchbowl, the National Cemetery of the Pacific, is the most visited site in the Islands. Each year it attracts five million people, many of whom come to pay their respects to nearly 35,000 American soldiers who fell in Pacific campaigns. For information, call 541-1430.

SPORTS

BICYCLING

Aloha Funway Rentals
025 Kalakaua Ave.,
Honolulu
• 946-2766

Ten-speed bike rentals in the heart of Waikiki, for $12.90 per day or $69 per week.
Open daily 8 a.m.-5 p.m.

Hawaii Bicycling
P.O. Box 4403,
Honolulu
• 988-7175

If you'd like some company while cycling on Oahu, a call to this cycling group will put you in touch with someone willing to share your enthusiasm for two-wheeled locomotion. The club also has regularly scheduled outings and events.

DIVING & SNORKELING

Aaron's Dive Shop
602 Kailua Rd.,
Kailua
• 261-1211

46-216 Kahuhipa,
Kaneohe
• 235-3877

This is not a "touristy" place, but it is interested in serving the needs of the recreational-diving enthusiast. One of the state's largest training facilities, Aaron's has been in business for twenty years, offering certification training from beginners to instructors, rental gear and retail. Willing to discount private certification classes for two or more people.
Open Mon.-Fri. 8 a.m.-8 p.m., Sat.-Sun. 8 a.m.-6 p.m. Introductory dive $65. Scuba certification classes $300.

Aloha Dive Shop
Koko Marina Highway Mall,
7192 Kalanianaole Hwy.,
Honolulu
• 395-5922

The closest dive shop to the state underwater park at Hanauma Bay, this full-service dive shop specializes in access to that body of water. The owner of the shop, singing and film star Jacqueline James, has had the place about twenty years and considers serving the diving community her second career.
Open daily 8 a.m.-5 p.m. Introductory boat dives $55; three-day certification program $325.

Haleiwa Surf Center
66-167 Haleiwa Rd.,
Haleiwa
• 637-5051

Multisport instructional center that teaches snorkeling, surfing, windsurfing and sailing and offers guided snorkeling tours. Also the county agency for information on water sports and facilities.
Open daily 9:30 a.m.-5:30 p.m.

Snuba Tours of Oahu
2233 Kalakaua Ave.,
Ste. 1271,
Honolulu
• 922-7762

This unique cross between scuba and snorkeling allows neophytes to enjoy the best of both, without the rigorous training required for scuba certification. Guided trips.
Tours daily. Mon.-Fri. morning tours $49.95, afternoon tours $59.95. Weekend tours $65 (includes lunch). All tours include hotel pick-up, all equipment, instruction by certified instructor and guided tour.

South Seas Aquatics
870 Kapahulu Ave.,
Honolulu
• 735-0437

One of the oldest and most respected dive shops on Oahu. A five-star PADI Instructor Training Facility. Offers not only all scuba-equipment rental, but also camera and video rental. There are interesting dive charters available on a 38-foot boat.
Open Mon.-Sat. 8 a.m.-6 p.m., Sun. 8 a.m.-5 p.m. Introductory boat dives $65.

Steve's Diving Adventures
1860 Ala Moana Blvd.,
Honolulu
• 947-8900

This five-star PADI center has been in business twelve years and features certification courses, dive charters, retail, and snorkeling rental. No scuba-equipment rental.
Open Mon.-Sat. 8 a.m.-5 p.m. Snorkeling equipment rental $5.20 per day.

Surf & Sea
62-595 Kamehameha Hwy.,
Haleiwa
• 637-9887

For divers intent on enjoying the less trammeled reefs of Oahu's North Shore, Surf & Sea is the place not only for rentals, but also for information on dive conditions in the area. *Open daily 9 a.m.-6 p.m. Full scuba equipment $35 per day.*

FISHING

A lthough Kona, on the Big Island of Hawaii, is the most famous spot in the state for big-game fishing, Oahu waters can produce excellent results, particularly from late March through October of each year. The largest marlin ever captured on rod and reel anywhere on the planet was landed by Captain Cornelius Choy off Oahu. The monstrous fish weighed 1,805 pounds! No saltwater-fishing licenses are required in Hawaii. Oahu also offers freshwater fishing in the 300-acre **Wahiawa Reservoir** near Scofield Barracks, and occasionally in other reservoirs. Wahiawa Reservoir is home to a fair population of largemouth bass (and other species) and even hosts a national bass championship every year. Freshwater fishing requires a license.

Brooke Kay,
Honolulu
Trolling, Inc.
33 S. King St., Rm. 515,
Honolulu
• 396-8257

Captain Toby Bento operates the tidiest charter boat in the Honolulu fleet and also produces some of the best catches. This fully rigged 38-foot Bertram sportfisher with full tuna tower is an excellent way to pursue big game in comfort. *Charter daily. Cost $350 for 4 hours, $400 for 6 hours, $450 for 8 hours, with a maximum of six passengers.*

Coreene-C Sport
Fishing Charters
802 Punahou St.,
Honolulu
• 536-7472

The largest and most comfortable sportfishing boat in Island waters, the Coreene-C is also one of the few that can legally carry more than six passengers for a day of sportfishing. This locally built *haole sampan* is gyro-stabilized for a smooth ride in the sometimes choppy waters. *Open daily 24 hours; fishing 7 a.m.- 3 p.m. Cost $95 for share charters; $525 exclusive charter for 8 hours.*

Division of
Aquatic
Resources
Dept. of Land and Natural Resources,
1151 Punchbowl St.,
Honolulu
• 548-5897

For information on fishing regulations, particularly those pertaining to freshwater fishing on Oahu and elsewhere in the state, contact the Division of Aquatic Resources. They will also be able to tell you if any of the normally inaccessible Oahu reservoirs are open, and where to obtain a freshwater fishing license. *Open Mon.-Fri. 9 a.m.-5 p.m.*

Kewalo Basin
Off Ala Moana Blvd.,
west of Ala Moana
Beach Park,
Honolulu

The bulk of the Oahu-based sportfishing fleet is housed in Kewalo Basin, and most charter operators maintain an information booth that is the best single source of information available on sportfishing off Oahu. Best time to be there is around 4 p.m. when the fleet returns with the day's catch.
Open Mon.-Fri. 9 a.m.-5 p.m.

GOLF

Ala Wai Driving Range
404 Kapahulu Ave.,
Honolulu
• 296-4653

Features a pro shop, video instruction, a PGA professional on the staff, lighted putting and chipping greens, automatic tee-up machines, 32 driving stalls and an authentic target green.
Open daily 6:30 a.m.-11 p.m. Cost $1.50 for 30 balls.

Ala Wai Golf Course
404 Kapahulu Ave.,
Honolulu
• 296-4653

One of three golf courses maintained by the City and County of Honolulu, this recently renovated par-70 course at the edge of Waikiki is a real bargain, if you can get on it. Tee times are chosen by lottery and generally well in advance. This moderately challenging course lacks only one thing required by many visitors: there are no rentals available.
Daily tee times begin 6 a.m. Cost $18 weekdays, $20 weekends.

Hawaii Kai Golf Course
8902 Kalanianaole Hwy.,
Honolulu
• 395-2358

This moderately challenging par-72, 6,350-yard course located between Sandy Beach and Makapuu Point is one of the most easily accessed golf courses available to visitors staying in Waikiki. It promises some beautiful vistas, well-designed fairways and greens and relatively inexpensive green fees, as well.
Daily tee times begin 6:30 a.m., last tee time 1:30 p.m. Cost $50 (includes cart).

Kahuku Golf Course
Kahuku
• 293-5842

This hidden nine-hole sleeper is one of the most enjoyable courses in Hawaii and easily the best bargain in the state. Managed by the City and County of Honolulu Department of Parks and Recreation and draped along the shore of Oahu's northernmost tip, this exotic little curiosity is a delight to both duffers and pros, with at least one hole unlike any on the planet, and a real kick to play. No pro shop, no rentals. For weekday play, don't call, just come. Call in advance for weekend mornings, the most popular times.
Open daily 7 a.m.-5 p.m. Cost $18 weekdays 18 holes, $14 for 9 holes; $20 weekends 18 holes, $14 for 9 holes.

Pali Golf Course

45-050 Kamehameha
Hwy.,
Kaneohe
• 261-9784, 296-7254

The most challenging and beautiful of the three golf courses maintained by the City and County of Honolulu. The par-72, 6,494-yard Pali Golf Course is also very popular with residents and therefore extremely difficult for visitors to access, though it is worth the effort. Tee times must be made at least a week in advance, rates are ridiculously reasonable, and you'll never forget the par five, 520-yard-long fifth hole.
Daily tee times begin 6:30 a.m. Fees $18 weekdays, $20 weekends, cart $11.

Sheraton Makaha Resort West Golf Course

84-626 Makaha Valley
Rd.,
Makaha
• 695-9544

It's a long drive out to Makaha from Waikiki, but worth it to see this beautiful valley and get in a round of golf on this spectacular par-72, 7,091-yard course. Challenging, especially the dog-legged fourth hole.
Daily tee times 7 a.m.-9 a.m., 11:40 a.m.-1:40 p.m., and 4:30 for night holes. Cost: $125 for non-Sheraton guests (includes cart).

Turtle Bay Hilton & Country Club

Kahuku
• 293-8574

Site of several LPGA tournaments over the years, this George Fazio–designed, par-72, 7,000-yard course can be plagued by strong, gusty winds and sudden torrential downpours. Our vote for toughest hole is the sixth, a par-4 that has a dog leg and bunker in front of the green (right into the wind, of course).
Daily tee times begin 7 a.m., last tee 1:15 p.m. in the winter and 1:45 p.m. in the summer. Fees $80 weekdays & $90 weekends (both fees include cart).

HIKING

Oahu has many fine hiking trails, most of which are well marked and easy to access. Caution should be exercised, though: stick close to the trail, because even experienced hikers get lost here each year when they venture off the beaten path. Recommended reading is Robert Smith's *Hiking Oahu* (Wilderness Press, 1978) for a comprehensive guide to all of Oahu's hiking trails and access points. Information and hiking-trail maps can be obtained from the following organizations: **City and County of Honolulu Department of Parks and Recreation** (650 S. King Street; 527-6343); **Division of Forestry & Wildlife** (1151 Punchbowl, Room 325, Honolulu; 548-8850), which offers free maps on hiking on Oahu; **Hawaii State Department of Land and Natural Resources**, State Parks Division (P.O. Box 621, Honolulu; 548-7455), which provides information on trails, hikes, camping and permits in all state parks; **Hawaiian Trail and Mountain Club** (P.O. Box 2238, Honolulu; 734-5515), which offers regularly scheduled hikes on Oahu; and the **Sierra**

Club (212 Merchant Street, Room 201, Honolulu; 946-8494), which regularly schedules club outings, including a variety of hikes into the remote areas of Oahu. Following are a couple of the better trails:

Puu Ohia Trail This relatively easy hike along the ridge between Nuuanu and Manoa valleys eventually crosses the Manoa Cliffs Trail near a thick bamboo forest, allowing either an out-and-back hike or a return onto Roundtop Drive. Both hikes take you through a variety of lush rain-forest vegetation with occasional view planes back over two of the most beautiful valleys leading out of Honolulu. Best in the morning. Be advised that the trail can become extremely muddy when it's raining. The hike begins at the top of Tantalus Drive—start near the locked gate on the Hawaiian Telephone Co. access road.

Waimano Trail This seven-mile trail that starts off disarmingly along an old irrigation ditch eventually climbs some 1,600 feet to an extraordinary spot overlooking nearly the entire windward side of Oahu. Swimming is possible en route. To get to this trail, turn off Kamehameha Highway onto Waimano Home Road, and continue two and a half miles until you see the irrigation ditch on the left.

HORSEBACK RIDING

Hilltop Ranch
41-430 Waikupanaha St.,
Waimanalo
• 259-8463

Lessons only. Learn either English or Western riding style from British Horse Society–accredited instructors. Riders must sign up for a minimum of four lessons. A safety helmet is provided, and you must wear jeans and closed-toe shoes.
Open daily, lessons by appointment. Lessons $25, minimum four lessons.

Kualoa Ranch
49-560 Kamehameha
Hwy.,
Kaneohe
• 237-8515

Meander through the mountain trails and pastures of a 4,000-acre working cattle ranch on guided tours. Reasonably priced. *Tours Mon.-Fri. 2 p.m., Sat. 9 a.m., 11:30 a.m., & 1:30 p.m. Cost $15 for 1 hour & $25 for 2 hours. Minimum age 12.*

Turtle Bay Hilton & Country Club
57-091 Kamehameha
Hwy.,
Kahuku
• 293-8811 ext. 36

Horseback riding on the beach! Tours last 45-55 minutes. *Daily tours 9 a.m.-3 p.m. Cost $20 hotel guests, $22 non-guests. Minimum age 9; minimum height 4 1/2 feet.*

ICE SKATING

Ice Palace
Stadium Mall,
4510 Salt Lake Blvd.,
Honolulu
• 487-9921

It may be hard to believe, but there is actually an ice skating arena in Hawaii. Moreover, it is remarkably popular with local residents (there is even a hockey league) and can be crowded. Rates are reasonable, and ice time includes skates, unless, of course, you brought your skates with you.
Open Mon.-Wed. 10 a.m.-3:15 p.m. & 7:30-9:30 p.m., Thurs. 10 a.m.-3 p.m., Fri. 9:30 a.m.-4:30 p.m., & 6-11:30 p.m., Sat. 10:45 a.m.-11:30 p.m., Sun. 10:45 a.m.-9:30 p.m. Adults $5 & children under 17 $4.50 (price includes skates).

KAYAKING

Kayaking clubs based on Oahu sponsor regularly scheduled outings and can provide useful information for visiting kayak enthusiasts. The following three are good clubs: **Hui Waa Kaukahi** (P.O. Box 88143, Honolulu 96744); **Kanaka Ikaika** (P.O. Box 438, Kaneohe 96744); and **Women's Kayak Club of Hawaii** (P.O. Box 438, Kaneohe 96744). If you want to brave the seas on your own, the **Kailua Sailboard Company** (130 Kailua Road, Kailua 96744; 262-2555) is one of the very few places on Oahu that rents kayaks. Cost is $35 per day for a two-person kayak. The shop is open daily from 8:30 a.m. to 5 p.m.

PARASAILING

Waikiki Beach Services
2169 Kalia Rd. (on the beach in front of Outrigger Reef Hotel), Honolulu
• 924-4941

See Waikiki from a bird's point of view, gliding through the air on a parasail.
Open daily 10 a.m.-5 p.m. Cost: 9 a.m. ride $36, 10 a.m.-4 p.m. ride $45.

RAFTING

Windward Expeditions
7192 Kalanianaole Hwy., Ste. 205A,
Honolulu
• 396-6450

Intrepid types will want to set aside an afternoon for Hawaiian-style white-water rafting, the usual adventure plus snorkeling. Trips are along Oahu's southeast coastline with all equipment and instruction provided. Reservations required at least a day in advance.
Open daily. Cost $35 an hour.

SAILING

Aikane Catamaran Cruises
677 Ala Moana Blvd.,
Ste. 502,
Honolulu
• 522-1533

Founded and operated by the king of the modern Hawaiian catamaran, Rudy Choy, this well-established business offers a variety of offshore cruises and sailing options on some of the most modern catamarans in the business. Sail with the man who put the catamaran on the map, and who presently holds the trans-Pacific sailing speed record to boot.
Tours daily 5:15 p.m. ($41) & 7:45 p.m. ($36).

Hilton Hawaiian Village Catamaran Sail
2005 Kalia Rd.,
Honolulu
• 949-4321

One of the island's longest-established sailing charter operators, the Hilton Hawaiian Village's Ale Ale Kai catamaran fleet offers large multipassenger catamaran sailing—for those who don't mind a crowd. The "Cat" holds up to 148 people and generally is filled for its Diamond Head Champagne Breakfast Sail (full breakfast, including champagne) and the Twilight Dinner Sail (open bar, dinner and hula show).
Sails daily, breakfast 8 a.m.-9:30 a.m. $19.50, dinner 5:30 p.m.-7:30 p.m. $39.

Honolulu Sailing Co.
45-995 Wailele Rd.,
Kaneohe
• 235-8264

For over fifteen years, the fleet from Honolulu Sailing company has provided weddings at sea, honeymoon cruises, sailing-snorkeling sails, private lessons, and private charters. Their fleet ranges from 44-foot to 71-foot yachts.
Charters and lessons by appointment. Charters start at $50 per person; lessons from $125 per day, per person.

Southern Cross Charters
1750 Kalakaua Ave.,
Ste. 3-525,
Honolulu
• 599-4757

Sail the 72-foot Alden schooner, a replica of the nineteenth-century trading schooner that plied the waters between Hawaii and California 100 years ago. Garner some hands-on sailing experience or just sit back and relax. There can be up to 49 passengers on the three-hour trip. Overnight trips and all-day sails also available.
Daily sails. Cost $19 per person for three-hour sail.

Tradewind Charters
1833 Kalakaua Ave.,
Ste. 612,
Honolulu
• 973-0311,
(800-777-2451)

There are myriad activities available on their half-day, full-day and sunset sails besides sailing: kayaking, swimming, snorkeling, windsurfing, scuba diving and more. Private charters for weddings, interisland sailing, and fishing also available. Their fleet ranges in size from 30-foot to 72-foot and can accommodate any size group.
Call for reservations. Rates begin at $59 per person.

SURFING & WINDSURFING

To get the straight scope on good surfing and windsurfing spots, your best bet is to call the **Haleiwa Surf Center** (66-167 Haleiwa Road, Haleiwa; 637-5051), open daily from 9 a.m. to 5 p.m. The local surf report number is 836-1952.

Aloha Beach Service

Sheraton Moana
Surfrider Hotel,
2365 Kalakaua Ave.,
Honolulu
• 922-3111

This classic hotel, built in 1901, and recently restored to all her splendor and glory, also offers complete beach services that combine the very best of the past with the present. Learn to surf from classic beach boys, on classic equipment fronting this classic structure—ah, the romance of it all! Windsurfing lessons run $25 for a two-hour group lesson and $25 an hour for private lessons. Windsurfer rental (9 a.m. to 5 p.m.) runs $15 for four hours, $20 for eight hours, $25 for 24 hours, $100 per week. Surfing lessons can be taken by the group for $15 an hour, or privately for $20 an hour. Or, if you're already an expert, surfboard rentals cost $5 for the first hour and $2 for each additional hour.
Open daily 9 a.m.-5:30 p.m.

Downing Hawaii

3021 Waialae Ave.,
Honolulu
• 737-9696.

George Downing is one of the foremost figures in the world of surfing in Hawaii. Surfboard rentals available for $15 a day.
Open Mon.-Fri. 10 a.m.-6 p.m., Sat. 9 a.m.-5 p.m.

Local Motion

1714 Kapiolani Blvd.,
Honolulu
• 955-7873

Koko Marina Shopping
Center,
7192 Kalanianaole
Hwy.,
Honolulu
• 396-7873

One of the top names in surfing equipment for years, Local Motion has also taken the plunge into windsurfing equipment as the popularity of the sport has grown. This full-service facility located in the heart of Honolulu is a "must-stop" for the serious practitioner or anyone interested in either activity. Surfboard rentals are available for $20 a day. Other Local Motion locations out of Honolulu are in Windward Mall (46-056 Kamehameha Highway, Kaneohe; 263-7873) and in Pearl Kai Center (98-199 Kamehameha Highway, Aiea; 486-7873).
Open Mon.-Fri. 9 a.m.-9 p.m., Sat.-Sun. 9 a.m.-6 p.m.

Prime Time Sports

Fort DeRussy Beach
(end of Paoa Place),
2055 Kalia Rd.,
Honolulu
• 949-8952

This group specializes in teaching windsurfing. With a maximum of three people per instructor, a one-and-a-quarter-hour lesson costs $30; for three-and-a-quarter hours it's $55. Equipment rental costs $18 for the first hour and $12 for each additional hour. Discounts given to military personnel.
Open daily. Lessons 9:30 a.m., 11:30 a.m., 1:30 p.m. & 3:30 p.m.

Surf & Sea
62-595 Kamehameha Hwy.,
Haleiwa
• 637-9887

A full-service marine center with surfing and windsurfing lessons for $35 per two hours. Surfboards can be rented for $18 a day; windsurfers for $40 a day. Also, diving and snorkeling rental and fishing charters.
Open daily 9 a.m.-6 p.m.

Waikiki Beach Services
Outrigger Reef Hotel,
2169 Kalia Rd.,
Honolulu
• 924-4941

What could be more romantic than learning to surf from a Waikiki beach boy? It is still possible and a really good idea. Waikiki is still the best place to try the sport of kings for the first time, and Waikiki Beach Services is a good place to start. For a one-and-a-quarter-hour lesson, you pay $20; for a private lesson, $30 an hour. Surfboard rental is $5 an hour.
Open daily 8 a.m.-5 p.m. Surfing lessons noon & 2 p.m.

Windsurfing Hawaii
156-C Hamakua Dr.,
Kailua
• 261-3539

The oldest and best-established windsurfing business in the Islands, this full-service facility is located in Kailua, close to the superb windsurfing areas of this Oahu bedroom community. Sales, rentals, instruction, repair and tips on where to go and when.
Open daily 9 a.m.-5:30 p.m. Lessons 9:30 a.m.-12:30 p.m. & 1 p.m.-4 p.m.; $40 for 3 hours (includes all equipment, plus a T-shirt). Rentals: $25 for 4 hours, $30 a day, plus $5 extra for high-performance.

TENNIS

There are some 106 free public tennis courts on Oahu, all of which are available to visitors as well as local residents. For a complete list of the locations in both the city and the county of Honolulu, and for advice on the best times to play, information on pending matches and so on, contact the **Department of Parks and Recreation**, 650 S. King Street, Honolulu; 523-4182. Following are two privately owned facilities:

Ilikai Sports Center
1777 Ala Moana Blvd.,
Honolulu
• 949-3811

One of the only major private facilities in the heart of Waikiki, the Ilikai Sports Center offers six excellent courts (one lit Omni and five hard surface), equipment sales, instruction, rentals and service. Private lessons are given for $37.50 an hour, semiprivate (for two) for $45 an hour, group for $12 an hour. Hourly rates for courts are $12 for singles, $16 for doubles; plus $2 extra for Omni lighting at night. Racket rental costs $5.50 a day; a session with the ball machine costs $10 for a half hour and $16 for an hour.
Open daily 7 a.m.-10 p.m.

Turtle Bay Hilton & Country Club
57-091 Kamehameha Hwy.,
Kahuku
• 293-8811 ext. 41

The Turtle Bay Hilton boasts ten courts, four of which are lighted. Somewhat windy conditions. For night courts, must make reservations in advance with pro shop. Private lessons are $20 for a half hour and $35 for an hour. Courts rent for $8 (singles) and $6 (per person, doubles). Equipment rental includes rackets for $5 a day, shoes for $5 a day, and a ball machine for $8 a half hour.
Open daily 8 a.m.-7 p.m.

WATERSKIING

Suyderhoud Water Ski Center
Koko Marina Shopping Center,
7192 Kalanianaole Hwy.,
Honolulu
• 395-3773

Developed and managed by a champion waterskier and located on the best waterways in the state for such activity, the Suyderhoud Water Ski Center in Hawaii Kai is not only the best place to carve a few turns and tune up your skills, it is about the only place to do so unless you know someone with a boat and skis, and access to some reasonably calm water.
Open Mon.-Fri. 9 a.m.-5 p.m., Sat. 9 a.m.-4 p.m. & Sun. 9 a.m.-3 p.m. Lessons $46 per half hour. Boat & equipment rental $78 an hour for up to 4 people.

BASICS

GETTING AROUND

Airport

The Honolulu International Airport is large, modern and busy. Located about nine miles west of Waikiki, it consists of two main areas, the Main Terminal and the Interisland Terminal. Transportation to and from the airport is moderately priced, but remember to allow enough time for heavy traffic! During the rush hour, the trip can take up to one hour. As of 1989, the **State Independent Drivers Association (SIDA) Taxi** has the airport taxi concession—$15 to $17 per carload to and from the Waikiki area (836-3535). **Airport Motor Coach** (836-3391) and other private bus transportation is also available for about $5 per person. Baggage areas in the main and interisland terminals have courtesy phones for calling ground transportation. The cheapest way to and from the airport is via **TheBUS**, the city bus system, at 60 cents, but you had better be traveling light—no baggage allowed!

The **Wiki-Wiki Shuttle** operates every 20 to 25 minutes, and carries people and baggage free between the main terminal, the interisland terminal, and the baggage areas. Just look for the signs.

Interisland flights (about $50 each way) depart frequently to Maui, Kauai, and the Big Island, and less frequently to Lanai and Molokai. The two major interisland carriers are **Aloha Airlines** (836-1111) and **Hawaiian Airlines** (537-5100).

When you leave Hawaii to go back to the mainland, your baggage will be subject to an agricultural inspection. This is now generally done by machine and is performed to help prevent the spread of plant diseases and pests to the other states.

Cars

Generally, you won't need a car in Waikiki. If you plan on staying elsewhere, or traveling around the island, the standard car-rental agencies provide a variety of cars at a variety of rates. Generally, a flat daily rate is charged with no extra charges for actual mileage. Here are the major companies: **Avis** (834-5536 at the airport, or 924-1688 for local rental locations), **Budget** (922-3600), **Hertz** (922-1158), **National** (834-7156). Other companies: **Dollar Rent-a-Car** (926-4200), **Honolulu Rent-a-Car** (941-9099), **Island World Rent-a-Car** (839-2222), **Thrifty Car Rental** (923-7383), **Tropical Rent-a-Car** (922-2385), **Ugly Duckling Rent-a-Car** (538-3825) and **United Car Rental** (922-4606). For exotic rentals: **Odyssey Rentals** (947-8036), **Silver Cloud Limousine** (524-7999), **Ferrari Rentals** (942-8725) and **Cruising Classics** (923-6446).

Public Transportation

TheBUS is the name of the city buses that go around all of Oahu, for a mere 60 cents. In the less populated areas of the island, you may ask your driver to stop and let you off anywhere, and you may flag down a bus from the side of the road. TheBus operates twenty hours a day, 365 days a year. For schedule and route information, call 531-1611.

Taxis

A large number of taxis and private and tour buses are available. Taxis are licensed by the City and County of Honolulu. Meters start at $1.40 for the first sixth of a mile, and 20 cents for each additional sixth of a mile. Drivers should be tipped about 15 percent. Major taxi companies are **Aloha State Taxi** (847-3566), **Americabs** (521-6680), **Charley's** (955-2211), **SIDA** (836-0011) and **TheCAB** (536-1707). Major tour operators include **Akamia Tours** (922-6485), **Gray Line Hawaii** (833-8000), **Robert's Hawaii** (947-3939) and **Waikiki Express** (942-2177).

FOREIGN EXCHANGE

When the banks are closed, money can be changed at the following places: **A-1 Foreign Exchange**, in the Hyatt Regency Waikiki (2424 Kalakaua Ave., Honolulu; 922-3327; open daily 8:15 a.m. to 11 p.m.); **Royal Hawaiian Shopping Center** (2301 Kalakaua Ave., Honolulu; 922-4761; open daily 9 a.m. to 5 p.m.); or **Deak International Ltd.**, which has several locations at Honolulu International Airport (834-1099; open daily 7 a.m. to 4:30 p.m. and 7 p.m. to 4:30 a.m.).

TELEPHONE NUMBERS

The area code for all numbers on the Islands is 808 .

Agricultural Inspection 541-2951
TheBUS 531-1611
Chamber of Commerce of Hawaii 522-8800
Civil Defense..523-4121
Coast Guard 536-4336
Dental Emergency 536-2135
Directory Assistance (local) 411
        (interisland 1-555-1212
Emergency
        (Ambulance, Fire, Police & Rescue) 911
Health Center (Waikiki) 922-4787
Honolulu International Airport (for overseas
        flight arrivals and visitors' information for all
        islands) 836-6413

Hospital (Queens Medical Center Emergency
  Services) 547-4311
Hyperbaric Center 523-9155
Immigration & Naturalization Service. 541-1379
Information Referral Center 521-4566
Library Information 548-4775
Lifeguard 922-3888
Marine Forecasts 836-3921
Paramedics .... 911 Parks, 548-3179
Poison Control Center 941-4411
Postal Information 423-3990
Surf Report 836-1952
Time 983-3211
Visitors Information Bureau 923-1811
Weather
  Honolulu 833-2849
  rest of Oahu 836-0121

GOINGS-ON

January

- **Family Sunday,** held the first Sunday of every month, on the Bishop Museum grounds; 847-3511.
- **International Bodyboard Championships,** on Oahu's North Shore; 396-8342.
- **Kodak Hula Bowl Football Classic,** usually the second Saturday, at Aloha Stadium. A concert attraction gives a postgame show, which is presented as a benefit for the University of Hawaii Foundation and other charities; 955-5541.
- **Narcissus Festival,** a tradition of the Chinese community, including a queen pageant at Neal Blaisdell Center Concert Hall and a coronation gala at a Waikiki hotel. A prelude to the Chinese New Year's celebration; 533-3181.
- **Queen Emma Museum Open House,** Honolulu; 595-6291.
- **Vietnamese New Year Festival,** late January, at Kapiolani Park Bandstand.

February

- **Ala Wai Canoe Challenge**, Honolulu; no-experience-required annual quarter-mile canoe race down Waikiki's Ala Wai Canal, including food booths, games, arts and crafts; 923-1802.
- **Aloha Run/Walk**, from the Aloha Tower to Aloha Stadium. A benefit for the variety school; 735-6092.
- **Cherry Blossom Festival** (late February through early March), Honolulu; a Japanese cultural celebration, includes a variety of events including the Tea Ceremony, Kabuki theater, martial arts and crafts; 522-4153.
- **Chinese New Year's Celebration** and **Chinatown Open House**, in Chinatown and at the Chinese Cultural Center. Maunakea Street is closed to vehicular traffic; food and craft merchants sell a variety of Chinese wares; the Chinese Lion Dance and fireworks herald the occasion.
- **Hawaiian Open Golf Tournament**, Waialae Country Club, Honolulu. A PGA tournament featuring top professional golfers; 836-0060.
- **Humpback Whale Awareness Month**, Sea Life Park; Oahu; 259-7933.
- **Mardi Gras**, celebration, featuring New Orleans Dixieland jazz and food, at Restaurant Row.
- **Music for Lovers**, Waikiki Shell. The Honolulu Symphony's annual Valentine's Day Concert; 537-6191.
- **NFL Pro Bowl**, Aloha Stadium, Honolulu. An annual all-star football game between the National and American Conferences of the National Football League; 486-9300.
- **Punahou Carnival**, a major fund-raiser for Punahou School, featuring rides, games, food, variety shows and the biggest white-elephant show in the Islands; 944-5753.
- **Punahou School Carnival**, the biggest and best-attended carnival, on the grounds of the Puna School. Sponsored by the junior class as a scholorship benefit; 944-5752.

March

- **Adopt a Duckie Race**, Honolulu; more than 15,000 rubber ducks start at McCully Street Bridge and race down the Ala Wai Canal in Waikiki. Sponsors of winning duckies win prizes such as trips and car rentals. Annual benefit for United Cerebral Palsy of Hawaii; 538-6789
- **Annual Hawaiian International Music Festival** (during spring break), Honolulu. Represents the best high school jazz, concert and marching bands;

dance and drill teams; and cheerleaders from Australia, New Zealand, Japan, Canada and the mainland; 842-8315 or contact World of Pageantry, (800) 854-8191.

- **Annual Kamehameha Schools Song Contest**, Honolulu. Features the finest in Hawaiian choral competitive singing and dance. Telecast live; 842-8211.
- **Annual Oahu Kite Festival** and **Hawaii Challenge National Stunt Kite Festival**, Kapiolani Park, Waikiki. A celebration with competitions, demonstrations, displays, workshops, games and entertainment. Flyers from around the U.S. compete; 924-0148.
- **Hawaii Polo Club Games** (every Sunday from March through August), Mokuleia, Oahu. Includes visiting international players and teams; 637-7656.
- **Prince Kuhio Day**, celebration at Prince Kuhio Federal Building, Honolulu. A state holiday; 546-7573.
- **Sandcastle Building Contest**, Kailua Beach Park, Oahu. Pits students from the University of Hawaii School of Architecture against professional architects; 948-7235.
- **St. Patrick's Day Parade**, March 17, beginning at noon from Fort DeRussy to Kapiolani Park.
- **World's Greatest Garage Sale**, featuring an array of goods at bargain prices, at the Neal Blaisdell Center Exhibition Hall. A benefit for the American Cancer Society; 531-1662.

April

- **Buddha Day**, closest Sunday to April 8, Oahu. Celebrated at Buddhist Temples on all islands with special services, pageants, dances and flowers; 538-3805.
- **Carole Kai Bed Race and Parade**, from Fort DeRussy to Kapiolani Park; decorated beds parade along Kalakaua Avenue and a colorful bed race follows, on a course along Kalakaua; 755-6092.
- **Easter Sunday**, sunrise service at the Punchbowl; 531-4888.
- **Hawaiian Highland Gathering**, Richardson Field, Pearl Harbor, Honolulu. A gathering of the clans for Scottish games, competitions, food, dancing, games and pipe bands; 523-5050.

May

- **Annual Festival of the Pacific,** late May or early June, Honolulu. Features athletic tournaments, music, songs, and dances of the multi-ethnic people of the Pacific; 395-7063.
- **Annual Koi Show,** Honolulu. Part of the Japanese Boy's Day celebration by the Hawaii Goldfish and Carp Association; 946-1641.
- **Cinco de Mayo Celebration,** May 5, at several venues, including Compadres Mexican Bar & Grill (538-1441), Restaurant Row (523-1307) and Merchant Street.
- **Hawaii State Fair,** late May or early June, Aloha Stadium, Honolulu. Exhibits, food booths, entertainment, arts and crafts; 486-9300.
- **Lei Day,** May 1, Kapiolani Park, Waikiki. The city's annual create-a-lei contest. There are statewide leicompetitions, exhibits, and the crowning of a Lei Queen; 521-9815.
- **Lei Day Concert with the Brothers Cazimero,** May 1, Waikiki Shell. Make a lei, buy a leiand wear a lei, then sit in on one of the most heavenly Hawaiian musical experiences. Presented by Mountain Apple Co.; 528-1888.
- **May Day/Lei Day,** Waimea Falls Park; 638-8511. Also at Sea Life Park; 259-7933.
- **Memorial Day Special Military Services,** National Memorial Cemetery of the Pacific, Punchbowl, Honolulu; 541-1430.
- **Na Hoku Nanohano Awards,** an evening saluting achievements in Hawaii's recording industry, site and date to be announced. Sponsored by the Hawaii Academy of Recording Arts; 524-4272.
- **Pacific Handicrafters Guild Spring Fair,** Ala Moana Park, Honolulu. Quality arts and crafts from Hawaii's finest artists, demonstrations, ethnic foods and entertainment; 732-4913.

June

- **Annual Friends of the Library of Hawaii Book Sale,** featuring a wealth of books at bargain prices, at McKinley High School cafeteria; 737-2300.
- **Fancy Fair,** featuring a Hawaiian marketplace, entertainment, arts and crafts, on the grounds of Mission Houses Museum, a missionary-built historic site; 531-0481.
- **King Kamehameha Day,** June 11, Kamehameha's birthday. State holiday that honors Kamehameha the Great, Hawaii's first monarch. Celebration on all islands with parades, chants, hula dances, foot races and exhibits; 536-6540.

- **Miss Hawaii Scholarship Pageant,** to be Hawaii's entrant in the Miss America Pageant, date and site to be announced.
- **TDK "Gotcha" Pro Surf Championships,** Sandy Beach, Oahu. International summer surfing event; 326-1011.
- **Wildest Show in Town,** a summer twilight concert series (every Wednesday through August), held at the Honolulu Zoo; 923-7723.

July

- **Annual Ukulele Festival,** Queen Kapiolani Park Bandstand, Waikiki; 487-6010. Features hundreds of ukulele players.
- **Fourth of July celebration,** including Hawaii's biggest fireworks display, at Sills Field, Schofield Barracks.
- **Hawaii State Farm Fair,** featuring carnival rides, food and game booths, produce, plat sales and displays of livestock as well as an auction, on the grounds of McKinley High School. Presented by the Hawaii Farm Bureau Federation; 848-2074.
- **Kailua Fourth of July Celebration and Parade,** featuring fireworks display on July 3 at Kailua Beach Park, and a parade through Kailua town on July 4.
- **Kalakaua Avenue Summer Block Party,** featuring entertainment stages and food booths on Kalakaua Avenue between Seaside and Kapahulu avenues; 923-1094.
- **Midsummer Night's Glean,** a nocturnal attraction combining entertainment beneath a full moon, at Foster Botanic Garden.
- **Prince Lot Hula Festival,** Maunalua Gardens, Honolulu; 839-5334. A festival honoring King Kamehameha V. Hula schools perform authentic ancient and modern hula. Also games, arts and crafts, exhibits.

August

- **Admission Day,** August 19. State holiday that celebrates Hawaii's admission as the 50th state; 923-1811.
- **Floating Lantern Ceremony,** Ala Wai Park; 595-2556. A Buddhist ceremony held on the anniversary of the end of World War II.
- **Ka Himeni Ana,** an a capella contest of old Hawaiian-style singing, site and date to be announced; 842-1131.
- **Queen Liliuokalani Keiki Hula Competition,** Kamehameha schools gym, Honolulu. Girls and boys ages 6 to 12 compete in ancient and modern hula; 521-6905.

- **Samoan Flag Day**, Keehi Lagoon Park, Honolulu. Includes a parade, ceremony, speeches, Samoan dances and singing; 545-7451.
- **Slack Key Festival**, a concert in the *ki ho alu* (slack-key) guitar style, at McKoy Pavilion, Ala Moana Park. Hawaii's legendary slack-key artists usually assemble for this event.

September

- **Aloha Week Festivals**, all islands, in September and October. Hawaiian pageantry, canoe races, street parties and parades; 944-8857.
- **Annual Celebration of the Hawaiian Canoe and Kayak Racers**, Heeia State Park, Kaneohe, Oahu. Crafts, foods, and exhibits; 842-5500.
- **Annual Okinawan Festival**, features dancing and exhibits; 546-8119.
- **Waikiki Rough Water Swim**, a two-mile swim from Sans Souci Beach to Duke Kahanamoku Beach. All ages and categories; 396-4008.

October

- **Annual Waimea Falls Makahiki Festival**, Waimea Falls Park, Oahu. Hawaiian games, crafts, music, foods and hula competition; 638-8511.
- **Bankoh Molokai Hoe** (Bank of Hawaii Men's Molokai to Oahu Canoe Race. About 50 international teams race across the rough Molokai Channel in outrigger canoes, finishing at Fort DeRussy in Waikiki); 842-5500.
- **Honolulu Orchid Society Show**, Blaisdell Center, Honolulu. Exhibition of thousands of varieties of orchids by Hawaii's growers; 527-5400.
- **Oktoberfest**, celebration at the Hibiscus Ballroom, Ramada Renaissance Ala Moana Hotel. Features Bavarian food and entertainment; 955-4811.

November

- **Academy Folk Art Bazaar**, late November to early December, Honolulu Academy of Arts. Sale of items from around the world; 538-3693.
- **Honolulu Symphony Radiothon**, a fund-raiser to benefit the symphony. KGU carries the broadcast.
- **International Film Festival**, late November to early December. Features Asian and U.S. films shown throughout Oahu; 944-7200.

- **Kamehameha Schools Hoolaulea** (celebration), features Hawaiian entertainment, arts and edibles, at the elementary school campus.
- **Mission Houses Museum Christmas Fair**, crafts, foods, books, gifts; 531-0481.
- **Surfing Championships**, including Pipeline Masters, Men's World Cup and Women's World Cup, late November to early December, North Shore; 842-5500. The world's greatest surfers compete on Oahu's North Shore. Beaches and dates are based on wave action.

December

- **Aloha Bowl Collegiate Football**; Aloha Stadium, Honolulu; 486-9509.
- **Annual Rainbow Classic**, Blaisdell Center, Honolulu. Invitational collegiate basketball; 948-7523.
- **Bodhi Day**, early December; Hawaii Buddhist Council. The traditional Buddhist Day of Enlightenment celebrated on all islands. Services in Japanese and English. Visitors welcome; 542-9200.
- **Christmas Water Show**, presented by Mermaids Hawaii, at the Hawaii Dynasty Hotel pool; 538-3255.
- **Festival of Trees**, Amfac Center, downtown Honolulu. A display and sale of Christmas trees and ornaments, the proceeds of which benefit the Queen's Medical Center Auxiliary.
- **Honolulu City Lights**, the city's annual tree-lighting ceremony and concert, at Honolulu Hale (city hall).
- **Honolulu Marathon**, early December. One of the most popular marathons in the U.S.; 734-7200.
- **Honolulu Wheelchair Marathon**, a part of the Honolulu Marathon, same course and distance; 734-7200.
- **Jingle Bell Run**; *Honolulu Advertiser*. A fun five-kilometer run with stops along the way for singing contests and awards. Entertainment, party afterwards; 525-8000.
- **Kamehameha Schools Christmas Concert**, Blaisdell Center, Honolulu; 842-8211.
- **Kaneohe Christmas Parade**, Kaneohe, Oahu. A two-hour parade with military and school bands, the Royal Hawaiian Band, and floats; 235-4543.
- **Pacific Handicrafters Guild Christmas Fair**, Honolulu; 732-4913.
- **Pearl Harbor Day**, December 7 (USS *Arizona* Memorial), Honolulu. A special service in memory of those killed during the Japanese bombing of Oahu in 1941; 422-0561.

MAUI

RESTAURANTS

For more information on how our rating system works, how we estimate meal prices and so on, turn to About the Restaurants, page 6. Also in that section is a Toque Tally, page 10, which lists all the restaurants in this book by rating.

BY CUISINE

AMERICAN

Dillon's Restaurant (*Paia*)
Leilani's on the Beach (*Kaanapali*)
Maui Outrigger (*Kihei*)

CONTINENTAL

Lanai Terrace (*Wailea*)
La Perouse (*Wailea*)
Swan Court (*Lahaina*)

FRENCH

La Bretagne Restaurant (*Lahaina*)
Chez Paul (*Olowalu*)
Gerard's Restaurant (*Lahaina*)
La Perouse (*Wailea*)

HAWAIIAN

The Lodge at Koele Dining Room
(*Lanani*)
Maui Outrigger (*Kihei*)
Plantation Veranda (*Kapalua*)

ITALIAN

Alex's Hole in the Wall (*Lahaina*)

JAPANESE

East-West Dining Room (*Kahului*)
Hakone (*Kihei*)

MEDITERRANEAN

Tasca (*Lahaina*)

NEW AMERICAN

Café Kiowai (*Kihei*)
Kapalua Bay Club Restaurant
(*Kapalua*)
The Lodge at Koele Dining Room
(*Lanai*)
Longhi's (*Lahaina*)
Plantation Veranda (*Kapalua*)
Prince Court (*Makena*)
Raffles (*Kihei*)
Sound of the Falls (*Lahaina*)

PACIFIC RIM

Avalon Restaurant & Bar (*Lahaina*)
Café Kiowai (*Kihei*)

SEAFOOD

Aurelio's (*Kahului*)
The Grill & Bar (*Kapalua*)

Island Fish House (*Kihei*)

Kapalua Bay Club Restaurant (*Kapalua*)

Kimo's Restaurant (*Lahaina*)

Lahaina Treehouse (*Lahaina*)

Mama's Fish House (*Paia*)

SUSHI

Hakone (*Kihei*)

THAI

Siam Thai (*Wailuku*)

STEAK HOUSE

Aurelio's (*Kahului*)

Kimo's Restaurant (*Lahaina*)

> *We're always interested to hear about your discoveries, and to receive your comments on ours. Please feel free to write to us, and do state clearly exactly what you liked or disliked.*

Alex's Hole in the Wall
834 Front St.,
Lahaina
• 661-3197
ITALIAN

9/20

Alex's is an old (since 1974) standby, which serves average, traditional-Italian dishes in a cozy, homey atmosphere. The upstairs dining room is filled with nostalgic tchochkes, and is quite comfortable; but don't get your hopes up about the food. This is red-sauce territory: lasagne, veal Parmigiana, sausage and peppers and various pastas. The portions are very generous, and they're not ripping you off here too terribly, at least by Maui standards. Dinner for two, with wine, is about $50.
Open for dinner Mon.-Sat. 5:30 p.m.-10 p.m. Cards: AE, MC, V.

Aurelio's Restaurant
55 Kaahumanu Ave.,
Kahului
• 871-7656
STEAK/SEAFOOD

11/20

It is a joy to find, across the street from the Maui Mall, Aurelio's, this very sweet and cozy family-run restaurant. The food is good—not great—but the friendly atmosphere and very pretty room contribute to making this a worthwhile dining experience. And bring the kids. The owners, Andres and Nancy Oania, go to great pains to accommodate families (and prices are pretty mild for Maui). The food is your basic, solid stuff: onion soup, a good Portuguese bean soup, various sandwiches and burgers, plate lunches and short ribs, Hawaii-style (heavy on the soy sauce). There's also a selection of seafood dishes, steaks and chicken—basically, something for everyone. After an afternoon of shopping at the mall, Aurelio's makes a nice rest stop. Dinner for two, with beverages, is about $40.
Open Mon.-Sat. 11 a.m.-9 p.m. Cards: MC, V.

Avalon Restaurant & Bar

844 Front St.,
Lahaina
• 667-5559
PACIFIC RIM

Avalon is like a much-needed breath of fresh air on the Lahaina restaurant scene, and we truly hope that it's a harbinger of things to come. The look is tropical/hip, with lots of bamboo, floral prints and a wonderfully airy atmosphere. The staff is young, friendly and surprisingly professional for this laid-back town. The menu is pretty ambitious, taking its cues from the likes of Roy Yamaguchi and Jeremiah Tower. There are culinary stops through the Pacific Rim, featuring various exotic ports: Thailand, China, Indonesia, India, Japan, as well as Hawaii. While the execution here isn't always perfect, the intentions are to be encouraged. And just the fact that someone's making an attempt to do creative, up-to-date food on this island is reason enough to come. The appetizers are delightful; order a mess of them and share. The Maui onion rings with a smoky-sweet homemade tamarind-chipotle ketchup are habit-forming, as are the skewers of Indonesian saté—tender chicken marinated in kecap manis, then grilled and served with a luscious Balinese peanut sauce. We also loved the fresh sugar-snap peas, wok-sautéed with a spicy Szechuan-chili sauce; and the Vietnamese summer rolls are richly done: fat, overstuffed pillows of shrimp, bean sprouts, rice noodles and fresh herbs barely held together in their rice paper wrapper, served with a Thai peanut sauce. Wisely, Avalon offers a platter of all these appetizers, served in half orders, so you get to sample them all. The salads are a hit here, too. Try the simple mixed green salad with Maui onions, cucumber and crispy rice noodles in a light ginger-sesame dressing for a refreshing palate cleanser; for a more substantial middle course, the lightly sautéed scallops and shiitake mushrooms on a bed of mixed greens with that same ginger-sesame dressing is a good bet. Avalon serves a nice selection of grilled dishes (steak, chicken breast, prawns and fresh local fish) that are prepared in several ways with various sauces; we preferred the garlic black-bean preparation. Other good entrées are the soft-shell crabs with garlic butter and herbs, the mixed seafood grill, and, on Friday and Saturday nights, the Chinese duck, served with soft, puffy bao. There is also a roster of vegetarian entrées. All of the dishes here can be prepared in varying degrees of heat. For the amount of food you get, as well as the quality, prices are most reasonable, especially considering that Avalon just may be the best restaurant in Lahaina. Dinner for two, with wine, will run about $90.

Open daily noon-midnight. All major cards.

I SELL SEA SHELLS

Among the many exotic local ingredients that are beginning to find their way into Hawaii's restaurant kitchens are *opihi*: small mollusks that come in black, red or yellow. Their chewy, briny-tasting meat is similar to that of the abalone, and even more expensive: a gallon sells for about $160. Hawaiians traditionally have eaten them raw or in salads, and chefs are now mixing them into dishes of fettuccine or angel-hair pasta.

La Bretagne Restaurant

off Front St., next to
the baseball field,
Lahaina
• 661-8900
FRENCH

10/20

La Bretagne, which was the home of a Maui sheriff early in the century, is too respectful of the culinary laws of the past. The place is charming enough, if a tad on the oppressive, fusty side, but the food really needs some revamping. Classical French is the name of the game here, with dinosaur dishes like duck à l'orange, fish en papillote and seafood en croute that are a bit, well, overprepared. Basically, the food is just too rich, especially for the climate. Nevertheless, La Bretagne maintains its reputation as an old favorite here, but if it's classic cuisine you're looking for, there are places on the island doing it with a lighter touch. Dinner for two, with wine, is about $90.
Open nightly 6 p.m.-10:30 p.m. All major cards.

Café Kiowai

5400 Makena Alanui
Maui Prince Hotel
Kihei
• 874-1111
PACIFIC RIM/
NEW AMERICAN

Café Kiowai is nominally the Maui Prince's coffee shop, but it's really a full-blown restaurant as far as we're concerned. For one thing, its indoor-outdoor setting, with streams stocked with koi winding through the room, and a terrace that overlooks tranquil pools and lush vegetation make the Café one of the prettiest places to dine on Maui. Another draw is the food—it's simply real cuisine, and far too sophisticated to be classed as mere coffee shop fare. Café Kiowai serves from dawn until dusk (including a between-meals snack menu), and while the food is consistent all day long, the Café really shines at dinnertime, with a menu that is all over the culinary map. There aren't too many places on the island (or the whole state, for that matter), where you'll find a bruschetta-loaf of warm peasant bread with extra-virgin olive oil and fresh mozzarella, marvelous Dungeness crab and corn cakes with an oven-roasted tomato coulis, or deep-fried soft-shell crabs in black-bean sauce with pineapple salsa. And those are just the appetizers. The Maui onion soup served in a hollowed-out loaf of bread is a must; so is the Caesar salad with homemade croutons. Or how about an open-faced duck enchilada with salsa and sour cream? These aren't gimmicks—this is really exciting food, beautifully done. The pastas are quite good here, as is the black-bean chili served with cheddar cheese and sweet Maui onions. They also do a bang-up job with fresh fish: the sesame-grilled catch of the day with wok-sautéed vegetables and shoyu butter is delicious, as is the seared-but-rare tuna with Maui ginger marmalade and sun-dried cranberries. For carnivores, don't miss the charbroiled lamb loin steaks with Maui wine-onion relish, or the house-smoked-and-barbecued pork ribs with warm pecan muffins. Get a side order of the potato-and-red-onion pancakes with sour cream and the Maui onion rings (which may be the best anywhere) for good measure. You won't be sorry. Café Kiowai puts many of Maui's more hotsy-totsy restaurants to shame; we really love this place. And it's not just good by Hawaii standards—there are a lot of chefs stateside

who could learn a few lessons here. Dinner for two, with wine, is about $75.
Open daily 6:30 a.m.-10:30 p.m. All major cards.

Chez Paul
Honoapiilani Hwy.,
Olowalu
• 661-3843
FRENCH

12/20

Chez Paul is a real favorite in Maui, and while its location is certainly intriguing (out in the boonies, where the petroglyphs are), the food really isn't. This charming, unpretentious room would do a lot better with less complicated food, and while the preparations of classic dishes are a lot more successful than they are at La Bretagne, for instance, this really isn't the kind of food we can enjoy in a casual, tropical land. The restaurant prides itself on the fact that you won't find any dread "trendy" ingredients, such as those wild sun-dried tomatoes, or those parvenues of the fungus world, shiitake mushrooms, on the menu. Yes, the duck à l'orange is lovely, as is the scampi and the poisson beurre blanc, but these dishes really are a bit tired, and who wants to eat this stuff when the reality of donning a bathing suit the next day looms overhead? Dinner for two, with wine, is about $70.
Open nightly 6:30 p.m. & 8:30 p.m. All major cards.

Dillon's Restaurant
89 Hana Hwy.,
Paia
• 579-9113
AMERICAN

9/20

Local color takes precedence over food at this Paia tradition unless bagels and cream cheese will do on the opening leg of the rollercoaster ride to Hana. Expatriate owners Chuck and Nancy Powell, having shed all but their Brooklyn accents in the move west, dish up adequate breakfast food—Kahlúa french toast—and such luncheon standbys as hamburgers, to stave off hunger pangs. When they venture into the more rarefied strata of gourmandise, however (such as lasagne, or anything with a sauce), the menehunes, ineptitude, or a combination thereof conspire against them and the hapless customer. Clam chowder, for example, a slightly curdled, not unpleasantly tart cream, provided lots more stringy bits of ham than shellfish. Lasagne managed to be both tough and flour-sticky. Anomalous clumps of meat afloat in an acidic tomato-paste sauce made us wish we had decided to go for the vegetarian version. Garlic bread leaves a film on the palate that remains faintly metallic as one saunters up and down Paia's two main streets to browse among artsy-craftsy emporia and allow the meal to settle. A glutinous mush-room sauce covers sautéed tuna and hamburger unless one asks for them plain, a course we'd recommend. Grilled and sporting a heap of french fries, the day's fresh fish, hamburgers and perhaps New York steak are better bets at dinner than more ambitious efforts such as pepper steak or pasta primavera. The large open room cut by waist-high bamboo balustrades sports a bamboo-sheathed bar under a bamboo simulacrum of a thatched roof. Well-worn chairs, tables and flooring equally worn and service casual to the point of indifference establish the prevailing tone, a kind of "just hang loose" atmosphere to which Tiffany-style overhead lamps and airport-quality New Guinea art, hung haphazardly, add a quirky phoniness. A pair of wanderers will leave about $50-60 lighter after dinner with beer or wine, tax and tip included.

Open daily 7 a.m.-9 p.m. Cards: AE, MC, V.

East-West Dining Room

Maui Beach Hotel,
170 Kaahumanu Ave.,
Kahului
• 877-0051
JAPANESE

The far windows look out on a dreary motel swimming pool. As the entrance from a parking lot is all motel, as well, it's best to focus on the food and the locals chattering away at a sea of tables in this capacious room. The term "chop suey" refers to the ethnic mix that pervades the Islands, and chop suey convenes for this superior buffet, filipino and filipina, the great-grandchildren of Portuguese and paki (Chinese) laborers, remnants of the Hawaiian stock that once ruled the land, among others. Oh, yes, and the Japanese, who virtually own the island but know a bargain when they taste it. The buffet goes well with Maui lager, whose malt tingle doesn't overwhelm the fish or savory vegetables. That buffet includes a few concessions to haole (white) tastes, notably creamy potato salad, a huge bowl of salad greens, string beans and three or four kinds of fresh fruit. These, however, aren't the reason for your presence. You are here to pile plate after plate with sesame-dressed spinach, soy-dunked chunks of snowy-white tofu, mildly pungent-and-sweet pickled cucumber. To these you'll add daikon turned saffron-yellow from its marinade, and beside them you'll place a small gray crackle-finish bowl heaped with wheat or buckwheat noodles drenched in mirin sauce. The aficionado will revel in magnificent sashimi, a great trencher of the yellowfin tuna or marlin, or both, on shredded cabbage to be given the smoldering benediction of wasabi, Japanese green horseradish, stirred into soy sauce. He'll also make a pass at tako slices (boiled octopus), platters of nori-wrapped sushi, spiky clusters of marinated black seaweed, chewy-tender rings of fish pudding and gobo, strands of wonderfully crunchy burdock root. Having done justice, and more, to these cold dishes, go on to the teppanyaki grill in the rear where a battery of chefs slice and stir-fry medium-rare beef, chicken and vegetables with scallops and deep-fat fry tempura shrimp, squid, sweet potato and zucchini. Miso soup, rice and

PINEAPPLE WINE

So, you thought that all wine was made from grapes? True, at Tedeschi Vineyards on Maui, most of the wines come from the traditional source, but Hawaii's only vintner is most famous for Maui Blanc, a wine made from fermented pineapple juice. If you don't happen to be near France for Beaujolais Nouveau mania, you can get a bottle of Maui Nouveau in early November. For information on tours, call (808) 878-6058, or write P.O. Box 953, Ulupalakua, Hawaii 96790.

stir-fried noodles at another station complete the assemblage of food, which ranges from good to superb. Parking in the motel lot can be a hassle on weekends, when it may seem as though the entire island has turned up. It's a hassle savvy locals unhesitatingly undertake and with good reason. The Imperial Teppanyaki Buffet with beer or saké will cost a couple $45 with tax and tip included.
Open nightly 5:30 p.m.-8:30 p.m. All major cards.

Gerard's Restaurant
174 Lahainaluna Rd.,
Lahaina
• 661-8939
FRENCH

This is one of our favorite restaurants on Maui, not only for the excellent nouvelle cuisine of Chef Gerard Reversade but for the romantic setting. Reversade moved from Oahu to Maui in 1982 and opened a small, very French restaurant. Overnight word got out about his excellent food. In 1987 he moved up the street into the Plantation Inn and his food only got better. Patrons can choose to dine inside in the small rooms; we recommend reserving a table outside on the lanai or on the garden patio. The white-wicker tables and chairs offer the feeling of dining in a French country inn. Gerard's menu, which changes frequently, is mainly French cuisine with an extensive use of Hawaiian produce. For example, he combines shiitake and oyster mushrooms into a puff pastry; a filet of beef is served with Maui onions and a red-wine butter; a rich confit of duck with wild mushrooms and garlic potatoes is served with a salad of Island greens and duck cracklings. Gerard has fallen in love with Hawaiian fish and continues to create new ways to serve it. The wine list is well thought out and reasonably priced by Lahaina standards. Premium wines and Champagne are also available by the glass. Book well in advance; every tourist who knows about the place wants to sample his food. Dinner for two, with a wonderful wine, will run around $125.
Open nightly 6 p.m.-9 p.m. All major cards.

The Grill & Bar
200 Kapalua Dr.,
Kapalua
• 669-5653
SEAFOOD

11/20

Overlooking Kapalua's award-winning golf course, the Grill and Bar is good for casual dining in a wood-paneled, open-windowed, fern-filled restaurant. Instead of a dinner menu, specials of the day are offered, which generally consist of four different fresh-fish dishes (seared, baked, broiled, or sautéed with a variety of sauces). Meals are always tasty, the wine list is nice, and eaters dress in everything from shorts and T-shirts to elegant resort-wear. Dinner for two, with wine, costs about $100.
Open daily 11:30 a.m.-3 p.m. & 5 p.m.-12:30 a.m. Cards: MC, V.

Hakone

Maui Prince Hotel,
5400 Makena Alanui,
Kihei
• 874-1111
JAPANESE/SUSHI

It's only fitting that the elegant, Japanese-owned Maui Prince Hotel should have a first-rate Japanese restaurant, and in Hakone, it certainly does. Designed with Zen spareness, with blond woods, lots of white, generously spaced tables and a beautifully laid out sushi bar, Hakone is quietly handsome, yet casual enough for comfort. The service is absolutely marvelous—you barely have to wiggle your eyebrow, and someone will be refilling your water, or bringing you a hot towel. Like all the restaurants in the Maui Prince, Hakone exudes class—and offers good food as well. The sushi is fresh, delicious and perfectly prepared by the chef. The cooked dishes equal the raw ones. Tempura came to table crisp and greaseless, and cooked to a turn. The chicken yakitori featured toothsome white meat interspersed with grilled vegetables and the chawan mushi, the steamed egg custard with chicken, shrimp, shiitake mushrooms and ginko nuts, was delicate yet flavorful. We also enjoyed the kaiseki dinner, which comes in three varieties: seven-course, nine-course or a sushi version. The sampling in these dinners is fairly panoramic and is just a fun way to graze—lots of little courses, lots of different tastes. A kaiseki dinner for two, with saké, will run about $90. And don't forget the dress code: no shorts, tank tops, culottes or bare feet.
Open nightly 6 p.m.-9:30 p.m. All major cards.

Hotel Hana-Maui Dining Room

Hotel Hana-Maui,
Hana
• 248-7264
PACIFIC RIM/
CONTINENTAL

12/20

We'll go a long way in pursuit of things culinary—even attempt the outrageously arduous and beautiful drive to Hana. This pursuit was made all the more intriguing, given the whispered beginnings of a new cuisine forming in Hawaii. So it was with hats in hand and expectation in our eyes that we arrived at the dining room of executive chef Amy Ferguson-Ota, one of the cuisine's most quoted progenitors. We expected a lot, and, unfortunately, we came away disappointed.

The dining room itself is splendidly tropical, but its open airy feeling and large size don't necessarily make for a great showcase. Tropical flowers pull the eye earthward from the lofty ceiling—nice. But if there isn't a crowd—and there wasn't—the place seems unnervingly empty.

The menu was limited for dinner. One Friday night there were three appetizers, two soups, two salads and five entrées. Asian influences were evident, as well as a mix of indigenous ingredients. One dish, bamboo-steamed mahimahi with date chutney and lime-butter sauce, says a lot about Pacific Rim cuisine.

But we expected so much more. From the specials menu, we were content with the Oriental duck salad. The sesame dressing and crisp wontons were inventive, but barely out of the ordinary. So, too, was the Cajun-style catfish that tasted of the local wood over which it was grilled. But we wondered why Cajun? We also balked at the other special—Norwegian salmon. It's a long way to drive for something so commonplace. Of course, if you're staying here, you are completely in Ferguson-Ota's hands.

While we're grousing, improper spelling has never been a successful apéritif: "wanton," "Norwiegen," and "waterchestnuts" are three examples from the menu. Anyone who's paying these prices deserves the courtesy and attentiveness that is overflowing everywhere else in this special resort.

The new wine list is small, but reasonably priced, with an interesting selection of California Chardonnays. For two, expect to pay $120 or more with wine.

Open daily 7:30 a.m.-10 a.m., 11:30 a.m.-2 p.m. & 6 p.m.-9 p.m. All major cards.

Island Fish House
1945 S. Kihei Rd.,
Kihei
• 879-7771
SEAFOOD

10/20

In among the jungle of fast-food outlets and horribly designed condominium projects on Kihei Road is an oasis for seafood and fresh-fish lovers, the Island Fish House. The interior is a little too dark and the tables too close together, but the fish is fresh and prepared in ten different ways. The chef's trio plate allows the *malihini* (newcomer) to sample three different types of fish. In addition to fish, they also serve beef, chicken and steak, but why go to a fish house to eat steak? Service can be hurried at times (let your waiter know you are in no rush). The wine list is a bit pricey but offers a good selection. They offer an early-bird special from 5 p.m. to 6 p.m., which substantially cuts the price of their dinners. Expect dinner for two, with wine, to run about $85.

Open nightly 5 p.m.-9 p.m. Cards: AE, MC, V.

Kapalua Bay Club Restaurant
1 Bay Dr.,
Kapalua
• 669-8008
SEAFOOD/NEW AMERICAN

Consider the epitome of elegance in paradise: a restaurant perched on a cliff overlooking the rolling waves of Kapalua Bay. The decor is warm wood, muted lighting and original artwork. Soft, classical music plays quietly in the background. The Kapalua Bay Club offers not only a haven of luxury but creative dishes found nowhere else on the island. For example, the chef has taken shrimp from the island of Molokai (visible across the channel) and filled it with Dungeness crab laced with a saffron sauce; we enjoyed the salpicon of pheasant with plum sauce. Even the salads are unique: thinly sectioned Maui onions, tomatoes, cucumbers and Brie cheese or fingers of avocado and papaya with raspberry vinaigrette. Although they offer excellent scaloppini of veal, filet mignon, lamb and chicken, we recommend ordering the fresh fish. The chef's innovative fish preparations include broiled with mango chutney butter and julienne of red and green bell peppers, sautéed with oysters and shrimp in a dill-flavored white-wine sauce, or poached with lobster sauce and mussels. The multipage wine list offers a selection of

the best wines in the world. Dinner for two, with a modest wine, will cost about $125.
Open daily 11:30 a.m.-2 p.m. & 6 p.m.-11 p.m. Entertainment 6:30 p.m.-10:30 p.m. All major cards.

Kimo's Restaurant
845 Front St., Lahaina
• 661-4811
STEAKHOUSE/SEAFOOD

10/20

On the water in historic downtown Lahaina, Kimo's is a dependably good fish- and steakhouse. The view (especially if you can get an oceanfront table) is exceptional at sunset. The menu is not particularily imaginative, but they do have a selection of fresh Island fish, the perennial lobster-and-steak combo and a range of steak, chicken and pork dishes. The downstairs bar is always crowded with a young singles crowd and dinner patrons waiting for a table (the restaurant, which is upstairs, usually has a long wait for dinner). Dinner for two, with wine, will set you back about $88.
Open daily 11:30 a.m.-2:30 p.m. & 5 p.m.-10:30 p.m. Cards: MC, V.

Lahaina Treehouse
Lahaina Market Place, 126 Lahainaluna Rd., Lahaina
• 667-9224
SEAFOOD

12/20

Yes, the Lahaina Treehouse is actually a treehouse—a gorgeous, massive ohia tree has been pressed into service to house this restaurant. With its campy Polynesian overtones, the Treehouse is kind of nutty, but very comfortable with an extremely friendly staff. The menu is voluminous, with dozens of seafood preparations to choose from (in fact, it rather resembles a laundry list). Whatever sea critter you choose can be prepared in any number of ways—grilled, battered, sauced, gumboed. Get the picture? There are also several pastas from which to choose, but stick to the fresh, local fish, such as ahi or mahimahi, although the shrimp can be very good, too. A meal for two, with beverages, will run about $60.
Open daily 11 a.m.-11 p.m. No cards.

Lanai Terrace
Maui Inter-Continental Wailea, Wailea
• 879-1922
CONTINENTAL

7/20

If Café Kiowai in the Maui Prince is the apotheosis of casual hotel dining, then the Lanai Terrace at the Inter-Continental must be the nadir. This was our singularly worst dining experience on all the islands—a textbook example of how not to run a restaurant. First off, the room has a sort of desultory feel to it; the view consists mostly of hotel rooftops. The service is sluggish and apathetic, but that was nothing compared to the food. The hotel must own a saltwater conversion plant; otherwise, there is no way to explain the oversalination of every dish that we tried. The Maui onion soup was thin and tasteless, except for its staggering salt content, which offered the only flavor it had. The Caesar salad was shameful—the lettuce was tired and limp, the commercially made croutons were stale, and the dressing was heavy and much too fishy. Not to mention way too salty. The cheeseburger was simply awful, a tough, congealed mess of meat and gluey cheese. We ordered it medium-rare; it arrived ultra–well done. The same thing happened at a table next to us; that party sent their burger back twice, and both times it was cooked to death. Another table sent back their saimin noodles—a dish that even the simplest plate-lunch joint manages to do well—with myriad complaints about saltiness and an off-taste. In fact, everyone around us seemed to be complaining about the food. And we were not thrilled by the fact that we practically had to lie down in the middle of the floor to attract our waitress's attention at any given point. Even if you're staying at the Inter-Continental, skip this place—Café Kiowai is just down the road. Lunch for two, with beverages, is about $30.

Open daily 6 a.m.-11 p.m. All major cards.

Leilani's on the Beach
Whalers Village, Kaanapali
• **661-4495**
AMERICAN

10/20

Overlooking the rolling surf on Kaanapali Beach, Leilani's specializes in smoking meat and fish in the koa-wood-burning oven, basting it with barbecue sauce and then broiling it to order. These folks do it right, and consequently the baby back pork ribs, prime rib and steaks are very popular. Leilani's also has a wide selection of fresh fish prepared either broiled or Cajun style. We recommend ordering the smoked fish of the day appetizer, followed by those tasty ribs. Dinners, which include bread, rice and soup or salad, are served upstairs from 5 p.m. For lighter meals, the downstairs, beachside grill has burgers, sandwiches and smaller portions of the popular smoker meat plate. Leilani's is frequently crowded, so make your reservations, especially if you want a window seat. Patrons, mainly visitors, dress casually. Dinner for two, with wine, comes to about $75.

Open 11:30 a.m.-10:30 p.m. Cocktail lounge: 11:30 a.m.-midnight. Cards: AE, MC, V.

Longhi's
888 Front St., Lahaina
• **667-2288**
NEW AMERICAN

11/20

Longhi's is a sort of amusement park ride of a restaurant, a place where the scene is far more interesting than the food. Unbelievably popular and successful, Longhi's is terrific looking, gets a lively crowd that ranges from teenagers to partying locals to gawking tourists, and even has live jazz on the weekends. But one wishes that the food were just a wee bit better. There's nothing terribly wrong with what's served (and you do get very large portions of it)—it's just eminently forgettable. Also forgettable is the actual menu. You see, Longhi's has adopted that most annoying policy of the recited menu. And not just the specials are named off by your waiter—the entire menu is. We got so frustrated trying to remember the items mentioned at the beginning that by the time the end of the list was reached (after having made the hapless waiter repeat it several times) we probably ended up ordering things we really didn't want, simply because they were the only ones we could recall. And watch your wallet—everything here is à la carte. Another caveat, aside from the suggestion that you learn shorthand in order to dine here, is to split dishes, as each portion is really large enough for two. Keep it simple; stick with the fresh fish (although our shrimp and ahi were overcooked), and ask for the pastas al dente. You'll probably want to order an extra helping of the jalapeño-cheese bread—it's disgustingly addictive. Dinner for two, with wine, is about $90.

Open daily 7:30 a.m.-10 p.m. All major cards.

Mama's Fish House

799 Kaiholo Pl.,
Paia
• 579-9672
SEAFOOD

11/20

Mama's has one of the best locations on the island: away from the resort areas, right on the ocean in the small residential community of Kuau, on the Hana Highway. A lush vine- and plant-filled corridor leads to a beautifully decorated woodsy restaurant. Mama specializes in fish. She offers chicken and steak, but her heart is in preparing fish, always fresh caught and prepared a variety of creative ways. We enjoy it steamed in a ti leaf with Asian seasonings and vegetables cut julienne-style. The wine list has offerings of limited- and estate-bottlings from California that are hard to find on the Islands. Everything about the place is top-drawer, but Mama we're mad at you: you've gotten greedy and continually upped your prices every year, until they are now astronomical when compared to other fine fish restaurants. It is a very nice experience, but it is definitely not "the biggest bang for your bucks." Dinner for two, with appropriate wine, can cost $125.

Open daily 11 a.m.-2:30 p.m. & 5 p.m.-9:30 p.m. Cards: AE, MC V.

Maui Outrigger

2980 S. Kihei Rd.,
Kihei
• 879-1581
AMERICAN/HAWAIIAN

12/20

The bar makes great banana daiquiris, and sunsets don't come much prettier than those that paint the channel, on clear days, in washes of gold, mustard, blood-orange, violet and, finally, bruise-purple. Try for a table on the patio. With luck, you'll be able to get a seat at the edge of the sand to ogle La as he gives up the ghost for another day. The salad bar runs to nineteen items, down from last year but respectable. There's a cream dressing rife with good domestic blue along with Italian and French, lots of clean lettuce, sprouts, fresh mushrooms, tangy pickled beets, at least one bean salad, potato or macaroni salad, or both, and the requisite croutons and bacon bits for a full-frontal assault on the palate. Though the early-bird dinner ($8.95, must be ordered by 6:30 p.m.) offers prime rib or chicken teriyaki as well as fish, there's little reason to deviate from the latter. Ono, a slab of almost veal-like white fish, takes particularly well to sautéeing, but ahi (tuna) is its equal either broiled or sautéed. The regular menu includes rock-lobster tails, sashimi, scampi sautéed in garlic-annointed butter and the usual pineapple-festooned brochettes and grills. Occasionally, uku, gray snapper, or Hawaiian sea bass will make an appearance, to the delight of the cognoscenti. We generally forgo dessert, electing to wind down with some fruit from the salad bar, but cream pies and ice cream keep the kiddies happy. Owner George Brunner displays some attractive pastel oils on the walls, all for sale, Island scenes in rose-pinks, cabbage green and sky-blue. A grotto-esque bar and lounge just to the right of the entrance serves booze and brews until 11 p.m., though the kitchen closes at 9 p.m. A couple can eat for $38 with a carafe of house wine, tip and tax included, and despite piling on tropical drinks and choosing the regular dinner rather than the Early Bird should not have to exceed $65.

Open daily 6:30 a.m.-9 p.m. All major cards.

La Perouse

Maui Inter-Continental
Wailea,
Wailea
• 879-1922
FRENCH/CONTINENTAL

11/20

Long a bastion of fine dining on Maui, expecially in that cultural cul-de-sac that until recently characterized Wailea, La Perouse seems stuck in a time warp. Not having gone forward, it has for all practical purposes, retreated. Frankly, the old girl shows her age: in the menu, in the service and in the setting. The menu promises little, which is odd given one of the finest wine lists on the island. Exactly six appetizers—one, Beluga caviar, at $85 a hit—grace the list, such dining dinosaurs as escargots bourguignonne and mushrooms gratin along with fresh foie gras, sashimi and shrimp with Big Island fiddleheads. We've had shrimp cocktails in motel dining rooms not much inferior to the latter dish, whose fiddleheads were thick and tough unlike the grass-and-mint savory specimens we've enjoyed on the mainland. Two soups amplify the appetizer list a bit. One, callaloo and crabmeat stroked with coconut milk, though pleasant, would not have been out of place on a cruise ship a few decades back. Nine entrées—no specials—exhausted the menu on our last visit. Beef tenderloin with something called "pepper cheese," spiny lobster tails in sherry sauce, veal with champagne cream? We surreptitiously pinch ourselves. No, we're not at a middle-class wedding circa 1965 or eating with 500 others at a sales convention. Well, opakapaka in puff pastry with dill sauce at least sounds good. It might have been but for puff pastry that never puffed and which, in consequence, could have passed for a layer of damp papier-mâché. Magret of duck, oddly, was quite good, rare and juicy yet crisped and well served by its ginger-spiked gravy. Side dishes of fried rice and mixed vegetables would have been at home on a cafeteria steam table. Desserts did not raise the average. Crème brûlée sported clumps of brown sugar on top rather than a baked-on praline. Chocolate meringue cake did better, but heavy-handed pear and apple tarts made us wonder why tropical fruit such as guava, lilikoi, or mango had not been chosen. The final blow was coffee, a slatey, musty-acrid brew unworthy of a serious restaurant. The interior bears no hint of Maui unless one considers a leaf-green mural reminiscent of the Douanier Rousseau isle-like. Divided into left, center and right, the room projects a forbidding, dark-wood club aura not greatly relieved by a pianistic background that flatters the dark keys and lower registers for 25 minutes at a stretch. A handsome foyer with parquet flooring leads diners to expect more than the room delivers. Water, which we had to request, came in glasses reeking of garlic. The replacements smelled merely of mediocre tap water. Our waiter neglected to mention whipped cream and cinnamon toppings while displaying the dessert trolley. La Perouse apparently remains content with laurels that have grown flat, weary, stale and, given the sea of empty tables we saw, unprofitable. It needs a shaking up on all levels to justify the upwards of $140 it will cost a couple to dine here with wine, tip and tax included.

Open Tues.-Sun. 6:30 p.m.-10 p.m. All major cards.

Plantation Veranda

Kapalua Bay Hotel,
1 Bay Dr.,
Kapalua
• 669-5656
HAWAIIAN/
NEW AMERICAN

Despite being domiciled in one of Maui's ultra-luxe hotels, the Plantation Veranda does, in fact, resemble a plantation veranda. Being home to an exemplary cellar of California wines seems no hindrance, either. Butt-joined hardwood laths for flooring, tea-rose pink walls and French doors that open onto red ginger set among Island ferns induce a willing suspension of disbelief. Upon the walls, five original Pegge Hopper murals look timelessly across the room. Harp glissandos drift through a rustle of conversation. It it were not that the serious business of wining and dining heads the agenda, we might ourselves drift toward the magic shores of reverie. The food, however, beckons imperiously, setting the standard for Island nouvelle up to dessert and coffee, which, unfortunately, drop precipitously from that standard. Chef Michael Anderson handles game adroitly. Kauai buffalo, kiawe-scorched while rare and tenderly fibrous inside, proves how satisfying such low-fat meat can be. Wild boar reveals itself to be a heightened and densely grained version of its domesticated cousin sautéed with truffles, artichoke and asparagus. A scallopine of Axis deer from the pineapple island, Lanai, receives an unctuous sauce compounded of Peter Herring cherry liqueur and sun-dried red cherries, an inspired variation of blueberry-based saucing. There's much more than game, though: capon with California chèvre, beef given the twin blessings of wild mushrooms and goose-liver pâté, fresh fish

poached, or broiled with macadamia nuts, or sautéed, or baked with a yin-yang saucing of champagne cream and sweet-pepper butter. Among the appetizers, we're partial to lobster medallion with briny-pungent and chewy squid-ink pasta and to a half dozen decadently rich oysters in Pernod cream, each topped by a dollop of Beluga caviar. But with only a baker's dozen of openers, including two soups and a quartet of salads, clearly the menu's emphasis is on entrées. In either case, the key word is harmony: island food integrated with off-island ingredients in modestly innovative rather than extravagant formulations. Only at the end have we been disappointed, as, for example, by an odd crème brûlée, tapioca-tough custard on a bed of flaky pastry, a touch soggy and topped by brown sugar innocent of the fire that might have glazed it appropriately. Fairly ordinary chocolate cakes and cheesecakes weigh down the dessert trolley; flamed items such as crêpes Suzette, which we haven't tried, undercut the dignity of the room but are quite popular. The sommelier knows his wares and will lovingly pursue possibilities with guests. Vichon Merlot 1987, listed at $30 but billed at $32 on our last visit, kept us happy, its velvety tannins propping up the ample fruit and elegant spice. Service as attentive as one expects at a restaurant of this class (but too often fails to receive) prevails, though wine may, on occasion, languish in the bottle. Complex cappuccino makes a better choice than the one-dimensional Kona coffee, and the petit fours served gratis are so surprisingly good that we're tempted to skip any other sweets. Two people will spend $135, including wine.
Open Wed.-Sun. 6:30 p.m.-9:30 p.m. All major cards.

Prince Court

Maui Prince Hotel,
5400 Makena
Alanui Rd.,
Makena
• 874-1111
NEW AMERICAN

The Maui Prince Hotel hunkers down among what used to be, a decade ago, a place we hiked to for a saunter along Maui's only nude beach. The setting now has been landscaped and golf-coursed to accommodate the clamorous and affluent hordes. To its credit, the hotel has exercised some restraint and taste in its desecration of the environment. The Prince Court dining room is a far cry, literally and figuratively, from its west-shore compeers. A biwing design in earth tones with white pillars and dropped ceiling, the room has been called austere. We'd prefer something such as "studied elegance." During the dinner hour, a small chamber group proffers Telemann, Boccherini and kin from an inner courtyard whose perimeter the restaurant hugs. A Japanese garden lends an extra measure of grace to the setting.

Roger Dikon's food is ambitious, worthy of comparison with mainland stylings. Homemade duck sausage heady with smoke from kiawe wood, comes serenaded by black beans served as a cake with tangy tomato salsa. Quail sidles up to a couscous enlivened by tart dried berries and wild greens while the sea-breeze flavor of butter clams is enhanced by roasted garlic cream. Those whose purses can stretch a bit, and a bit more, should try the whole baby abalone, at $18. Chef Dikon coats it with macadamia-nut flour, sautés it and serves the mildly acrid, fibrous shellfish laden with sliced shiitake mushrooms. Something very like spa cuisine turns up as a trio of entrées: clams, shrimp and scallops in a bamboo steamer; Dungeness crab rolls; and mixed seafood on Hawaii's famous "shave ice" flavored with peppery shallot sauce. Those made of sterner stuff will turn to the wild-game grill, for specials such as papio (baby ulua) in white-truffle cream sauce, salmon grilled in ti leaves, rack of lamb with Maui-onion relish or sesame-crusted duckling seconded by a chutney of savory poha berries, an Island specialty reminiscent of East Coast beach plums. Lapses do occur. Rabbit and caribou have been dry and not notably flavorful; a strawberry tart held woody fruit that should never have seen the dining room. For the most part, though, the food is tasteful in presentation and on the palate. Chocolate-macadamia-nut-caramel pie is a happily vulgar prize-winning confection. While the extensive wine list isn't strong on half bottles, a decent Sauvignon Blanc in the 375 ml. size can be combined with a Joseph Phelps zinfandel, for barely more than the cost of a full-size bottle of either. Service comfortably walks the line between formal and casual. The Sunday brunch, steep at $25, takes a run at the Kapalua Bay Hotel's Mayfair Buffet ($16.50), which was up to now the island's best. A three-course meal for two with wine, tax and tip will come to about $140.

Open daily 6 p.m.-10 p.m. All major cards.

GRANO 1015 Y

Who would have ever thought that the lowly onion could make a name for itself? Yet there it is, a culinary star right up there with macadamia nuts and taro chips. Enthusiasts say that the Maui onion is the sweetest in the world, and the world seems to agree: demand for the 1990 crop of one-million pounds exceeded the supply.

Raffles

Stouffer Wailea
Beach Resort,
3550 Wailea Alanui Dr.,
Kihei
• 879-4900
NEW AMERICAN

Continental cuisine has taken quite a few knocks of late (many of them from us, and many well deserved), but Raffles is doing quite a bit to restore some of the luster to this much-abused genre. The restaurant takes its name and decorative cues from the infamous Raffles in Singapore and looks the way the original would if it were restored to its former glory. Though it is lushly elegant, with an entryway hewn from Athenian verde marble, plush, oversize banquettes and bespoke Axminster carpets, Raffles doesn't feel the least bit stuffy. Anything seems to go garb-wise here, from women in little black dresses and gents in suits to folks in Bermuda shorts. However, we tend to feel

somewhat uncomfortable when the waiter is dressed better than we are, so it may be best to err on the side of sartorial seriousness. The service here is friendly without being overly chummy; the waiters are true professionals. When one of our party was cut by an errant shard of glass on the banquette, our eagle-eyed waiter attended the wound with the *sangfroid* of a paramedic. Executive chef Horst Fuetterer, a veteran of European kitchens, does a marvelous job here; the menu is a pleasant one. From the yummy herb-Parmesan toasts brought at the start of the meal to coffee, things are really done right. The fresh fish preparations are perfectly done, from the yellowtail sashimi with pink ginger and daikon radish sprouts to the roasted ono topped with sweet, caramelized garlic, papaya and a yellow tomato coulis. The tricolor ravioli of lobster and grilled shiitake mushrooms is alternately silky and musky, enveloped in a thin sheet of pasta, and the seafood chowder is light and fresh. Even the seafood cocktail is gorgeous, beautifully arranged in a green coconut husk. The wine list is large and well chosen. Other good bets: the roast rack of lamb with a tart mango chutney, fresh mint and Brie potatoes and the mahimahi sautéed with macadamia-nut butter and young Maui leeks. In fact, we didn't find one clinker in the bunch. And don't forget to order your hot soufflé for dessert at the start of your meal, as they are truly divine. Dinner for two, with wine, is about $100.
Open nightly 6:30 p.m.-9:30 p.m.; Sun. brunch 9 a.m.-1 p.m. All major cards.

THE *POI*-FECT STAPLE

China has its rice, India has its breads, Mexico its tortillas, Italy its pasta; in Hawaii, the ubiquitous carbohydrate staple is poi. It's made from the starchy taro root, which is boiled and then mashed or pounded into a gray, glutinous substance reminiscent of baby mash, and is served with almost anything. Taro root is also used to make chips, biscuits, turnovers and so on, and its greens are eaten as a vegetable, boiled and seasoned with coconut milk.

Not even the snails that live in taro fields escape the cook's pot: these small creatures (called—you guessed it—taro snails) are prepared like escargots, or stir-fried with ginger and garlic. Taro snails must be soaked overnight in water before cooking, however, or they taste, literally, like mud.

Siam Thai
123 N. Market St.,
Wailuku
• 244-3817
THAI

12/20

Popular with both locals and visiting celebs (if Robert Redford's photographed kisser on the wall is any indication), Siam Thai serves up Thai cuisine hot enough to make a grown man who eats jalapeños as an avocation cry—but we just keep coming back for more. Many call this the best Thai restaurant on the island, and they may be right: the curries are superb, as are the satés, soups and spring rolls. As hot as the food is, that's how cool the prices are: two can dine sumptuously, with beverages, for about $50.

Open Mon.-Fri. 11 a.m.-2:30 p.m., nightly 5 p.m.-9:30 p.m. All major cards.

Sound of the Falls

Westin Maui Hotel,
2365 Kaanapali Pkwy.,
Lahaina
• 667-2525
NEW AMERICAN

Ask for a table set on one of the marble-clad peninsulas that jut into the pool. Flamingos cluster under the palms, and swans paddle industriously about the tables looking for handouts. Further in, a carpet in rust arabesques, loops of rolled gilt fabric between art-deco mirrors and pastels modulating into earthtones set a mood that the pianist underscores with light classics and show tunes.

A complimentary appetizer, perhaps magret d'oie and crusty sourdough rolls, helps while away the time looking over the menu, which, though brief, achieves a commendable balance. Marinated Island snapper demands yet belies comparison with gravlax. A rosette of parchment-thick oval slices dressed with red peppercorns and a suave vinaigrette savors of the sea but suggests heaven. Tea-smoked duck breast laid over fresh green pasta dressed with shiitake mushrooms isn't far behind. Long pocketbooks may opt for Beluga Malossol caviar eaten from blue-corn blinis, to a vodka accompaniment, while the penurious settle for crayfish bisque at one-fourteenth the price. Entrées include such obvious, and expensive, possibilities as poached Maine lobster or lamb roast accented by wild mushrooms. Of greater interest to us are sautéed opakapaka spiked with lemon and capers, or fresh Hawaiian shrimp alternating with ocean scallops, the combination sparked by a green lemon sabayon of disarming simplicity. Molokai venison compares favorably with Texas axis deer, and roast moulard duck heightened by passion fruit puts new life into a culinary cliche. The dessert of choice may be a jellyroll-wrapped blanc mange, the custard given a pleasantly down-to-earth touch of raspberry jam. We find the more popular caramel-and-chocolate macadamia-nut pie overwhelming after a rich meal. Wines tend to be pricey. Look for Jekel Vineyards Cabernet Sauvignon. Listed as 1985, a magnificent 1982 actually appeared. A fount of heady red and black cherry checked by a light oaky underpinning, this wine deserves to chaperone roast meat or fowl. Service, generally brisk and friendly, can unaccountably sink into moments of what we suppose is *dolce far niente*, Island-style. Dinner for two, with wine, will hover around $130.

Open daily 6 p.m.-10 p.m. Sun. brunch 10 a.m.-2 p.m. All major cards.

Swan Court

**Hyatt Regency Maui,
200 Nohea Kai Dr.,
Lahaina
• 667-7474**
CONTINENTAL

8/20

The Swan Court boasts one of the most stunning settings on Maui—and some of its lousiest food. The multitiered dining room faces out on lushly landscaped waterfalls and ponds, complete with graceful swans; if you stop here for a cup of coffee, you'll be in good shape. You'll just get into trouble if you make the mistake of actually dining here. Aside from being terrible, the fare is shamefully expensive. And don't be fooled by the lines of people clamoring to get in. For brunch, there are dozens of items offered—heaping islands of breads, muffins and sweet rolls, egg dishes, potatoes, crêpes—and none of them are any good. You won't fare too much better at lunch and dinner, when tired, overcooked versions of beef medallions, rack of lamb and roast duckling hold sway. Service is efficient yet brusque, and the entire effect is of a bad attempt at a culinary Disneyland. At least at Disneyland you don't feel ripped off when you leave. Dinner for two, with wine, is about $90.
Open daily 6:30 a.m.-9:30 p.m. All major cards.

Tasca

**608 Front St.,
Lahaina
• 661-8001**
MEDITERRANEAN

12/20

Tapas has finally made the scene in Maui, along with flamenco on the sound system, and a very "in" crowd scattered among the ubiquitous tourists. The food actually stretches the term "tapas" considerably, and the waiter is quick to correct any misimpression, by saying that the offerings are "Mediterranean." Whew! That helps explain such dishes as saffron bouillabaisse and ratatouille. Alas, it doesn't help much with dishes such as marinated back ribs or broiled ahi with pineapple salsa. Well, it seems to make no difference in paradise.

Papio heaped with fine strands of purple onion tangled with red pepper takes to a fiery vinaigrette beautifully. Sweet and tart, the dish rivals its Mexican progenitor, ceviche. Opakapaka "Grenoblaise" doesn't come off quite as successfully, the thinly sliced snapper toughened from too much fire, with the flavor obscured by a tart glaze. It's Tasca's version, we suppose, of the lemon slices and capers properly used for trout Grenobloise. Redskin potatoes have been exemplary in their caper-and-garlic mayonnaise caparison, but the paella lacked sufficient saffron and could have used the earthy vigor of a Spanish çigalla (crayfish). For dessert, go for the clean, eggy flan. The wine list offers a fine Macon Lugny for $22. Up front, the white walls are adorned with scads of local art; in back, raw wood beams are surmounted by corrugated iron sheeting. Two can spend $70 for a complete meal with wine.
Open Mon.-Sat. 11:30 a.m.-midnight, Sun. 5:30 p.m.-midnight. Cards: AE, MC, V.

QUICK BITES

BAKERY

The Bakery
991D Limahana Pl.,
Lahaina
• 667-9062

The Bakery is a charming little French-style café that is a real Maui favorite. This is a perfect stop for a light lunch or snack—the pastas, salads, sandwiches and other savory goodies are very good, as are the myriad pastries. In fact, if you're planning a day at the beach, this is a terrific place to purchase your picnic provisions. Lunch for two, with beverage, is about $15.
Open Mon.-Sat. 7 a.m.-5 p.m., Sun. 7 a.m.-noon. No cards.

CAFES & COFFEEHOUSES

Lahaina Coolers
180 Dickenson St.,
Lahaina
• 661-7082

This breezy, casual café is open for breakfast, lunch and dinner and has a pretty lively bar as well. There's a good omelet made with Portuguese sausage, Maui onion, tomato and sour cream; and the snack foods, like won tons with peanut and plum sauces, calamari with herb dipping sauce and garlic-Parmesan bread, are fun. If you're feeling highly adventurous, there's a green-apple-and-Brie quesadilla with walnuts—it's better than it sounds. The menu also has lots of pizzas, pastas and salads; and the prices are very reasonable, especially by Lahaina standards: a meal for two, with drinks, is about $25.
Open daily 7 a.m.-midnight. All major cards.

The Original Maui Sweet Baked Ham Co.

190 E. Alamaha St.,
Kahului
• 877-HAMS

The OMSBHC is an absolutely charming, spic-and-span café/deli/gourmet shop based around—you guessed it—ham. The hardwood-smoked ham is basted with their "sweet secret glaze," as they call it, and is quite delicious. Aside from the yummy ham sandwiches served here, there are roast beef, turkey, tuna, pastrami, and vegetarian sandwiches, as well as a selection of deli salads and Maui chips. This is also a fun place to browse in; the OMSBHC has an awesome collection of pig mugs, T-shirts, salt and pepper shakers, and aprons for sale, as well as gourmet deli items. A meal for two, with beverage, is about $12.
Open Mon.-Fri. 9 a.m.-6 p.m., Sat. 9 a.m.-6:30 p.m., Sun. 9 a.m.-4:30 p.m. No cards.

Pappoule's Restaurant

Lahaina Cannery
Shopping Center,
Lahaina
• 661-4300

The friendly folks at this little stand serve up some pretty good Greek fast food—gyros, shish kebabs, sausages and pastries—at very low prices. Lunch for two, with beverage, is about $10.
Open daily 9:30 a.m.-9 p.m. No cards.

C.D. Rush's Café

Kaahumanu Shopping
Center,
275 Kaahumanu Ave.,
Kahului
• 877-3978

Formerly Idini's, an entrenched local favorite, aside from the name nothing has changed much here. Although we find this café a tad dismal, it's popular among the locals, and it does serve very good coconut cake, pies and cookies, along with soups, salads and sandwiches. A meal for two is about $16, with beverage.
Open Mon.-Sat. 9 a.m.-10:30 p.m., Sun. 10 a.m.-5 p.m. Cards: AE, MC, V.

Sir Wilfred's

Lahaina Cannery
Shopping Center,
Lahaina
• 667-1941

Sir Wilfred's is the hangout of choice in the Cannery mall—you'll always find a small crowd of locals chewing the fat at the espresso bar. Good for a snack stop, Sir Wilfred's serves various coffee drinks and pastries, and also sells coffee by the pound. A snack for two, with coffee, is about $6.
Open daily 9 a.m.-9 p.m. Cards: AE, MC, V.

Whaler's Book Shoppe & Coffee House

658 Front St., No. 168
(Wharf Cinema Center),
Lahaina
• 667-9544

A nice place for a browse and a cup of java. This charming shop not only carries a great selection of books, magazines and local publications, but serves up some terrific coffees and pastries. When you get tired of endlessly cruising Front Street, this is a good place to stop. A snack for two is about $6, with coffee.
Open daily 9 a.m.-9:30 p.m. All major cards.

DELIS

Maui Bagel Co.
201 Dairy Rd.,
Kahului
• 871-4825

Run, don't walk, to Maui Bagel. This is what we thought Hawaiian Bagel on Oahu would be like but wasn't. Maui Bagel, however, is the real deal. We stopped here on the way up to Haleakala and absolutely fell in love with the place. It looks like a bare-bones deli, but you forget about that once you catch a whiff of the yeasty fragrance of bagels baking and pick up on the enthusiasm of the crowd around the counter, who consider Maui Bagel akin to a religious experience. They may be right. The bagels (water, onion, garlic, raisin and so on) are perfectly crusty outside and meltingly chewy inside. You can get your bagel with a choice of delicious, flavored cream cheeses: Maui onion (our favorite), garlic, herb, strawberry, green olive, lox, or yummy cinnamon-walnut-raisin. Also available are sandwiches (on both bagels and bread), fabulous pastries such as poppyseed cake, brownies, fruit turnovers and walnut coffee cake. They even bake challah on Fridays. We could go into even more raptures over Maui Bagel, but we'll let you discover its joys for yourself. A meal for two, with drinks, is about $8. *Open Mon.-Sat. 6:30 a.m.-6 p.m., Sun. 6:30 a.m.-2 p.m. No cards.*

New York Gourmet Deli
Dolphin Plaza,
2395 S. Kihei Rd.,
Kihei
• 879-1115

Ignore the dismal mall that New York Gourmet Deli is located in, and you'll enjoy yourself here. This cute deli is a real treat, with its red-and-white checked tablecloths, charming clutter and hip rock-and-roll in the background. The food is a treat, too: sandwiches, bagels, pastas and deli sandwiches, along with giftware (including Alessi teapots) and to-go gourmet items. A meal for two, with beverage, is about $15. *Open daily 9 a.m.-8 p.m. No cards.*

HAMBURGERS

Cheeseburger in Paradise
811 Front St.,
Lahaina
• 661-4855

A newcomer to Front Street, Cheeseburger in Paradise lives up to the laid-back sense of bonhomie implied by its appropriation of the Jimmy Buffett song title that is its name: when we asked the hostess for the street address here (it's not on the front of the building), neither she nor any of the staff seemed to know it. Everyone thought it was pretty funny, and we got a good chuckle out of it as well. This upstairs, veranda-type café is an airy, casual, fun place for an easy lunch or dinner. The menu is terse—burgers are the crux of what they do here, along with a chicken sandwich, fries, onion rings, desserts and the requisite nutty cocktails. We really enjoyed this one. A meal for two is about $12, with beverage.

Open daily 11 a.m.-11 p.m. Cards: AE, MC, V.

The Sports Page Bar & Grill
Kamaole Beach Center,
2411 S. Kihei Rd.,
Kihei
• 879-0602

This new hangout in Kihei gets quite a lively crowd, is good-looking, and is another good destination for sports junkies. The foodstuffs are of the genre found in *Restaurants & Institutions* magazine: prefab Buffalo wings, zucchini sticks, cheese sticks and teriyaki steak on a stick, along with rather nondescript sandwiches and salads. But the hot dogs are pretty good, and there's a decent international selection of beers. A meal for two, with beverage, is about $20.

Open daily 11 a.m.-midnight. All major cards.

MEXICAN FAST FOOD

Chico's Cantina
Whaler's Village,
Kaanapali
• 667-2777

Your typical, commercial Mexican-style eatery, Chico's is none-theless a good and inexpensive choice if you've got the kids in tow. The food is better than average; you'll find the usual tostadas, tacos, combo plates and guacamole, but there are also fajitas and burgers on the menu. A meal for two, with drinks, is about $25.

Open daily 11 a.m.-10 p.m. All major cards.

PIZZA

Wiki-Wiki Pizza and Sports Bar
1285 Front St.,
Lahaina
• 661-5686

This is a happening kind of place, with a large sun-deck, big-screen TV televising all sorts of sporting events, and oh yes, they serve pizza, too. Wiki-Wiki is great for teens and sports-addicted adults, and the pizza is pretty decent, as are the sandwiches. A meal for two is about $20.

Open daily 11 a.m.-10 p.m. No cards

HOTELS & CONDOMINIUMS

CONDOMINIUMS

Hana Kai-Maui Resort
Uakea Rd.,
Hana 96713
• 248-8426
(800) 346-2772
No fax

To us, the word "resort" means tennis, golf, horseback riding and the like. In this case, you get none of that. This is a nineteen-unit condo, and nothing more or less. The good news is that it's beautifully situated, within steps of the Hana surf, as it crashes onto a picturesque rock beach. The bad news is that the units are drab at best, with small kitchens and a sense of having been passed by in the development of Maui. However, this presently is the only condo in the Hana area.
Doubles: $80; suites: $95.

Kapalua Bay Villas
One Bay Dr.,
Kapalua 96761
• 669-5656,
(800) 367-8000
Fax 669-4694

A fair argument can be made that it was the Kapalua Bay Hotel (which these "villas" adjoin) that turned Maui into one of the trendiest vacation destinations in the world. Before the Kapalua was created out of what had been a pineapple plantation for most of the nineteenth century, Maui was a sleepy spot where adventurous tourists weary of Waikiki would go to get away from it all. After the Kapalua was built, Maui became the island of choice for the rich and the super-rich, and Maui was never the same again. To this day, the Kapalua remains one of the class acts on Maui, a world away from the theatrics of the Hyatt Regency. Surrounding the 488 condos here are eighteen well-tended acres of greenery where you can lose yourself, along with one of the best beaches on the island. One could do worse, as well, than eating at the Plantation Veranda and the Bay Club, though do note that a jacket is required for the former (a rarity for casual Maui).
Doubles: $185-$335; suites: $210-505.

Napili Kai Beach Club

5900 Honoapiilani Rd.,
Lahaina 96761
• 669-6271,
(800) 367-5030
Fax 669-5740

This unusual 136-unit facility is actually half a hotel and half a condo complex. On the one hand, the units are a bit smaller than those we usually identify as condos; on the other hand, there's no room service, which is one of the identifying factors that makes a hotel a hotel. In any case, this is a very pleasant place to stay, spread out across eight two-story buildings, with five swimming pools, two tennis courts and a golf course right across the street. And this complex is more about Hawaii than most of the new resorts; the Napili Kai Foundation is run out of here, the purpose of which is to teach the fundamental tenets of Hawaiiana to the next generation.
Doubles: $150-$195; suites: $180-$450.

Wailea Condominiums

3750 Wailea Alanui Dr.,
Wailea 96753
• 879-1595,
(800) 367-5246
Fax 874-3554

This is actually an association of several condominium villages, run by a company called Destination Resorts Wailea. We mention them simply because they are, with the exception of the condos at the Kapalua Bay Hotel, the best condos on the island. You have a choice between the Wailea Ekolu, above the Blue Golf Course; the Wailea Ekahi, above Keawakapu Beach; and Wailea Elua, on Ulua Beach. All told, there are 594 units, ranging from studios to three-bedroom units.
Doubles: $130; suites: $365-$450. Minimum stay is three nights.

The Whaler on Kaanapali Beach

2481 Kaanapali Pkwy.,
Lahaina 96761
• 661-4861,
(800) 367-7052
Fax 661-8315

One of the most consistently popular condos resorts in the Kaanapali area, this matched set of twelve-story buildings is known for its pleasant furnishings (lots of wicker and Polynesiana), its excellent views and its first-rate beach access, with smashing views of Molokai and Lanai. Unfortunately, its popularity doesn't guarantee you a lot of peace; in this case, you're right in the middle of the whole tourist muddle. Still, the resort has held up well, with 360 units to choose from.
Doubles: $160-$240; presidential suite: $525.

LUXURY

Hotel Hana-Maui

Hana 96713
• 248-8211,
(800) 321-HANA
Fax 248-7202

Not all highways lead to heaven, but there is at least one exception—the Hana Highway and its terminus, the Hotel Hana-Maui. Anyone who's stayed at other Rosewood-operated hotels, such as the Bel-Air in Los Angeles and the Mansion at Turtle Creek in Dallas, knows what to expect at the Hana-Maui—absolute and complete pampering. Also expect a warm family welcome from Clyde and Hilda Min, the husband-and-wife management team, as well as from the rest of the staff. If you're interested in this family affair, check out the family tree that hangs near the lobby. Many of the staff members are related. The staff will show you how the old comic-book character Richie Rich must have felt. This is one of those hotels that spoils you "rottenest"; after the Hana, even the best doesn't look quite the same. Moreover, the Hana recently was buffed and polished, thanks to a $24-million renovation. You'll stay in lush bungalows, surrounded by a profusion of sweet-smelling blooms. You'll swim in the heated pool, nodding politely to the likes of Don Johnson or Jack Nicholson. You'll sink into your sunken Jacuzzi, facing out onto your private garden. Of course, the staff will be busy caring for your every need: carrying your snorkeling gear to the beach; bringing you a cold drink; massaging your deal-weary muscles. There's also pitch-and-putt golf, tennis, horseback riding and a private beach, which you'll be driven to in a 1929 Packard. The bungalows don't offer TVs, clocks or air conditioning (which by anyone's count is unnecessary anyway). The only modern device that will connect you to the workaday world is the telephone.

If you really want to go whole hog (or should we say first class?) rent the Plantation House as an executive master suite for a mere $3,000 per day. This hilltop structure is the meticulously restored home of Hana's first sugarcane farmer, who did not enjoy the privilege of having his own private butler, which you will. Prices include three meals a day.

Doubles: $445; suites: $685 & $920.

PINEAPPLE WINE

So, you thought that all wine was made from grapes? True, at Tedeschi Vineyards on Maui, most of the wines come from the traditional source, but Hawaii's only vintner is most famous for Maui Blanc, a wine made from fermented pineapple juice. If you don't happen to be near France for Beaujolais Nouveau mania, you can get a bottle of Maui Nouveau in early November. For information on tours, call (808) 878-6058, or write P.O. Box 953, Ulupalakua, Hawaii 96790.

Hyatt Regency Maui

200 Nohea Kai Dr.,
Lahaina 96713
• 661-1234,
(800) 228-9000
Fax 667-4498

This twenty-acre combination hotel and theme park has been described as Disneyland, Maui-style. The Kaanapali Beach branch of the Hyatt chain isn't so much a hotel as it is a nonstop series of rides and amusements. The landscaping is pure Hollywood, with swinging rope bridges, cascading waterfalls, burbling streams, even a wide assortment of birds tended by a staff ornithologist. Add to that a constant profusion of conventioneers and tour groups, and you have a hotel that some find less than a taste of paradise. In either case, more has been put into the grounds than the rooms, which are functional and fine, but not much beyond that. There are 815 rooms, spread out over three towers that run from seven to nine stories each. There's lots of beach, though most guests seem to prefer the pool, which can resemble Grand Central Station at peak moments.

Doubles: $195-$355; suites: $260-$2,000.

Kapalua Bay Hotel

One Bay Dr.,
Kapalua 96761
• 669-5656,
(800) 367-8000
Fax 808-669-4694

A fair argument can be made that it was the Kapalua that turned Maui into one of the trendiest vacation destinations in the world. Before the Kapalua was created out of what had been a pineapple plantation for most of the nineteenth century, Maui was a sleepy spot where tourists weary of Waikiki would go to escape. After the Kapalua was built, Maui became the island of choice for the rich and the super-rich, and Maui was never the same again. To this day, the Kapalua remains one of the class acts on Maui, a world away from the theatrics of the Hyatt Regency. Subdued is the operative word, from the quiet colors in the rooms, to the three-story open lobby. There are 374 rooms, spread out over a relatively low-profile structure (plus 488 condos). And there are eighteen well-tended acres of greenery where you can lose yourself, along with one of the best beaches on the island. One could do worse than eating at the Plantation Veranda and the Bay Club; note that a jacket is required for the former (a rarity for casual Maui).
Doubles: $205-$385; suites: $750-$1,250.

Maui Inter-Continental Wailea

3700 Wailea Alanui Dr.,
Wailea 96753
• 879-1922,
(800) 367-2960
Fax 879-7658

This is one of the very first hotels to start the current expansion toward the south of Lahaina, along the strip ending with Makena Beach, at the base of the towering Haleakala Volcano. Most of the rooms are in a seven-story tower, though if high-rises are not your idea of a good time, you can easily nest in any number of low, cozy buildings, which are dropped down like so many Monopoly pieces over this sprawling resort. There's a distinct sense of openness found at the Inter-Continental that you won't encounter at, say, the nearby Stouffer's; you can wander about the grounds here for a while, without running into another tourist. As at most of the Wailea/Makena resorts, expect an assortment of golf courses and a tennis complex, along with condos, homes and an entire shopping village. The beach is good, and not overly populated. The rooms are adequate enough, though not a lot better.
Doubles: $185-$275; suites: $350-$1,200.

Maui Marriott

100 Nohea Kai Dr.,
Lahaina 96761
• 667-1200,
(800) 228-9290
Fax 667-2047

No matter where it is, a Marriott is a Marriott is a Marriott. What we have here is a 720-unit, double nine-story structure, arranged into something of a V, with two swimming pools, a beach and lots of flowers. That's all fine and well. But the generally tacky state of the rooms, the worn-looking grounds, the lackadaisical service all leaves us colder than winter in Wyoming. The Marriott is popular with large groups, which act just like large groups and drink too much to notice the lack of amenities. All things (or even just a few things) considered, you can do better.
Doubles: $195-$285; suites: $400-$1,000.

Maui Prince

5400 Makena Alanui
Dr.,
Kihei 96753
• 874-1111,
(800) 321-MAUI
Fax 879-8763

There was a time, not that long ago, when Makena Beach was known far more for its nude sunbathers than for its hyperbolic resort hotels. But that was then, and this is now. And these days, there's hardly a hippie to be found anywhere near Makena. Instead, there's what might be called Kaanapali South, one of the linchpins of which is the pleasantly isolated Maui Prince, the first hotel to break ground in this formerly uncharted territory. Though the rooms are decidedly unremarkable, they do have wholly remarkable ocean views; you can sit on your lanai looking out on the islands of Molokini, Kahoolawe and Lanai. Despite the increased growth along Makena, the Prince remains nicely set apart, a good if not very spectacular place to go for swimming, tennis, golf and horseback riding along the beach. And, of course, towering overhead is Haleakala, with its fringe of clouds. One can do a good deal worse.
Doubles: $190-$290; suites: $350-$700.

Royal Lahaina Resort

2780 Kekaa Dr.,
Lahaina 96761
• 661-3611,
(800) 621-2151
Fax 661-6150

Actually, this aging Maui relic is more of a tennis resort with a hotel attached than the other way around. The pride of the Royal Lahaina, one of the original Kaanapali hotels (which means it dates back all the way to 1969), is its tennis ranch, comprising eleven courts and a stadium. For those who live for tennis, it is the place to stay. For the rest of us, this is a decent, if not overly exciting hotel, with 514 rooms spread out over 23 buildings, mostly two-story cottages, built around the twelve-story Lahaina Kai Tower. Amenities are sufficient, and both Chopsticks and Moby Dick's are decent restaurants, though no better than you should expect, considering the location.
Doubles: $150-$200; suites: $500-$1,000.

Sheraton-Maui

2605 Kaanapali Pkwy.,
Lahaina 96761
• 661-0031,
(800) 325-3535
Fax 661-0458

Along with the Royal Lahaina, this is one of Kaanapali's first hotels, and it is by far the better of the two. Both have seen better days. But the Sheraton is definitely preferred, first of all because it's a better-kept hotel, and secondly because it's the best-situated hotel in the area. As most guides readily point out, the Sheraton-Maui is built on and around an 80-foot-tall lava formation called Black Rock, from which you can see just about forever. Beyond Black Rock is one of the finest beaches on Maui, a long strand of silky sands and calm seas. This is one hotel where a pool is wholly redundant (though there are two of them). There are 435 rooms here, but the best of them are to be found in the cottages near the beach, where you can virtually step out of bed and into the ocean. The area around Black Rock is also fabled for its snorkeling; and for the many legends about sacrifices and native rituals.
Doubles: $190-$300; suites: $400.

Stouffer Wailea Beach Resort

3550 Wailea Alanui Dr.,
Wailea 96753
• 879-4900,
(800) HOTELS-1
Fax 879-6128

As a rule, we haven't found ourselves liking the Stouffer's chain of hotels very much; they seem as packaged and chilly as their frozen entrées, and about as nourishing. That said, the Stouffer Wailea Beach isn't bad—for a Stouffer. The location, right off Mokapu Beach, is pretty impressive. The structure, with its homage to the Great God Maui, is hokey, but dramatic. The fifteen-acre site is landscaped with an assortment of waterfalls, bridges and tropical plants—where once there was no paradise at all, now paradise flourishes. There are 347 rooms here, which means you don't feel overly crowded. Even the hotel's restaurant, Raffles, is much better than expected—not great, mind you, but at least you don't feel they're defrosting your meal when you order it.
Doubles: $165-$360; suites: $500-$1,200.

Westin Maui

2365 Kaanapali Pkwy.,
Lahaina 96761
• 667-2525,
(800) 228-3000
Fax 661-5831

Before 1987 this was known as the Maui Surf, a decomposing, old structure that may never have seen better days; it just seemed tired. The Westin people pumped in $155 million worth of fresh blood, turning the newly named 762-room Westin Maui into one of the main destinations along the Kaanapali Coast. The hotel, an eleven-story structure, is probably best known for featuring the largest swimming pool on the island; it looks more like one of the Great Lakes, complete with waterfalls, islands and grottos. But it also offers a wonderful lagoonlike beachfront, plenty of shopping and a decent restaurant called Sound of the Falls. As you might expect, this is also a popular spot with large group tours. Caveat emptor.
Doubles: $185-$375; suites: $500-$1,500.

PRACTICAL

Heavenly Hana Inn

P.O. Box 146,
Hana 96713
• 248-8442

The best-known hotel on the Hana end of Maui is, of course, the luxurious Hana-Maui. The best-kept secret, though, is even farther off the beaten path, a diminuitive four-suite inn appropriately named Heavenly Hana. Except for the tropical setting, it wouldn't be hard to imagine that you were staying at a small Japanese country inn on the outskirts of Fujinomiya. In this case, the accommodations are plusher than what you'd find at your basic *ryokan*. Each suite, for instance, comprises two bedrooms, a living room and a kitchenette, instead of the usual one-room setup found in Japan. Still, the overall effect is of utter peace and tranquillity, in a setting far away from the rest of the world (it's even two miles from the nearest beach).
Suites: $75.

Pioneer Inn
658 Wharf St.,
Lahaina 96761
• 661-3636
Fax 667-5708

The Pioneer Inn is a perfectly dreadful place to stay, especially if you're the sort who enjoys the pleasures of a good night's sleep. This nineteenth-century landmark dates back to Maui's whaling days, when salty tars would slaughter whales by day and drink rum by night. These days the whalers are gone. But the rum shops aren't. They're filled with tourists who make a lot of noise. The rooms sit atop the Old Whaler's Grog Shop, where the mai tais flow until one in the morning. At the Inn, you sleep much like the old salts did, in tiny cribs with an overhead fan. Some of the rooms have private bathing facilities. It's all very quaint when you check in. And it is cheap. But you'll hate yourself in the morning.
Doubles: $25-$70.

NIGHTLIFE

BARS	153
DANCING	154
LUAUS	155

BARS

Banana Moon
Maui Marriott
100 Nohea Kai Dr.,
Kaanapali
• 667-1200

It's always a full moon at Banana Moon, a hangout for residents and visitors alike. Casual is the password, in dress and in attitude. *Open nightly 9 p.m.-2 a.m. No cover charge. All major cards.*

Chico's Cantina
Whaler's Village,
Kaanapali
• 667-2777

Between shopping and sightseeing, there's nothing better than a tall, cool one, with or without booze, and Chico's serves a variety of tropical-fruit drinks as well as a hefty margarita. You may sit in the taco bar or in the dining room. People-watching is a voluntary sport here.
Open daily 11:30-midnight. Cards: AE, MC, V.

Longhi's
888 Front St.,
Lahaina
• 667-2288

Depending upon what you go for, Longhi's is fun, fantastic or frustrating. The sidewalk-café spirit makes for informality; the menu boasts Italian dishes served with savvy and pride (see Maui Restaurants, page 134). Service tends to be slow, however, and

if you're in the mood for partying once the sun goes down and the music-format begins, be prepared to wait.
Open Fri.-Sat. for live entertainment 9 p.m.-10 p.m. No cover charge. Cards: AE, MC, V.

La Perouse
Maui Inter-Continental
Hotel,
Wailea
• 879-1922

Frank Withalm mans the grand piano in this fine dining room (see Maui Restaurants, page 136). His repertoire runs the gamut from classics to show tunes to standards. Happily, he'll take requests—and the birthday and anniversary celebrants never should be shy to ask for a special favor.
Music Tues.-Sun. 6:30 p.m.-10:30 p.m. All major cards.

Maui Tropical Plantation
Honoapiilani Hwy.
(Hwy. 30),
Waikapu
• 242-8605

A country plantation barbecue, with a Hawaiian-flavored paniolo show featuring Buddy Fo's Hawaiian Country Revue, unfolds daily amid a marketplace. Grab a tram ride through the plantation and see fields of sugarcane, pineapple and papaya; then partake of a steak-and-chicken barbecue buffet. Cameras are suggested for taking keepsake snapshots.
Shows Mon., Wed., Fri. 5 p.m.-8 p.m. $42 per person. All major cards.

Sunset Terrace
Hyatt Regency Maui,
200 Nokea Kai Dr.,
Kaanapali
• 661-1234

"Drums of the Pacific," a romantic journey through Polynesian ports of call, is stunningly costumed, and features an attractive cast. Grab a rum punch and go with the flow; the outdoor setting on a warm Polynesian night is the stuff of which dreams are made.
Shows Mon.-Wed. & Fri.-Sat. 7:30 p.m.; dinner seating at 5:30 p.m. Dinner package $42, cocktail package $24. All major cards.

DANCING

Inu Inu Lounge
Maui Inter-Continental
Hotel,
Wailea
• 879-1922

The dance spot on the west side of Maui, the Inu Inu is traditionally a gathering place for locals. Visitors will find the site appealing: you may sip cordials, "talk story" (local pidgin for "gossip"), dance or just listen to the music. On Sundays, there's big-band sounds with a live orchestra; Espree is the house band Tuesdays through Saturdays; Sundays there's a big-band format.
Open Mon.-Thurs. 6 p.m.-1 a.m., Fri.-Sat. 9 p.m.-1 a.m., Sun. 5 p.m.-7:30 p.m. No cover. All major cards.

Makai Bar

Maui Marriott Hotel
100 Nohea Kai Dr.,
Kaanapali
• 667-1200

Locals flock to this popular bar for fun and festivity; there's Hawaiian-accented, hang-loose entertainment during happy hour from 4:30 p.m. to 8:30 p.m. The spirit and the tempo pick up after 8:30 p.m. when a contemporary combo takes over. There's dancing, too.

Open nightly 4:30 p.m.-1 a.m. No cover. All major cards.

Spats

Hyatt Regency Maui,
200 Nokea Kai Dr.,
Kaanapali
• 661-1234

You can start with an Italian dinner, then boogie the calories off in the sico. Expect throngs during the weekends, when the younger set takes over the dance floor.

Open Sun.-Thurs. 6:30 p.m.-2 a.m., Fri.-Sat. 6:30 p.m.-4 a.m. All major cards.

LUAUS

Jesse's Luau

2945 Kihei Rd.,
Kihei
• 879-7227

Jesse Nakooka, an Island son, is host and star of a tropical parade of songs and dances from Hawaii, Samoa and Tahiti. Sure, it's tailor-made for tourists, but Nakooka is an authentic Hawaiian "find," displaying a voice and spirit that are the essence of the Islands. The cost is $78 for two.

Open Sun., Wed. & Fri. 5:30 p.m.-8:30 p.m. All major cards.

GOING WHOLE HOG

Almost every luau features what must be one of the most memorable of Hawaiian feasts: kalua pig. Kalua ("baked" or "to bake in a ground oven") pig is prepared in a lengthy, festive procedure outdoors, not unlike a New England clambake. The ceremony begins with the digging of an *imu,* a pit six feet wide and four feet deep, which is lined with wood and lava rocks. When the wood has burned down to coals, the pig (usually about 60 pounds) is sliced open, salted and stuffed with some of the sizzling rocks. The pit is lined with banana leaves and the moist pieces of a banana-tree stump, which create steam for cooking. The pig is then wrapped in leaves and wire, hoisted into the pit and covered with tea leaves, banana leaves and hot stones (and sometimes dirt, burlap or canvas). It's left to cook for about four hours, to smoky succulence.

SHOPS

ANTIQUES

The Gallery Ltd.
716 Front St., Lahaina
• 661-0696

The atmosphere in this purveyor of Chinese antiques is hushed, the built-in wall display cases are literally crammed with material, and a ten-sided minipavilion occupies the center of the room. The material is pricey but not outrageous, and occasionally does approach museum quality. It's worth a visit, whether or not you buy, to be able to compare, for example, nine different ivory doctors' models (undraped women on which modest Chinese women would point out where they were hurting), hundreds of netsukes, lapis lazuli horses, rose-quartz dogs two or more feet long and an endless array of Sumi ink paintings, nineteenth-century porcelain, jade jewelry, snuff bottles and gilt temple foo dogs. One small room in the rear is devoted to older porcelains from the Sung dynasty to the beginning of the Ch'ing dynasty. There's also an extensive collection of pearl and coral jewelry.
Open Mon.-Thurs. 9:30 a.m.-4:45 p.m., Fri. 9:30 a.m.-9:30 p.m.

South Seas Trading Post
851 Front St., Lahaina
• 661-3168

Here you'll find genuine New Guinea masks, hook carvings, statues, yam fans and penis sheaths. In another section of the shop you may come across children's paintings from Bali, or neolithic bowls from China. Wander farther, and you'll doubtless see jade carvings and Chinese porcelains, not to mention silver filigree jewelry, an assortment of baskets, bark paintings and a plethora of touristic whatnots. Owner Joan McKelvey and manager Pat Warshauer travel frequently to southeast Asia and sometimes return with wonderful goodies. Well worth a visit.
Open daily 8:30 a.m.-10 p.m.

CARTIER FOR THE TABLE

CARTIER, THE KING OF JEWELERS,
BRINGS ITS ARTISTRY TO
THE TABLE AND PRESENTS
AN EXTRAORDINARY NEW
COLLECTION CALLED
"LES MAISONS DE CARTIER®".
CHINA, CRYSTAL, SILVER,
IN BRILLIANT DESIGNS
REFLECTING THE GREAT
CREATIVE PERIODS OF THE HOUSE:
NEO-RENAISSANCE, ART NOUVEAU,
ART DECO, CONTEMPORARY.
OBJECTS OF RARE BEAUTY
TO GRACE ANY TABLE.
AND EACH SIGNED CARTIER.
THE ART OF LIVING,
THE ART OF GIVING,
THE ART OF BEING UNIQUE.

les maisons de Cartier

Cartier

THE ART OF BEING UNIQUE

AT CLUB MED, WE TAKE DINING SERIOUSLY.

Exquisite cuisine prepared by our specially-trained chefs, served to you in a sunny sea-side bistro, or under an evening sky blanketed by stars—that's dining, Club Med-style.

For breakfast, freshly-baked croissants, danish, and *pain au chocolat*. Eggs, any style, with sausage and bacon. Crepes and French toast. The ripest fruits.

For lunch, bottomless buffets. Dozens of salads, grilled meats and fish, savory local specialties, and the freshest vegetables and fruits.

For dinner, delicious appetizers from our salad buffets, and lavish main courses starring scrumptious fare from the four corners of the globe.

Did we mention the fresh-from-the-oven breads and rolls, baked right on the premises by our hand-picked *boulanger*? And the tempting assortment of pastries created daily by our own pastry chef? Or free-flowing wine and beer at lunch and dinner?

Between meals, there's every sport under the sun. From windsurfing and scuba diving to golf and tennis, complete with modern equipment and expert instruction. Laugh-out-loud games and activities like picnics, arts and crafts, boat rides, and classical music concerts on CD video discs. After dinner, there are Broadway-style extravaganzas, comedy shows, theme parties. In exotic, tropical settings as sumptuous as our cuisine.

Pre-paid and hassle-free. So you can enjoy your vacation, and your meals, without having to reach into your pockets.

If you now have a craving to sample a bit more of the Club Med vacation, simply call your travel agent or 1-800-CLUB MED.

CLUB MED®
The antidote for civilization.℠

Traders of the Lost Art
158 N. Market St.,
Wailuku
• 242-7753

Head honcho of Wailuku's budding association of antique gallery owners, Tye Hartall has come a long way from his native Illinois. His rock group, The Sharks, finally turned belly up, which left him free to haggle with headhunters and reputed cannibals in Papua, New Guinea, for the tribal art that stocks his Market Street shop. Storyboards from the Kalahari, Tamburan canoe prow carvings, mud bowls, yam masks, gable figures and food hooks stare down from the walls and up from the floor. When we last dropped in, the doorstop was a massive limestone fragment, which Tye reluctantly dragged out of the sun and priced for us. Mostly recent—few pieces date back as far as World War II—these affordable artifacts are often powerful expressions of non-Western culture.
Open daily 1 p.m.-6 p.m. & by appointment.

ARTS AND CRAFTS

Coast Gallery
Maui Inter-Continental Wailea,
13700 Wailea Alanui Dr.,
Kihea
• 879-2301

For us, interest in this gallery generally goes three ways. We particularly like the woodwork, notably the jewelry chests of Marcus Castaing and Todd Campbell's massive hand-turned wooden bowls of Norfolk pine. We're also partial to the taro fields, pineapple patches and ramshackle houses Pam Andelin evokes in brash pinks, greens and yellows. Last, by no means least, is the collector's room where Rembrandt and Whistler rub shoulders with Yoshida, whose satirical evocations of modern Japan use traditional woodblock techniques. Mr. Patrick Robinson, managing director, happily answers all questions and keeps out of the way of browsers. Seventy-five percent of the artists represented are Hawaiian. We are, however, less than enchanted by the occasional glitzy, Lahaina-style art that creeps in from time to time. The best we can do is to admit that it probably helps pay the bills.
Open daily 9 a.m.-9 p.m.

Hui No'eau
2841 Baldwin Ave.,
Makawao
• 572-6560

There's a small gift shop on the ground floor of this old plantation house that serves as an art center for some of the island's most talented artists. Local pottery, tie-dyed T-shirts, blouses and dresses, silk blouses, dresses and scarves, graphics (oils, watercolors, prints) and, of course, handmade jewelry crowd the tiny space given over to the shop. The real reason for coming here, however, is to look at the exhibits, mostly by Mauians, which demonstrate extraordinary ability, and which change frequently. The setting is exquisite, just below Makawao on a gentle slope, lush and green, harkening back to an earlier, more serene Maui far from the hurly-burly of Kihei and Lahaina. *Hours vary, call ahead.*

Maui Crafts Guild
43 Hana Hwy.,
Paia
• 579-9697

This two-floor plantation home is stocked with some of the island's best craftsware. Baskets made of island grasses, leaves and ferns, wooden bowls and cutting boards by Takeo Omuro, graphics by David Warren and other Maui artists and a handsome selection of pottery by a variety of potters. Some exceptionally lovely tie-dyed silk blouses and caftans occupy a small rear gallery, and unique handmade sterling silver jewelry fills a case and part of one wall. The gallery is a collaborative project, and the person who answers your questions and takes your money will most likely be one of the artists represented in the gallery.
Open daily 9 a.m.-6 p.m.

The Village Gallery at the Cannery
Lahaina Cannery
Shopping Center,
1221 Honoapiilani
Hwy.,
Lahaina
• 661-3280

Although under the same management as the Village Gallery on Dickinson Street (see next entry), and consequently exhibiting many of the same artists, it is well worth a separate visit just to see the beautiful flowers by Margaret Bedell, the explosive landscapes by Diana Lehr, the baskets by Theo Morrison, and the breathtaking wooden bowls carved by Ron Kent, primarily from Norfolk pine.
Open daily 9:30 a.m.-9:30 p.m.

The Village Gallery in Lahaina
120 Dickenson St.,
Lahaina
• 661-4402

This is a gallery for wandering. Aisles and corridors sprout at odd turns making the interior a pleasant maze. High quality and relatively low prices keep us coming back to the powerful female images Sara Lawless sculpts, the oil paintings Pamela Andelin imbues with intense Island colors, art glass, collages and a delightful collection of handmade jewelry. Friendly, knowledgeable salespeople add to the fun. If you want to see what local artists are up to these days, this is the place to go, whether it's ceramic pots, wooden bowls, baskets or graphics.
Open daily 9 a.m.-9 p.m.

CLOTHES

Silks Kaanapali
Whalers Village,
Kaanapali
• 667-7133

Those who think that "art-to-wear" has had its day ought to pop into Silks Kaanapali. Artists such as Stuart Epstein, Rhonda Valeri and Eva Ananda create lush and lovely canvases of diaphanous silk, which designer Ann Moore transforms into comfortably elegant blouses, dresses, pants and scarves. Prices are reasonable, considering the quality. Silks begin at $30 for a

top and top out at $675 for a one-of-a-kind Eva Ananda signed crepe shirt-and-pants set. Items made from rayon, batiked in Bali, and cotton, hand-painted by part-owner Bev Barefoot, are no less lovely and considerably easier on the pocketbook.
Open daily 9:30 a.m.-9 p.m.

FOOD

Paradise Fruit
1913 S. Kihei Rd., Kihei
• 879-1723

Just across the road from an almost life-sized humpback whale in Kalama Park, our favorite all-night basic food stand waits for our snack attacks. We go here for papayas and pineapple and Kula onions, of course, but also for linguesa (Portuguese sausage) and whole-grain Island breads when the munchies descend unexpectedly in the wee hours. Tucked away in corners, on shelves and in bins, there's a respectable selection of nuts, both raw and roasted, dried fruit and honey, as well as Maui potato chips and Maui-style chips (once you've crunched the real thing, made in small batches, by hand, it's hard not to become a chip snob). A variety of sprouts and sandwich fixings round out the offerings.
Open daily 24 hours.

Rocky Mountain Chocolate Factory
Lahaina Cannery Shopping Center, 1221 Honoapiilani Hwy., Lahaina
• 661-8420

They claim their chocolates are always fresh, and after a tasting, we believe them. No preservatives or waxes sully these caramels, macadamia-nut clusters, fruit creams and fudges. Definitely worth the calories, in our book.
Open daily 9:30 a.m.-9:30 p.m.

Sir Wilfred's
Lahaina Cannery Shopping Center, 1221 Honoapiilani Hwy., Lahaina
• 667-1941

Sir Wilfred's carries seventeen to twenty varieties of coffee, including one of our favorites, Kona peaberry. A small café pours one exotic coffee each day and dishes up quiches, cheesecakes, muffins and bagels. Tea lovers won't feel slighted here—there's jasmine, Irish breakfast, Darjeeling and apricot, among others, in addition to an assortment of herbal brews. A walk-in humidor in back offers 92 varieties of cigars. This, by the way, is the only commercial walk-in humidor in the entire state.
Open daily 9 a.m.-9 p.m.

GIFTS

By the Bay Gift Gallery
Kapalua Shops,
Kapalua
• 669-5227

A rare golden cowrie at $650 and an even rarer spotted cowrie at $1,200 share a cabinet with a textile cone at $3. Fossils 25 to 500 million years old range from $2 for a shark's tooth to $45 for a fossil ammonite. For a mere $50, you can bring home a South Pacific Amphora, about 12 inches long, eight inches high, in a brown, beige and gold checkered design. A few ceramic and glass sculptures, and here and there a coral tree, complement the shells.
Open daily 9 a.m.-6 p.m.

Distant Drums
Kapalua Shops,
124 Bay Dr.,
Kapalua
• 669-5522

Handcrafted ceramic fish made on Maui consort with hand-carved and painted wooden fish from Sri Lanka. Thai buddhas, New Guinea ceremonial pieces, baskets galore and silver jewelry fill up the small but carefully arranged interior. Occasionally an authentic piece will lurk among the modern imitations. Prices are moderate.
Open Mon.-Sat. 9 a.m.-7 p.m., Sun. 9 a.m.-6 p.m.

Haimoff and Haimoff
Kapalua Shops,
130 Bay Dr.,
Kapalua
• 669-5213

This gallery shows the work of Harry Haimoff, the most award-winning jeweler in Hawaii, who has also won two awards at the prestigious international pearl design competition in Japan. His original pieces feature unusually cut amethyst, blue topaz, rodalite and other stones, all of them set in eighteen-karat gold. Prices reflect the quality of the workmanship—high.
Open daily 9 a.m.-6 p.m.

Return to Paradise
845 Front St.,
Lahaina
• 667-5811

Something of a new boy on the block, Return to Paradise markets cultured Tahitian pearls aggressively, using the by now familiar gimmick of automatic markdowns, 50 to 60 percent routinely knocked off ticketed prices. The customer is alternately flattered and bullied. Ring after ring appears set with round or oval or baroque pearls in lemony purple, gold flushed by pink, or steely gray and bearing price tags ranging from the low thousands to five digits. An automatic buy-back policy reassures customers. It's an excellent sales device and seldom invoked once the buyer has returned to Keokuk or Hackensack with memories and a small piece of the South Seas set in gold.
Open daily 9 a.m.-9 p.m.

Wholesale Coral Outlet
991 4G Limahana Pl., Lahaina
• No phone

Out-of-the-way places such as this appeal both to our sense of adventure and the almost universal love of a bargain. Carrying relatively low overhead away from Front Street's carnival atmosphere, this shop sells lapis and biwa pearls, malachite and coral at swap meet prices. Gold and precious stones go for one-third of the ticket price, an innocuous gimmick, while costume jewelry sells for whatever is marked. Triple strands of natural peach or lavender freshwater pearls have been $105 (marked $315), an intense blue lapis set against a fourteen-karat gold band will cost about $300, and earrings and chokers of volcanic glass fired to an opalescent glow sell for $18 and up.
Open daily 9:30 a.m.-5:30 p.m.

MISCELLANEOUS

Going down Baldwin Avenue from Makawao Highway, there's **Crater Gallery** (crafts more than art), **Collections** (gifts, clothing, inexpensive jewelry), **Mountain Fresh Market** (organically grown produce and other comestibles), **Rodeo General Store** (meat and fish market, gourmet groceries, and wine), **Country Flowers**, **Coconut Classics** (clothing and local collectibles such as bottles, wickerware, lace and aloha shirts), **Maui Child: Toys and Books** (hand-crafted), **Stan Ort's Studio** (portraits and oil paintings), **Maui Moorea** (custom resort wear), **Goodies** (primarily clothing and accessories), **David Warren's Studio and Gallery**, **Gecko Trading Company** (another boutique), and **Klein, Fein, and Nikki Gallery**, which carries a small but extremely well-crafted line of original wooden bowls, ceramic pieces, and bold-to-splashy-to-tacky Island scenes in oils. This part of the island has not been "discovered," though that's not far off, so go while prices are modest and the dusty road still retains some charm.

Wings on the Wind
Kukui Mall
1819 S. Kihei Rd., Kihei
• 874-5050

Owners Ron and Nancy Scheidler like to call their shop the one-stop fun shop. Though toys of all sorts abound, the emphasis here is on kites, which begin at $2.50 and soar to $250. Whether a craving strikes for a long-tailed dragon, or for a box kite, or for the old reliable triangle and diamond-shaped affair remembered from too long ago to name, they've got it. They'll even instruct novices gratis on Kamaole III beach when the wind is right.
Open Mon.-Sat. 10 a.m.-8 p.m., Sun. noon-6 p.m.

SIGHTS

AMUSEMENTS

Maui Tropical Plantation
Rte. 1, Box 600, Wailuku
• 244-7643

The best way to learn about all of Hawaii's tropical agricultural products is by touring this well-planned, 120-acre agricultural park. We recommend the guided tours through lush miniplantations featuring virtually all of the tropical fruits of Hawaii. One of the few visitor-oriented places where inquisitive children are welcome.
Open daily 9 a.m.-5 p.m. Admission free, tour $8; barbecue, Mon., Wed. & Fri., with Hawaiian country show 5 p.m.-8 p.m. $42.

Lahaina-Kaanapali and Pacific Railroad (The Sugar Cane Train)
Honoapiilani Hwy., Lahaina
• 661-0089

It ain't the Chattanooga Choo-Choo, but kids will be enthralled riding this authentic 1890-era sugar train. The hour-long ride provides a nostalgic tour through the sugar plantation above Kaanapali, complete with historical narrative about what was once Lahaina's major industry.
Open daily 8:30 a.m.-4:30 p.m. Reservations not required for the six one-hour round-trips from Lahaina to Kaanapali. Adults $9, children over 3 $4.50.

BEACHES

D.T. Fleming Beach Park
Honoapiilani Hwy.,
Honokahua
• 661-4685

Far from the madding, blanket-to-blanket beach crowds, this exquisite white-sand beach has a large ironwood-shaded, grassy area for picnicking and a view of the island of Molokai just across the channel. Excellent bodysurfing in the winter months when waters are rougher (care should be exercised by the uninitiated). Lifeguard not always on duty.

Hamoa Beach
Hana Hwy.,
between Hana & Seven
Pools at Kipahulu
• 248-8211

This exquisite salt-and-pepper-sand beach is maintained by the *très*-chic Hotel Hana Maui and offers superb bodysurfing and boogie boarding in the winter, great swimming and snorkeling in the summer.

Honolua Bay/Mokuleia Beach
Honoapiilani Hwy.,
northwest of Kapalua,
Honolua
• 661-4685

One of the few Marine Life Conservation Districts in Maui County, this lovely bay and associated beach are flanked by steep valley walls. Honolua is famous for its superb snorkeling (best in spring and summer), which improves significantly in the outer bay, and as you round the point that separates Honolua from the adjacent Mokuleia Bay to the east. The protected status of these areas precludes all consumptive uses, making sea life inordinately unconcerned with intruders. (In other words, you snorkel nose-to-nose with the fish.) Honolua is also well known for its world-class surfing in the winter months (which precludes snorkeling but is great for spectators). Winter also makes it great for bodysurfing, but experts only, please. Mokuleia Bay is otherwise known as "Slaughter House Beach" after the slaughter house once located on the cliff above the bay. This lovely pocket of sand nestled against sea cliffs is a good sunbathing, swimming and snorkeling beach, though access is a bit tricky down the rough trail from the highway.

Hookipa Beach
Hana Hwy.,
east of Paia
• 572-8122

Hookipa is one of the most famous wave-jumping sites on the international windsurfing circuit, and a number of major competitions are held annually. Park on the dirt lot off the highway or in the parking lot on the cliffs to the left of the park to enjoy the spectacular board-sailing tricks and freestyle expressions. The shallow reefs off the park are good for diving when there are no waves.

Kaanapali Beach

Kaanapali Resort,
Honoapiilani Hwy.,
Lahaina

Smack dab in front of Maui's most famous glut of hotels and condominiums is one of the prettiest white-sand beaches on the island. With easy snorkeling near Black Rock on the north end and safe swimming in the near-shore waters year-round, virtually every ocean recreation amusement conceivable is available from vendors. For people who don't mind a crowded beach, it offers the best people-watching on the island.

> ### A SOUL'S LEAP
>
> There is a significant site in Hawaiian legend known as Black Rock, or Puu Kekaa. A volcanic cylinder cone that stands prominently on the hill above Kaanapali Beach, it's a famous *leina a ka uhane*, or "soul's leap,"—one of many on the Islands. Hawaiians believe that as a person lies dying, his soul goes to a lein a ka uhane such as Puu Kekaa, and leaps into the next world. At the exact moment of the leap, physical death comes to the individual's body.

Kanaha Beach Park

East of Kahului, off
Keolani Pl.,
Kahului
• 243-7389

This conveniently located, extensive beach park facility is an excellent place to picnic. Broad shaded lawns, picnic tables and barbecue pits, public rest rooms and showers flank a picturesque, mile-long white-sand beach. Kanaha is unfortunately located adjacent to Maui's main airport and is therefore noisy. The park attracts windsurfers from all over the world, thanks to dependably windy conditions, and the ambience of butterfly-winglike sails, skittering over the water is awe inspiring. The central location also attracts local residents and their families for a day at the beach. On weekends it is extremely crowded. Midweek it is less populated. Be sure to leave nothing in your car, as this is a prime area for theft.

Makena Beach

Makena Rd.,
east of Wailea/Kihei

Easily Maui's most spectacular white-sand beach. The deep-blue, gin-clear water vies for attention with views of the nearby islands of Molokini and Kahoolawe. You can bodysurf when the waves are up or snorkel when no surf is present. The fact that this gorgeous public beach has no facilities is a function of near criminal neglect by the State of Hawaii, despite more than twenty years of lobbying by the people of Maui. At the west end of Makena, access "Little Beach" at the foot of Puu Olai by scrambling over the boundary headland. This is known as a clothing-optional beach; but skinny-dipping is illegal in Hawaii, and the area is occasionally "raided" by the police. Nude sunbathers are charged with lewd conduct.

Wailea Beaches
Kihei Rd.,
fronting the Wailea
Resort,
Wailea
• 879-4461

The good news about Wailea beaches is the excellent snorkeling off the rocky points (when winter surf is not stirring things up) and the beautiful sand beaches with access to all manner of facilities and ocean recreation activities. The bad news is the beaches can be so crowded during high tourist season that you can barely walk without stumbling over the supine hordes who blanket the beach.

EXCURSIONS

Hana Highway
Hana Hwy.,
Kahului-Kipahulu

If you don't make the day-long tip to Hana, you really haven't seen Maui. The most scenic drive in the Hawaiian Islands meanders along the north Maui coastline past spectacular ocean vistas, through lush tropical rain forest over one of the poorest excuses for a road you'll ever traverse, to the very Hawaiian town of Hana and beyond to Oheo Gulch in Kipahulu. This famous spot is commonly called the Seven Sacred Pools, a name invented by the visitor industry. (There is nothing "sacred" about this series of waterfalls.) The apparently short distance on a map (51 miles) belies the time required as vehicular speed rarely exceeds 25 miles per hour. Don't be surprised if you end up in the middle of the longest caravan you've ever seen. Allow a minimum of three hours from Kahului to Hana and another hour to Kipahulu. (The most popular-selling T-shirt at the Hasegawa General Store in Hana proclaims "I survived the Hana Highway.") Leave early to miss the traffic, pack a lunch. Some fabulous stops are: Twin Falls, a perfectly formed swimming hole about 20 miles from Kahului; Waikamoi Ridge, good picnic spot and hiking trail; Puohokamoa Falls, next to a waterfall and swimming hole; Kaumahina State Wayside, nestled in the trees overlooking Honomanu Gulch and Keanae Peninsula; Keanae Arboretum, botanical gardens; and Puaa Kaa State Park, another picnic area complete with waterfall. Take your time and plan to spend a *long* but enjoyable day in tropical paradise. Return the way you came, the road beyond Kipahulu is unsafe, tortuous, often closed completely, and your rental car is probably not insured to traverse it anyway.

A VISUAL MAP

Maui, the "Valley Isle," is defined by the 10,000-foot volcano Haleakala on one side and the ancient West Maui Mountains on the other. The isthmus between sprouts miles of waving sugarcane fields. Modern resorts line the beaches on the western or "leeward" shores, and lush tropical rain forests flank the eastern or "windward" side of Haleakala.

Upcountry
Paia-Makawao-
Haiku-Pukalani-Kula-
Ulupalakua

A different part of Hawaii, located on the verdant slopes of Haleakala. Start in the historic plantation village of Paia, peruse the eclectic mix of shops and bargains, then drive up Baldwin Avenue to the cowboy town of Makawao. A horse tied to the hitching post outside one of the shops is not unusual. Then continue up the slopes through the pineapple fields and flower-growing regions of Kula to Hawaii's only winery, Tedeschi Vineyards (878-6058) at the historic Ulupalakua Ranch, high on the slopes above Wailea and Makena. The Tasting Room is open daily. Side jaunts through the lush residential areas of Haiku or up Olinda Road are beautiful excursions. Check Maui "Goings On" section, page 189, for events like the Makawao Rodeo (Oskie Rice Arena) and polo matches in the area.

Molokini Crater The spectacular half-moon islet of Molokini is located halfway between the Wailea resort area and the island of Kahoolawe. This half-crater of an extinct volcano is a marine preserve and one of the most exquisite snorkeling and/or scuba diving areas in the Pacific—unfortunately it's also one of the most popular. Excursions leave from Wailea Beach, Kihei, Maalaea Small Boat Harbor and Lahaina Harbor daily. Morning runs offer better water clarity. Many different purveyors; ask about slow days and the more uncrowded trips. At times there may seem to be more snorkelers and divers in the water at Molokini than marine life.

Historic Lahaina The centuries-old whaling port of Lahaina was once the capital
Lahaina of the Kingdom of Hawaii and boasts a wide variety of historic sights, most within easy walking distance. A ticky-tacky of modern tourist meccas and some rather unusual art galleries also compete for your attention—and bucks. The town has been a National Historic District since 1962, and the Lahaina Restoration Foundation has fought to keep the historic buildings and atmosphere in a booming tourist town. The Lahaina Restoration Foundation also runs the Baldwin Home on Front Street (661-3262), which has a map of the many historic sites they maintain in the town, ranging from the restored brigantine Carthaginian to the Wo Hing Chinese Temple. In the late afternoon, a stroll along Lahaina Harbor will provide information on the day's catch of the sportfishing fleet and all the details of the many and varied ocean activities based there. Next to the harbor is the historic Pioneer Inn, built in 1901, which wraps around a turn-of-the-century-style courtyard. Once inside, visitors are confronted with the original "house rules": "Women is not allow in you room," (sic) and "Only on Sunday you can sleep all day." They still offer rooms, which are located above the boisterous bar, and occupancy runs nearly 100 percent year-round. Across from the Pioneer Inn is a 100-year-old banyan tree, one of the oldest and largest in Hawaii, covering an acre of land. Planted in 1873 by Sheriff William Smith for the 50th anniversary of the first Christian Mission in Lahaina, the giant tree seems to come to life at sunset when hundreds of

mynah birds gather for a cacophonous chorus to usher in the evening. In the basement of the Old Courthouse, next to the banyan tree, is the Old Jail, which now houses an art gallery featuring local artists. Also note the stone ruins on the sides of the courthouse, which are the remainder of the Old Fort, constructed during the 1830s to protect Lahaina from the drunken antics (like firing cannon balls) of the whalers and their crew.

Wailuku Town
Wailuku

Maui's center of business and government is located in the historic town of Wailuku. The funky and historic community is in the midst of restoration. Market Street winds down into scenic Happy Valley, formerly a "red light" district that has retained the cheeky charm of its bygone days. Main street runs up past the Kaahumanu Church, the oldest church on Maui, built in 1837. Continuing up Main, stop at Hale Hoikeike, the Maui Historical Society Museum, housed in the 1834 Bailey House. A half mile beyond the Bailey House the road forks; take the left to Kepaniwai Park, a park and cultural center combined. With the towering Iao Needle in the background, the park features Japanese and Chinese monuments, arched bridges, oriental gardens and buildings and a swimming pool. At the end of the road is the Iao Valley State Park, whose main feature is the 2,250-foot Iao Needle jutting up from the valley floor. The park can offer a quiet respite near Iao Valley Stream or it can be jam-packed with tour buses. Best time to go is early in the morning; you'll have the park to yourself.

LUAU

Jesse's Luau
2945 Kihei Rd.,
Kihei
• 879-7227

Jesse Nakooka, an Island son, is host and star of a tropical parade of songs and dances from Hawaii, Samoa and Tahiti. Sure, it's tailor-made for tourists, but Nakooka is an authentic Hawaiian "find," displaying a voice and spirit that are the essence of the Islands. The cost is $78 for two.
Open Sun., Wed., Fri. 5:30-8:30. All major cards.

MUSEUMS

Alexander and Baldwin Sugar Museum
3957 Hansen Rd.,
Puunene
• 871-8058

Displays and memorabilia from the earlier days of what is one of the most productive and successful sugar companies in the Hawaiian Islands. Included are displays (and no small amount of propaganda) on plantation life.
Open Mon.-Sat. 9:30 a.m.-4:30 p.m. Adults $2, children 6-17 $1.

Bailey House Museum-Maui Historical Society Museum

2375-A Main St.,
Wailuku
• 244-3326

Old houses converted to museums tend to be mildew-smelling, boring and run by hawk-eyed old ladies—not so here. The Maui Historical Society, which manages the Bailey House Museum (also known as Hale Hoikeike), has converted this 1834 house into a very appealing living historical record. Displays detailing the missionary period of Hawaiian history include nineteenth-century Hawaiian artifacts and photos. Very knowledgable docents let their love of Hawaiian history show in their exuberance.

Open Mon.-Sat. 10 a.m.-4:30 p.m. Donations requested.

Baldwin Home Museum

Front/Dickenson St.,
Lahaina
• 661-3262.

Nestled among the dozens of seemingly identical art galleries, copious T-shirt shops and overpriced jewelry stores lies Maui's oldest building, the coral-and-stone 1830 Baldwin home. The Lahaina Restoration Foundation has done a remarkable job of saving and renovating this house into an interesting glimpse into Maui's missionary era. The original home of Rev. Dwight Baldwin, the museum is furnished with pieces and family heirlooms from that era. Rev. Baldwin, in addition to spreading the word of Christianity, was also a doctor. Be sure and check out his "medical" instruments (the tools could be props from a *Nightmare on Elm Street* horror flick).

Open Mon.-Sat. 9 a.m.-4:30 p.m., Sun. 11 a.m.-4 p.m. Adults $2, children free.

Carthaginian II

Lahaina Harbor,
Lahaina
• 661-8527

Even if the thought of spending one minute in a museum makes you want to retch, you should see this shipboard museum in the steel-hulled schooner just like the many that anchored off Lahaina during the height of the whaling industry in the late 1800s. This 93-foot Swedish ship replaced the Carthaginian I, which went aground on the reef in 1972. A wonderful place for children, the floating museum has various exhibits, including excellent information on whales.

Open Mon.-Fri. 9 a.m.-4 p.m., Sat.-Sun. 9:30 a.m.-4:30 p.m. Adults $2, children free.

Hale Pai

Lahainaluna School,
Lahaina Luna Rd.,
Lahaina
• 661-7040

The truth is we found looking at old printing presses at Hale Pai (House of Print) boring. But we still recommend going there because of the unbelievable panoramic view from the top of Lahaina, the best view from the west side. You can see the entire coastline, the boats in the Lahaina Roadstead, and Molokai and Lanai in the distance. OK, for the fans of old printing presses, this is the first printing shop on Maui, built in 1836 and recently restored. For years the print shop was connected with Lahainaluna School, the oldest school west of the Rockies,

started in 1831 by missionaries. And even back then it was the best place for a view of West Maui.
Open Mon., Wed., & Fri. 10 a.m.-4 p.m. Donations requested.

Whalers Village Museum
Whalers Village,
Kaanapali
• 661-5992

Buried in the heart of Kaanapali's largest tourist shopping mall is this museum dedicated to the historic whaling industry, which was so important to Hawaii and Lahaina in particular around the turn of the century. The display includes a completely reticulated whale skeleton and a superb collection of historic whaling industry artifacts.
Open daily 9:30 a.m.-10 p.m. Admission free.

Wo Hing Temple Museum
858 Front St.,
Lahaina
• 661-5553

This former gathering place for the Chinese of Lahaina dates back to 1912. Today it has been restored and is a museum of the Chinese and their culture in Hawaii. Next door to the museum, in the old cookhouse, old films of the Islands are shown.
Open daily 10 a.m.-4 p.m. Admission $1.

PARKS & GARDENS

Haleakala National Park
Crater Rd.,
Kula
• 572-9306,
572-7749 (recording)

This immense national park is dedicated to the preservation of the many and varied ecosystems unique to Maui's largest volcano, Haleakala. Sunrise on Haleakala is a unique, soul-lifting phenomenon. The view from the crater rim is otherworldly—well worth the early drive. Morning viewing is best (before the clouds obscure the view). The road to the top of Haleakala is unique in itself: it is the only road in the world that rises from sea level to 10,000 feet in just 37 miles. Just before the entrance to the park, at 7,000 feet, is a scenic campground area called Hosmer Grove. After you pass the toll gate, be sure to stop at park headquarters for descriptive information and hiking trail details. You can also find out about camp sites and cabin rentals in the crater, but these are usually booked months in advance. As you continue up the circuitous road, the terrain becomes barren and moonlike. The first peek inside the crater is at Leleiwi Overlook, at 8,800 feet. The multicolored crater, with swirls of reds, browns and charcoal grays, is filled with cinder cones, lava flows and several smaller craters. The next view into the abyss is at 9,325 feet at the Kalahaku Overlook. Be sure to stop here, not only to see the crater but also to experience the silversword plants. Related to the sunflower family, these spiky, silver-leafed plants are found only on the volcanoes of Maui and the Big Island. For the first two decades of their lives, the plants are low, porcupinelike bush plants, then suddenly they bloom into tall

A SLOW SUN

Maui's most visual landmark, Haleakala ("House of the Sun"), sports a legend known to nearly every schoolchild in Hawaii. The sun used to traverse the sky so quickly in ancient times that the people were not able to get their work done. The goddess Hina went to her son, Maui, for help, and Maui figured out a plan.

He stealthily climbed the mountain and waited for the sun to make its appearance in the eastern sky. As the first rays broke across the horizon, Maui quickly threw out a rope of woven coconut fiber and lassoed the sun. The glowing ball begged for mercy, and Maui extracted a promise for his release—that he would travel more slowly across the sky. To this day, sunlight in Hawaii varies from eleven hours in the winter to nearly thirteen hours in the summer.

flowering stalks (between May and November) and then die. The best view of the entire Haleakala Crater is at the Visitors Center, where the full crater—seven miles long, two miles wide and 21 miles in circumference—can be seen in all its glory. The drop from the top to the floor is 3,000 feet. The Visitors Center also features an exhibit on Haleakala and volcanoes. The crater summit at Puu Ulaula Lookout is ideal for viewing Maui, Lanai, Molokai and the Big Island. Bring a warm jacket: at 10,000 feet, it's much colder than at sea level.
Open daily. Headquarters open 7:30 a.m.-4 p.m. Visitors Center at the Crater Rim open 6 a.m.-3 p.m. Fee: $3/car, $1/bike or hiker.

Iao Needle State Park

Iao Valley Rd., Wailuku
• 244-4352

The Iao Needle is a tropical retreat situated alongside the gurgling Iao Stream. The serene setting at the base of verdant cliffs makes a wonderful picnic spot. But, with its full facilities, it's also a popular stop on the tour bus circuit. The parking lot, as well as the park, is filled to capacity from 9 a.m. to 4 p.m. daily. If you want to enjoy the serenity, get there early. Never leave valuables in your car here (even if you lock the doors and trunk). This area periodically experiences a series of car break-ins, usually by juveniles looking for cameras, cash and other easy-to-dispose-of items.
Open daily.

Kula Botanical Garden

Upper Kula Rd., Kula
• 878-1715

For a one-stop look at native species of Hawaii and numerous horticultural wonders including the alien-looking protea, tropical birds of paradise, exotic orchids and other blooms popular in the international cut-flower markets, make the drive up to the Kula Botanical Garden. It's a great place to picnic, and *after* you eat, be sure to check out the "Taboo Garden" filled with poisonous plants.
Open daily 9 a.m.-4 p.m. Adults $3; children 6-12 50 cents.

TOURS

Akamai Tours
532 Keolani Pl.,
Kahului
• 871-9551

Ever wonder about those ubiquitous little yellow vans, crammed with sweating, overweight tourists that seem to be coming and going everywhere in Hawaii? Well, hey, you can join them for the Haleakala Sunrise if you want to load up at your hotel at 3:25 a.m., stop at Sizzler for breakfast Dutch treat (we're not making this up) and return to your hotel room at about 11 a.m., for as little as $39 per person (plus breakfast). Fun? How about a nine-hour van ride to Hana with a lunch consisting of beef, chicken or fish, rice, salad and coffee or tea for $55.50 a head? Remember you can rent a car, call your own shots, eat wild guavas (or a gourmet box lunch) and do the same thing with four of your friends in a convertible for $49.99 a day, but the convertible may not be yellow, so you choose.
Tours daily.

Captain Zodiac
115 Dickenson St.,
Lahaina
• 67-5351

The originator of the now immensely popular inflatable-boat adventure trips in Hawaii, Captain Zodiac is still the king of the genre. While their morning snorkel and whale-watch (winter season) trips are generally a real gas, rubber boats are best left to Navy frogmen when the water is rough or the distance is formidable. No shade, so cover up and carry plenty of sunscreen. All snorkel gear provided, as are drinks and snacks.
Open Mon.-Sat. 7 a.m.-9 p.m., Sun. 8 a.m.-6 p.m. Snorkel trip (3.5 hours) daily 9 a.m. &1 p.m. Adults $50, children under 12 $35. Circumnavigate Lanai (7.5 hours) Tues. & Sat. Adults $95, children under 12 $55. Deluxe (3.5-hour) whale-watch daily 9 a.m. & 1 p.m. (winter only). Adults $53, children under 12 $40.

Cardinal Helicopters
910 Honoapiilani Hwy.,
Lahaina
• 661-0092,
(800) 448-1232

Cardinal Helicopters has more than a few good things going for it. To start with they save you money and keep their rates extremely low by eschewing the normal activities desk that charges usurious rates for their "services." (Cardinal provides referral to all of the top activities on Maui at no cost.) They also offer a video tape of each individual flight, complete with the pilot's continuous narration and the comments made by you and your flight-mates. Cardinal has a number of superb pre-planned flights or they can design private charters to your specifications. And they will pick you up from your hotel free if you are staying in the Kapalua to Wailea area.
Open daily 7 a.m.-9 p.m. Haleakala crater–Hana rain forest (40 minutes) $88 per person. West Maui, Waihee Valley flight (70 minutes) $144 per person. Private charters $550 per hour.

Club Lanai

355 Hukilike St.,
Kahului
• 871-1144

What was once a simple beachcomber's delight, an adventure to a little piece of untouched Hawaii, has evolved into a miniature Waikiki in a few short years. Club Lanai is an idyllicly located stretch of beach just across the channel from bustling Lahaina and Kaanapali. Unfortunately, it attracts large numbers of visitors scrambling to get away from the clutter, the vendors and the crowd. If you are visiting in the off season, make the trek midweek or you can get a body count from the company before you book; it could be a most enjoyable experience. A Continental breakfast is served en route, and a beach buffet lunch at noon, with live entertainment. Hammocks, sun shades, lounges, beach mats, water toys and access to miles of beach, as well as a glass-bottomed boat with snorkeling gear are all part of the deal.

Open daily 7:30 a.m.-10 p.m. Adults $89; children 5-12, $25.

Hike Maui

Box 330969,
Kahului
• 879-5270

This is our top choice for natural history buffs or anyone interested in the biology, archaeology, geology, oceanography, even the philosophy of Hawaii—or just anyone who loves to hike. Ken Schmitt runs a simple, very complete one-man operation, guiding no more than six intrepid travelers at a time onto the trails. He'll guide you across ridges and mountain tops, into the valleys and craters, through forests and waterfalls or down to the shoreline, imparting his powerful sense of the surroundings. Hikes into every conceivable kind of area, hikes at all levels of difficulty are offered, as well as hikes custom-tailored to meet your special desires. Day packs, ponchos, water and gourmet snacks and food are provided (supplemented from the wild, of course) as is transportation from a central meeting point. The longest hikes are twelve miles across Haleakala Crater and the Oheo Gulch Hike to the falls above Kipahulu. The shortest jaunts are the West Maui Valley Hike, Mountain Hike and Coastal Hike of two to five miles over five hours. Schmitt offers the only way to experience the real Maui, naturally.

Tours daily. Adults $50-$90; children under 16 $30-$55.

Maui Helicopters

Box 1002,
Kihei
• 879-1601

Maui Helicopters is a local company with some unique packages in their repertoire. They offer a fly/drive package that allows you to take a helicopter tour of the island, land in Hana and then drive back in an air-conditioned vehicle or vice versa, avoiding half of the arduous drive to that unique little piece of Hawaii. The trip includes a gourmet lunch at Hana Bay. Another rare opportunity is their Whole Island Tour, which includes a stop on private land in remote Kaupo with a champagne reception.

Open daily 7:30 a.m.-4 p.m. Hana-Haleakala Fly/Drive (5.5 hours) $149 per person; Whole Island Tour $200 per person.

**Papillon
Helicopters**
Box 1690,
Lahaina
• 669-4884

Papillon is a division of the largest helicopter sightseeing company in the world, and they really show it with high levels of professionalism rarely found in locally based operations. Papillon exclusively flies Aerospatiale ASTAR helicopters, which offer the best view and the most comfortable ride of any helicopter in the business. Most flights depart out of their own heliport located above Kapalua, just 10 minutes from Kaanapali; others take off from Kahului airport. Superb service, professional attitude and well-maintained equipment make these tours delightful—especially the Hana Day package, which includes the use of a Jeep in Hana and lunch at the exquisite Hotel Hana Maui and a champagne reception on your return to base; or the Sunrise Circle Island, which includes a Haleakala Sunrise and breakfast in Hana.

Open daily 7 a.m.-7 p.m. Half-hour West Maui Fantasia $99 per person; two-hour Circle Island Tour $205 per person; two-hour Sunrise-Hana $245 per person; Hana Package, $395 per person.

SPORTS

BICYCLING

Cruiser Bob's Downhill Bicycle Tour
505 Front St.,
Lahaina
• 667-7717

For a family adventure, unique to Maui, take grandma and the kids on an original Haleakala downhill bicycle safari. Accept no substitute. Cruiser Bob's is absolutely the best of the downhill bike tours. Float down the slopes from the 10,000-foot peak of Haleakala past flower farms, pineapple fields and historic communities on custom-made downhill cruisers with knowledgeable, safety-conscious guides. Hotel pickup and appropriate meals included. A safe no-strain activity suitable for just about anyone. Book in advance.
Tours daily. Hotel pickup for either sunrise tour with breakfast or afternoon ride with lunch. Cost $92.70 (includes transportation, wheels and meals).

Maui Downhill
333 Dairy Rd.,
Suite 201E,
Kahului
• 871-2155

If you can't get into Cruiser Bob's Tour, Maui Downhill is the next best. Coast for 38 miles down the flanks of Haleakala dropping from 10,000 feet to sea level in a half-day bicycle trip anyone can complete. Free transportation and an all-you-can-eat buffet are included.
Tours daily for either sunrise or day tours. Cost $93.

DIVING & SNORKELING

Central Pacific Divers
780 Front St.,
Lahaina
• 661-8718

One of Maui's oldest and most reputable scuba-diving operations, Central Pacific Divers has operated very professionally out of the same storefront in Lahaina since 1971. They feature a pair of large, comfortable, fast interisland dive boats, complete sales and rentals, diver training at all levels and a unique and very luxurious dive lodge facility in Lahaina called the Plantation Inn.
Open 6:30 a.m.-9 p.m. 2-tank dive to Molokini $73 (includes Continental breakfast and lunch); 3-tank dive on Lanai $87 (includes meals); single-tank outside of Lahaina $57.

Hawaiian Watercolors
50 Koki St.,
Kihei
• 879-3584

Widely published underwater photographer Ed Robinson offers specialized scuba charters designed specifically for beginning and advanced underwater photographers. His highly personalized and knowledgeable service, which caters to small groups (maximum of six passengers in his 21-foot Boston Whaler), is conservation oriented.
Charters daily. Two-tank dives $80, including all equipment, Continental breakfast, snacks and refreshments.

Lahaina Divers

710 Front St.,
Lahaina
• 661-4505

One of Maui's few Five Star PADI-IDC facilities is also one of the most professionally managed scuba-dive operations on an island where they really proliferate. Complete classes from introductory to full certification and advanced skill levels, two of the fastest dive boats in the Islands, daily interisland trips to Molokini and Lanai.

Open daily 8 a.m.-9:30 p.m. Scuba charter to Molokini or Lanai, 2-tank dive with rolls and coffee for breakfast $79 (includes weights and tank); extra equipment rental $3.50 each.

Maui Dive Shop

Azeka Plaza Shopping
Center,
Kihei
• 879-3388

Lahaina Cannery
Shopping Center,
Lahaina
• 661-5388

Maui's largest diving retailer offers professional scuba diving instruction, charters and services (primarily to the Kihei and Wailea resort areas) and four shops to choose from. Maui Dive Shop is a PADI Five Star facility with a proven reputation and excellent access to all the top dive spots.

Open Mon.-Fri. 9 a.m.-5:30 p.m., Sat. 8 a.m.-5 p.m. 2-tank dives to Molokini $75, including all equipment.

Ocean Activities Center

1325 S. Kihei Rd.,
Ste. 212,
Kihei
• 879-4485

Ocean Activities Center is one of Maui's largest ocean recreation companies. Operating out of a number of Island bases, they offer an extensive array of snorkeling charters and the entire gamut of ocean activities. They were the first to offer group snorkeling trips to Molokini, and still rate as one of the best for that unique trip.

Tours daily 7 a.m.-11 a.m. Tour $36.95; deluxe tour (7:15 a.m.-12:15 p.m.) with Continental breakfast, deli lunch, open bar, transportation from hotel and stop at two snorkeling spots $60.

FISHING

Aerial Sportfishing

Lahaina Harbor,
Lahaina
• 667-9089

Fish one of Hawaii's true classic sportfishing boats out of the historic whaling port of Lahaina. The boats in Capt. Chris Rose's fleet range in size from 36 feet to 44 feet.

Charters daily. Cost $65 (half-day shared boat) to $550 (full-day exclusive charter).

Excel Charters

Maalaea Harbor,
Maalaea
• 877-3333

Choose from either sportfishing combined with party-boat fishing in the morning or party-boat bottom-fishing in the afternoon on the comfortable Excel. Excel caters to small groups, and all gear is provided.

Charters daily. Morning combination sport-and-party-boat fishing $95, passengers not fishing $47.50 (includes breakfast and lunch). Afternoon bottom-fishing $65.

Finest Kind and Exact Charters
Lahaina Harbor,
Lahaina
• 661-0338

Capt. Dave Hudson runs the most professionally managed sportfishing fleet in Maui waters, including the 37-foot Merritt Finest Kind. His vessels are consistent producers of good catches and large fish, and the boats are always meticulously maintained. *Charters daily. Share-boat, six-hour trip $100; eight-hour trip $125; nonfishing passengers half price. Exclusive boat (up to 6 passengers) 6-hour trip $475, 8-hour trip $600. During slow seasons they may discount rates.*

Maalaea Activities
Maalaea Harbor,
Maalaea
• 242-6982

This cooperative charter operation books virtually all of the sportfishing boats out of Maalaea Harbor, close to the Kihei and Wailea resort areas. Top choices include Capt. Joe Yurkanin's No Ka Oi III and Capt. David Ventura's Maui Diamond. *Charters daily. Cost $70 (half-day share-boat) to $500 (full-day exclusive cruise).*

Robalo One
Box 10253,
Lahaina
• 669-0776

Capt. Kenny Takashima runs the only small-boat, light-tackle (twelve-pound test) charter operation on Maui. He draws enthusiastic reviews from spin, plug and bottom fishermen who have enjoyed his productive trips. Drift bottom-fishing, half-day shares or exclusive full days. *Charters daily. Half-day share $70 (includes all equipment); full-day exclusive $350-$450.*

GOLF

Kapalua Bay and Village Golf Courses
Kapalua Resort,
Kapalua
• 669-8044

Scene of the Isuzu-Kapalua International and the Kirin Cup World Championship of Golf, these two golf courses are not only challenging but worth a tour just to catch the scenery. The Bay Course is a par-72, 6,761-yard championship course, with a world-famous fifth hole that overlooks a small ocean cove. Even the pros have trouble with the 205-yard, par-three hole. The Village course is a par-71, 6,632-yard championship course, with a scenic sixth hole overlooking a lake and the ocean in the distance. The tee is between two rows of Cook Pines. No golfer should leave Maui without playing one of these two spectacular courses. *Tee times begin daily around 6 a.m., last tee time for 18 holes 2 p.m. Pro shop open daily 6:30 a.m.-8 p.m. Cost $60 for resort guests & $90 for visitors (includes mandatory cart).*

Makena Golf Course
Makena Resort,
Makena
• 879-3344

This par-72, 6,739-yard championship course is at the southern end of Maui's gold coast of golf courses. Its signature hole is the scenic 15th, a par-3, with a view of the Molokini Crater looming in the background. Maui's newest golf course, Makena also has attracted the Senior's PGA tour with its Epson Seniors Stats Match every December.
Daily tee times start 6:36 a.m., last tee around 1:40 p.m. Cost $55 for guests of Makena Prince Hotel, $90 for others (cart included). Pro shop open daily 6:45 a.m.-6:30 p.m.

Royal Kaanapali North and South Golf Courses
Kaanapali Resort,
Kaanapali
• 661-3691

This is golfing resort-style. The courses can be somewhat challenging but also a blessing for the high handicappers. The North Course, a par-72, 6,305-yard course, has a tricky 18th hole (par 4, 435 yards) with a water hazard on the approach to the green. The somewhat easier par-72, 6,250-yard South Course also has a water hazard on its final hole, causing the score to be in question until the final putt is sunk. Every December the GTE Kaanapali Classic, a PGA Seniors event, is played here.
Daily tee times vary (around 7 a.m.) Last tee time around 2 p.m. for 18 holes. Pro shop open daily 7 a.m.-7 p.m. Cost $90 for hotel guests and nonguests.

Wailea Golf Courses
Wailea Resort,
Wailea
• 879-2966

Wailea offers a choice of courses: either the par-72, 6,810-yard championship Orange course, with narrow fairways and several tricky dogleg holes; or the par-72, 6,743-yard championship Blue, a flatter, open course dotted with bunkers and water hazards.
Daily tee times begin 6:36 a.m., last tee time around 2 p.m. depending on the time of year. Cost $45 for guests at Wailea Resort, $90 others (includes cart). Pro shop open daily 6:20 a.m.-6:30 p.m.

HIKING

For information on various trails and hikes, contact one of the following organizations: the **Hawaii Geographical Society** (Box 1698, Honolulu; 538-3952), which offers a packet on trails throughout the state for $6; **Hawaii State Department of Land and Natural Resources** (Box 1049, Wailuku; 244-4352); **Hawaiian Trail and Mountain Club** (Box 2238, Honolulu; 734-5515), which offers a packet on hiking on all islands (just send $1 and a self-addressed, stamped envelope); and the **Maui County Department of Parks and Recreation** (1580 Kaahumanu Ave., Wailuku; 243-7230). On the following page are some of Maui's better trails:

Haleakala National Park
Box 369,
Makawao
• 572-9306

Hike into the belly of a dormant volcano. Some 32 miles of marked hiking trails, two campsites and three cabins offer an outdoor adventure like nothing else on the planet. The terrain varies from cinder cone to lava tubes and prehistoric-looking rocks. The Hawaiians considered Haleakala a sacred place. One walk through the moonlike surroundings and you will see why. The three main trails in the park are: Sliding Sands Trail, a steep trail of slippery cinder beginning at the Visitor Center and descending 3,000 feet in ten miles to the Paliku Cabin; the Kaupo Trail, an eight-mile descent out of the crater to sea level in the small hamlet of Kaupo; and Halemauu Trail, a ten-mile switch-back trail from the crater floor to the rim. Camping and cabin rentals all require a permit from the national park.

Hana-Waianapanapa Coastal Trail
Waianapanapa State Park
to Hana Bay,
Hana
• 244-4354

Hike back in time: see the coastline as it looked to the Hawaiians hundreds of years ago. Beginning in the Waianapanapa State Park, this six-mile round-trip coastal hike passes forests of lauhala trees, caves buried in the rocks, a blow hole and a heiau or sacred temple.

Iao Valley
Iao Valley State Park,
Wailuku
• 244-4354

Come early or after 4 p.m. to enjoy a quiet hike through the Iao Valley Park. The trail begins at the parking lot, then climbs 500 feet to the park lookout shelter for a view of the valley. Or take the side trail up the Iao Stream, crisscrossing the shallow water by rock-hopping up the stream.

Kahakuloa Valley Trail
Kahekili Hwy.,
Kahakuloa

In the nearly untouched scenic valley of Kahakuloa, where Hawaiians still grow taro and live a life-style that hasn't changed for generations, is a great place to hike. The trail begins across the street from the church and climbs up through guava trees and passion-fruit vines, passing old burial caves and former agricultural sites. The round-trip hike is approximately four miles.

Kanaha Pond Wildlife Sanctuary
Haleakala/Hana Hwy.,
Kahului
• 244-4352

Believe it or not, sandwiched between the Kahului Airport and a sewer treatment plant is a wildlife sanctuary for Hawaii's endangered birds. With a permit you can wander along both of the mile-long loop trails inside, observing the endangered Hawaiian stilt, Hawaiian coot and other birds.

King's Highway Coastal Trail
La Perouse Bay to Kanaloa Pt.

The Hawaiians had trails circling the entire island at one time. The trail along this 1790 lava flow is still very well marked. Beginning at La Perouse Bay, the eleven-mile round-trip trail follows the ocean, through thorny kiawe groves, over dusty cattle land and across lava flows to Kanaloa Point. This is a strenuous hike, with no fresh water along the way, so come prepared. Good fishing off some points. After Kanaloa, the coastal property is all private and fenced.

Polipoli State Park
Box 1049,
Wailuku
• 244-4352

Polipoli State Park is just part of the 21,000 acres of the Kula and Kahikinui Forest Reserve on the upper western and southern slopes of Haleakala. Originally this area was composed of koa, ohia and mamane trees; but overlogging to meet the demands of greedy traders and overgrazing by animals destroyed the native forests in the nineteenth-century. In the 1920s a major reforestation program planted redwood, Monterey cypress, ash, sugi, cedar and other pines. The result is a cool area, with muted sunlight filtered by the towering trees. It's hard to believe that you are in Hawaii here. Of the area's numerous well-marked trails, our favorite three: Redwood Trail—almost two miles shrouded in giant redwoods, some nearly 100 feet tall and four feet in circumference (markers identify the species of trees). Connecting with the Redwood Trail at the ranger's cabin, the Plum Trail is named for its plums that ripen in June and July. The Plum Trail is approximately 2.3 miles long and connects to the Haleakala Ridge Trail, which offers the best views of the island; Haleakala Ridge Trail is 1.2 miles long. Tent camping and cabins are available at Polipoli Park. Permits must be obtained in advance.

Waihee Ridge Trail
Camp Maluhia
Kahekili Hwy.,
Wailuku
• 244-4352

This very strenuous, nearly six-mile round-trip hike, will take approximately three hours and gain 1,500 feet in altitude. A sign marks the trail head next to the Boy Scout Camp and the markers continue every half mile. Wear rain gear, hiking boots and long pants as the trail is often overgrown with vegetation. The views along the way are worth the climb: Waihee Canyon, Central Maui, Makamakaole Gulch and the north side of the island.

Waimoku Falls
Seven Sacred Falls,
Hana Hwy.,
Hana
• 248-8251

About 100 yards south of the "Seven Sacred Pools" (as the tourist industry generally calls Oheo Gulch) is a gate marking the beginning of the two-mile trail. The hike goes up a jeep road, crisscrosses the stream over and over and ends up in a singing bamboo forest. When the stream is flowing, bring a bathing suit to take advantage of great swimming holes.

HORSEBACK RIDING

Adventures on Horseback
Box 1771,
Makawao
• 242-7445

Spectacular adventure rides through rugged ranch lands, into tropical rain forests and to remote swimming holes. Day-long tour with breaks for breakfast, lunch and swimming is suitable for small groups; up to six people.
Daily ride 10 a.m. & 3 p.m. Cost $125. No children under 12, weight limit 275 pounds.

Hana Ranch Stables
Box 278,
Hana
• 248-7238

Choose either the regular one-hour guided trail rides through heavenly Hana's lush ranch lands and along the rugged coastline or create your own personalized experience, which can include anything from a tour into ancient Hawaiian archaeological sites to a ride to a sunset luau.
Daily rides. Cost regular 1-hour rides $25, personalized rides $50 per hour.

Kaanapali Kau Lio Horseback Riding
Box 1065,
Lahaina
• 667-7896

This is one of those memorable experiences that stays with you for years. Not only is this one of the most beautiful trail rides in the West Maui mountains (panoramic views of the West Maui resort area and the islands of Molokai and Lanai) but the guides are screamingly funny. Whether you're a novice or an expert, you'll laugh until your sides ache. Free Kaanapali resort pickup.
Daily rides. 3-hour rides $53; 4-hour rides (including an hour for lunch) $67; sunset rides (1 1/2-hour ride plus 1-hour hors d'oeuvres) $67. Minimum age 8. No weight limit as long as the rider can balance on a horse.

Pony Express Tours
Box 535,
Kula
• 667-2200

Tour Haleakala Crater on horseback or take a one- to two-hour ride across Haleakala Ranch land, located at 4,000 feet in the lush upcountry area.
Rides Mon.-Sat. Half-day Crater tour $95, including lunch; full-day Crater tours $120, including lunch. 1-hour ranch tours $25, 2-hour ranch tours $45. Minimum age 10. Weight limit 235 pounds.

SAILING

Kamehameha Catamaran Sails
577 Luakini St.,
Lahaina
• 661-4522

Cruise on a classic 40-foot Hawaiian beach catamaran. Operating regular sailing and snorkeling trips out of historic Lahaina Harbor, the Kamehameha offers a shaded, cushioned cockpit as well as the net "trampoline" area between the bows and lots of deck space. Daily sailing areas are dictated by wind conditions, but you can count on a superb Maui vista in any event. The sunset cruise is a pure sailing adventure. The morning and the longer midday sail/snorkel trips include free snorkeling equipment and the free use of an underwater camera (bring your own 110 film). All trips include snacks and soft drinks. Trips depart from Slip 67 in Lahaina Harbor.

Tours daily. Snorkel/sail 9 a.m.-11 a.m. & noon-3 p.m.; sunset sail (varies with season) 4 p.m.-5 p.m. Sunset sail & morning snorkel/sail: adults $24, children under 12 $18. Midday snorkel/sail: adults $34, children under 12 $24.

Maui Classic Charters
101 N. Kihei Rd.,
Kihei
• 879-8188

If classic sailboats attract you, the 60-foot topsail pilot schooner Lavengro may be of interest. This fine old vessel (built in 1926) has been fully restored and carries up to 27 passengers on daily snorkel/sail trips to Molokini Crater. It is also available for everything from sunset cruises and whale watching (winter season) to private charters that feature an extensive choice of menus. Morning snorkel/sail includes a fine Continental breakfast and a big buffet lunch as well as an array of beverages. All gear is provided including underwater cameras. This true classic sailing vessel is docked at Slip 55 in Maalaea Harbor.

Tours daily. Molokini snorkel/sail 7:30 a.m.-12:30 p.m. Adults $57, children under 12 $36.

Pardner Charters
57 Loa St.,
Napili
• 661-3448

These luxury sailing charters aboard a customized Cal 2/46 are limited to just six passengers. Plan your own three-hour sailing trip with snorkeling stops if you like or whale watch (in the winter season). Sunset champagne cruises are also delightful. Prices include snacks, soft drinks and beer; the sunset cruises include champagne and mai tais as well. Full-day cruise includes full deli lunch. All snorkeling equipment provided, including underwater cameras.

Sails daily 9 a.m.-noon & 1 p.m.-4 p.m., $48; full-day sails daily 9 a.m.-3 p.m., $80; sunset sail (times vary) $30. (Prices 15 percent less for children under 8.)

Scotch Mist Charters
Box 831,
Lahaina
• 661-0386

Sail aboard the winner of the 1982 Victoria B.C. to Maui Yacht Race, one of the finest and fastest racing sailboats in the Islands. Scotch Mist offers personalized offshore adventures that can include snorkeling, whale watching and champagne sunset cruises, as well as occasional full-moon cruises. Destination and sailing areas can be dictated by wind conditions but generally include snorkeling off Lanai. All gear is provided, as is instruction and soft drinks, beer, wine and snacks. Yacht carries no more than 19 passengers; private charters can be arranged.

Tours: Lanai snorkel/sail 8 a.m.-noon ($50), 12:30 p.m.-3:30 *p.m. ($40) & sunset sail (varies seasonally, $30). (All prices less $10 for children under 12.) Private charters start at $195 per hour, two-hour minimum.*

Suntan Special Sailing Charters
145 N. Kihei Rd.,
Kihei
• 874-0332

Thrill to the speed of a fully race-rigged Santa Cruz 50 as it skims the dependable afternoon breezes off Maalaea and Kihei. This modern high-tech sailing machine is certified to carry as many as 25 passengers, but management limits the load to sixteen to assure its special brand of personalized service and passenger comfort. Daily sails include a morning trip for snorkeling at Molokini Crater that departs from the Kealia Beach Center and returns with an invigorating sail after the best deli lunch on any of Maui's snorkel/sail vessels. Not only is all snorkeling gear provided, but the company offers a money-back guarantee that it is unlikely ever to have to meet. This is a top-end experience. Afternoon trips that offer a genuine sailing experience are also available as are private charters, catered to your exacting whims, for groups of as many as 25.

Tours: Molokini snorkel/sail 7:30 a.m.-1 p.m.; Adults $59, children 13-18 $39. Afternoon-sunset sail 2 p.m.-dark $200 plus $25 per person. Private charters $200 boat plus $25 per person.

LIFE'S A BEACH

Question: Okay, how many beaches are there in Hawaii?

Answer: 280. If you don't believe us, you have permission to start counting yourself.

Trilogy Excursions
180 Lahainaluna Rd.,
Lahaina
• 661-4743

What is unquestionably Maui's finest sailing and snorkeling adventure is operated by the Coon family on their fleet of custom-built, stable and comfortable multihull sailboats. Personal service and the genuine enthusiasm of your crew makes this the best single way to spend your day while on Maui. Day-long trips to Lanai include a breakfast complete with the family's world-famous homemade cinnamon rolls, snorkeling instruction at one of the most exquisite beaches in the state (Manele Bay, which Trilogy Excursions is the only charter operator licensed to use), an Island-style barbecue lunch, a van tour of the world's largest pineapple plantation and Lanai City, and a fun sail back to Lahaina with memories that will last a lifetime. In Maui's all-too-plastic visitor industry, this operation stands well above all the others by reflecting a genuine aloha spirit and the best single adventure available to visitors to the island. Trips depart and return to Lahaina Harbor.

Tours: Mon.-Fri. 6:45 a.m.-4:30 p.m. (no weekend trips); Adults $125 per person, children under 12 $67.50.

SURFING

R emember that many of Maui's windsurfing shops also rent and sell surfboards and surfing accessories and can also arrange for surfing instruction.

Hunt Hawaii
Box 989,
Paia
• 579-8129

Doug Hunt has been around the surfing world for years and his little shop in Paia rents surfboards and boogie boards (as well as windsurfing gear) at reasonable rates. His quality shop offers lots of accessories and beachwear as well as manufacturing quality custom boards.
Open daily 9 a.m.-6 p.m. Surfboards $20 per day; boogie boards $12.

Maui Beach Center
1295 Front St.,
Lahaina
• 661-4941

The home of surfing equipment and ocean recreation rentals, located on the water near The Cannery on Front Street in Lahaina.
Open daily 9 a.m.-6 p.m. Surfboard $20 per day, rent five days get two days free; boogie boards $5.

Surfing Beaches

Honolua Bay
West of Kapalua on the
Honoapiilani Hwy.

Honolua is home to some of the world's most revered waves when the winter swell pours into the picturesque little bay. It is also an excellent place to observe surfing from the close vantage point of the cliffs overlooking this unique bay.

Hookipa
East of Paia, on the
Hana Hwy.

This is an easily accessible break that is great for beginners until it gets over about five feet in height, at which point it offers an array of wave types, speeds and break directions for the more practiced wave riders. Can be crowded by board sailors when the wind and waves are up.

Lahaina Harbor
Just off the channel
entrance at Lahaina
Harbor

This is one of the little breaks on Maui, when the summer south swell is producing wave action. It gets very crowded when school gets out and the local kids hit the water.

Maalaea
Near Maalaea Small Boat
Harbor entrance

This fast, tight south swell break is another of Maui's most famous surf spots. Maalaea is famed for producing one of the cleanest, fastest rideable lefts in Island waters.

TENNIS

The **Maui County Department of Parks and Recreation** maintains many public courts all over the island. All are available for play from daylight until sunset, and those with lighting systems are available until 10 p.m. nightly. All courts are available on a "first come, first served" basis. Local rules dictate no more than 45 minutes' use when there is someone waiting to play on any court. Public courts are located in Lahaina (on Front Street and at the Civic Center), Kihei (Kalama Park and behind the Maui Sunset condominium), Haliimaile, Makawao (Eddie Tam Gym), Wailuku (War Memorial Gym and at Wells Park), Kahului (near the Kahului Post Office) and in Hana. Contact the Maui County Department of Parks and Recreation, 200 S. High Street, Wailuku 96793. Or call 243-7232 (Central Maui), 661-4685 (Lahaina area), 879-4364 (Kihei area) or 572-8122 (East Maui).

Kapalua Tennis Garden
Kapalua Resort
• 669-5677

The well-maintained courts at Kapalua are the home to the Kapalua Open, which features the largest prize purse in the state (Labor Day weekend), and the Kapalua Betsy N. Aglesen Tennis Invitational Pro-Am in November. There are a total of ten courts available at Kapalua; four have lights for night play. Dress code dictates shirt with sleeves for men; no cut-offs, bathing suits or running shoes.
Open daily 7 a.m.-9:30 p.m. Cost $10 per person, $9 for resort guests. Pro shop open daily 7:30 a.m.-8 p.m.

Makena Tennis Club
5415 Makena Alanui Rd.,
Makena
• 879-8777

Located at the new Maui Prince Hotel near Wailea, these six hard courts are among the newest on the island. Dress code dictates tennis attire and disallows tank tops and bathing suits.
Open daily 7 a.m.-6:15 p.m. Cost $8 per person per day, $5 for resort guests. Pro shop open when courts are open.

Wailea Tennis Club
131 Wailea Ike Pl.,
Wailea
• 879-1958

Three of the best grass courts on the island and an additional 11 Plexi-pave courts (three with night lights) await at the Wailea Tennis Club in the Wailea Resort area. Services include a complete pro shop and a tennis academy (taught by head pro Joe Violette and a staff of three teaching professionals).
Open daily 7 a.m.-9 p.m. (grass 10 a.m.-5 p.m.). Cost $10 per day for guests at the Wailea resorts, $12 per day for visitors.

WINDSURFING

Hawaiian Island Windsurfing
460 Dairy Rd.,
Kahului
• 871-4981

This well-established professional operation features a rental inventory of more than 200 sailboards and better than 300 sails, as well as a full-service repair facility and retail store with everything for the windsurfer. This shop features Jimmy Lewis sailboards and Gastra sails and is also home of Windsurfing West, one of the best instructional schools on the island. Rentals include board, sail, complete rig, harness and car roof racks. *Open daily 9 a.m.-6 p.m. Rentals: $40 per day, $225 per week. Beginning lessons $49 (3 hours, gear included). Advanced lessons $44 per hour.*

Hawaiian Sailboarding Techniques
230 Hana Hwy.,
Kahului
• 871-5423

Maui's best board-sailing school, Hawaiian Sailboarding Techniques is owned and operated by one of the top professional board sailors ever to evolve out of Maui waters, Alan Cadiz. His success on the local and international board-sailing circuit has been translated very well into success as an instructor, particularly in refining a student's technique. Alan and a team of certified instructors use video tape, instructor-to-student radio communications and beach-based wave simulators. Classes limited to three students. *Open Mon.-Sat. 8:30 a.m.-12:30 p.m. Beginners classes $60 (2.5 hours); advanced classes (3 hours) $90; ongoing instruction (10 hours in 4 lessons) $225; private instruction $45 per hour.*

Hi-Tech Sailboards
230 Hana Hwy.,
Kahului
• 877-2111 or 579-9297

This growing name on the international board-sailing circuit was founded on Maui and still manages the oldest windsurfing shop on the island in Paia. Both shops offer complete sailboard manufacture, service and rental programs, featuring Hi-Tech sailboards, Simmer, North and Neil Pryde sails. A complete line of beachwear and sailboarding accessories is also available. Hi-Tech sponsors the Maui Slalom race series every other Saturday, June through August; races are open to the public. *Open daily 9 a.m.-6 p.m. Introductory lessons (2.5 hours) $60, equipment included; private lessons $45/hour.*

Hunt Hawaii
Box 989,
Paia
• 579-8129

This handy little board-sailing and surf shop in the plantation town of Paia offers everything the visiting windsurfer could want—from custom sailboards (including high technology carbon/epoxy slalom boards) by Doug Hunt to a complete rental inventory, accessory sales and beachwear section. They can also arrange for lessons through Hawaiian Sailboarding Techniques. *Open daily 9 a.m.-6 p.m. Rentals: $35 per day, including board, sail, rig, harness and roof racks.*

The Maui Windsurf Co.

520 Keolani Pl.,
Kahului
• 877-4816

This top-ranked board-sailing business features a full-service retail store, rental facility, service center and also incorporates Maui Magic Windsurfing Schools, one of the best of its kind on the island. The rental service offers a unique program of unlimited free exchanges to take into account skill increases or changing conditions. All rentals include two sails, rig, board, harness and roof rack. The company also features on-beach videos at Kanaha Beach Park. Maui Magic Windsurfing Schools pioneered the use of customized waterproof radios to allow instructor-to-student communications on separate channels. This is a first-class operation.

Open daily 8:30 a.m.-5:30 p.m. Rentals: $40 per day; $175 for five days. Lessons: $55 for a three-hour introductory course, gear included; three full lessons $150.

Second Wind Windsurfing

111 Hana Hwy.,
Kahului
• 877-7467,
(800) 852-7467

A "do-it-all" facility with the most delightful radio advertisement in the business, Second Wind buys, sells, rents, trades and consigns all manner of sailboarding gear. They also offer some of the promptest, most efficient board and gear repair on the island and a pleasant retail atmosphere that offers everything for the board sailor including beachwear and wetsuits. Gear rented as complete sets or by the piece. Rental prices include board, sail, rig, harness and roof racks.

Open daily 9 a.m.-6 p.m. Rentals: $35 per day, $200 per week. Lessons: Arranged through Hawaiian Sailboarding Techniques.

WHERE THE WATERS RUN RED

The ancient Hawaiian legends tell of a tragedy on the southern shores of Haleakala. A terribly cruel Hawaiian chief, Ka'akea, accused his wife, Popo'alaea, of having had an affair with another man and, as punishment, he would beat her. Finally, Popo'alaea fled to the Wai'anapanapa ("Glistening Water") Cave. Inside the cave was a hidden chamber that could be reached only by swimming underwater. At night her attendants would come out of the cave and search for food. One night Ka'akea spotted them on their midnight run. In a rage, he dove into the water, swam to Popo'alaea and killed her. When her servants returned they saw that the cavern waters had turned red, and they knew immediately what had happened.

Even today, when the spirit of Popo'alaea returns to the scene of her death, the waters of the Wai'anapanapa are said to be red.

BASICS

GETTING AROUND

Airport

If you have decided not to rent a car, taxis are available at the taxi stand at Maui's main airport in Kahului, or you can contact them from special phones within the terminal. At West Maui Airport, the **Kapalua West Maui Airport Trolley** runs daily from 8:15 a.m. to 5:15 p.m. and will take you at no charge to the Kaanapali hotels and resorts. The Kapalua Bay Resort has a free shuttle service for its guests. The Hotel Hana-Maui will pick up guests at Hana Airport.

Cars

Rental cars are generally readily available at or near Kahului Airport from national and local agencies, and most do not charge for mileage. Several agencies operate out of the West Maui and Hana airports, and at hotels and resorts as well. Airport listings: **Alamo** (877-3466); **Andres Rent-a-Car** (877-5378); **Atlas U-Drive** (877-7208); **Avis** (871-7575); **Budget** (Kahului Airport, 871-8811; and West Maui Airport, 669-7044); **Dollar** (Kahului Airport, 877-2731; West Maui Airport, 669-7400; Hana Airport, 248-8237); **Hertz** (877-5167, Kahului Airport and West Maui Airport, 669-9042); **Kamaaina Rent-a-Car** (877-5460); **National** (871-8851); **Payless Rent a Car** (877-5600); **Thrifty** (871-7596); **Tropical** (Kahului Airport, 877-0002; and West Maui Airport, 661-0061). Luxury cars can be rented from **EuroClassic**

(871-7467) and **Sunshine** (871-6222). Four-wheel drive vehicles are not necessary, but are available at **Adventures** (877-6626) **and Maui Sights & Treasures** (879-6260).

Taxis

There are no public buses on Maui. Because of distances and traffic, taxis can become expensive. They are metered at $1.40 for the first sixth of a mile and 20 cents for each additional sixth of a mile or minute of waiting, plus 25 cents for each bag handled by the driver and $3 per surfboard or bicycle. Be forewarned: from the airport at Kahului to a Kaanapali hotel can easily run as high as $50. Many companies, including most taxis, offer sightseeing tours. The major taxi companies are **Alii Cab** in Kaanapali (661-3688), **Kaanapali Taxi** (661-5285), **Kihei Taxi** (879-3000) and **Yellow Cab** in Kahului (877-7000).

TELEPHONE NUMBERS

The area code for all numbers on the Islands is 808 .

Chamber of Commerce 871-7711
Civil Defense 243-7285
  (after hours) 244-6400
Coast Guard .... (800) 331-6176
Crisis Center 244-7407
Directory Assistance (local) 411
  (interisland) 1-555-1212
Emergency
  (Ambulance, Fire, Police, Rescue) ... 911
Hana Airport 248-8208
Hospital 242-2036
Hyperbaric Center 1-523-9155
Kahului Airport 877-0078
Library Information 877-5048
Marine Forecasts 877-3477
Poison Control Center .. (800) 362-3585
Postal Information 244-4815
Time 242-0212
Visitor's Information Bureau . 871-8691
Weather 877-5111
West Maui Airport 669-0228

GAULT MILLAU GUIDES:
WE LEAD YOU TO THE GOOD LIFE

"You will enjoy their prose" - *US News &World Report*
"Breezy, honest, specific" - *Chicago Tribune*
"Gault Millau is the authority" - *South China Morning Post*

Also available:

The Best of Chicago
The Best of London
The Best of Los Angeles
The Best of Paris
The Best of San Francisco
The Best of Washington, D.C.

MORE *GAULT MILLAU* "BEST OF" GUIDES

The guidebook series known throughout Europe for its wit and savvy now reveals the best of major U.S., European and Asian destinations. Gault Millau books include full details on the best of everything that makes these places special: the restaurants, diversions, nightlife, hotels, shops and arts. The guides also offer practical information on getting around and enjoying each area. Perfect for visitors and residents alike.

Please send me the books checked below:

- ☐ The Best of Chicago $15.95
- ☐ The Best of France $16.95
- ☐ The Best of Hawaii..$16.95
- ☐ The Best of Hong Kong $16.95
- ☐ The Best of Italy $16.95
- ☐ The Best of London $16.95
- ☐ The Best of Los Angeles $16.95
- ☐ The Best of New England $15.95
- ☐ The Best of New Orleans $16.95
- ☐ The Best of New York $16.95
- ☐ The Best of Paris $16.95
- ☐ The Best of San Francisco..$16.95
- ☐ The Best of Washington, D.C. $16.95

PRENTICE HALL TRADE DIVISION
Order Department - Travel Books
200 Old Tappan Road
Old Tappan, NJ 07675

In the U.S., include $2 (UPS shipping charge) for the first book, and $1 for each additional book. Outside the U.S., $3 and $1.

Enclosed is my check or money order made out to Prentice Hall Press, for $_____

NAME _____

ADDRESS _____

CITY _____ STATE _____

ZIP _____ COUNTRY _____

GOINGS-ON

February

- **Maui Marine Art Expo,** a prestigious and extensive exhibition of works by national marine artists. Runs through February and March; Maui Inter-Continental Wailea Hotel; 879-1922.

March

- **O'Neill Invitational Professional Boardsailing Competition,** featuring the best windsurfers, held in March or April; 475-7500.
- **Prince Kuhio Day** (March 26), state holiday celebrating Hawaii's first delegate to the U.S. Congress; 871-8691.

April

- **Aloha State Archery Association Annual State Field Archery Championships,** in which all islands vie for state champion; Kahului; 871-8691.
- **Art Maui,** a prestigious juried show including paintings, drawings, prints, photographs, collage, sculpture, fiber art, ceramics and glass; Makawao; 572-6660.
- **Buddha Day,** celebrated by Buddhist temples on all islands; 871-8691.

May

- **Annual Barrio Festival,** a Filipino community cultural celebration with arts and crafts, games, contests and food booths, Wailuku; 871-8691.
- **Kaupakalua Roping Club's Memorial Day Weekend Rodeo,** with a full schedule of rodeo events; 572-5951.

June

- **Annual Up-country Fun Fair,** an old-fashioned farm fair, featuring 4-H farmer's products, a fun run, sports tournaments, entertainment and food booths; Makawao; 572-8883.
- **Bon Season,** June through August. Buddhist temples host colorful bon dances. Check newspapers; 871-8691.

- **Kamehameha Day Archery Tournament**, the state's largest outdoor archery tournament; Kahului; 871-8691.
- **Kamehameha Day Celebration Parade**; Lahaina; 871-8691.
- **Kapalua Music Festival**, chamber music by acclaimed musicians from across the U.S.; Kapalua Bay Hotel; 669-5273.
- **Victoria-to-Maui Yacht Race**, during even-numbered years the yachts leave Victoria, British Columbia, in late June and arrive in Lahaina about twelve days later; 661-3557.

July

- **Annual Maui Jaycees Carnival**, featuring games, rides, entertainment, food and merchandise booths, and an opening-day parade; Kahului; 244-5505.
- **Fireworks Display at Whalers Village**, Kaanapali Beach Operators Association; 661-3271.
- **Great Kalua Pig Cook-Off**, a Fourth of July competition with $1,000 cash prize for the best pig roaster in the state. Watch participants prepare pigs and *imus* (underground ovens), with a full day of entertainment and parade; free canoe and pony rides, craft and food booths; Royal Lahaina Hotel; 661-3611.
- **Kapalua Wine Symposium**, a July gathering of wine and food experts for a series of formal tastings and panel discussions; Kapalua Bay Hotel; 669-0244.
- **Kihei Fourth of July Parade**; Kihei; 871-8691.
- **Makawao Statewide Rodeo**, one of the best, plus annual Fourth of July Rodeo Parade; Oskie Rice Arena, Makawao; 572-9689.
- **Old-fashioned Fourth of July Celebration and Crafts Fair**; Makawao; 572-6560.

August

- **Admission Day**, a state holiday celebrating Hawaii's admission as the 50th state; 871-8691.
- **Haleakala Run to the Sun**, an uphill run of 36 miles, finishing at the top of Haleakala National Park; Kahului; 877-5827.

September

- **Aloha Week**, celebrated September and October on all islands; 871-8691.
- **Hana Relay**, a 54-mile team run; Kahului to Hana; 242-6042.

- **Kapalua Open Tennis Championship**, a Hawaii Grand Prix event featuring the state's largest tennis purse for Hawaii's top players; Kapalua Tennis Garden; 669-0244.
- **Polo season begins**, through mid-November, weekends; Oskie Rice Arena, Makawao or Kula Polo Field; 871-8691.

October

- **Aloha Classic Boardsailing Competition**, Hookipa; 475-7500.
- **Halloween**, Maui goes all out for this holiday! Best place to see and be seen is on Front Street, Lahaina.
- **Maui County Fair**, Kahului; 871-8691.
- **Wailea Hoolaulea**, an annual two-day event celebrating the Hawaiian heritage. Pau Parade, ancient and modern hula, Hawaiian games and food, lei contest and entertainment; 1-531-9723.

November

- **Isuzu Kapalua International Golf Championship**, world's leading golfers compete for the Super Bowl of golf and a purse of over $650,000; 669-4844.
- **Kapalua Betsy Nagelson Pro-Am Tennis Invitational**, a select field of professional and amateur women competing in pro-doubles and pro-am doubles tournaments; Kapalua Bay Resort; 669-5677.
- **Maui Classic**, the preseason showcase for college basketball. Thanksgiving weekend. Televised nationally; Lahaina Civic Center; 661-4685.
- **Michelob Polo Cup and Barbecue**, an exhibition match of highest-rated players; Olinda Outdoor Polo Field, Makawao; 877-3987.
- **Na Mele o Maui**, a five-day festival of Hawaiian music, dance, arts and crafts, cultural displays, canoe races and luaus; 871-8691.

December

- **Bodhi Day**, the traditional Buddhist Day of Enlightenment; 1-522-9200.

BIG ISLAND

RESTAURANTS

For more information on how our rating system works, how we estimate meal prices and so on, turn to About the Restaurants, page 6. Also in that section is a Toque Tally, page 10, which lists all the restaurants in this book by rating.

BY CUISINE

AMERICAN

Aloha Café (*Kainalui*)
Bree Garden Restaurant (*Kamuela*)
Harrington's (*Hilo*)
Harrington's (*Kawaihae*)
Kona Provision Co. (*Kohala*)
Kona Ranch House (*Kailua-Kona*)
Quinn's Almost By The Sea
(*Kailua-Kona*)

CONTINENTAL

Batik Room (*Kawaihae*)
Beach Club (*Kailua-Kona*)
Bree Garden Restaurant (*Kamuela*)
Eclipse (*Kailua-Kona*)
Edelweiss (*Kamuela*)
Gallery Restaurant (*Kohala*)
Huggo's (*Kailua-Kona*)
Jameson's by the Sea (*Kailua-Kona*)
Kona Hilton Beach and Tennis
Resort (*Kailua-Kona*)
The Terrace Restaurant (*Keauhou*)

CREOLE

Roussel's (*Hilo*)

FRENCH

La Bourgogne (*Kailua-Kona*)
Roussel's (*Hilo*)

HAWAIIAN

Canoe House (*Kohala*)
Fisherman's Landing (*Kailua-Kona*)

ITALIAN

Donatoni's (*Kohala*)
Phillip Paolo's (*Kailua-Kona*)
Poki's Pasta (*Kailua-Kona*)

JAPANESE

Kanazawa-tei (*Kailua-Kona*)

NEW AMERICAN

Hartwell's at Hale Kea (*Kamuela*)
Merriman's (*Kamuela*)

PACIFIC RIM

Kilauea Lodge and Restaurant
(*Volcano Village*)
The Terrace Restaurant (*Keauhou*)

SEAFOOD

Fisherman's Landing (*Kailua-Kona*)
Gallery Restaurant (*Kohala*)
Huggo's (*Kailua-Kona*)
Jameson's by the Sea (*Kailua-Kona*)
Kona Inn Restaurant (*Kailua-Kona*)
Quinn's Almost by the Sea
(*Kailua-Kona*)

SUSHI

Kanazawa-tei (*Kailua-Kona*)

THAI

Batik Room (*Kawaihae*)
Poo Ping Thai Cuisine
(*Kailua-Kona*)

WHAT'S IN A NAME?

Ordering fish in a Hawaiian restaurant can be akin to sailing into uncharted waters. All those strange names can have a numbing effect on the brain, so we've produced this simple guide to make sure that your palate doesn't suffer. We're only including the most popular, so don't look for the likes of hapuu or oio, please. All are saltwater fish.

AHI - Here's one Hawaiian fish that has made it onto mainland restaurant menus, along with mahimahi. Usually served grilled, a yellowtail tuna can weigh up to 300 pounds. The white, firm flesh is also delicious as sushi.

AKU - This is another type of tuna. Much smaller than the yellowtail, it averages around twenty pounds.

AKULE - In Hawaii, the bigeye scad has to be over seven inches to be called "akule." Those in the five-to-seven-inch range are known as "maau," while those that are up to five inches are referred to as "halalu."

MAHIMAHI - You might just remember this as the world's most delicious fish, or be horrified by the translation as "dolphin." No, it's not the same dolphin that we all know and love, and, yes, it is the tastiest fish in the world, thank you.

ONAGA - Occasionally seen on Island menus, the onaga is none other than the ubiquitous red snapper. The average size is about four pounds.

ONO - Some folks love the flavor of the six-foot-long wahoo, but all others can say is "watch out for the numerous bones." It's a great fish for display cooking.

OPAKAPAKA - Did you realize that besides the red snapper, there is also a blue snapper? This delicious fish is usually served in filets.

ULUA - You probably know him best as jack crevalle, but in Hawaii this tasty jack goes by a different name. The young fish is called "papio."

Aloha Café

Aloha Theater Building,
Hwy. 11,
Kainaliu
• 322-3383
AMERICAN

12/20

In the cool mountain town of Kainaliu (a one-street village south of Kailua-Kona taken right out of the 1940s), the Aloha Café is as close to culinary heaven in a bistro as Hawaii can offer. Situated in a historical theater, the tiny café produces excellent breakfasts, lunches and dinners at extraordinarily low prices. Grab a table on the outside covered *lanai* for the view, a panorama that stretches from rolling hills out to sportfishing boats on the horizon. People-watchers might prefer to sit in the French bistro–style interior, which features rotating displays of eclectic works by local artists. Forget the menu; instead, check out the daily specials, such as the "Father Guido Sarducci" breakfast omelet—ricotta and Parmesan cheese, artichoke hearts, mushrooms, garlic and basil, topped off with a home-made banana muffin and delicious home fries (with or without more garlic). For lunch and dinner don't pass up the fresh fish. Choice of tuna marinated in a spicy tamari sauce or mahimahi in a ginger-and-cashew sauce. Leave room for the homemade desserts: an assortment of cakes, pies, pastries and oversize cookies. The Aloha is one of the few restaurants anywhere in the state to serve real, 100-percent, locally grown Kona coffee. The clientele holds your interest—local coffee farmers in faded, torn T-shirts and boots to elegantly dressed businesspeople on expense accounts, with a few camera-toting tourists thrown in. The waiters are mostly struggling actors, all helpful, but some-what slow when the restaurant is filled to capacity. A small but interesting wine list emphasizes California Chardonnays. The selection of imported beers is one of the best on the island. Dinner for two, with a bottle of wine, is about $60, worth every penny.
Open Mon.-Sat. 8 a.m.-8 p.m. Cards: MC, V.

Batik Room

Mauna Kea Beach Hotel,
Kawaihae
• 882-7222
CONTINENTAL/THAI

8/20

The Mauna Kea Beach Hotel earned itself a reputation for exceptional quality. At first glance, the Batik Room is in keeping with that level of excellence. Male patrons are required to don jackets, which adds a certain monied esprit de corps to the place. The restaurant's decor is understated, with Indonesian-Thai artifacts, and the menu lists page after page of creative, exotic dishes. But beware, as disappointment looms straight ahead. We soon found our food to be overcooked, oversauced and over-priced, which made us say "over and out" to the chic Batik. The fresh fish of the day, which according to the menu is "harvested daily from our Island waters," tasted, to our palates, not so. The special appetizer of the day, abalone from a nearby aquaculture farm, was a tiny portion floating in an ocean of cream sauce. The spinach salad was creatively laden with carrots and shiitake mushrooms, but there was barely a nouvelle-size serving of spinach on the plate. The curried tomato soup with whipped minted cream sounded divine, but plummeted into an imaginative mix of ill-combined tastes. Desserts were equally misguided. Rumor has it that many of the ancien régime dishes featured on the menu, such as the various curries, are kept there because returning patrons—many of whom vacation here every year—demand it. But we are sure that even the most loyal will soon begin to demand competent cooking as well. Even with excellent service and relaxing surroundings the Batik Room is disappointing, especially when you have to pay $150 for two with wine. Instead, try The Garden, where the promise is fulfilled.

Open daily 7 p.m.-10 p.m. All major cards.

Beach Club

Kona-by-the-Sea
Condominium 75-6106
Alii Dr.,
Kailua-Kona
• 329-0290
SEAFOOD/
CONTINENTAL

9/20

When Chef Mark Tuhy was creating new and magical dishes here, it was the hottest restaurant on the Big Island. But Tuhy's no longer here. Of course, the location, right on a white-sand beach (you are seated amid swaying palm trees, the sand beneath your feet), is still the most romantic in Kona. Nothing beats seeing the moon glow on the rolling surf. The menu has retained traces of Tuhy's creative cuisine: Aztec shrimp with papaya relish, fisherman's minipizza with local seafood and cheese, spicy Thai salad with hot strips of filet of beef. Or pastas such as "ragin' Cajun" or black calamari with sun-dried tomatoes and goat cheese. Our favorite dishes were the blackened fish on a painted plate, New Orleans style with three-color sauce, or half-cooked ahi (tuna) with fresh cumin, jalapeño rice and Mexican vegetables. Desserts include the usual suspects: brownies, apple pie and Häagen-Dazs ice-cream bars. Owner Margo Elliopoulos has been busy with her successful catering business, leaving no one to mind the store, and the lack of service has been appalling. We had to beg our waiter six times for water during a recent night when the restaurant was not even a third full. We waited 23 minutes after the table had been cleared to get our check while the staff chatted among themselves. Once a bargain at any price, now we find that dinners for two, approximately $125, including wine, are not worth the tariff or the indignity.

Open Tues.-Sat. 6 p.m.-9 p.m. Cards: AE, MC, V.

La Bourgogne

Kuakini Plaza South,
Kuakini Hwy. &
Nalani St.,
Kailua-Kona
• 329-6711
FRENCH

8/20

It's French cooking the old-fashioned way, from the old school where calorie-filled sauce was king and no one even imagined that the word "cholesterol" existed. Down another Pernod, light another Gitanes and let's talk politics. Understandably, La Bourgogne caters to an older crowd. Patrons walk through a time warp from Hawaii into a decor that is suitably dark, rich and heavy. The menu carries French onion soup baked with cheese and homemade pâté for starters; entrées run the whole

gamut of French classics from coquilles St-Jacques Provençale and roast saddle of lamb with either garlic dressing or creamy mustard sauce, to sweetbreads of veal with Madeira sauce. The key word here is sauce, plenty of it. Desserts are in keeping with the high-calorie family: cherries jubilee, custard-cream pudding and amaretto cheesecake. The service is friendly and attentive. Dinner for two, with wine, is about $100.
Open Mon.-Sat. 6 p.m.-10 p.m. All major cards.

Bree Garden Restaurant
64-5188 Kinohoa St., Kamuela
• 885-5888
AMERICAN/
CONTINENTAL

12/20

Bernd and Diana Bree have planted a cozy, quaint oasis in what once was inhospitable territory for the palate. We like to arrive a little before our reservations to have a drink in the comfortable bar, where patrons sink into overstuffed couches and watch the rain pelt the old-fashioned windows. The main dining room features ceiling-to-floor windows overlooking a giant banyan tree in the courtyard. Muted lighting creates a dreamy atmosphere for clients who range from elegant, older Waimea residents to yuppie tourists, sporting sunburns acquired at the nearby Kohala resorts. The wine list is small but complete with a number of 1986 California Sauvignon Blancs. If you can't decide from among the many choices on the main menu, there is a prix-fixe menu. For starters, think of the angel-hair pasta with fresh tomato-and-basil sauce and a brunoise of carrots, or the seared cajun carpaccio sprinkled with black-olive pesto. Unusual is the pepper-broiled salmon steak, which has been marinated in olive oil and peppercorns, then laced with a watercress-mustard butter. The meat-and-potatoes crowd will relish the smoked pork chops served with juniper-apple sauerkraut. Desserts here are deemed "naughty treats," and justly so. The naughtiest is the Triple Passion Delight: macadamia-nut butter crust filled with passion fruit and cream cheese. Sinfully delicious. Dinner à la carte for two, with wine, will cost around $100; prix-fixe dinner is $33 per person.
Open daily 4:30 p.m.-8:30 p.m. Cards: AE, MC, V.

Canoe House
Mauni Lani Bay Hotel, Kohala
• 885-6622
HAWAIIAN

Just off the beach in a covered, open-air setting, the Canoe House emphasizes Island cuisine in casual elegance. Expect to receive a lei before being seated. The ancient koa canoe of the restaurant's name hangs from the open-beamed ceiling. In addition to chef Alan Wong's regular menu, the Canoe House has a sushi bar. Sample from the creative menu that includes a range of local food presented with culinary flourish. For example: from the Orient, wok-fried Kohala-coast snapper wrapped in nori with wasabe sauce and kim chee; from Indonesia, chicken saté; from the mainland (with an Island twist)—rack of lamb

glazed with poha jelly. Combination sushi-sashimi plates are available for those who want a meal and their sushi, too. The wine list carries some 75 labels from California and France, by region. Service is impeccable. The dessert plate is a treat: samples of all the desserts on the menu. All this, plus an ocean view. Dinner for two, with wine, is about $120.
Open nightly 5:30 p.m.-10 p.m. All major cards.

Donatoni's
Hyatt Regency Waikoloa,
One Waikoloa Beach Resort,
Kohala
• 885-1234
ITALIAN

12/20

If you're looking for Donatello's, try San Francisco. Here in Hawaii—with some legal persuading—it's Donatoni's, the Hyatt's upscale Italian eatery. The restaurant is located near the swankier rooms and has an exterior design that's vaguely *faux* Italianate. In keeping with the evening's romantic theme, ride the gondola to Donatoni's door.

The food is good average Italian, but could bring back the taste of home, especially if you're tired of eating local fish. There's nothing new on this menu, so don't be intimidated by all of the Italian words.

For example, under the antipasti category, the calamari fritti tasted very much like fried squid. The antipasto salad was fine. Pizzas reminded us of the scale of the hotel—gigantic. Just right for carbo-loading after a day of golf, tennis, dolphin encounters and walking, if you missed the boat to the restaurant. Also, go right ahead and order the pasta of your choice, since they all taste pretty much the same. Seafood-lovers can pick the linguine alla pescatore (or try the cioppino); vegetarians will enjoy the trenette al filetto di pomodora.

Desserts are optional after this heavy meal. The wine list is comprehensive, with a number of Italian wines by the glass. One word of caution for late romantics and diners—get there before Spats disco erupts. The music is louder than Kiluaea on the other side of the island. For two, count on spending $100.
Open daily 5:30 p.m.-9:30 p.m. All major cards.

Eclipse
75-5711 Kuakini Hwy.,
Kailua-Kona
• 329-4686
CONTINENTAL

8/20

A Kona institution for more than a decade, the Eclipse is packed with the business-lunch crowd during the week and is one of the few late dancing spots on the weekends. The menu features predictably all right but uninspired food: the usual fresh fish, prawns, scampi, steaks and chicken. The fern-filled restaurant has a quiet, comfortable bar area, and service is generally quick and pleasant, but as you would expect from the name, this Eclipse doesn't shine much. Dinner for two, with wine, runs about $78.
Open Mon.-Fri. 11 a.m.-2 p.m. & 5-9 p.m., Fri.-Sun. 5 p.m.-9 p.m. All major cards.

Edelweiss

Rte. 19,
Kamuela
• 885-6800
CONTINENTAL

10/20

In the climate of Waimea, the domain of Chef Hans-Peter Hager, who began his apprenticeship at age 13 in Germany, Edelweiss features alpine creations to good effect. The chaletlike restaurant usually has a long waiting line for dinner; so come prepared to linger in the crowded bar (they do not take reservations). Once seated, don't spend too much time looking at the menu—your waiter or waitress will tell you all about the day's half dozen specials, usually German-Swiss cuisine based on venison, game birds, veal and chicken. Sautéed veal, lamb, beef and bacon with pfifferling (chanterelle mushrooms) and rack of lamb basted in garlic, mustard and herbs constitute the basic fare here. In the past, we have found the chef to have a heavy hand with the salt shaker. Dinner for two with wine will run about $85. Light dinners (bratwurst with sauerkraut; veal and pork sausage with Rösti) are also available for $10, with coffee. *Open Tues.-Sat. 11:30 a.m.-1:30 p.m. & 5 p.m.-9 p.m., Sun. 11:30 a.m.-1:30 p.m. & 5 p.m.-8 p.m. Cards: MC, V.*

HOME BREW

Question: What is the only coffee grown in the United States?
Answer: Good old Kona coffee, grown on 2,600 acres of volcanic slopes, near Kealakekua on the Big Island.

Question: What is the second most traded commodity in the world, after oil?
Answer: Coffee.

Fisherman's Landing

Kona Inn Shopping Village,
75-5744 Alii Dr.,
Kailua-Kona
• 326-2555
SEAFOOD/HAWAIIAN

10/20

In a very romantic setting on the veranda of the old Kona Inn (now a shopping center), right on the ocean, Fisherman's Landing is a seafood-lover's cornucopia. As you walk into the open-air restaurant you pass an iced display of the day's fresh catches. In the evening, Hawaiian music plays gently in the background. The creative menu, designed by Chef Harry Yoshida, features a blend of Asian and Island cuisine, such as the dragon-roll appetizers (a mixture of Asian shrimp and vegetables wrapped in won ton pi, then deep-fried) or sweet-and-sour shrimp lychee. Other "must tastes" are the shellfish sauté sec (crab claws, scallops, shrimps, mussels and clams with fresh basil, shallots, garlic, mushrooms and wine served over fettuccine) and the fresh fish Creole. They also serve a wide selection from the butcher's block, such as steaks and prime ribs. The drawbacks to this ocean-view restaurant are its size (too big and open for a quiet, romantic dinner) and the service (slow and often untutored in the intricacies of local fish). Complete dinner for two, with dessert and wine, runs about $75. *Open Sun.-Thurs. 11:30 a.m.-2 p.m. & 5:30 p.m.-10 p.m., Fri.-Sat. 11:30 a.m.-2 p.m. & 5:30 p.m.-10:30 p.m. All major cards.*

Gallery Restaurant

Mauna Lani Resort, Kohala
• 885-7777
SEAFOOD/
CONTINENTAL

Exotic Hawaiian ornamental flowers punctuate the muted pastel decor. Faint background music and indirect lighting soften the sounds and the shapes of this restaurant. Elegantly dressed waiters and waitresses speak in hushed tones. Patrons usually include the upscale guests of nearby Mauna Lani Resort and other expensive Kohala hotels. Reservations are a must in this dining oasis. Executive Chef Ann Sutherland, who turned to cooking after studying law and is a graduate of the well-regarded California Culinary Academy in San Francisco, offers one of the most creative mixes of Hawaii's indigenous food. Try the shrimp-phyllo appetizer in a lemon beurre blanc, Cajun pasta of shrimp and scallops or Thai beef. Even a simple thing such as a spinach salad has Sutherland's special touch: a honey-curry dressing that imparts a tantalizing sweet-and-spicy flavor. Her magic combinations with seafood are responsible for the Gallery's reputation—locally caught fish broiled with tomato-shrimp sauce or macadamia-nut pesto, or (our favorite) broiled with papaya-and-lemon-butter sauce. Other dishes we recommend are the wok-charred ahi (half-cooked spicy sashimi served with an Island-fruit-and-scallion relish), lilikoi scallops (sautéed with passion-fruit butter and cilantro) and Hawaiian shrimp (stir-fried with garlic sauce on taro leaves). Desserts include a delightful double-chocolate cake with raspberries and a passion-fruit custard with meringue topping. The large wine list includes a good selection of Champagnes, such as Veuve Cliquot Pompardin, Taittinger Contes de Champagne and (according to the French, this is a sparkling wine) Schramsburg Blanc de Noir from California. Dinner for two, with wine, costs about $125.
Open daily 6 p.m.-9 p.m. Cards: AE, MC, V.

Harrington's

Kawaihae Shopping Center,
Kawaihae
• 882-7997

135 Kalanianaole St., Hilo
• 961-4966
AMERICAN

10/20

Harrington's has been an institution in Hilo for years. It recently added a second restaurant in the Kawaihae shopping center to serve the visitors to the Kohala coast. The new restaurant is decorated in old-Hawaiian-plantation style: small-paned windows open to overlook the sunset on the coast, high wooden ceiling and pastel prints along the walls. The menu offers everything from seafood (lobster, prawns, scallops, calamari) to their specialties: steak, prime rib and chicken. Daily specials include fresh fish, stir-fried chicken and teriyaki dishes. Harrington's gained quite a reputation for its slavic steak (a sirloin steak broiled, then sliced thin and topped with garlic-mushroom-butter sauce). The wine list is ample and reasonably priced (they also offer a half dozen premium wines daily by the glass). The Kawaihae location has a special children's menu. Two will spend, with a bottle of wine, about $75.
Open nightly 5:30 p.m.-10 p.m. Cards: MC, V.

Hartwell's at Hale Kea

Kawaihae Rd.,
Kamuela
• 885-6095
NEW AMERICAN

8/20

Fostered in the recently renovated former home of Laurance Rockefeller, Hale Kea is a combination of unique boutique shops and Hartwell's restaurant. Restaurant seating is in various rooms of the 1897 house: the library, *paniolo* (cowboy) room, dining room and outdoor lanai. With the exception of tourists at nearby tables, the atmosphere has remained true to an old plantation home, and many old photographs help add to that ambience. The menu features locally grown food. One of the specialties of the house that we do not enjoy seems to be to substitute dishes without consultation. We ordered ahi carpaccio (fresh tuna, thinly sliced in a balsamic vinaigrette, with avocado), only to receive sashimi. When we pointed this out to our waiter, he merely shrugged and said there was no ahi carpaccio tonight, something that did not seem important to him when we placed our order. The fresh fish of the day came to the table dead on arrival, a victim of merciless overcooking. Hale Kea is a wonderful place to wander around (get there before dark to see the exquisitely landscaped gardens) and shop. Watch the sunset or come after dinner for coffee and dessert (Waimea strawberry mousse, gingerbread with warm lilikoi sauce). Dinner for two, with wine, will cost about $115. *Open daily 11 a.m.-10 p.m. Cards: AE, MC, V.*

Huggo's

75-5828 Kahakai Rd.,
Kailua-Kona
• 329-1493
SEAFOOD/
CONTINENTAL

10/20

Huggo's is not just on the ocean, it extends out over the ocean. With an elegant wood interior and a panoramic view of the Kona shoreline, this spot features dependably good food and excellent drinks. Founded by Huggo von Platen, a Hawaiian "Hemingway" and Kona resident, Huggo's used to be the "in" spot for fishermen and charter-boat captains. The food was plain but plentiful fare, and drinks were cheap. Several years ago, Huggo turned the restaurant over to his son, Eric, who redecorated, renovated and revamped it. When the bartenders started pouring fine French and California wines by the glass, the beer-swilling fishermen moved on and the business crowd moved in. With its seafront location, it's only natural that Huggo's features fresh fish daily, and good steaks as well. Seafood comes grilled, broiled, sautéed or blackened (with Chef Paul Prudhomme's blackened-fish recipe). Huggo's also is known for its salad bar, which can be ordered as a meal in itself. Lunches are alive with Kona's business and financial community. Reservations are a must for dinner, as the restaurant is as popular with local residents as it is with tourists. At night a spotlight on the reef outside the restaurant attracts manta rays that dance in the surf. Wine and dinner for two costs around $95. *Open Mon.-Fri. 11:30 a.m.-2:30 p.m. & 5:30 p.m.-12:30 a.m., Sat.-Sun. 5:30 p.m.- 12:30 a.m. All major cards.*

Jameson's By The Sea

**77-6452 Alii Dr.,
Kailua-Kona
• 329-3195**
CONTINENTAL/
SEAFOOD

9/20

Overlooking Magic Sands Beach, Jameson's is a brightly lit but cozy restaurant right on the water. Reserve a table outside on the lanai where you can watch the crashing surf. A popular spot for tourists and longtime Kona residents, Jameson's offers an array of seafood: fresh fish, scallops, clams, shrimp and also veal, chicken and beef. The food is generally good, but not all that creative, with dishes gleaned from the meat-and-potatoes/fish-and-rice school of cooking. But there are a few selections on the menu that present a pleasant departure: the Yokohama soup, which is a hearty fish soup with fresh spinach and cream; and the shrimp curry with mango chutney (shrimp and vegetables in a curry sauce topped with bacon and chutney). Lunch, featuring hot and cold sandwiches and salads, attracts tourists who come to ogle the fantastic ocean view. Complete dinner for two, with wine, comes to around $100.
Open Mon.-Fri. 11 a.m.-10 p.m., Sat.-Sun. 5 p.m.-10 p.m. All major cards.

Kanazawa-Tei

**75-5845 Alii Dr.,
Kailua-Kona
• 326-1881**
JAPANESE/SUSHI

10/20

One of a handful of traditional Japanese restaurants in Kona, Kanazawa-Tei includes a sushi bar. Tourists, most of them Japanese, like this place, which is located directly across the street from the Kona Hilton. The service remains fast and friendly, although communications frequently have to be made with signals or gestures. The Japanese staff forgot to take English lessons. If you ask any questions, the waiter will find a translator who can speak English. Pricing here also seems geared toward Tokyo: if you have a yen for sushi, plan on spending the big bucks. The best deal is lunch—one bento lunch can feed two, with a couple of sushi orders on the side. Dinner for two, with saké, ranges from $85 to $105.
Open Mon.-Fri. 11:30 a.m.-2 p.m. & 6 p.m.-9:30 p.m., Sat.-Sun. 6 p.m.-9:30 p.m. Cards: AE, MC, V.

Kilauea Lodge and Restaurant

**Volcano Village (off Hwy. 11),
• 967-7366**
PACIFIC RIM

12/20

Thirty-two Pacific Rim countries shipped rocks to the YMCA in 1938 to erect a fireplace, baptised purposefully the "fireplace of friendship," in this lodge perched on the mist-filled mountaintop volcano. Since this date many a fireplace has turned into a bonfire of illusions. The structure has the feel of old Hawaii: polished wooden floors echo when you walk on them, high-beamed ceiling and walls lined with plantation-style, small-paned windows. But the three-course meals blend old-fashioned country cooking with splashes of the 1990s: crab-filled mushroom caps or blackened sashimi as an appetizer, followed by broiled marlin with mango relish or, on the traditional side, filet mignon béarnaise. Vegetarians will be happy with eggplant supreme (eggplant, onion, green peppers, tomatoes and fresh basil topped with a choice of cheeses) or fettuc-

cine primavera. Chilly temperatures at the 3,750-foot elevation and, more often than not, rainy weather make selecting from the lodge's limited wine list difficult. Save room for the home-cooked desserts; if the macadamia-nut pie is on the menu, don't hesitate. Dinner for two, with wine, runs about $75.
Open Tues.-Sun. 5:30-9 p.m. Cards: AE, MC, V.

Kona Hilton Beach & Tennis Resort
75-5852 Alii Dr.,
Kailua-Kona
• 329-3111
CONTINENTAL

10/20

Usually all-you-can-eat buffets conjure up images of down-on-your-chips Las Vegas: huge smorgasbords, formica tables, screaming children and piles of day-old food simmering tastelessly in rows of stainless-steel chafing dishes. Thankfully, this is not the case during the Kona Hilton weekend buffets. In fact, it's one of the very few food "deals" left in Hawaii: Chef Sam Choy's well-prepared, fresh local food at prices a family can afford. On Friday, it's pasta; Saturday, prime rib; Sunday, an international buffet (call ahead and reserve an oceanside table—otherwise you'll feel as if you're eating in a dark cave). Local entertainers play quietly in the background: a xylophonist entertained us the night we dropped in. The crowd is mainly tourists and the dress ranges from casual resort wear to shorts and T-shirts. The salads feature local exotica in season such as tree fern shoots and spicy Japanese vegetables. The pastas are made to order with a variety of sauces from pesto to marinara. But the desserts are what makes it all worthwhile: more than twenty different kinds, from chocolate-raspberry cake to fruit tarts. Expect to spend around $55 for two, including wine.
Open Fri.-Sun. 5:30 p.m.-8:30 p.m. All major cards.

Kona Inn Restaurant
Kona Inn Shopping Villge,
75-5744 Alii Dr.,
Kailua-Kona
• 329-4455
SEAFOOD

9/20

The decor here conjures up the steamship days. The now defunct Kona Inn was a twenty-room establishment, built by the Inter-Island Steam Navigation Company in 1928 for its passengers. The open-air restaurant overlooks rolling surf along the Kona coast. High-back wooden and rattan chairs seem snatched from an earlier, slower era, when wooden fans interconnected by leather belts would suffice to slowly stir the air into motion. The bar is the hottest singles spot on the coast. The bill of fare features fresh, dependably good fish from local waters, plus chicken and steak. We don't complain about the broiled fresh fish, but there is one weak point: the Kona Inn's version of Cajun-style fish relies heavily on black pepper, light on additional spices, and the result is not Cajun but nearly inedible fish. The wine list of some 40 vintages is not bad and is reasonably priced. Dinner for two, with a bottle of wine, will cost about $90. Lighter fare (sandwiches, salads and soups) is available from the café menu.
Open daily 11:30 a.m.-midnight (café menu), dinner 5:30 p.m.-10 p.m. Cards: AE, MC, V.

Kona Provision Company

Hyatt Regency Waikoloa,
One Waikoloa Beach
Resort,
Kohala
• 885-1234
AMERICAN

10/20

Of all the restaurants in the new Hyatt Regency Waikoloa complex, we like the Kona Provision Company—not only for the fresh local food that's served, but because it is one of the best places to watch the sunset. Perched on a rocky ledge at one end of the massive resort, the Kona is decorated as if it were an old Hawaiian country store, complete with a shop full of local products. Wood floors, big windows and tropical ferns round out the relaxing atmosphere. Everything on the menu is good, but not great: it features fresh local fish, and the beef, veal and lamb are fine but without creative surprise. The staff is quick and friendly. The wine list, with French and California selections, is a little on the pricey side. Dinner for two, with wine, will be about $100.
Open daily 11:30 a.m.-2:30 p.m. & 5:30 p.m.-10:30 p.m. All major cards.

Kona Ranch House

75-5653 Ololi St.,
Kailua-Kona
• 329-7061
AMERICAN

9/20

The Kona Ranch House looks the part, and the grits are down-home as well. It's one of our favorite places to eat breakfast in Kailua-Kona, and you can have lunch and dinner, if you like. The hearty and plentiful food of the *paniolos* (Hawaiian cowboys) comes to table: prime rib, steaks, sirloin and a barbecue-platter special of the day. No one leaves here hungry, since dinners come with soup or salad and a choice of additional rib-stickers from baked potatoes to baked beans, a house specialty. Residents who know the Ranch House offers good, dependable food pack the place for breakfast and lunch. Dinner draws more tourists. Attire is casual, service is quick, and prices remain in keeping with a cowboy's pay. For dinner for two, with house wine, plan to spend around $55.
Open daily 6:30 a.m.-9 p.m. Cards: AE, MC, V.

Merriman's

Opelo Plaza,
Rte. 19,
Kamuela
• 885-6822
NEW AMERICAN

Early in 1990, chef Peter Merriman recently left his position as executive chef at the Gallery Restaurant to open his own, which is devoted to "regional American cuisine" featuring local produce, fish and meats of the island of Hawaii. He has a certain touch. In fact you can watch him at his tactile best: the restaurant wraps around an exhibition kitchen, and Merriman is the guy in the painter's cap, always smiling, with his arms and hands moving at the speed of light. For this neck of the woods, the menu is exceptionally creative. Scrumptious appetizers, such as roasted peppers with Puna goat cheese; lager-steamed shrimp and clams; marlin ceviche marinated in lime with peppers and cilantro; and smoked-salmon linguine served in a garlic-cream-and-dill sauce delight. Merriman's love of the local produce really shows in the salads, which include a spinach salad with hot balsalmic vinaigrette and pipikaula (dried beef), a vine-ripened lokelani tomato salad, topped with Maui onions and a

MACADAMIA MANIA

As well as being the most expensive nut in the world, the macadamia nut must be one of the richest, sweetest, most buttery nuts in the universe. The nut is popping up on menus all over the world, as more and more chefs experiment with it, in salads, as a hidden thickening agent in sweet-hot sauces, as a "breading" for chicken or fish filets, in tarts, waffles and pancakes, and so on.

More than 65 percent of the world's supply of macadamia nuts comes from the Islands. It seems as if these heavenly morsels must just shower down from Hawaii's blessed skies, but in reality the crops are cultivated at great expense. The trees take about five years to bear fruit, and then another ten to reach the peak of productivity. Moreover, the nuts' shells are so tough that it's a difficult and delicate process to break them open without damaging the meat; to do this, the nuts are dried, until the meat separates slightly from the inside of the shell, and then subjected to 300 cubic pounds of pressure. Macadamia nuts are a rare commodity, and Hawaii has a virtual monopoly on their world production, so there isn't exactly price competition. But we say they're worth every penny!

wild-rice-and-watercress salad with Puako-lime vinaigrette. The fish, which is purchased fresh daily from the Kawaihae harbor twenty minutes away, might come grilled with warm shiitakes, sautéed with lemon capers, baked in phyllo dough and served with a saffron-dill sauce, steamed with garlic and ginger or wok-charred (blackened on the outside, raw on the inside). Also tempting are the sea scallops and the Thai shrimp curry. Since Merriman's sits in the middle of Hawaii's cattle country, it's no wonder that Peter offers good beef. Try the tasty steak served with Cabernet Sauvignon and Gorgonzola sauce, the New York strip served with Maui onions and herb butter, or the Kahua Ranch lamb, which comes prepared as a shepherd's pie. Then, there's the dessert extravaganza: our favorite is chocolate decadence, a chocoholic's divine dream crafted from fudge mousse with a coffee-cream sauce, topped with whipped cream and macadamia nuts. The wine list includes 80 labels priced in the $16-to-$65 range, plus a few treasures in the three-digit range. Reservations are a must here, as tourists and Island residents alike enjoy Merriman's fare. Dinner for two, with wine, is about $85.

Open Mon.-Fri. 11:30 a.m.-1:30 p.m. & 5:30 p.m.-9 p.m., Sat. 5:30 p.m.-9 p.m., Sun. 10:30 a.m.-1 p.m. & 5:30 p.m.-9 p.m. Cards: AE, MC, V.

Phillip Paolo's
Waterfront Row,
75-5770 Alii Dr.,
Kailua-Kona
• 329-4436
ITALIAN

10/20

Italian music, from classical to 1940s tunes, wafts out of Phillip Paolo's located on the top floor of Waterfront Row. Inside, vine-covered trellises adorn the walls and scenic art draws the eyes. Smells of garlic, olive oil and basil remind you that there's a little bit of Italy in Kailua-Kona. Pastas are made fresh daily. The manicotti florentine (pasta crêpe filed with ricotta cheese and spinach) comes on a bed of spinach with tomato sauce, and the fettuccine montefiascone combines crispy vegetables, shrimp and calamari in a marinara sauce. There also are good renditions of the ubiquitous fresh fish (request that the chef cook the fish medium, or he may dry it out), plus a range of Italian veal, chicken and steak dishes (such as veal messina and chicken parmigiana). Each entrée is an overflowing plateful—but do save room for the cheesecake served with fresh fruit. Dinner for two, with wine, costs about $75.

Open daily 11:30 a.m.-2:30 p.m. & 5:30 p.m.-10 p.m. Cards: AE, MC, V.

Poki's Pasta

75-5699F Alii Dr.,
Kailua-Kona
• 329-7888
ITALIAN

9/20

Hidden among the mini-malls along Alii Drive is an Alice in Wonderland–size restaurant that features endless Italian food. Poki's Pasta is the child of Poki and Bob Gould, longtime Big Island cooks. Every morning Poki is up to her elbows in semolina flour making linguine, lasagna noodles, ravioli and spinach noodles. Their tiny restaurant, which seats only 22, is chock-a-block for dinner. In fact, people form a line and wait on weekends for Poki's lasagne, ravioli and cannelloni. Start with the baked elephant garlic and follow with the eggplant parmigiana or calamari steak. Take a chance by ending with whatever dessert of the day Poki has whipped up. Poki's doesn't have a liquor license, but you may bring your own wine. Dinner for two is about $40.

Open Mon.-Fri. 11:30 a.m.-9 p.m., Sat.-Sun. 4 p.m.-9 p.m. Cards: MC, V.

Poo Ping Thai Cuisine

Kona Inn Shopping Village,
75-5744 Alii Dr.,
Kailua-Kona
• 329-2677

Kamehameha Square,
75-5626 Kuakini Hwy.,
Kailua-Kona
• 329-0010
THAI

12/20

Both locations of Poo Ping Thai Cuisine have as much atmo-sphere as a school cafeteria, but the food is tasty when compared to other Thai restaurants, so you won't be looking any further than your plate. Owners Nop Kanchanawat and his wife created a one-acre garden in Kona to grow the Thai vegetables and spices that can't be imported into the United States. These home-grown ingredients are the secret that gives their dishes zip and authenticity. Mee krob crunches with justly crisp noo-dles and sweet-and-sour sauce. The assorted Thai soups, curries (red, green, yellow and sweet) and noodle dishes are appealing. Also pleasant is their fresh fish of the day cooked Poo Ping–style, with ginger, mushrooms and chili sauce. Which brings up an important point: All dishes come in mild, spicy or very spicy versions. Unless you were born and raised in Bangkok and sport an asbestos palate, start with the mild and work up. Of the two locations, we prefer the Kona Inn Shopping Center. The Kamehameha Square restaurant offers an all-you-can-eat lunch buffet on weekdays for $5.95 and turns into a disco joint at 10 p.m. Dinner for two, with Singha Thai beer, is around $45.

Kona Inn Shopping Village branch: open nightly 5 p.m.-9:30 p.m. Kamehameha Square branch: open Mon.-Sat. 11 a.m.-3 p.m. & 5 p.m.-9 p.m., Sun. 5 p.m.-9 p.m. All major cards.

Quinn's Almost by the Sea

75-5655A Palani Rd.,
Kailua-Kona
• 329-3822
SEAFOOD/AMERICAN

11/20

Psst! Quinn's is a secret: a favorite of locals, rarely discovered by visitors. Located across the street from the King Kam Hotel, Quinn's looks like a hole-in-the-wall joint, which is exactly what it is: a small, crowded bar, usually populated by local fishing-boat captains who are swapping lies about the day's catch, swigging beer and watching "the game" on the overhead television. Behind the bar, nearly hidden in the back, is a covered open-air lanai where some of the best meals in Kona are served: daily fresh fish, prepared four different ways (broiled, sautéed, stir-fried or as sashimi), the best burgers in town and a menu full of salads and low-calorie plates for the weight conscious. Quinn's is the only place you can eat in Kailua-Kona at midnight, or past 10:30 p.m., for that matter. Dinner for two, with wine, costs $50.
Open Mon.-Sat. 11 a.m.-1 a.m., Sun. 11 a.m.-midnight. Cards: MC, V.

THE *POI*-FECT STAPLE

China has its rice, India has its breads, Mexico its tortillas, Italy its pasta; in Hawaii, the ubiquitous carbohydrate staple is poi. It's made from the starchy taro root, which is boiled and then mashed or pounded into a gray, glutinous substance reminiscent of baby mash, and is served with almost anything. Taro root is also used to make chips, biscuits, turnovers and so on, and its greens are eaten as a vegetable, boiled and seasoned with coconut milk.

Roussels

60 Keawe St.,
Hilo
• 935-5111
FRENCH/CREOLE

12/20

Roussel's successfully melds New Orleans' Creole cooking with a touch of Hawaii. Housed in a renovated bank with polished maple floors, sixteen-foot-high ceilings, muted lighting and classical music playing in the background, Roussel's sets the ambience for an elegant dinner. The classic French Creole cooking features yesteryear's trendy blackened fish (the chef personally goes to the fish auction every morning to select the fish of the day), gumbo and shrimp Creole, with a wine selection to match each creation. Chef Andrew Oliver favors trout Alexander, a poached filet in a cream sauce of lobster, shrimp, mushrooms and sherry. In addition to steaks and chicken, Oliver, who cooked in New York City and New Orleans for twenty years before moving to the Islands, also prepares a duck dish in a rich veal stock seasoned with rosemary and cracked pepper. Expect to see local businesspeople, dressed in everything from muumuus to business suits. Service responds when you need things and knows to remain pleasantly absent when you want to linger over coffee and dessert. Intimate parties can be accommodated cozily in the old vault. Dinner for two with wine is around $80.
Open Mon.-Fri. 11:30 a.m.-4:30 p.m., Mon.- Sat. 5 p.m.-10 p.m. All major cards.

The Terrace Restaurant
Kanaloa at Kona
Condominium,
78-261 Manukai St.,
Keauhou
• 322-1003
CONTINENTAL/
PACIFIC RIM

11/20

Right at the ocean's edge (in fact during high surf, at the outer tables, you can almost feel the foaming waves), the Terrace Restaurant offers a Hawaii Visitor's Bureau poster of dinner in paradise. Swaying palm trees, setting sun and gentle rolling surf—even if they didn't serve fine meals this would be a great place to visit. Fortunately, the meals do not betray the setting. We love the ono hollandaise baked in phyllo and the Korean-style short ribs marinated in a spicy sauce. We have enjoyed the chicken-and-prawn stir-fry. Don't forget breakfast: you might swoon over the Belgian waffles, which have whatever fruit is in season on top, or you might have to be content with just macadamia nuts. The Terrace is also open for lunch. You will enjoy this stopover on your tour of the Big Island, mostly because of the location. Dinner for two, with wine, is $80. *Open daily 8 a.m.-2:30 p.m. & 5 p.m.-9:30 p.m. Cards: DC, MC, V.*

QUICK BITES

CAFES & COFFEEHOUSES

Bear's Coffee
106 Keawe St.,
Hilo
• 935-0708

This is a bear-memorabilia fan's heaven. But bears aren't the only reason to come to this quaint, tiny place in downtown Hilo. It offers the town's best breakfasts, pastries, hot chocolate and 26 different kinds of coffee. We love the light, fluffy steamed eggs (made on their espresso machine) and oversized home-made muffins. Lunch features deli sandwiches, "designer" bagels (you design the topping) and crispy salads (the Greek salad is divine). Breakfast for two, with the coffee of the day, $11; lunch for two with caffè latte, $12. *Open Mon.-Fri. 7 a.m.-5 p.m., Sat. 8 a.m.-8 p.m. No cards.*

Ken's House of Pancakes
1730 Kamehameha
Ave.,
Hilo
• 935-8711

Ken's looks like one of those chain coffeehouses with vinyl booths and plastic menus, but the food is lip-smacking good. This big family-style restaurant is nearly always crowded, except in the wee hours of the morning, and with good reason. The 24-hour-a-day breakfasts feature an array of perfectly cooked egg dishes, as well as Ken's renowned pancakes (macadamia-nut, banana and coconut, to name a few). Next to breakfast, burgers and sandwiches are the best sellers. Ken's winning combination? Soul-satisfying food, cheap prices, quick service and a shop that's always open. Breakfast for two, with endless coffee, runs about $12. Lunch for two, with Ken's frothy milk shakes, is about $14.
Open daily 24 hours. All major cards.

Naalehu Coffee Shop
Naalehu
• 929-7238

Don't let this old coffee shop with its tacky tourist decor and merchandise put you off. The food is good and inexpensive, featuring fish caught just a few miles away at South Point, and the desserts are homemade (the place is famous for its so-called banana bread, more precisely a banana cake with freshly sliced bananas and whipped cream between the layers). We recommend the ahi burgers, fresh tuna ground up into a patty. Be sure and check out the lush garden in the back. About $20 for lunch for two with fresh-brewed coffee.
Open Mon.-Sat. 8 a.m.-3 p.m. & 5:30 p.m.-8 p.m. No cards.

Sibu Café
75-5695-E Alii Dr.,
Kailua-Kona
• 329-1112

Sibu is a small indoor-outdoor café near the big banyan tree across from the seawall, featuring the best in Indonesian cuisine, with items like Balinese chicken, stir frys, satés and daily specials. There's plenty here for the vegetarian and extra spicy items for the brave. The small but interesting domestic and imported beer list and a very limited wine list complete the menu. Lunch or dinner for two with a couple of bottles of exotic beer, $22.
Open daily 11:30 a.m.-9 p.m. No cards.

HAMBURGERS & FAST FOOD

Captain Cook Inn
Rte. 11,
Captain Cook
• 323-2080

Drive through or stay put in this remodeled "Kentucky Fried Chicken" building, which has a typical fast-food burger, chicken, ribs and fish type of menu, but it's all good and made to order. There are a few unusual items: Loco Moco, a local favorite consisting of fried eggs served on top of a burger patty over rice and smothered in gravy, or the mahimahi tempura sandwich. Breakfast for two will set you back about $9, lunch about $11.
Open daily 7 a.m.-8 p.m. No cards.

Don Drysdale's Club 53

Kona Inn Shopping Village,
75-5744 Alii Dr.,
Kailua-Kona
• 329-6651

Don Drysdale's Two

Keauhou Shopping Village,
78-6831 Alii Dr.,
Kailua-Kona 96740
• 322-0070

Both Drysdale's branches are good stops for quick burgers and sandwiches. The Club 53 is an open-air restaurant with an ocean view in a shopping village, usually filled with tourists who are spending money in the numerous boutique shops. Drysdale's Two is in another modern shopping center, farther south. A quieter, less bustling place, this one's the hangout for sports fans (big overhead televisions monitor every baseball, football and basketball game). Food is adequate; most sports fans don't care as long as the burgers are hot, the beer cold and their favorite team is winning. Lunch for two, with a brew, is about $14.
Open daily 10 a.m.-midnight. Don Drysdale's Two: open daily 11 a.m.- 12:30 a.m. Cards: AE, MC, V.

Hong Kong Chop Suey

Kealakekua Ranch Center,
Captain Cook
• 323-3373

A typical Chinese restaurant with zilch decor, but the food is surprisingly tasty, inexpensive and filling. You have your choice of ordering at the counter from their variety plate-lunch menu (including pork tofu; beef and tomatoes; egg foo yung; or char siu roast pork, plus fried rice or noodles for under $4 each) or table service from their menu of nearly 100 items. Full lunch or dinner for two, with the required tea, about $25.
Open Mon.-Sat. 10 a.m.-8:30 p.m. No cards.

Manago Hotel & Restaurant

Rte. 11,
Captain Cook
• 323-2642

If you want to get away from the tourist haunts, this old hotel and restaurant might be the place. The dining room looks like a bygone school cafeteria. The menu changes daily, and the only place it's written is on the blackboard. Breakfast prices are so cheap, you'll swear someone made a mistake. Lunch and dinner consist of pork chops, liver and onions, fresh fish and local foods, served family style. Good, remarkably inexpensive food and an adventure you won't forget. Dinner for two, with a brew, will set you back $14.
Open Tues.-Thurs. 7 a.m.-9 a.m., 11 a.m.-2 p.m. & 5 p.m.-7:30 p.m., Fri.-Sun. 7 a.m.-9 a.m., 11 a.m.-2 p.m. & 5 p.m.-7 p.m. Cards: MC, V.

Naalehu Fruit Stand

Naalehu
• 929-9009

We like this funky place, housed in an old wooden building complete with rickety steps. Not only does it feature submarine sandwiches, home-baked fruit breads, brownies, salads and pizza, it also sells an eclectic assortment of herb teas and remedies, fresh fruit and vegetables, ice cream and cards by local artists. This is a good place to grab some take-out munchies for your trip to or from the volcanoes. Two submarine sandwiches and fresh-brewed Kona coffee will set you back $8.50.
Open Sun. 9 a.m.-5 p.m., Mon.-Thurs. 9 a.m.-6:30 p.m., Fri.-Sat. 9 a.m.-7 p.m. No cards.

Ocean View Inn
Kailua Village (across
from the sea wall)
• 329-9998

The oldest restaurant in West Hawaii, this establishment is very popular with local people, mainly because it serves "local" food: combinations of American, Hawaiian and Chinese. White sticky rice is served with everything (including breakfast), teriyaki sauce is poured on every imaginable meat, and the helpings would please a sumo wrestler. Decor is nonexistent: formica tables, drab walls and linoleum floors. But the service is quick and friendly, and prices are low. The bar does a brisk business in the evenings. Beer and sandwiches for two rings up to $14. *Open Tues.-Sun. 6:30 a.m.-2:45 p.m. & 5:15 p.m.-9 p.m. No cards.*

Wakefield Gardens Restaurant
Rte. 160,
Honaunau
• 328-9930

Located on the highway leading to the Place of Refuge, this eclectic restaurant run by Arlene Wakefield is open for lunch only. Arlene puts out a good spread for lunch: fresh roast turkey (which makes for a wonderful turkey-avocado sandwich), not to mention great soup, burgers, Mexican food and our favorite, fresh-fruit salad. All desserts are homemade and irresistibly priced at only $2. Sandwiches, drinks and dessert for two will set you back about $20.
Open daily 11 a.m.-3 p.m. No cards.

MEXICAN FAST FOOD

Réal Mexican Food
Kealakekua Ranch
Center,
Captain Cook
• 323-3036

The western side of Hawaii is not known for its Mexican food, but you can get good, quick simple Mexican food at the little "stand" on the lower level of this shopping center. Tacos, burritos, tostadas, taquitos and combination plates to take out, or you can eat at the red-and-white, plastic-tableclothed picnic benches. Lunch for two, washed down with a soft drink (no alcohol allowed on the shopping-center grounds) will set you back about $10.
Open Mon.-Fri. 11 a.m.-7 p.m., Sun. 11 a.m.-4 p.m. No cards.

PIZZA

Café Pesto
Kawaihae Shopping
Center
• 882-1071

Not far from Hapuna Beach is a little restaurant with pizza, pasta and interesting sandwiches. Café Pesto started out as a deli called "We're Talking Pizza." Remnants of the old deli are still to be seen when you walk in: a long refrigerated deli case and cash register up front. The next room is filled with red-and-white checkered tablecloths and decor pretending to be Italian.

In addition to their regular pizzas (with a crust to die for—a blend of white, rye and wheat flours, extra-virgin olive oil and honey), they have gourmet pizzas featuring sun-dried tomatoes, marinara sauce, exotic cheeses and fresh-picked herbs. Pizza for two, with a couple of glasses of Chianti, will total about $25. *Open Sun.-Thurs. 11 a.m.-9 p.m., Fri.-Sat. 11 a.m.-10 p.m. Cards: MC, V.*

Tom Bombadil's Food & Drink
75-5864 Walua Rd.,
Kailua-Kona
• 329-1292

What a location! It's right across the street from the Kona Hilton with an ocean view. Here's a good place to grab a pizza: This eatery offers a selection of creative combinations (we recommend the meatless marvel with onions, mushrooms, tomatoes, black and green olives and green peppers on a whole-wheat-honey crust), or you can create your pizzas from the long list of toppings. Also on the menu are sandwiches, burgers, chicken, fish and salads. Eat here and enjoy the view or take your grub out. A huge television screen in the bar shows sporting events. Pizza for two, with a couple of beers, $17. *Open daily 11 a.m.-10 p.m. Cards: MC, V.*

GETTING A PARDON, HAWAIIAN STYLE

Ancient Hawaii was governed by a set of sacred laws called *kapu*. Some kapu were conservation measures that controlled fishing or the gathering of scarce foodstuffs. Others forbade women to eat pork, coconuts, bananas or shark meat; eating with men was also off-limits.

Other kapu called for commoners to avert their eyes in the presence of royalty, and to lie prostrate before a king. One kapu forbade commoners to step on the shadow of *alii* (royalty).

The penalty for breaking a kapu was death. Some kapu called for specific means of execution: stoning, clubbing, strangling, being buried or burned alive. Sometimes a kapu-breaker was singled out as a sacrificial victim to appease a certain god or as a warning to potential criminals.

There was, however, one chance of salvation. If he could reach a *puuhonua* (a place of refuge), the criminal would be spared. The Hawaiians believed that a person's *mana* (spirit) remained in his bones after death. So, naturally, a burial ground hosted a collection of powerful spirits. And a puuhonua was sacred because it was the burial site of royalty. On the Big Island, the Pu'uhonua O Honaunau (Place of Refuge of Honaunau), which dates to 1550 and served as a temple mausoleum until 1818, is now a national park.

HOTELS & CONDOMINIUMS

BED & BREAKFASTS

Adrienne's Bed & Breakfast
85-4577 Mamalahoa Hwy.,
Captain Cook 96704
• 328-9726
No fax

Here's heaven for movie buffs—the owner used to work in a video store and has 1,000 movies for the VCRs. On Route 11 just a mile south of the road leading to the Place of Refuge (Route 160), Adrienne's has four units, including a single in the loft of the main house that has a secret: a fabulous 180-degree ocean view. The other three bedrooms all have private entrances and baths. Other amenities include a whirlpool bath. Adrienne bakes breads for breakfast and serves them with fresh fruit juices. No smoking, no pets.
Rooms: $30-$60.

Holualoa Inn
Box 222,
Holualoa 96725
• 324-1121
No fax

Just five miles from Kailua-Kona in the artists' town of Holualoa, this bed-and-breakfast is in a custom-designed wooden home. Secluded and private, the home is at the 1,200-foot elevation on a 40-acre working coffee farm. The house features a rooftop gazebo, with panoramic views of the countryside and those delicious Hawaiian sunsets. Each of the four guest rooms has a private bath. Breakfast always includes fresh-roasted Kona coffee and Island fruit juice.
Singles: $60; doubles: $75-125.

Ishigo's Inn

Box 8,
Honomu 96728
• 963-6128
No fax

Located on the main street of the tiny sugar-plantation village of Honomu (and on the way to Akaka Falls), Ishigo's is not only a bed-and-breakfast but also a country general store and bakery. A few years ago Sam Ishigo revived the old store, which his grandfather founded in 1910, and added four guest rooms. The rooms are clean and simple; three share a bath, and one has a private half-bath. Breakfast is the best part: just-baked pastries come from the bakery downstairs with endless cups of Kona coffee.
Rooms: $20-$25.

Kilauea Lodge

Box 116,
Volcano 96785
• 967-7366
No fax

This place rings our chimes and, in fact, is our favorite bed-and-breakfast on the Big Island. Located in the high-mountain rural village of Volcano, at 4,000 feet, this deluxe four-bedroom spot features fireplaces (complete with wood, kindling, newspaper and matches), well-designed private baths and country-inn decor. A one-bedroom cottage is also available. Thankfully, we wake up hungry, since breakfasts include local fruit, a main course and local (as in Kona) coffee. Unfortunately, others also find it wonderful, so book your reservation a month in advance.
Rooms: $75-$90.

The Log House

Box 2307,
Kamuela 96743
• 775-9990, 885-1224
No fax

The two-story, 3,200-square-foot Log House in Ahualoa remains popular with Kailua-Kona and Honolulu residents who want a change of climate and terrain. Five rooms are available, three with shared bath and two suites with private baths. TVs are available, but most guests take advantage of the fireplace room in this misty, cool mountain climate (10 miles from Kamuela, the heart of the Big Island cattle country and some good restaurants). A hearty breakfast is included in the rate. As the owner puts it, "This is not for the party animal."
Rooms: $60-$80.

My Island

Box 100,
Volcano 96785
• 967-7110, 967-7216
No fax

My Island, located at the edge of Hawaii Volcanoes National Park, offers six rooms. Three have shared baths in a 100-year-old historic, missionary-style home surrounded by botanical gardens and a lush, fern-filled jungle. The other three rooms are garden apartments with private baths and entrances. My Island, Inc. also serves as reservation headquarters for 21 Big Island bed-and-breakfasts.
Singles: $25-$30; doubles $45-$50.

Reggie's Tropical Hideaway

Box 1107,
Kealakekua 96750
• 322-8888
No fax

So you want to get away from it all? This charming older Hawaiian-style house has two rooms for rent in the main house and a separate two-bedroom house. The grounds include two acres, with ocean and mountain views and banana and coffee plants.
Rooms: $40-$60.

Volcano Bed & Breakfast

Box 22,
Volcano 96785
• 967-7779
Fax 967-7619

Here's a big rambling three-story house with three rooms (shared bath) in a peaceful mountain setting. Lush vegetation surrounds this home in the heart of the cool climate. Rooms are open, airy, clean and comfortable. Continental breakfast includes homemade bread, muffins, fruit and coffee.
Rooms: $45-$50.

Waimea Garden Cottage

Box 563,
Kamuela 96743
• 885-4550
No fax

Just eight miles from Hawaii's best beach, this cottage rests on more than an acre of ground, with its own stream at the foot of the Kohala Mountains. Now for the indoor niceties: TV, phone, French doors, patio, barbecue. Towels, robes and backrests for the beach are provided. You cook your own breakfast, but owner Barbara Campbell will stock your refrigerator with your favorite food. She reckons that this way, guests can sleep as late as they like and have a leisurely breakfast when they want it.
Rooms: $85, 3-night minimum.

CONDOMINIUMS

Aston Royal Sea Cliff Resort

75-6040 Alii Dr.,
Kailua-Kona 96740
• 329-8021
No fax

These luxuriously appointed studios and one- to two-bedroom units sit right on the ocean. Several of the 154 units have wheelchair access. Air conditioning, television, a full kitchen and quality furnishings are included in each unit. Amenities on the property include tennis courts and a pool.
Rooms: $150-$425.

Kanaloa at Kona

78-261 Manukai St.,
Keauhou 96740
• 322-2272
Fax 322-3818

These one-, two- and three-bedroom luxury condos border a golf course on one side, a secluded bay for snorkeling on another and the blue waters of the Pacific on the third side. The well-appointed and -decorated units have garden or ocean views, and the ocean units include separate wet bars and Jacuzzis. Each unit features koa-wood interiors, ceiling fans and

television sets. Other amenities include an excellent restaurant on the premises (The Terrace, see Big Island Restaurants, page 209), tennis courts, barbecue facilities, pool, recreation-meeting rooms and shoreline access (although there is no sandy beach). The units are first class, and the grounds are impeccable. One of the best condominums in all of Kona.
Rooms: $115-$220.

Kona-by-the-Sea
75-6106 Alii Dr.
Kailua-Kona 96740
• 329-0200

Facing a scenic but rocky beach, this 80-unit condominium features one- and two-bedroom units, with a pool and restaurant (The Beach Club) on the property. The units are spacious with private lanais and complete kitchens.
Rooms: $140-$195.

Kona Tiki Hotel
75-5968 Alii Dr.,
Kailua-Kona 96740
• 329-1425

One of the best buys in Kona: an apartment/hotel right on the ocean with only seventeen units. Rooms are either standard or with kitchen. Amenities include a swimming pool and great views. Keep in mind that you get what you pay for: the place is old and has neither air conditioning nor room phones.
Rooms: $40-45.

Kona White Sands Apartment/ Hotel
77-6467 Alii Dr.,
Kailua-Kona 96740
• 329-3210
Fax 326-4137

These old units get a lot of return business, because of their location on Alii Drive adjacent to the White (or Magic or Disappearing) Sands Beach. They're cheap, and the people are friendly. There are only eight units, five of which are vacation rentals, so you'll need to reserve early. Rates drop a bit for "low season" (May to November). All have kitchen areas (some nicer than others) and lanais. Every unit faces the ocean, which will either lull you to sleep or keep you awake!
Doubles: $45-$50.

Mauna Lani Point Condominiums
2 Kaniku Dr.,
Kamuela 96743
• 667-1400

Located in the luxurious Mauna Lani Resort, these one-, two- and three-bedroom units offer 1,000 to 1,500 square feet of living space and include oversize baths, fully equipped kitchens with European cabinetry, washer and dryer and central air conditioning. One travel survey ranked these condominium units sixteenth in the world as best places to stay. Guests have the use of the Racquet Club, the Francis I'i Brown Championship Golf course, Olympic-size pool, weight room, Jacuzzi and sauna. The grounds are well manicured, the resort divine. Staying here is heavenly.
One bedroom $225-$275; 2 bedrooms $295-$350; 3 bedrooms $400.

Mauna Lani Terrace Condominiums
South Kohala 96743
• 882-1066
Fax 882-7676

Adjacent to the Mauna Lani Bay Hotel, these one-, two- and three-bedroom condominium units scream luxury, and contain all the amenities one would expect in a plush condo: exquisite decor, private lanais, wet bars, complete laundry facilities and central air conditioning. Access to all of the resort's sports activities (golf, tennis, health club, pool). Ask for a discount if you plan to stay more than seven nights.
Rooms: $235-$380.

SeaMountain– Colony One
Punaluu Black Sand Beach,
Pahala 96777
• 928-8301

Punaluu is one of the lovely black-sand beaches offered up by Big Island volcanoes. Of the 76 SeaMountain condominium units, nearly half are available for daily rentals. The units, from studio to two-bedroom suites, are privately owned and vary from basic amenities to opulently furnished homes. Swimming pools abound on the resort property, and the condos are a one-minute drive or a seven-minute walk from the beach (which is not good for swimming due to the strong surf and dangerous currents). The SeaMountain Golf Course is nearby, and the area's only restaurant, the Punaluu Black Sand Restaurant, is within walking distance (the meals are pretty ho-hum). The closest town is Pahala, about five miles away. This is a very dramatic area with a black-sand beach, wind-swept vegetation and thundering surf. It's a spot that stirs up the imagination and allows glimpses into what ancient Hawaii must have been like.
Rooms: $66-$140.

LUXURY

Hyatt Regency Waikoloa
One Waikoloa Beach Resort,
South Kohala 96743
• 885-1234
Fax 885-5737

The people at Hyatt refuse to call this a hotel, and, they gush, neither is it "just a resort." They market it as the "ultimate fantasy resort" of the 1990s. Poppycock; it's Disneyland gone Beach Blanket Bingo (and like Disneyland, it offers a "back of the house" tour that you shouldn't miss). Just imagine 62 oceanfront acres on Waiulua Bay, covered with crumbling black lava. The hotel opened in September 1988 to enthusiastic reviews. In the words of writer James A. Michener: "This is the kind of place that God would have built if he had sufficient cash flow." Some two years and $360 million later, picture a massively landscaped, mega-amenities, art-infested resort. Arriving guests are draped with exotic flower leis and are offered a tropical concoction before they even reach the check-in desk of the indoor-outdoor lobby. Baggage disappears and the guests are directed to their rooms via a modernistic tram or mahogany motor launch, or by walking along the mile-long art-filled hallway to one of the 1,241 rooms. The hotel has seven restaurants, twelve lounges (including a disco), eight tennis courts, three swimming pools (one nearly an acre in size) and two golf courses. The spacious rooms sport king-size beds, a settee with coffee table and extra chairs. If all that's not enough, the staff will arrange anything else you want, through what they call their fantasy vacation service, which can book a charter helicopter to watch the erupting volcano or arrange a hunting safari on nearby Mauna Kea. But remember: 2,000 other guests may be trying to book what you want. This congestion spills over into the resort's restaurants, golfing, tennis. . . .

We can't work up quite as much enthusiasm about the Hyatt Waikoloa as Michener did. Yes, the place is visually spectacular, but for $360 million, one would think a resort in Hawaii would be fronting a gorgeous beach. Nope, no beach here! Guests have to wait for the bus to take them to and from the beach, which is a mile away. You also spend time waiting for the tram or boat to return you to your room (after one ride the idea becomes old real fast). After a few days, the ultimate fantasy resort began to wear on us.

Doubles: $215-380; suites: $550-$2,700.

Kona Village Resort

Kaupulehu-Kona
96740
• 325-5555
Fax 325-5124

This is our favorite resort in all of Hawaii. Kona Village exists for people who really want to escape. The resort, located on the site of an old Hawaiian village that escaped damage during a volcanic eruption in the late 18th century, contains 115 thatched-roofed Polynesian *hales* (houses). Each separate hale reflects one of the Pacific island cultures in design and decoration: Hawaii, Tahiti, Tonga, Fiji, New Caledonia, New Hebrides, Samoa, Palau and the Marquesas. Each hale is exquisitely decorated: king-size beds, coffee-maker, refrigerator, lanais, separate dressing area, comfortable chairs and usually a hammock or two nearby. To maintain your sense of escape, none of the rooms has a phone, radio or television. Also, the rooms have no keys, as Kona Village is isolated from the rest of the world by a lava field, and the guard at the gate house allows only guests and workers to enter. (Most of the employees at Kona Village not only are related to each other but have worked at the Village since its opening in 1965.) There are also tropical gardens, a lagoon, exotic birds, cultural artifacts, tennis courts, two pools, lounges and restaurants (the daily buffet lunch served outdoors on the patio is fabulous). If you can afford a few days of paradise, there is nothing else like it in Hawaii.

Rooms: $345-565 (for two, including all meals).

Mauna Kea Beach Hotel

South Kohala 96743
• 882-7222
Fax 882-7552

Consistently appearing at the top of nearly every list of the world's best resorts, the elegant Mauna Kea Beach Hotel, with its fine beach and beautiful championship golf courses, remains a wonderful way to vacation in the islands. Since Laurance Rockefeller opened the resort in 1965, it has set a standard of excellence for Hawaiian resorts. The man behind it all— through various owners, too—is the affable Adi Kohler, who twenty years ago went from a hotel in Paris to Phoenix, Arizona, to learn English, a necessary requirement for his promotion to assistant front-desk manager. Lucky stars led to his recruitment by Rockefeller while in the United States. Today Kohler is one of the most respected general managers in the business.

The hotel itself, consisting of 310 rooms and four restaurants, has earned stacks of well-deserved awards from nearly every travel publication in the world. Every aspect seems to embody excellence. Its golf facilities are consistently high ranking in America's Best Golf Courses by *Golf* magazine. As for tennis, *Tennis* Magazine rates Mauna Kea as one of the "50 Great Tennis Resorts in America." Of course, there is more to life than just eighteen holes and a net. Other activities include: horseback riding, water sports on one of the most stunning white-sand beaches on the Big Island, historical and cultural tours (the resort owns a fabulous collection of Pacific and Asian art) and a fitness center. Like the matriarch of Big Island hotels that she is, this service-oriented, luxurious resort seems to get better with age. The guests, nearly all independent travelers of some wealth, generally are older, conservative types who have seen the best resorts in the world and continue to return to Mauna Kea Beach. Don't even try to get reservations for Christmas week; it's a sort of old-timers' event, when veterans of twenty or more visits sit on the beach and reminisce about the way things used to be in the old days—and still are at the Mauna Kea.

Modified American Plan (includes accommodations, breakfast and dinner) double: $355-$520; European Plan (accommodations only) available mid-April-Dec. single or double: $230-$395.

A CENSUS CONSENSUS

Up the slope from Rockefeller's lush resort is a mysterious site called Ahu a Umi. In the fifteenth century, Umi became the first known ruler of the Big Island. After he conquered district after district, Umi went to a desolate, windswept spot on the slopes of Mauna Kea, a dormant volcano. Here he ordered a census taken; servants brought up stones from various regions, which represented the number of people, animals and amount of land. Later, these heaps (*ahu*) of stones were fashioned into a place of worship. According to the old legend, Umi was directed by the gods to this spot, from which, because of an optical illusion, three of the Big Island's volcanoes, Mauna Kea (13,796 feet), Mauna Loa (13,677 feet) and Hualalai (8,271 feet) appear nearly the same size.

Mauna Lani Bay Hotel

South Kohala 96743
• 885-6622
Fax 885-4556

This resort is the epitome of elegance and excellent service. Developed by Japanese with an exhausting attention to detail, the 351-room resort is located on a luxuriously landscaped charcoal lava flow fronting Makaiwa Bay Beach. The guest rooms are spacious and decorated with an eye to practicality as well as design: double-sink bathrooms, oversize televisions and spectacular views. Amenities include award-winning restaurants, cocktail lounges (with some of the best entertainers on the island), tennis courts, shops, meeting rooms and the fine Francis I'i Brown Golf Course. Guests tend to be younger and more active than those at nearby Mauna Kea Beach Resort. *Rooms: $250-$395; suites: $600-$2,500.*

The Royal Waikoloan

P.O. Box 5000,
Waikoloa 96743
• 885-6789
Fax 885-7852

Formerly called the Sheraton Royal Waikoloa, the Royal Waikoloan has some heavy competition in the Kohala gold coast of megabuck resorts. However, this place does have an advantage or two: the resort is right on Anaehoomalu Bay, a crescent-shaped white-sand beach; and the area is loaded with Hawaiian artifacts and ancient history. Royal Resorts president Gordon Hentschel has oriented his entire resort to the beauty and culture of Hawaii. The beach offers every conceivable water activity, including the best windsurfing on the Big Island. Two golf courses, six tennis courts, horseback riding and historical, garden and cultural tours and special events are what Hentschel hopes will keep the guests from ever leaving. The spectacular entrance to the hotel is through an open-air lobby that overlooks the pool and gardens. Rooms, which were recently renovated, are attractively furnished and face either the ocean, mountains or manicured gardens. Best reasonably priced accommodations on the burgeoning Kohala Coast. Nonsmoking rooms are available. *Doubles: $155-$300.*

FIRST CLASS

Kona Hilton Beach & Tennis Resort

75-5852 Alii Dr.,
Kailua-Kona 96740
• 329-3111
Fax 329-9532

This 452-room hotel sits on a precipice jutting out into Kailua Bay, and not only offers vistas of the ocean and the bay but is within walking easy distance of Kailua village. The open-air lobby is filled with the sounds of running water in the artificial lagoons and streams. Entrance to the rooms is through an open-air courtyard, and all rooms have views of either the ocean or the mountains. Rooms are neat and clean, with televisions, refrigerators and complimentary coffee-and-tea-making facilities. Other amenities include restaurants (the coffee shop overlooks the ocean), bars, tennis courts, shops and meeting rooms. *Doubles: $119-$185; suites: $200-$470.*

PRACTICAL

Dolphin Bay Hotel
333 Iliahi St.,
Hilo 96720
• 935-1466
No fax

Located in a quiet residential section of Hilo called Puueo, only four blocks from downtown Hilo, this eighteen-unit hotel is one of our favorites. Don't expect a phone in the room or, for that matter, a pool or a restaurant, but every room does have a complete kitchen (the management encourages you to sample the fruit from the garden out back), and most rooms have Roman baths. The powers that be are friendly and helpful to visitors—they pride themselves on repeat guests—and they'll gladly help you decide what to see and where to eat. It's only 40 minutes from Hawaii Volcanoes National Park.
Studios: $40-$50; 1-bedroom apartment: $60; 2-bedroom apartment: $70.

Hawaii Naniloa Hotel
93 Banyan Dr.,
Hilo 96720
• 969-3333
Fax 969-6622

They've renovated the 400-room Naniloa, located on the water along scenic Banyan Drive. And it's beautiful. A huge, airy lobby with a bright pastel color scheme greets visitors. Amenities include a large, new swimming pool and a new Japanese restaurant with fast, efficient service and a modern sushi bar. The best location on Hilo Bay.
Rooms: $80-$120; suites: $170-$500.

Hotel King Kamehameha
75-5660 Palani Rd.,
Kailua-Kona 96740
• 329-2911
Fax 329-4602

A central location in the heart of Kailua village, coupled with reasonable rates, makes this 460-room hotel a popular choice. Close to shopping, restaurants and a small beach, it's very convenient for those who don't wish to rent a car. The rooms are nothing to brag about, but they suffice. On the hotel grounds is an air-conditioned mall with shops and Hawaii's only major department store, Liberty House. We recommend requesting a room overlooking the Kailua Pier where charter sport fishing boats unload their daily catch. Amenities include restaurants (the coffee shop is one of the few restaurants to serve 100-percent pure Kona coffee), cocktail lounges, tennis courts (with one of Kona's best tennis pros) and a pool. The clients range from tour groups to independent travelers.
Rooms: $95-$480 (three-bedroom suite). Children under 17 free if sharing existing beds.

The "Big Island," which actually is the island of Hawaii, is the newest and largest of the Islands, and is the southernmost in the chain. It is more than twice the size of all the other islands combined. Here, every type of geographical terrain known can be found (except the deserts of the Sahara and the extreme ice of the Arctic).

Kamuela Inn
Kawaihae Rd.,
Kamuela 96743
• 885-4243
No fax

Located in the cool high-country of Waimea, this 31-room country inn is still just fifteen minutes from Hapuna Beach, one of the best white-sand beaches in Hawaii. Standard rooms and kitchenettes all have television. There is no restaurant on the property, but it's within walking distance of many fine restaurants and sights in historic Kamuela (also known as Waimea). *Rooms: $44; suites: $72-$118.*

Keauhou Beach Hotel
78-6740 Alii Dr.,
Kailua-Kona 96740
• 322-3441
Fax 322-6586

Recently purchased by a Japanese firm that promises to renovate this former beauty, the Keauhou Beach Hotel is, for now, an adequate budget hotel. Popular with local interisland travelers for its low rates, the Keauhou Beach is a fading shadow of its former self. The 310-room property is situated on a stark, rocky coastline that is dotted with tidal pools. Other amenities include lushly landscaped gardens, tennis courts, a restaurant, pool and quick access to one of Kona's best snorkeling beaches, Kahaluu. *Doubles: $77-135; suites: $195-345.*

Kona Seaside Hotel
75-5646 Palani Rd.,
Kailua-Kona 96740
• 329-2455
No fax

In the heart of Kailua-Kona, this newly renovated 255-room hotel offers reasonable room rates and room-car packages, two pools, a laundromat, Stan's Restaurant and a lounge. The rooms are clean, feature very basic furnishings and are simply decorated. A good budget hotel. *Rooms: $42-$79.*

Kona Surf Resort
78-128 Ehukai St.,
Kailua-Kona 96740
• 322-3411
Fax 322-3245

This 535-room resort has seen its ups and downs over the years, but it is generally well maintained and situated in a lovely spot at the edge of Keauhou Bay, about seven miles from Kailua village. The architectural design of the resort is fabulous, centered around lush, tropical gardens and pools that can be seen from all levels, so you always feel as if you're outside. The ocean-view rooms provide breathtaking panoramas. Other amenities include tennis, golf, freshwater and saltwater pools, restaurants, bars, disco, shops and the largest convention facilities in Kona. Although the Kona Surf is right on the ocean, there is scant beach access; but wander to the edge of the lava rock at night to see manta rays playing in the surf. *Doubles: $99-$155; suites: $350-$850.*

Manago Hotel

Rte. 11,
Captain Cook 96704
• 323-2642
No fax

Situated in the historic coffee town of Captain Cook, the Manago exudes old Hawaii. The three-story hotel, owned and operated by the Manago family since it was built in 1917, has wonderful ocean views, a voluptuous garden and old-fashioned hospitality. A new wing was added in 1977, bringing the room total to 42. Some rooms have private baths, while some must share the community bath; none of the rooms has a phone. The charm of the Manago Hotel is in its family-style restaurant and bar, where guests sit and "talk story" with the local residents. Also, the Managos staff the hotel themselves. More than a bargain, the Manago is a taste of a quickly disappearing Hawaii. *Doubles: $29-$35. (Rates go up with floor level.)*

Parker Ranch Lodge

P.O. Box 458,
Kawaihae Rd.,
Kamuela 96743
• 885-4100
No fax

When we went to press, this small country motel had twenty rooms, with plans to add another twenty by 1991. The rooms are pleasantly furnished with king-size or double beds, phones and pleasant views. Located in the middle of Kamuela (Waimea), it's within walking distance of restaurants, bars and other attractions (no restaurant on the property). *Singles: $63; doubles; $77; kitchenettes: $70-80.*

Shirakawa Motel

Waiohinu 96772
• 929-7462
No fax

This is for the adventuresome traveler, who would like to experience the true aloha spirit of an earlier era in a 1930s house. Mrs. Shirakawa rents out thirteen rooms, most sharing the bathroom at the end of the hall. The rooms are not exactly elaborate: a bed, perhaps a straight-back chair and a single bulb hanging from the ceiling. But a night at Shirakawa's is not about luxury and elegant room service. It's a trip to another time, where people sit in the kitchen and "talk story" about the old days and Mrs. Shirakawa greets each guest like a favorite relative. On a recent visit, we had to leave quite early in the morning, even before the nearby roosters began their chorus. The night before she had expressed concern that we wouldn't be able to get breakfast, but when we awoke the next morning we found that Mrs. S. had risen before us and baked a pineapple upside-down cake (with fresh pineapple) for our morning meal. *Twins: $28; kitchenettes: $32. Extra bed in room, $9.*

Volcano House

Hawaii Volcanoes
National Park 96718
• 967-7321
No fax

Volcano House is the world's only hotel perched at the edge of an active volcano. This 37-room rustic country lodge, located on Crater Rim Drive within the National Park (and thus subject to room-rate regulation by the U.S. Government), contains the original old building with a large lobby and fireplace and a newer, rather characterless, extension, which could definitely use some serious soundproofing. A few small rooms soon will be available in a separate building located between the main hotel and the Visitor Center. The hotel has a snack bar and a good restaurant (especially for breakfast and dinner, but beware lunch time when buses fill the parking lot and tourists fill the restaurant seats). The rooms are clean, spacious and well kept (request one of the rooms with the crater-rim view; they're worth the extra cost). Staying in the cool, misty climate is an experience that stays with you long after your tan has faded. *Doubles: $60-$102.*

NIGHTLIFE

BARS	225
DANCING	226
DINNER SHOW	227
LUAUS	227

BARS

Huggo's
75-5828 Kahakai Rd.,
Kailua-Kona
• 329-1493

With an on-the-water location, Huggo's is splendid (see Big Island Restaurants, page 202). You can watch the sun go down or listen to the waves lapping on the lava shores below. Happy hour, from 4 p.m. to 6 p.m., is convivial conversation. Connie Skinner tickles the ivories in the informal piano bar later in the evening, on Tuesday through Saturday evenings. *Open daily 4 p.m.-12:30 a.m.*

Kona Provision Co.
Hyatt Regency
Waikoloa,
One Waikoloa Beach
Resort,
Kohala Coast
• 885-1234

Its edge-of-the-hill location overlooking the Pacific makes the KPC a grand escape (see Big Island Restaurants, page 205): on the one side, there's a sweeping view of the Pacific; on the other, a perspective of the pool and the hotel towers. A Hawaiian duo provides idyllic background serenades during the evening. *Open nightly 5:30 p.m.-9:30 p.m. All major cards.*

Lehua's Bay City Bar & Grill
11 Waianuenue Ave.,
Hilo
• 935-8055

On weekends, there's a variety of entertainment along with the burgers and sanwiches. The good times range from chalangalang (old-fashioned backyard jams) to stand-up comedians. The "stage" is minuscule, but the spirit is sincere.
Open Fri-Sat. 9 p.m.-10 p.m.

Roussel's
60 Keawe St.,
Hilo
• 935-5111

On Saturdays, there is guitar and piano music to go along with the French and Creole cooking in an old bank building (see Big Island Restaurants, page 208).
Open Sat. 5 p.m.-10 p.m.

DANCING

Fiasco's
Waiakea Square Warehouse,
Hwy. 11 (near Banyan Dr.),
Volcano
• 935-7666

For locals and visitors alike, this restaurant/club is ideal for quick meals and after-work partying. Let's also include nighttime dancing. The bar is cooler and quieter than the dining room. On Thursdays, Fridays and Saturdays, the upstairs club opens for dancing to the nostalgic sounds of the 1950s and 1960s.
Open nightly 8:30 p.m.-1:30 a.m. Cover charge. All major cards.

Reflections Restaurant
101 Aupuni St.,
Hilo
• 935-8501

There's a little something for everyone here: a large-screen TV for those in search of live-via-satellite sports programs; an "attitude-adjustment hour" between 4 p.m. and 8 p.m. weekdays for smoothing out your problems; and music for listening and dancing from 8 p.m. Tuesdays through Saturdays. Prime rib is the staple on the buffet line.
Open nightly 5 p.m.-11 p.m. Cards: AE, MC, V.

Spats
Hyatt Regency Waikoloa,
One Waikoloa Beach Resort,
Kohala
• 885-2134

The most popular gathering spot for the young and the young-at-heart. The dance floor is crowded on weekends and holidays, but there's ample space for a tête-à-tête in nooks furnished with tables and sofas. The speakeasy decor is accented by a stand-up bar for those who like to hoist one with the bartender's blessing.
Open nightly 8:30 p.m.-2 a.m. No cover. All major cards.

Water's Edge
Hyatt Regency Waikoloa,
One Waikoloa Beach Resort,
Kohala
• 885-1234

If you enjoy the musical standards and cheek-to-cheek dancing, this is the place. A combo or a small orchestra, depending on the season, provides the live music. The club lives up to its name at the edge of an artificial lagoon. Access is from a landing deck, a stone's throw from the monorail or motor launch.
Open nightly 6:30 p.m.-10:30 p.m. No cover. All major cards.

DINNER SHOW

**King
Kamehameha
Court**
Hyatt Regency
Waikoloa,
One Waikoloa Beach
Resort,
Waikoloa
• 885-1234

"Legends of Polynesia," the splashiest Polynesian production on the island, is an eye- and ear-filler, with numbers that are both poignant and fiery. Even larger-than-life-size *menehunes*—Hawaiian "leprechauns"—perform. This gem from Tihati Productions will cost $92 for dinner, $48 for cocktails only.
Open Mon., Wed. & Fri. 7:30 p.m.-10 p.m. All major cards.

LUAUS

**Hotel King
Kamehameha**
75-5660 Paleni Rd.,
Kailua-Kona
• 329-2911

The food is not as lavish as at the Kona Village luau, but it is authentic (with some American dishes thrown in). Plan on spending $79 for two adults.
Luaus Sun., Tues. & Thurs. 5:30 p.m. All major cards.

**Kona Hilton
Luau**
Kona Hilton
75-5852 Alii Dr.,
Kailua-Kona
• 329-3111

An outdoor feast, with all the ritual of an old-fashioned Island-style party, heralds guests to sample not only liquid spirits (mai tais) but a cultural menu as well. There are hulas and chants, plus contemporary cocktail-hour music by the Freitas Brothers.
Luaus Mon., Wed. & Fri. 6 p.m.-10 p.m. All major cards.

**Kona Village
Resort Luau**
Kona Village Resort,
P.O. Box 1299,
Kailua-Kona
• 325-6787

Can one visit Hawaii and not attend a luau? Yes, but a good luau really shouldn't be missed. The best luau on the Big Island (and some say in all of Hawaii) can be found on Friday nights at the secluded Kona Village Resort. The menu includes traditional food prepared in the ancient way, such as kalua pig (baked in an *imu* pit), chicken prepared with taro tops and coconut milk, laulau (pork, fish and taro tops steamed in ti-leaf bundles), poisson cru (a Tahitian dish of raw fish marinated in coconut milk and lime juice), steamed ulu (breadfruit), aama crab, tako poke (raw octopus in a chile-pepper marinade) and kulolo (taro pudding, steamed in banana leaves). Cost is $99 for two.
Luau Fri. 5:30 p.m. All major cards.

**Volcano
Grounds**
Royal Waikoloan,
off Kaahumanu Hwy.
(Hwy. 19),
Waikoloa
• 885-6789

An *imu* ceremony, where the luau pig is fittingly removed for serving, is a must-see. The spirited Polynesian cast offers conventional luau entertainment with zestful appeal. The dinner package for two is $80; the cocktail package is $40.
Luau Sun. 6 p.m. All major cards.

SHOPS

ANTIQUES

The Hawaiian Shop
Mamane St.,
Honokaa
• 775-7703

Next door to Handcarved Museum Replicas and under the same management, the Hawaiian Shop holds down the fort, about two or three times as large, and consequently stuffed with two or three times as much junk. We'd single out the chair in the form of a hand, long-case clocks, porcelain of almost every kind and description, and enough shell leis to outfit your own hula show.
Hours vary. Call for an appointment.

Louise Dumaine Antiques
140 Keawe St.,
Hilo
• 935-9604

Carnival glass, poi bowls, costume jewelry (some precious stones), quilts, kimonos and Island-style furniture—the kind of miscellaneous clutter that accumulates in a life and is eventually sold by puzzled executors—fills up this one-room shop.
Open Mon.-Sat. 9 a.m.-5 p.m.

ARTS & CRAFTS

Ackerman Gallery
P.O. Box 961,
Kamuela
• 889-5971

Enter through a stylized marble archway that debouches onto a miniature grotto graced by a fountain and a glass Naiad, and you'll find yourself in a well-laid-out gallery that features alabaster sculptures by Sara Lawless, paintings by owner Gary Ackerman, handwoven baskets by Mika McCann of Maui and wooden boxes by Greg Pontino. If you go deeper into the shop, you'll get to another section, called the Ackerman Collection, which purveys upscale women's clothing and tastefully designed costume jewelry, most of it made on the Big Island. *Open daily 9:30 a.m.-5:30 p.m.*

Artists' Studio
Mamane St.,
Honokaa
• 775-9191

This is a combination school and store—local people take classes here in silk screening, clay modeling and papier-mâché in addition to drawing, painting and photography. Sales are by arrangement with the artist. A lot of the art leans toward surrealistic or wildly impressionistic tropical landscapes. The last time we looked, a magnificent papier-mâché pony painted in blues, greens and yellows by Julie Melko caught our eye, as well as what appeared to be a blue plumeria with a tangled jade-green stem, lying on its side, all 3 1/2 feet of it, done by Louise Block. *Open Mon.-Fri. 1 p.m.-7 p.m., Sat. 11 a.m.-1 p.m.*

Fiberarts
Expresso
Gallerie/
Topstitch
Parker Ranch Shopping
Center,
Kamuela
• 885-7666, 885-4482

Separated by an arched doorway, these shops spill over into each other. The keynote here is taste. The small selection of wood, mainly milo, koa and Norfolk pine, is nicely finished. The Hawaiian quilts would be handsome as wall hangings or bed-spreads. Small items such as fabric bouquets and sachets make fine small gifts, as does the nice selection of Hawaiian books and Pacificana. *Open Mon.-Fri 9:30 a.m.-5 p.m., Sun. 10 a.m.-3 p.m.*

Gallery of Great
Things
Parker Square,
Kamuela
• 885-7706, 885-6171

We like to wander through the rooms of this old tin-roofed shack, where modern track lighting lines the beamed ceiling, picking out here a rice-paper woodblock print, there an etched glass panel, there a coconut scraper. The quality is top notch, whether you're looking at silk scarves and caftans by Susun Schulze and others, or wooden bowls and boxes or authentic Panama hats. You'll also find some genuine antiques—celadons from Thailand, for example—and some authentic artifacts from New Guinea and elsewhere, including Polynesia and the Phillipines, some of it of museum quality. *Open Mon.-Sat. 9 a.m.-5 p.m.*

Gallery of
Pacific Art
2 Mauna Lani Dr.,
Kohala Coast
• 885-7779, 885-5757

Set among fields of desolate lava-rock rubble, this handsomely arranged gallery sells high-quality art at astronomical prices, such as the photographs and small bronzes for upwards of $12,000. At openings, jazz concerts are held on a little deck overlooking a golf course and, beyond that, the ocean. Part of the collection constitutes a museum of Asian and Greco-Roman antiquities, not for sale, but beautiful to behold. You'll find paintings and sculpture by some of Hawaii's top artists, jewelry

by Richard Lawless and photographs by Brett Weston, son of Edward Weston. Exhibits change frequently.
Open daily 9 a.m.-6 p.m., and by appointment.

Gamelan Gallery
277 Keawe St.,
Hilo
• 969-7655

Open in 1990, this shop specializes in objects from Indonesia and Thailand. Sterling-silver jewelry and handwoven ikats (some of which have been made into vests) make up the bulk of the offerings, but a few Indonesian masks and some intricately hand-carved, hand-painted medicine cabinets also clamor for attention.
Open Mon.-Sat. 9 a.m.-5 p.m.

Hawaiian Artifacts
R.R. 1, Box 139,
Papaikou
• 964-1729

About six or seven miles outside of Hilo, on the scenic route going north to Honokaa, you'll find Paul and Barbara Gebhart's little gallery. Paul, a former student of Dan Deluz, carves fish and birds, in addition to the usual wooden bowls, and strings palm seed and kukui-nut leis. A wide shelf displays local shells and another contains shells from all over the world.
Open Mon.-Sat. 9 a.m.-5 p.m.

Hawaiian Handcraft Shop
760 Kilauea Ave.,
Hilo
• 935-5587

Museum-quality pieces—mainly bowls, with some platters—carved from koa, milo and Norfolk pine, are owner and proprietor Dan Deluz's stock-in-trade. A veritable museum of Island woods—pheasant, tulip and mango, for example—carved by Mr. Deluz occupies one wall. These are not for sale, but a collection of 40 similar pieces can be ordered for a mere $10,000. For $6,000 you can get a set of 40 smaller pieces with covers. Just about whenever you drop in, Mr. Deluz will be happy to take you on a tour of the workshop.
Open daily 9 a.m.-5 p.m.

Kama'aina Woods
P.O. Box 982,
Honokaa
• 775-7722, 885-5521

The entranceway features a small aviary and, usually, a diminutive black cat who enjoys attention. Inside, the space is devoted almost entirely to bowls, mainly koa. Prices are moderate.
Open Mon.-Fri. 9 a.m.-4:30 p.m., Sat. 9 a.m.-5 p.m.

The Potter's Gallery
95 Waianuenue Ave.,
Hilo
• 935-4069

There's a lot of pottery by Randy Morehouse, one of the owners, and other Big Island artists, with raku ware and irridescent glazed vases and pieces emphasized. A few representational pieces, such as a humpback whale in a naturalistic grayish metallic glaze, lurk about, as well as some fiber art. One of our favorite Island sculptors, Sara Lawless, exhibits here, and it's worth the trip just to see her mythological figures.
Open Mon.-Sat. 9 a.m.-5 p.m.

Waipio Wood Works

P.O. Box 5091,
Kukuihaele
• 775-0958

Here, browse among a fine selection of exotic wood bowls and trays, notably some of pheasant wood and tamarind by Scott Hare Schuler, a few oils, photographs and prints, as well as art glass, pottery and the ubiquitous T-shirts and costume jewelry. The two-room shop has a marvelous back view of tin-roofed shacks and an anomalous collection of weather-beaten vehicles. *Open daily 9 a.m.-5 p.m.*

CLOTHES

Big Island Hat Company

Kona Inn Shopping Village,
75-5744 Alii Dr.,
Kailua-Kona
• 329-3332

Whether you fancy a Panama (not a fino), a woven-fiber cloche accented by a broad pink band, or a jaunty number reminiscent of the one Maurice Chevalier tipped in many a movie, they're all here and more. There are also simpler visor-brimmed hats for the beach and a small selection of thongs. We suspect that the latter are there so they can truly claim to outfit you from head to foot . . . so long as you leave out everything between. *Open daily 9 a.m.-9 p.m.*

Christel's Collectibles

Kona Inn Shopping Village,
75-5744 Alii Dr.,
Kailua Kona
• 885-8870

In addition to one of the handsomest collections of tie-dyed pants and shirts we've seen in a while, Christel sells lacy lingerie from France and Italy made exclusively for her shop. Bar Viani designs from Chicago round out the cosmopolitan selection. *Open daily 9 a.m.-9 p.m.*

Noa Noa

Kona Inn Shopping Village,
75-5744 Alii Dr.,
Kailua-Kona
• 326-7577

The owner of this shop, Joan Simon, designs the shoes, mixes the dyes, and weaves the fabrics herself. Everything's an original, handmade in Bali, where Simon resides. In addition to brightly colored muumuus, shirts, shorts, skirts and snakeskin shoes, you'll find a shelf of twelfth-century to nineteenth-century Asian ceramics. Simon has two other outlets, but the shoes and antiques are sold only here. *Open daily 9 a.m.-9 p.m.*

Sig Zane Designs

140 Kilauea Ave.,
Hilo
• 935-7077

Sig Zane designs the fabrics here, which begin at $10 a yard for 100-percent cotton, and then turns them into elegant, tasteful dresses that go for $15 to $200. Florals predominate—hyacinths, Tahitian gardenia and a variety of Hawaiian exotics. And if dresses strike you as too formal, there's sure to be a *pareo*, T-shirt, or sarong that will turn you on. Fabric slip-on moccasins, called pedi-cozies, and a small but varied assortment of aloha shirts complete the collection. *Open Mon.-Sat. 9:30 a.m.-4:30 p.m.*

FOOD

Big Island Candies
500 Kalanianaole Ave.,
Hilo
• 935-8890

This is the only retail outlet for some of the best chocolate on the island. Though the company has been in business over a decade, supplying bakeries and other commercial enterprises, this open-to-the-public factory is a more recent addition. Our favorites are macadamia nuts from Kona hand-dipped in milk and dark chocolate and shortbread macadamia-nut cookies, also dipped in chocolate. A small snack shop on the premises offers counter service for visitors.
Open daily 8:30 a.m.-5 p.m.

The Candy Store
Prince Kuhio Plaza,
Hilo
• 959-6060

Everything for the sweet tooth, including licorice-flavored dried mango, candy-filled coffee mugs with tropical palm motifs, all-day suckers, sweet-potato chips, rainbow peek-a-boos and the world's smallest jelly beans in a variety of flavors, including root beer and watermelon. There's even cherry and apple cider to wash it all down.
Open Mon., Tues., Wed., Sat. 9:30 a.m.-5:30 p.m., Thurs.-Fri. 9:30 a.m.-9 p.m.

The Chocolate Bar
98 Keawe St.,
Hilo
• 961-5088

Stop here to pick up homemade chocolates on the way to Akaka or Rainbow Falls. Having originated chocolate-covered fortune cookies, a dubious distinction, the shop will customize them for you, baking in fortunes geared for weddings, birthdays and the like. A sweet sushi bento box (made with coconut and chocolate rather than rice and seaweed) goes for $4.50, or you can buy a roll of chocolate sushi wrapped in bamboo. Those who are tired of Gummi bears can get gummy dinosaurs here, or edible "prehistoric dinosaur eggs" to nibble on.
Open Mon.-Sat. 10 a.m.-5 p.m.

Hawaiian Holiday Macadamia Nut Co.
P.O. Box 707,
Honokaa
• 775-7743

You'll know you're approaching the Macadamia Nut Factory when you see the sign that reads "Watch out for nuts crossing the road." The usual cookies, candies and the eponymous are the mainstays here. We hanker for, but have never allowed desire to overwhelm judgment of, the "World's Largest Macadamia-Nut Candy Bar," which weighs in at 60 pounds and checks out for $495. You can watch the process of chocolate-making through glass panels that separate the factory from the sales area. Be warned—prices here may equal or exceed those charged in town.
Open daily 9 a.m.-6 p.m.

Suzanne's Bakeshop
75-5702 Alii Dr.,
Kailua-Kona
• 329-3365

Early birds and night owls alike gravitate toward Suzanne's Bake Shop, where they can munch on bear claws, butter cookies, apple pie and health-foody bar cookies with a cup of Kona coffee, or take them out to eat while strolling along Alii Drive. The quality of goodies here is several notches above the usual fare.
Open daily 4:45 a.m.-9:30 p.m.

GIFTS

Crystal Gallery
75-5699 Alii Dr.,
Kailua-Kona
• 329-8188

Howard Ritchie guarantees that his blown-glass sculptures are made from oven-annealed Pyrex, which gives his sailfish, or the hummingbird delicately thrusting its beak into a lilac-colored flower, or the ship inside the bottle a better-than-even chance of getting home intact. Ornaments and bells begin at $7, while complicated pieces can cost as much as $500.
Open daily 8:30 a.m.-9:30 p.m.

The Futon Connection
104 Keawe St.,
Hilo
• 935-8066

Wall hangings in natural fibers, floral fans in pastels, Japanese dolls, macramé, handmade costume jewelry, whimsical footstools supported on sneaker-shod legs and, of course, futons, typify the items that come and go in this store more reminiscent of southern California than sleepy Hilo.
Open Mon.-Sat. 9 a.m.-5 p.m.

Handcarved Museum Replicas
Mamane St.,
Honokaa
• 775-7703

Just when we thought we'd escaped from the honky-tonk and kitsch that entices tourists throughout the Islands, we came upon this place halfway between Hilo and Kona. Here junk junkies' wildest dreams come true. Rampantly inauthentic tikis rub shoulders (if you'll pardon the expression) with nubile young maidens that once might have served as ships' figureheads. Owner Jim Rice, who can spin a yarn with the best of them, carves many of the pieces himself. Carousel horses, Balinese wood carvings, modern Canton ware and too similar *faux* objets d'art pack the interior of the one-room shop.
Hours vary. Call for appointment.

Hawaiian Island Candle Co.
Prince Kuhio Plaza,
Hilo
• 959-8805

Owner Bruce Kramer designs and makes most of the candles, our favorite being a baleful black-wax volcano with fissures exposing an interior of yellow wax that glows like molten lava when the candle is lit. T-shirts designed by local artists, including Annenberg, drape one wall and koa wood bowls by a variety of craftspeople from the Big Island line the counters.
Open Mon., Wed. & Sat. 9:30 a.m.-5:30 p.m., Thurs.-Fri. 9:30 a.m.-9 p.m.

Jack Ackerman's Original Maui Divers
Kona Inn Shopping Village,
Kailua-Kona
• 329-9442

Here's one of the best selections of coral you'll find in Kona, including mottled beige tiger coral and rosy-cheeked apple coral. There's also a small selection of volcanic obsidian jewelry, plus the usual pink and black coral rings, necklaces and earrings. Black coral, by the way , is the Hawaiian state gem.
Open 9 a.m. to 9 p.m. daily.

Kimura Lauhala Shop
P.O. Box 32,
Holualoa
• 324-0053

Everything that can be made or woven from *lauhala* or split bamboo is likely to find a place in this mountain aerie. Hats, mats (both for table and floor), baskets, planters, trays, cigarette cases, wallets and purses—all will be found here, stuffed into one corner or another.
Open Mon.-Sat. 9 a.m.-5 p.m.

Lyman Museum Gift Shop
276 Haili St.,
Hilo
• 935-5021

A fairly large collection of books on Hawaii, including children's books, are the main reason for coming here. They also stock a strong collection of geodes and modern quilts and a fairly ordinary selection of shell leis, rocks, T-shirts and pottery.
Open Mon.-Sat. 9 a.m.-5 p.m.

Waimea General Store
P.O. Box 187,
Kamuela
• 885-4479

Pop into the back room called "The Clay Bodies" for hand-thrown platters by Lisa and Lex Morriss, the owners. In the outer room, you'll find a potpourri of kitchenware, toys, gift cards, yarn and wooden bracelets.
Open Mon.-Sat. 9 a.m.-5 p.m., Sun. 10 a.m.-4 p.m.

MISCELLANEOUS

Outdoor Wilderness Supply
Mamane St.,
Honokaa
• 775-7765

Those who want to explore the hiking trails and nearby hill country can get some useful tips on conditions here, whether they're in the market for a tent or not. Hunting bows are sold for shooting wild pigs that forage not too far from town.
Open Mon.-Sat. 9 a.m.-4 p.m.

Waipio Valley Wagon Tours
Mamane St.,
Honokaa
• 775-9518

The taro fields and colorful farm houses that dot the valley floor reappear on T-shirts that are sold as souvenirs, but Waipio Valley Wagon Tours's main purpose is to ferry the curious through this beautiful country.
Open 7:30 a.m.-5:30 p.m.

SIGHTS

BEACHES

The shoreline of the Big Island mimics its dramatic and varied interior. More than 100 beaches—of white, black and even green sand—are found along the 361-mile coastline. These beaches range from those with full public facilities, including parking lots, rest rooms and showers, to nearly inaccessible, remote locations on private land, or at the base of steep cliffs. Needless to say, each beach has a personality of its own.

Anaehoomalu
Fronting Royal Waikoloan Hotel, Kohala Coast
• 885-6789

Residents and visitors flock to this long, white-sand crescent, dotted with black-lava fragments and bordered by waving palm trees. The beach slopes gently down to deeper waters offshore, where swimming, snorkeling, near-shore scuba-diving, windsurfing and sometimes surfing are excellent. Equipment rental and instruction in snorkeling, scuba and windsurfing are available at the north end of the beach. There's a small park with rest rooms, showers and picnic tables at the south end. Parking is near the hotel.

Coconut Island Park
Center of Hilo Bay, Hilo
• 961-8311

The ancient Hawaiians claimed that swimming around the rock that lies offshore from Coconut Island could cure any illness. Today most of the swimming is centered around the diving tower, but this grassy, tree-lined area is popular with picnickers and fishermen as well as swimmers. Facilities include a pavilion with rest rooms, picnic tables, benches and a parking lot adjacent to the grounds of the Hilo Hawaiian Hotel.

Hapuna Beach State Recreation Area

Queen Kaahumanu
Hwy.,
north of Waikoloa
• 882-7995

Hapuna is the kind of perfect white-sand beach that central casting would choose for a movie set in paradise. Clean sand stretches for half a mile between the black-lava promontories that mark its boundaries. In the summer, the beach is 200 feet wide (the widest beach on the Big Island). In the winter, the surf gobbles up most of the white sand but leaves a few feet for beachgoers. May through September, residents from all over the island flock to this beach for swimming, snorkeling and scuba-diving. Facilities include a half-dozen A-frame cabins for overnight camping, paved parking lots, picnic pavilions, restrooms and showers. Winter totally changes Hapuna. From around October until April, high surf pounds the beach, generating a thundering shorebreak and extremely powerful rip currents. There is no lifeguard, and every winter people unfamiliar with the angry waters of Hapuna get into trouble.

Hookena Beach Park

Off Hawaii Belt Rd.,
Hookena
• 961-8311

This is a beach off the beaten path, tricky to find and a long ride down the mountain from the Hawaii Belt Highway. It's to Hookena that Hawaii residents bring their families to relax in the small park, complete with rest room, showers, picnic tables and shade trees. The beach, which is a combination of very fine black and white sand that blends into gray, allows easy entry and exit for swimmers. The best snorkeling and scuba-diving is north of Hookena Beach Park along the rocky shoreline.

Kahaluu Beach Park

Adjacent to Keauhou
Beach Hotel,
Alii Dr.,
Keauhou
• 961-8311

Shallow water, extraordinary reef structure and schools of colorful fish make Kahuluu Beach Park the most popular snorkeling spot in Kona. Even the most timid swimmers are comfortable here: they can stand up if they panic. The white-sand beach fills up quickly with sunbathers and families. On weekends, nearly every foot of space is occupied, including the picnic pavilion and parking area. County lifeguards warn the inexperienced that during high surf a strong rip current can pull swimmers outside the bay. When the surf's up, more rescues are made at Kahaluu Beach Park than at any other beach in Kona.

Magic Sands

Alii Dr.,
Kailua-Kona
• 961-8311

Magic Sands, also called White Sands or Disappearing Sands, gets its name from the periodic flushing of sand from this small beach. During the winter, violent waves can literally remove the sand within one 24-hour period, leaving bare rock: the sand "disappears" overnight. In the summer, the sand generally washes back. This tiny beach, the largest along the seven-mile coast from Kailua to Keauhou, is excellent for swimming; a small shore break on the sandbar offers small "training" waves for beginning bodysurfers and bodyboarders. In the winter, powerful waves—up to ten feet—roar through this small cove, providing excellent bodysurfing conditions. The facilities include rest room, showers, a lifeguard tower, tiny parking lot and small coconut grove.

Spencer Beach Park
Below the Puukohola Heiau,
Hwy. 19,
Kawaihae
• 882-7094

What was once one of the Big Island's fabulous beaches has fallen into disrepair and squalor, primarily due to homeless squatters who use the facilities. Lying in the shadow of the giant temple Kamehameha built before uniting all the Hawaiian islands is a white-sand beach. Its protection from the prevailing winds and offshore waves makes for exceptional swimming, snorkeling and diving conditions. The somewhat disheveled facilities include rest rooms, picnic tables, showers, tennis courts, a roofed pavilion, parking lots, camping area and lifeguard tower. We hope that Hawaii County will restore the facilities and surrounding area to its once pristine condition.

EXCURSIONS

Hilo
Hwy. 19

Who needs a time machine? A trip to Hilo is a trip to Hawaii circa 1939. Curving around the crescent bay at the base of Mauna Loa and Mauna Kea is the Big Island's capital city, Hilo. Lush with orchids that thrive in its rainy weather, Hilo has streets lined with old tin-roofed, wooden buildings from a more leisurely era. Home to more than 42,000, Hilo is the county seat, the location of a state university and the main port of the island. The city's people, who are a mixture of Japanese, Chinese, Hawaiian, Filipino and Caucasian, still believe in smiling at strangers and taking time to stop and talk to their neighbors. Don't be surprised when shopping in some of the old wood-front stores downtown if your selection is tallied with paper and pencil, an abacus or an old-fashioned cash register that "rings" up your purchase. Take time to wander through the numerous tropical gardens and historical museums. Time in Hilo is not measured in hours and minutes but in seasons. As one Hilo resident puts it: "Warning, Hilo's slow pace of life can become habit forming."

HAWAII'S ARTHUR

Ancient chants foretold of a warrior who would come one day to unify all the Hawaiian Islands. Islanders would know this warrior by his strength. The royal Naha clan was in charge of the Naha Stone, a two-and-a-half-ton stone that stood in front of a temple. Any young noble with aspirations of grandeur could try his luck at moving the stone. It's a little like the Arthurian legend, except instead of pulling out Excalibur, contenders needed considerably more heave-ho. The legend claims that when King Kamehameha was a young boy, he overturned the giant stone. It can still be seen today, even though the *heiau* is gone, fronting the Hawaii Public Library on Waianuenue Avenue in Hilo. No one has been able to budge the stone since.

Ka Lae
Southern tip of the Big Island

Down an eleven-mile road from Highway 11, along unfenced range lands where cattle roam freely, lies the southernmost point of the United States, Ka Lae. The windswept point was the first landfall made by the Polynesian voyagers. An arduous three-mile hike east from South Point through dry grass over a constantly windy plain leads to the famous Green Sand Beach. An entire cinder cone of olivine collapsed into the bay, resulting in this oddity. Good for swimming and picnicking, the beach faces miles of open ocean, where the next landfall is thousands of miles away.

Kohala Coast
Queen Kaahumanu Hwy. to Rte. 270

For a taste of ancient Hawaii, a half day's drive up the Kohala Coast is your ticket to the past. Starting at Puako, near Kawaihae, stop and view the petroglyphs, the ancient Hawaiian rock carvings depicting people, animals, historical and religious events, maps and nearly every aspect of daily life. North of Puako, just before Kawaihae, lies the Pu'ukohola Heiau, the temple Kamehameha the Great built in 1790 to honor the war god Kukailimoku and thus insure his domination of all the Hawaiian Islands. Traveling north, stop at Lapakahi, Hawaii's only state historical park, between Kawaihae and Mahukona on Highway 270. This small coastal fishing village has been preserved to demonstrate Hawaiian life as it was lived 600 years ago. The final and most mysterious stop on the tour is the Mo'okini Heiau, near the Upolu airfield on the northern tip of the island. This temple, once the site of important ceremonies and human sacrifices, is over 1,500 years old. It is built of water-worn basalt stones that come from Pololu Valley, more than ten miles and several valleys away. Oral history recounts that it was built in just one night by a human chain, which passed stones hand over hand ten miles to the site.

Kona Coffee Country
Hwy. 180 & Hwy. 11, Holualoa & Kealakekua

Up the slopes where lush tropical vegetation blankets the hillside lies Kona coffee country. A twenty-mile mile belt of land, beginning at 700 feet and rising to 2,500 feet, wraps across the flanks of two volcanoes, Hualalai and Mauna Loa. Little has changed in the growing and milling of coffee since the first trees came to Kona in 1828. The towns along the coffee belt have remained sleepy villages. Start on Route 180 at the northern end of coffee country in Holualoa, a one-street village with clusters of art galleries. Drive south past the flowering coffee trees, tall avocado trees, blooming yellow ginger plants and dew-kissed ferns to Kainaliu on Highway 11. Another place time has forgotten, Kainaliu seems like a town from the 1940s. The stores still have names like "dry goods" and "mercantile," and their proprietors know most of their customers' first names. Coffee country ends just past Kealakekua, which overlooks the bay where Captain Cook was killed. This is the home of Kona coffee, and tasting rooms abound. The best is the Kona Kai Farms Tasting Center on Highway 11, whose tasting room adjoins the coffee drop-off center. During coffee season (September to January), you can watch farmers deliver and weigh their coffee cherries.

Mauna Loa Macadamia Nut Co.
Off Hwy. 11, Hilo
• 966-8612

Don't trek all the way here hoping for a free handout—if you're struck by the urge to binge on the heavenly nut after visiting the plant, you'll have to pay dearly for them at the gift shop. But even if your interest in the nut is purely academic, a visit to Hawaii's largest producer of macadamia nuts makes for an enjoyable excursion; the visitors center's diversions include a "nature walk" through the orchards, a video on the nut's history and a self-guided tour of the processing plant next door. To get there, take Highway 11 about five miles south of Hilo and turn left on Macadamia Road. You'll meander three miles through macadamia orchards to reach the visitors center. *Open daily 8:30 a.m.-5 p.m. Admission free.*

G'DAY, MACADAMIA

Since almost every macadamia nut you've ever seen was probably in a jar labeled Mauna Loa, you thought they were Hawaiian nuts, right? The name "macadamia" even sounds exotic enough and sports enough vowels to be properly Hawaiian. Actually, the nut is native to Australia, and was named after Australian chemist John Macadam. The nut was brought to the Big Island from Down Under in 1882, but wasn't produced commercially until 1948. Now Hawaii's crops account for more than 65 percent of the world's production; the Islands' contribution in 1989 was 55 million pounds of in-shell nuts.

Milolii Fishing Village
Hwy. 11

Down a steep, winding road on the southwest flank of the Big Island lies the sleepy fishing village of Milolii. Ramshackle houses and motorized outrigger canoes line the beaches. The sound of ukuleles, the surf and children's laughter fills the air. Most of the Milolii residents, Hawaiians who escaped a 1920s eruption and settled here, make their living from the sea. Material possessions are not important; for some, electricity and running water are something to be enjoyed only in "town" (Kailua). Residents prefer to tinker with old cars, drink beer on the dilapidated porches of the homes or sit in the shade of a tree and "talk story" with neighbors. Journey to this special place not only to view this lifestyle but to feel the strong sense of community among these openhearted people.

Suisan Fish Auction
85 Lihiwai, Hilo
• 935-8051

Catching the Suisan Fish Auction may mean getting up a tad earlier than your usual vacation schedule allows, but it's worth it. It's a culture within itself. Wholesale buyers bark out bids in a staccato rhythm, language punctuated with hand gestures and poker-face looks, as the commercial catch from Hilo's fleet goes on the block. Fat yellow-fin tuna, giant marlin, swordfish and various kinds of deep-water snapper are inspected, graded and sold. The whole process can take as little as 30 minutes if the catch is off or last for hours when the fishing is good. If all of this auctioneering makes your mouth water, go next door to the retail shop and do a little bidding of your own.
Open Mon.-Sat. 8 a.m. Closing time varies.

Waipio Valley Shuttle & Services
End of Rte. 240, Waipio

Once a favored spot of Hawaiian royalty as well as a center of cultural and political life on the Big Island, Waipio Valley is now a retreat into the past. Neat geometric taro fields line the pastoral valley, bordered by 2,000-foot cliffs on one side and the waves of the Pacific on the other. This is a Hawaii of bygone days. Only four-wheel-drive vehicles can traverse the steep access road into the valley. Waipio Valley Shuttle offers excellent guided tours.
Open daily 9 a.m.-4 p.m. with tours every hour. Adults $20.

LUAUS

Can one visit Hawaii and not attend a luau? Yes, but a good luau really shouldn't be missed. The best luau on the Big Island (and some say in all of Hawaii) can be found on Friday nights at the secluded **Kona Village Resort**, north of Kailua-Kona. The menu includes traditional food prepared in the ancient way, such as kalua pig (baked in an *imu* pit), chicken prepared with taro tops and coconut milk, laulau (pork, fish and taro tops steamed in ti-leaf bundles), poisson cru (a Tahitian dish of raw fish marinated in coconut milk and lime juice), maki sushi (a Japanese favorite, rice rolled in seaweed wrappers), steamed ulu (breadfruit), aama crab, tako poke (raw octopus in a chile-pepper marinade) and kulolo (taro pudding, steamed in banana leaves).

The luau starts at 5:30 p.m. with a tour of the archaeologically rich grounds of Kona Village Resort. At 6:15 the uncovering of the imu pit begins. The food is served at 7 p.m., and a traditional Polynesian show starts at 8 p.m. The entire program (luau, imu ceremony, tour and show) is $49 for adults (includes tax, tip and house wine with dinner), $24.50 for children ages 6 to 12 and $12.25 for ages 2 to 5.

If for some reason you can't make the Kona Village luau, our second favorite luau is at the **Hotel King Kamehameha**, located in Kailua-Kona. The food is not as lavish as at the Kona Village luau, but it is authentic (with some American dishes thrown in). The luaus are every Sunday, Tuesday and Thursday beginning at 5:30 p.m., with a Polynesian show at 7:45. Cost is $49.50 for adults and $24 for children ages 5 to 12.

MUSEUMS

Hulihee Palace
75-5718 Alii Dr.,
Kailua-Kona
• 329-1877

For the price of admission, you, too, can be Queen (or King) for a Day. Home and summer residence of Hawaiian royalty, this coral and lava structure was built in 1838 by Gov. John Kuakini. The elegant two-story structure, which is furnished in Victorian and Hawaiian antiques reflecting the styles of the period, is surrounded by a broad lawn and fronts Kailua Bay. *Open daily 9 a.m.-4 p.m. Adults $4, seniors over 65 $3, students $1, children under 12 50 cents.*

Kamuela Museum
Rte. 19 & Rte. 250,
Kamuela
• 885-4724

This museum was founded by the great-great granddaughter of the founder of Parker Ranch, Harriet Solomon, and her husband, Albert. The Solomons curate this very eclectic collection themselves. It isn't so much the material assembled (which ranges from artifacts of Hawaiian royalty to pure junk) but the stories and commentary given by the Solomons that make this a fabulous stop. These folks are a treasure trove of information on Hawaiiana and Island life. Plan to spend at least a couple of hours wandering through the collection of European and Oriental art objects, moon-flight relics and Hawaiian artifacts. Don't leave without getting Albert Solomon to show you his rare lava stone—which is heavy but floats in water. *Open daily 8 a.m.-4 p.m. Adults $2.50, children under 12 $1.*

Kona Historical Society's Museum
Hwy. 11,
Kealakekua
• 323-3222

The old Greenwell Store has been preserved as a museum by the Kona Historical Society and features items from the store, antiques, relics from Captain Cook's visit and photo displays of this ranching and agricultural community in the nineteenth and early twentieth centuries. *Open Tues.-Fri. 9 a.m.-3 p.m., Sat. 9 a.m.-noon. Donation requested.*

Lyman House Memorial Museum
276 Haili St.,
Hilo
• 935-5021

Built in 1839 by one of the first missionaries to Hawaii, Rev. David Lyman, this two-story house displays antiques of life during the missionary era in Hawaii. Next door is the Lyman Museum, housing the Island Heritage Gallery, which uses modern display techniques and realistic settings to present the treasures, tools, implements, handcrafts, methods of dress and other cultural contributions of the various ethnic groups in Hawaii. Exhibits trace the story of Hawaii from the arrival of the first Polynesians. *Open Mon.-Sat. 9 a.m.-5 p.m. Adults $3.50, children 13-18 $2.50, children 6-12 $1.50.*

PARKS & GARDENS

**Akaka Falls
State Park**
Hwy. 19,
Hilo

This is as close as you may ever get to the Garden of Eden—66 acres under a rain-forest canopy: wild bamboo groves, dewy ferns, brilliant ti plants and tropical trees, the scent of ginger in the air. The highlight is the 420-foot cascade known as Akaka Falls. If you want a spot for a fabulous picnic, this is it.

**Hawaii Tropical
Botanical
Gardens**
P.O. Box 1415,
Onomea Bay
• 964-5233

Pathways carved out of the jungle meander through this exotic nature preserve. Streams, waterfalls and more than 1,000 plant species, including extensive collections of palms, bromeliads, gingers, exotic ornamentals and rare plants fill this natural wonderland. The park borders rugged coastline, where giant sea turtles may be seen.
Open daily 8:30 a.m.-4:30 p.m. Adults $10, children under 16 free.

**Hawaii
Volcanoes
National Park**
Hwy. 11,
Volcano
• 967-7311

Home of Pele, the Hawaiian fire goddess, this is a "must" on every visitor's list. Established in 1916, the 229,000-acre Hawaii Volcanoes National Park sprawls down Kilauea's southern and eastern flanks and up the slopes of Mauna Loa to the 13,677-foot summit. Within the park's boundaries are scenic drives, 150 miles of hiking trails, a comprehensive visitors center at park headquarters, the Thomas A. Jaggar Museum, Hawaii Volcano Observatory, campgrounds, the Volcano Art Center and the 37-room Volcano House, perched on the rim of the Kilauea caldera. Pele is currently in the midst of a temper tantrum that started in January 1983, one of the longest continuous eruptions ever recorded. In addition to her recent eruption from the Puu O Kupaiianaha and from vents on the side of Kilauea, the park is dotted with sights of this ever-changing geology: hissing roadside fumaroles, smoldering pits, pungent sulfur banks and miles of black, crusted lava. Eruptions vary from spectacular "curtains of fire" to underground rivers of molten lava, visible only at night. In addition to watching the eruption, visitors can enjoy one of the best hiking areas in Hawaii. The air is cool and brisk at 4,000 feet, the numerous trails lead across small craters, down Devastation Trail, into the 1,400-foot Thurston Lava Tube and even up to the top of Mauna Loa. For nonhikers, most of the park's points of interest are also reachable by car.
Open daily 24 hours. Visitor Center open daily 7:45 a.m.-5 p.m. Admission $5 per car per week. Cars with visitors 65 or older get in free.

A WORD ABOUT EARTHQUAKES:

The Big Island is subject to relatively frequent earthquakes generated by its active volcanoes. You may feel one while you are here, but few actually cause damage.

Liliuokalan Gardens

Banyan Dr.,
Waiakea Peninsula
Hilo

Here is the largest formal Oriental garden—30 acres—outside of Japan. This magnificent cultural park, named after Hawaii's last reigning monarch, Queen Liliuokalani, was built in the early 1900s as a memorial to the immigrant Japanese who came to work at the old Waiakea Sugar Plantation. The gardens feature both Hawaiian and Asian trees, pagodas, arched bridges, a ceremonial teahouse, carved stone lions, Japanese stone lanterns and reflecting lagoons.

Panaewa Rain Forest Zoo

Just off Hwy. 11 on
Stainback Hwy.,
Hilo
• 959-7224

Panaewa is one of the few tropical rain-forest zoos in the United States. Wander through this tiny zoo, which features several rain-forest species in a natural environment, such as: African pygmy hippopotami, rain-forest monkeys, a tapir, jungle parrots, rain-forest tigers and endangered Hawaiian birds including the nene goose, Hawaiian stilt and Koloa duck.
Open daily 9 a.m.-4 p.m. Admission free.

Puuhonua o Honaunau (Place of Refuge of Honaunau)

Off Hwy. 11,
Honaunau
• 328-2288

This ancient Hawaiian place of refuge once was a sanctuary for law-breakers—if one could enter, he would be spared from death. During times of war it also became a sanctuary for those who couldn't fight or those defeated in battle. Honaunau was the residence of the ruling chief, and his palace grounds adjoined the refuge. Inside the refuge was a mausoleum that housed the dead bodies of royalty. The ancient Hawaiians believed that the spiritual power of chiefs remained within their bones after death. Today this sacred site is preserved as a 181-acre national park. Many of the arts and skills of old Hawaii are performed, including the pounding of *tapa* (cloth made from bark) and the weaving of *lauhala* (pandanus-leaf) into baskets or mats.
Visitor center open daily 7:30 a.m.-5:30 p.m. Park grounds open daily 6 a.m.-midnight. Admission $1 (free after 4:30 p.m.)

TOURS

Captain Beans' Cruises

Kailua Pier,
Kailua-Kona
• 329-2955

Captain Beans' is an institution in Kona. The trademark red crab claw-shaped Polynesian sails have been cruising the waters of Kona for a couple of decades. Captain Beans' offers three types of excursions: the glass-bottom snorkeling trip (complete with lunch and Polynesian show), the glass-bottom trip for which a diver goes over the side to feed fish under the viewing windows, and the dinner sunset sail (lots of entertainment, hula dancers and never-ending refills on your mai tai). The 150-foot *Tamure* can hold up to 200 people.
Snorkel cruise daily 8:30 a.m.-1 p.m. $25. Glass-bottom tour daily 1:30-2:30 p.m. $10. Dinner sunset sail daily 5:15 p.m. $42.

Captain Zodiac

Honokohau Harbor
Kailua-Kona
• 329-3199

Twice a day, the 23-foot inflatable raft leaves Honokohau Harbor for the four-hour journey along the Kona coast. Hugging the coastline, the Captain reels off Hawaiian legends and points out the places of interest to his sixteen passengers. At Kealakekua Bay, the boat stops for snorkeling in the calm waters. All gear and a bit of instruction is provided. After snorkeling, a snack (such that it is—fruit, chips, pretzels and juice) is served. The cruise continues down to Honaunau Bay, site of the Place of Refuge. The trip back is a bit rough and bumpy (they refuse to take pregnant women and people with bad backs as passengers). Good way to see the coast up close; not for the infirm. Great during whale season—November to March. *Leaves Honokohau Harbor daily 8 a.m. & 1 p.m. Cost $52 for adults, $41.60 for children under 11.*

Hawaiian Eyes Big Island Bicycle Tours

P.O. Box 1500
Honokaa
• 885-8806

Owner Willy Senerchia likes to take people for a ride, a bike ride that is. He offers a variety of bicycle tours for groups of up to ten people to scenic, rural settings. Every tour begins with a get-acquainted lesson on how to use his mountain bikes. He stresses safety and backs it up by having two skilled guides leading and following each tour in radio communication with each other. His tours, open to people ages 10 to 65, vary from novice to intermediate in difficulty. One of his most scenic and easy tours is the all-downhill ride from the Hawaii Volcanoes National Park down the S-turns to the black-sand beach. This is a six-hour tour: three and a half hours on the bike, the rest in the van going back up the mountain. It includes a gourmet picnic lunch. The Saddle Road tour, 23 miles between the island's tallest mountain and its biggest landmass, starts at 7,000 feet and traverses down to 2,700 feet. One of his most scenic tours is the Kohala Mountain ride, fifteen miles of gradual downhill, which includes a stop for ice cream. In addition to the pastoral rolling hills of Kohala, in the winter months you may spot humpback whales offshore. Depending on the trip, Willy will pick you up or arrange to meet at a convenient spot.

Tours daily, times vary. Cost Volcano to the Sea $99, Saddle Road $90, Kohala Mountain $60.

A MOVING EXPERIENCE

Hawaiian chants and legends are filled with the wondrous deeds of King Kamehameha the Great. Indeed, he seems to be supernatural even in death. In 1880 an American sculptor working in Italy completed a statue of the great Hawaiian king and sent it to Hawaii. On the journey, the monument was lost at sea. Craftsmen completed a copy and placed it in front of the Judiciary Building in Honolulu. Then—egads—the original statue was found. Hawaiians argued that Kamehameha was behind the loss and recovery because he wanted the statue to be placed in Kapaau, near his birthplace. The original statue stands there today, and no one dares move it.

Kenai Helicopters
Waikoloa Heliport, Waikoloa
• 329-7424

With the volcano erupting, the most popular tour is a two-hour volcano flight from the active vent, down to where the hot molten lava hits the sea in an explosion of primal force, plus a flyover of valley waterfalls and the meadows of Parker Ranch on the return. Kenai has been flying on the Big Island for thirteen years and has found a few hidden spots to take their clients, especially along the steep, lush valleys of the Hamakua Coast or up to the top of Manua Loa summit for an early-morning greeting of the sun.
Open daily 7:30 a.m.-sunset. Volcano deluxe tour $245 per person, Hamakua Coast $140. Children under 2 free.

Mauna Kea Helicopters
P.O. Box 1713, Kamuela
• 885-6400

Ask for pilot Scott Shupe, one of the best helicopter pilots in Hawaii. Scott's customers always leave with a smile after a ride in the sky. Our favorite tours are the Valley Adventure, a 35-minute ride that covers all eight of the dramatic Hamakua valleys and the Kilauea Show Stopper, a tour of the active volcano, plus the Valley Adventure. Every seat in Scott's craft is a window seat.
Tours daily. Valley Adventure $110 per person, Kilauea Show Stopper $265 per person. Minimum of two, maximum of four per flight. Flights leave the Waimea Airport.

Papillon Hawaiian Helicopters
Waikoloa Heliport, Waikoloa
• 885-5995

The three best tours are the Kohala Coast (50 minutes of exploring inaccessible, hidden valleys filled with tumbling waterfalls and majestic scenery); the Volcano (eyeballing the blood-red lava flows and hovering next to the explosive blasts of steam, as the 2,000-degree magma flows into the 80-degree Pacific Ocean); and the Kilauea-Kohala Deluxe, a combination of the previous two, plus the rain forests of Hilo and the grazing lands of Parker Ranch.
Open daily 6 a.m.-6 p.m. Kohala Coast $145, Volcano $245 and Kilauea-Kohala Deluxe $295.

Paradise Safaris
P.O. Box A-D, Kailua-Kona
• 322-2366

Sunset star-gazing tour atop Mauna Kea. Pickup provided for South Kohala hotels. They also provide warm parkas and hot drinks as you drive to the top of Hawaii's tallest volcano for a magnificent sunset and a two-hour tour of the heavens through a high-tech telescope. Note: the company will not take pregnant women or anyone with respiratory or heart problems.
Tours daily 3 p.m.-11 p.m. $80 per person. Must be 17 or older.

Parker Ranch Tours

Parker Ranch,
Kamuela
• 885-7655

For the first time in the 142-year history of Parker Ranch, the family has opened up its historical homes and facilities to the public. One of the largest privately owned ranches in the United States, Parker Ranch represents a period of history in Hawaii when *paniolos* (cowboys) working cattle ranches were part of a major industry and lifestyle in the Islands. The Paniolo Shuttle Tour offers a look at the Ranch Museum (featuring large-screen videos on the family) and the Duke Kahanamoku Room (trophies and medals of the Olympic swimmer from Hawaii). A van then takes visitors to the Puukalani Stable area (in addition to the animals, the stable has a collection of antique surreys, and an orphan-calf program that will melt your heart). Then you visit Puu Opelo, the ranch owner's exquisite home with his priceless collection of art, ranging from Impressionist paintings to Ming Dynasty antiques. Next door is the Mana Home, the original home of the founder, John Palmer Parker I. Built in the 1840s, the home is constructed of rare koa wood and is a prime example of the simple but elegant lifestyle of the nineteenth century. The home is filled with memorabilia of six generations of the family. For the more deluxe Paniolo Country Tour you must book reservations in advance. This tour includes all of the above, plus a trip to the original two-acre homestead, which was a grant from King Kamehameha III. The tour includes a journey through the pastoral ranch lands, a stop at the family cemetery and picnic lunch.

Open daily 10 a.m.-3 p.m. Visitors center only $4.50, Paniolo Shuttle Tour $16.50. Paniolo Country Tour daily 10 a.m.-1:30 p.m. & 1:30 p.m.-5 p.m. Cost is $32.

> ## THAR SHE BLOWS
>
> The Big Island of Hawaii is the only spot in the U.S. where new land is being added by the minute. It's all thanks to Kilauea, the volcano that has been erupting on and off since the early 1980s, and the centerpiece of Hawaii Volcanoes National Park. To find out what's happening currently, call the "hot line" at (808) 967-7311.

Volcano Heli-Tours

Volcano Golf Course,
Volcano
• 967-7578

Located a mile and a half south of the entrance to the Hawaii Volcanoes National Park, this is the closest helicopter tour to the eruption. The tour features a 45-minute flight to the eruption site and around the entire Volcanoes National Park. *Open daily. Trips by arrangement. Cost is $105.*

Wilderness Hawaii

P.O. Box 61692,
Honolulu
• 1-737-4697
(Honolulu)

A four-day backpacking expedition for neophytes along the coast of Hawaii Volcanoes National Park. They provide all ground transportation, equipment, food and expert guide service.
Tours by arrangement. Cost is $300 (interisland air fare is additional). Maximum 10 people.

SPORTS

BICYCLING

Dave's Bike & Triathlon Shop
74-5588 Pawai Pl.,
Kailua-Kona
• 329-4522

Mountain-bike rental, some racing bikes.
Open Mon.-Fri. 9 a.m.-5 p.m., Sat. 9 a.m.-1 p.m. Closed Sun.
Rentals: $12 per day, $50-$60 per week.

DIVING & SNORKELING

Atlantis Submarines
Hotel King Kamehameha,
Kailua-Kona
• 329-6625

For those unable to plunge underwater in the flesh, or for those looking for a one-of-a-kind experience, Atlantis has brought in an 80-ton submarine and operates it daily off the shores of Kailua-Kona. A shuttle boat takes 48 passengers to the sub, which dives as deep as 150 feet. The vessel prowls around the reef as the passengers view the subterranean world from large portholes during the 55-minute ride. Even ardent divers have been impressed with the tour.No children under 4 allowed.
Departs Kailua Pier daily 10 a.m.-3 p.m. (Wed. 6:30 p.m. night dive.) Adults $67, children 4-12 $33.50.

Captain Cook Cruise
74-5543 Kaiwi St.,
Kailua-Kona
• 329-6411

The longest-running cruise on the Kona coast, the four-hour, round-trip excursion to Kealakekua Bay is geared for 175 passengers. After lunch, the crew will teach you how to snorkel. It's a great introduction to the brilliant underwater life in this marine preserve. All snorkeling gear provided. Lunch is not much to brag about, but the trip down the coast and the superb snorkeling in the bay are well worth the price.
Departs Kailua Pier 8:30 a.m. Adults $36.40, children under 12 $18.20, children under 2 free.

Fair Wind
78-1128 Kaleopapa Rd.,
Keauhou
• 322-2788

This is one of the most friendly snorkel-cruise trips available. Although the 50-foot trimaran is Coast Guard certified for 149 passengers, the Fair Wind books only 100 on their morning and afternoon cruises. The boat leaves palm-lined Keauhou Bay and sails to the marine preserve in Kealakekua Bay. A fruit snack is offered en route to the bay. After mooring, the crew gives a short snorkeling lesson to anyone interested. After an hour in the water, a barbecue lunch is served. More snorkeling follows lunch. This tour is set up for everyone, even nonswimmers. All snorkeling gear, including tubes and viewers if you don't want to put your head in the water, are provided. Scuba lessons are also available. The morning cruise is four and a half hours; the afternoon cruise is three and a half hours (no lunch). The best time to go is in the morning, when the sun is high overhead (for better viewing) and the waters are calmer.
Departs daily 8:30 a.m. & 1 p.m. Cost: morning cruise $54, afternoon cruise $34. Scuba lessons with gear $95, without gear $70.

Gold Coast Divers
Kona Inn Shopping Village,
Kailua-Kona
• 329-1328

Not only does Gold Coast Divers rent equipment, but it will suggest good dive spots.
Open daily 9 a.m.-9 p.m. Complete scuba equipment $21 per day. Fins, mask & snorkel $6 per day or $15 per week.

King Kamehameha Divers
Hotel King Kamehameha,
75-5660 Palani Rd.,
Kailua-Kona
• 329-5662

In addition to equipment rental, this dive shop has an excellent dive-charter boat.
Open daily 7 a.m.-7 p.m. Complete scuba equipment $40 per day. Fins, mask and snorkel $7.50 per day or $15 per three days. Weekly rates available.

Kona Aggressor
75-5864 Walua Rd.,
Kailua-Kona
• 329-8182

Live aboard a luxurious 110-foot yacht for a week with unlimited diving. Specializing in underwater photography, this luxury boat even has onboard photographic processing. Food is prepared by a professional chef, and after diving a bubbling Jacuzzi makes one wonder what ordinary mortals are doing. Diving areas range from Upolu Point at the northern tip of the Big Island all the way down to Ka Lae, the southernmost tip. The 25 to 30 divers on each trip vary from rank beginners to experts. *Departs weekly. Complete package (including all meals) $1,595. Scuba certification instruction for beginners $250.*

Kona Coast Divers
75-5614 Palani Rd.,
Kailua-Kona
• 329-8802

You can't miss this five-star PADI facility; it looks like a light house, though it's located half a mile from the ocean. This shop offers everything from classroom and training-pool instruction for certification to gear rental, retail sales and charter boat dives. Private scuba certification lessons are available. *Open daily 7 a.m.-6 p.m. Certification classes $323-$449. Dive charters $49.50-$59.40, including equipment.*

FISHING

The Kona coast is internationally famous for the quality of its big-game fishing. Giant marlin weighing more than 1,000 pounds have been caught in these prolific waters. Big yellowfin tunas have also been hauled in, as well as mahi mahi, ono and ulua. No fishing license is required to fish in Hawaiian salt waters. The best way to choose a charter fishing boat is to book through a top-flight charter desk. It can lead you through the maze of boats and options, and help you to select the one appropriate for you. We advise at least a full day of fishing to maximize your opportunity.

Kona Charter Skippers Assn.
75-5663 Palani Rd.,
Kailua-Kona
• 329-3600

Located right across the street from the weigh-in area on the Kailua Pier, KCSA not only books charters, it also has a selection of T-shirts, hats and other souvenirs. This is a cooperative association of some of the most well-established operators in sport fishing. *Open daily 8:15 a.m.-6 p.m. Rates vary from a low of $85 for a half-day share charter to a high of $1,200 for the most deluxe, overnight fishing adventure.*

Kona Coast Activities
Kona Inn Shopping Village,
Kailua-Kona
• 329-2971

Located next to Drysdale's in the Kona Inn Shopping Village, this small kiosk is the heart of the top charter-boat and activities booking operation. Even if you don't want to book a boat, wander by and listen to the crackling radio reports of lucky

fishermen swapping fish tales over the radio waves.
Open daily 7 a.m.-9 p.m. Rates vary from $87.50 (half-day share on six-passenger boat) to $500 (full-day exclusive charter).

GOLF

Mauna Kea Beach Golf Course
Mauna Kea Beach Hotel, Kohala Coast
• 882-7222

A Robert Trent Jones championship course now covers what once was a wasteland of lava and scrub. Continually rated one of the top courses in the United States, this par-72, 7,114-yard championship course is not only challenging but breathtaking as well. Our favorite hole is the third, where the sign reads 175 yards from the middle tee, but the Pacific Ocean and craggy cliffs between the tee and the green make it seem twice as long. *Tee times daily 7 a.m.-1:45 p.m. for 18 holes, 7 a.m.-4 p.m. for 9 holes. Fee $115 for nonhotel guests, $65 hotel guests (includes cart & green fees).*

Mauna Lani Frances I'i Brown Championship Course
P.O. Box 4959, Kawaihae
• 885-6655

This par-72, 18-hole championship course was literally carved out of ancient lava flows to create one of the toughest courses on the coast. Spectacularly beautiful, this course hosts the PGA Seniors Tour every year. Our vote for the most challenging yet beautiful hole is the sixth, located at the edge of a cliff. The greens are 180 yards and a blue ocean cove away. We won't mention the par. *Tee times begin daily 7:10 a.m. & conclude 2:30 p.m. for 18 holes, 4 p.m. for 9 holes. Fees $130 for 18 holes, $65 for 9 holes, half price for hotel guests.*

Volcano Golf & Country Club
Hawaii Volcanoes National Park, Volcano
• 967-7331

Hawaii's most unusual golf course is on the rim of Kilauea Volcano at 4,000 feet. Where else in the world will you be able to say you played golf on a fuming volcano? Designed by Jack Snyder, this par-72, mildly challenging course meanders among scarlet blossoms of blooming ohia trees and looks out on panoramic, often otherworldly, vistas. *Tee times begin daily 7 a.m. & conclude 2:30 p.m. for 18 holes, 3:30 p.m. for 9 holes. Fees $35 for 18, $20 for 9.*

Waikoloa Beach Golf Course
Waikoloa Resort, Kohala Coast
• 885-6060

Another Robert Trent Jones course, this par-71 course incorporates archaeological sites and lava formations. We found the most challenging hole to be the par-five twelfth hole, which is right on the ocean's edge.

*Tee times daily 7 a.m.-2 p.m. for 18 holes & 4 p.m. for 9 holes.
Fees $95 for 18 holes ($60 for hotel guests) & $60 for 9 holes ($45
for hotel guests).*

HIKING

For information on trails, hiking and camping in parks around the Big Island, contact the **Division of State Parks** (75 Aupuni St., Hilo; 961-7200); the **Hawaii County Department of Parks and Recreation** (25 Aupuni St., Hilo; 961-8311); the **Hawaii Geographic Society** (P.O. Box 1698, Honolulu; 1-538-3952), which has a $6 information packet on trails and hikes throughout the state; or the **Hawaiian Trail and Mountain Club** (P.O. Box 2238, Honolulu; 734-5515), which offers regularly scheduled hikes. Following are some of the Big Island's better trails:

Crater Rim Trail
Hawaii Volcanoes National Park, Volcano
• 967-7311

This is a good introduction to the national park. The 11.6-mile well-marked trail begins at park headquarters, encircles Kilauea crater, passing steam vents, lava flows and fern forests. Excellent for photography.

Halemaumau Trail
Hawaii Volcanoes National Park, Volcano
• 967-7311

One of the best hikes in the park, this 3.1-mile trail offers a view right into the bubbling Halemaumau crater, home of Pele, the fire goddess. The trail begins near the Volcano House and descends into Kilauea Crater, crosses the crater floor and climbs back out again.

Kilauea Iki Trail
Hawaii Volcanoes National Park, Volcano
• 967-7311

A short two-mile jaunt from the Thurston Lava Tube parking lot into the Kilauea Iki crater, where the trail passes next to a steaming vent before returning back to the top.

Mauna Loa Trail
Hawaii Volcanoes National Park, Volcano
• 967-7311

This is for the hardy only: a three-day, eighteen-mile trek to the top of the world's largest volcano. On day one you trek seven miles from Mauna Loa Strip Road to Red Hill. At 10,035 feet there is a cabin. On day two you'll hike another eleven miles to the second cabin at Mokuaweoweo caldera, just below Mauna Loa's summit. On day three it's time to turn around. This is for the physically fit only, and cold weather gear is a must. The trip back takes a minimum of one day, but most hikers take two.

Waimanu Valley Trail
Waipio

A trip into the wilderness, this seven-mile trail begins up the northern cliffs of Waipio Valley. The start is rough, straight up a 1,200-foot cliff in a series of dizzying switchbacks. At the top, it descends into lush Waimanu Valley. Your best bet is to head for the beach: chances are you'll have it all to yourself in a tropical jungle wonderland.

Waipio Valley Trail
Waipio Valley

Former home of Hawaiian royalty, the valley today houses a few taro growers. Once you step into this valley you will see why Hawaiian kings chose this spot from which to govern. The wide four-wheel-drive trail begins at the Waipio lookout at the end of Route 24. The trail drops steeply for about a mile to the valley floor. Here one trail winds through the lush valley, and the other trail goes to the beach.

HORSEBACK RIDING

Ironwood Outfitters
Entrance to Kohala Ranch (Mile Marker 11 on Hwy. 250), Kohala
• 885-4941

The Outfitters prefer to match people to horses and to trail rides. This is not a nose-to-tail-type operation. Instead, they have numerous types of rides and access to 30,000 acres of ranch land to enjoy it on.
Guided tours daily. Rates vary from $30-$65.

Waiono Meadow Trail Rides
Rte. 180, Holualoa
• 324-1544

In addition to the scenic rides through the 1,800-acre working cattle ranch, Waiono Meadow offers fishing for bass and trout at their well-stocked, private pond. Any type of ride can be arranged, including lunch prepared on pastoral sites. Minimum age is eight years; maximum weight limit is 250 pounds per rider.
Tours daily; times vary. Rates vary from $20.80-$35.36.

PARASAILING

Kona Water Sports
Banyan Court Mall, 75-5695G Alii Dr., Kailua-Kona
• 329-1593

To most people the thought of sailing 300 to 600 feet in the air above the ocean is terrifying. But once customers who sign up for the ten-minute ride climb into the air and scan the view, Kona Water Sports reports that 95 percent lose all their nervousness and ask for the extended ride. No skill required, just sit back, relax, and the custom-made boats will have you airborne in seconds.
Open daily 8 a.m.-5:30 p.m. Cost $34.95-$44.95.

Kona Winds Parasailing
75-5669 Alii Dr.,
Kailua-Kona
• 329-1007

The only company offering double-chair rides for two, Kona Winds will take children, no age limit.
Open daily 9 a.m.-3 p.m. Adults $39, children under 12 $29; boat ride only, $10.

SAILING

Discovery Charters
75-293 Aloha
Kona Dr.,
Kailua-Kona
• 326-1011

Private, upscale sailing charters on board a 45-foot luxury yacht. In addition to sailing to deserted bays, Carol and Bob Hogan, the owners/operators, offer a range of ocean toys to play with, including a kayak and snorkeling equipment. Catered gourmet meals on request; also available for birthday parties, barbecues, beach cookouts, wedding receptions or private parties.
Charters on request. Rates start at $375 for four hours; two-hour Sunset Sail $275.

Hawaii Sailing Academy
74-381 Kealakehe
Pkwy.,
Honokohou Harbor,
Kailua-Kona
• 329-9201

Michael Dangerfield manages Kona's only charter-sailing instruction business out of the main harbor on the west side of Honokohou. Sailing lessons range from private to groups of four and can be as short as one hour or as long as you like. He offers a range of chartered sailboats, complete with skipper for day-sails or interisland cruising. Bare-boat charters (without a skipper) are available, but the client must be qualified.
Open Mon.-Fri. 8 a.m.-5 p.m. Rates vary.

SURFING & WINDSURFING

Ka'u Wind
Hwy. 11,
Naalehu
• 929-9517

Ka'u Wind is the southernmost surfing and windsurfing store in the United States. Jim Penner, the owner, loves to windsurf, and if you spend any time in his store he'll talk you into trying it. His phone number doubles as a 24-hour wind-and-surf report recording. Located in the middle of Naalehu, which looks as if it were a farm town in a Norman Rockwell painting, Ka'u Wind has everything from private lessons to rentals. All you need is the wind and the waves.
Open daily 8 a.m.-1 p.m. Private lessons, rates vary, surfboard rental $25 per day, windsurfing equipment (roof rack, foot protectors, sail and board) $55 per day or $210 per week.

Ocean Sports
Royal Waikoloan,
Kamuela
• 885-5555

On the grounds of the Royal Waikoloan Hotel, Ocean Sports rents all sorts of ocean toys from windsurfing equipment to kayaks, wave skis and boogie boards—everything but surfboards. The surf isn't too great in front of the hotel, anyway.

Windsurfing lessons include use of their simulator on land before you take to the water.
Open daily 7 a.m.-sunset. Lessons $38, sailboard rental $19 per hour, $60 for 4 hours, $80 for 8 hours.

Orchid Land Surfboards
832 Kilauea Ave.,
Hilo
• 935-1533

Surfing rental only; no windsurfing equipment. Huge selection from bodyboards to 7-foot-6-inch surfboards.
Open Mon.-Sat. 9 a.m.-5 p.m. Rental surfboards $12 per day & bodyboards $10 per day.

TENNIS

The **Hawaii County Department of Parks and Recreation** can provide a detailed list of all the county tennis courts on the island. Its best courts are in Hilo at the **Hoolulu Tennis Stadium**, located next to the Civic Auditorium on Manono Street. It includes eight indoor courts. In Kona, try the courts at the **Old Airport** (at the Kailua end of the Kuakini Highway). The atmosphere is nill, but the courts are well kept. For details, contact the Parks Department (25 Aupuni St., Hilo; 935-8213). Many of the major resorts in the Kona-Kohala area have gorgeous tennis facilities, but these are generally reserved for hotel guests only. In slack seasons, some hotels may open up their facilities to nonhotel guests, but generally the policy at hotels is "no hotel room key, no play." Following are two private facilities open to the public:

Hotel King Kamehameha
75-5660 Palani Rd.,
Kailua-Kona
• 329-2911

The place to go in Kailua-Kona. The well-maintained courts are surrounded by sweet-smelling flowers and lush landscape. The pro shop has everything: lessons, equipment rental and comments on your backhand.
Open daily 8 a.m.-6 p.m. Lessons: $20 per half hour, $40 per hour, or $80 for series of five half-hour sessions. Court rental: $5 per person per day. Equipment rental: $5 per day for each racket.

Mauna Lani Racquet Club
Mauna Lani Resort,
Kohala
• 885-7765

The grass court is open to nonhotel guests. While you're here, check out the excellent facilities the hotel guests get to enjoy. The ambience is tropical, but 90 percent of the time strong winds plague the courts.
Open daily 7:30 a.m.-6 p.m. Court rental $5 per person per hour. Equipment rental: $6 per hour for each racket.

BASICS

GETTING AROUND

Airport

Your options are a rental car, a taxi or a hotel limo, from either Hilo or Kona Airports. Some of the tour bus/limo companies provide airport transportation, but there are no regularly scheduled shuttles. Make reservations a day before or through your travel agent. Try **Roberts** (Hilo, 935-2858; Kailua-Kona, 329-1688), or **Gray Line** (Hilo, 935-2835; Kailua-Kona, 329-9337). The **Waimea-Kohala Airport** is a small commuter airport served by **Aloha Island Air** (800-652-6541).

Cars

The Big Island is big. It takes more than two hours to drive between Hilo and Kailua-Kona, without doing any sight-seeing. Unless you plan on staying within the confines of your hotel or relying exclusively on tour services, a rented car is really a must. Big Island car-rental agencies include: **Alamo** (Hilo, 961-3343; Kailua-Kona, 329-8896), **Avis** (Hilo, 935-1290; Kailua-Kona, 329-1745), **Budget** (Hilo, 935-6878, Kailua-Kona, 329-8511), **Dollar** (Hilo, 961-6059; Kailua-Kona, 329-2744), **Hertz** (Hilo, 935-2896; Kailua-Kona, 329-3566), **National** (Hilo, 935-0891; Kailua-Kona, 329-1674), **Phillip's U Drive** (Hilo, 935-1936; Kailua-Kona, 329-1730), **Tropical** (Hilo, 935-3385; Kailua-Kona, 329-2437) and **World** (Kailua-Kona, 329-1006).

To see the Big Island's most beautiful beaches and back roads, you will need four-wheel drive, perhaps for a day or so. Hertz, Avis and Budget rent four-wheel drive Jeeps or similar vehicles. If you pick up your rented car at Hilo Airport and return it to Kona Airport, or vice versa, you will be charged a drop-off fee of about $40.

For personalized tour service: **Luana Limousine** (326-5466), **Phantom V Rolls Royce Limousine** (325-7244) or **VIP Limousines** (322-6579), all of which are in Kailua-Kona; or **Hawaii Resorts Transportation** (885-7484) in Kohala.

Public Transportation

Hawaii County's Mass Transit Department provides **The Hele On** ("Get Moving") service around the island, but it is limited. Schedules are available at visitors centers and hotel lobbies. A trip to Hilo from Kailua-Kona or vice versa costs $6. Service within Hilo is available for 75 cents. Call 935-8241 for information and schedule.

Taxis

Taxis are available in all areas of the Big Island. Many also do sight-seeing tours. Most taxis are metered, beginning at $2 for the first eighth of a mile, and 20 cents each additional eighth of a mile. You may encounter some taxis that charge by zone. In Hilo, try **A-1 Bob's Taxi** (959-4800) or **ABC Taxi** (935-0755). In Kona, call one of the following: **Kona Airport Taxi** (329-7779), **Marina Taxi** (329-2481) or **Paradise Taxi** (329-1234).

TELEPHONE NUMBERS

Airports
Hilo 935-0809
Kona 329-2484
Waimea (Kamuela)–Kohala 885-4520
Airport Visitor Information Program
Hilo 935-1018
Kona 394-3423
Chamber of Commerce
Hilo 935-7178
Kona/Kohala 329-1758
Civil Defense 935-0031, 935-3311
Coast Guard 935-6370, (800) 331-6176
Crisis/Help Line 329-9111
Directory Assistance (local) 411
(interisland) 1-555-1212
Emergency
(Ambulance, Fire & Rescue) 961-6022
Hele On Bus 935-8241

Hospitals

Hilo 969-4111
Kona Hospital 322-9311
Hyperbaric Center (Honolulu) 1-523-9155
Immigration 961-8220
Information 935-5407
Marine Forecasts.................................935-9883
Poison Control Center .... (800) 362-3585
Police
Hilo 935-3311
Kona 329-3311
Postal Information
Hilo 935-2821
Kailua-Kona 329-1927
Visitors Information Bureau
Hilo 961-5797
Kailua-Kona 329-7787
Weather
Hilo 935-8555
Big Island 961-5582

GOINGS-ON

January

- Keauhou Open Pro-Am Golf Tourney, 329-7787.
- Kilauea Volcano Wilderness Marathon and Rim Run, two separate events held (third Saturday in January) in the spectacular Volcanoes National Park; 967-8222.

February

- Mauna Kea Ski Meet, February or March depending on snow conditions; 737-4394.

March

- Kona Stampede, two days of rodeo action in mid-March at the Honaunau Arena, Honaunau; 885-7941.

- **Prince Kuhio Day** (March 26), a state holiday. For information on local celebrations, including a ski competition on Mauna Kea, call the Hawaii Visitors Bureau, Hilo; 961-5797.
- **Saddle Road 100K Relay & Ultramarathon** (held in March or April), a 62.1-mile run across the rugged Saddle Road; Hilo to Waimea; 935-7356.

April

- **Buddha Day**, the closest Sunday to April 8. For information on Big Island celebrations, call Hawaii Visitors Bureau; 961-5797.
- **Merrie Monarch Festival**, a major ancient and modern hula event paying tribute to Hawaii's last king, David Kalakaua. Tickets are very inexpensive but hard to get. This wonderful event is also televised. Held near Easter at Edith Kanaka'ole Auditorium, Hilo; 935-9168.

May

- **Outrigger Canoe Season**, May through September. Nearly every Saturday, short- course or long-distance canoe races start from piers in Hilo, Kailua-Kona, Kawaihae, Honaunau and Keauhou; 961-5797.
- **Western Week**, the week prior to Memorial Day. Seven days of activities, including parade, rodeo, market day, contests and dance, Honokaa; 775-7722.

June

- **Bon Season**, from June to August, when Buddhist temples host colorful bon dances, honoring their ancestors each weekend throughout the season; 961-5797.
- **Hawaii Light Tackle Tournament**, usually in June, pits light tackle anglers against billfish, ahi, ono and mahimahi, Kailua-Kona; 325-5000.
- **King Kamehameha Day**, June 11, a state holiday commemorating Kamehameha I who united the Hawaiian Islands. Includes parade in Kailua-Kona, ceremonies at the Kamehameha statue in Kapaau, and entertainment and festivities on Coconut Island; Hilo; 961-5797.
- **King Kamehameha Holua Ski Special**, ancient Hawaiian snowboard races; Mauna Kea; 737-4394.

July

- **Annual Big Island Bonsai Show**, with displays of this ancient Japanese art form, Wailoa Center, Hilo; 961-7360.
- **Hawaii State Horticulture Show**, the Big Island's best flowers on display, plus plant sale, usually late July or early August, Edith Kanaka'ole Auditorium, Hilo; 961-5797.
- **Hilo Orchid Society Show**, a top-notch amateur and professional show. Fourth of July weekend, Butler Building near the Afook-Chinen Civic Auditorium, Hilo; 935-8213.
- **International Festival of the Pacific**, a pageant of nations, including costumes and dances of Japan, China, Korea, Portugal, Tahiti, New Zealand and the Philippines. Centered around a ship in port. Arts, crafts, foods, parade, Hilo; 961-6123.
- **Parker Ranch Rodeo and Horse Races**, top entertainment by *paniolos* (Hawaiian cowboys) from one of the largest privately owned ranches in the United States; Paniolo Park, Waimea, Kamuela; 885-7655.

August

- **Admission Day**, August 18, a state holiday recognizing Hawaii's becoming the 50th State in 1959; 961-5797.
- **Establishment Day Cultural Festival,** an annual festival offering hula, lei making, Hawaiian language and other ancient skills (second week in August); Puukohala Heiau, Kohala; 882-7218.
- **Hawaiian International Billfish Tournament,** the world's leading international marlin-fishing tournament and parade. Daily catch weighings at Kailua-Kona pier. Based on best moon and tides (usually first or second week of August); 1-836-0974.

September

- **Aloha Week,** celebrated on all islands in September and October; 961-5797.
- **Hawaii County Fair**, Hilo; 961-5797.
- **Polo Season** begins, continuing through mid-December. Sunday-afternoon polo matches at Waikii or Kohala Ranch's polo fields; 329-9551.

October

- **Annual Karaoke Festival Finals,** a popular show with amateur singers and dancers performing to prerecorded music. Participants are winners from all Islands' Karaoke competitions; Civic Auditorium, Hilo; 935-0505.
- **Bud Light Ironman Triathlon,** the 2.4-mile swim, 112-mile bicycle race and 26.2-mile marathon, starting and finishing at Kailua-Kona Pier; 329-0063.

November

- **Annual Lei Making Contest,** celebrating King David Kalakaua's birthday; Volcanoes National Park; 967-8222.
- **King David Kalakaua Kupuna-Keiki Hula Festival,** a growing event featuring authentic hula by seniors and children from Hawaii, California, Canada and Japan, Keauhou-Kona; 329-7787.
- **Kona Coffee Cultural Festival,** an annual week-long event featuring international food bazaar, entertainment, recipe contest, parade, donkey races and the crowning of the Miss Kona Coffee Queen, in celebration of the gourmet coffee, Kailua-Kona; 325-7998.

December

- **Bodhi Day,** all islands celebrating Buddha's Enlightenment in early December; 1-542-9200.
- **Christmas arts and crafts shows;** 961-5797.
- **Christmas parades,** nearly every weekend in Waimea (Kamuela), Kainaliu, Kailua-Kona; 961-5797.
- **Mauna Lani Bay Hotel Golf Tournament,** 885-6622.

KAUAI

RESTAURANTS

For more information on how our rating system works, how we estimate meal prices and so on, turn to About the Restaurants, page 6. Also in that section is a Toque Tally, page 10, which lists all the restaurants in this book by rating.

BY CUISINE

AMERICAN

Brennecke's Beach Broiler (*Poipu*)
Mangos Tropical Restaurant & Bar (*Koloa*)
Ono Family Restaurant (*Kapaa*)
Plantation Gardens (*Poipu*)
Shell House (*Hanalei*)

CONTINENTAL

Gaylord's Restaurant (*Lihue*)

FRENCH

The Masters (*Lihue*)

HAWAIIAN

Ono Family Restaurant (*Kapaa*)
Tahiti Nui (*Hanalei*)

ITALIAN

Casa Italiana (*Lihue*)
Sirena del Lago (*Lihue*)

JAPANESE

Hanamaulu Restaurant/ Tea House/ Sushi Bar & Robata

Naniwa (*Poipu*)
Tempura Garden (*Lihue*)

MEXICAN

Charo's (*Haena*)
Flamingo Cantina (*Poipu*)
Norberto's El Café (*Kapaa*)

SEAFOOD

Beamreach Restaurant (*Princeville*)
Brennecke's Beach Broiler (*Poipu*)
Duke's Canoe Club (*Lihue*)
Hanalei Dolphin (*Hanalei*)
House of Seafood (*Poipu*)
Inn on the Cliffs (*Lihue*)
Kapa'a Fish Chowder House (*Kapaa*)
Mangos Tropical Restaurant & Bar (*Koloa*)
Plantation Gardens (*Poipu*)
Shell House (*Hanalei*)

STEAKHOUSE

Beamreach Restaurant (*Princeville*)
Duke's Canoe Club (*Lihue*)
Hanalei Dolphin (*Hanalei*)
Tahiti Nui (*Hanalei*)

SUSHI

Hanamaulu Restaurant/ Tea
House/ Sushi Bar & Robata
(*Hanamaulu*)

THAI

King and I (*Kapaa*)

*We always like to hear about
your discoveries and to receive
your comments about ours.
Please feel free to write to us ,
stating clearly what
you liked or disliked.*

Beamreach Restaurant

Box 283,
Hanalei
• 826-9131
STEAKHOUSE/SEAFOOD

8/20

The theme and decor of the Beamreach is nauseatingly nautical, with oversize photos of sailboats in blustery conditions and assorted marine paraphernalia hanging from the walls and ceiling. In fact, we wanted our captain's hat so we'd feel at home. Unfortunately, there is no ocean view to go with it all; in fact, there is no view whatsoever, except of a small condominium pool outside the restaurant. Oddly, Beamreach's specialty is steak, especially filet mignon, which is flown in weekly from the Midwest. Fresh fish of the day varies from mediocre to mundane. The wine list is limited. During the height of winter tourist season, the place is packed. Service is fast and efficient. If you don't have a reservation be prepared to sit in the bar for an hour. Dinner for two, with wine, about $90. *Open nightly 6 p.m.-10 p.m. Cards: AE, MC, V.*

Brennecke's Beach Broiler

2100 Hoone Rd.,
Poipu
• 742-7588
SEAFOOD/AMERICAN

12/20

You can't visit Poipu without eating at Brennecke's, a local landmark combining a superb beach/ocean view with lots of conviviality and good seafood. Like practically every other place on the island, Brennecke's markets itself aggressively; it advertises frequently, has its own gift shop/tourist center and, in the restaurant, sells all manner of clothing emblazoned with various Brennecke's insignias. But this self-promotion is so good-natured that even the staunchest antitourist cynics find themselves weakening and buying a Brennecke's T-shirt. It's a place that manages to be all things to all people: thoroughly casual yet not a dive, has a dreamy view for lovers, big tables and kid's portions for families, a full bar for merry imbibers (mai tais are big here), simple grilled fish for the seafood purist, pastas and fancier dishes for those sick of simple grilled fish, and mud pie for those on a splurge. It's best to stay away from the more complicated dishes (the pastas are ho-hum). Instead, start with the excellent ahi sashimi (served at almost every Kauai restaurant, and, actually, almost always excellent) or the ceviche—that is, only if you're pretty hungry, since dinners come with salad or clam chowder and pasta primavera. Meat eaters can order steaks or ribs, but most opt, and rightly so, for the unadorned grilled Pacific fish: ahi, ono, mahimahi, opakapaka and so forth.

The selection is always perfectly fresh; ask for your fish a bit undercooked if you don't want it a bit overcooked. The prices are high for the informal setting, but not by Hawaiian tourist-area standards: about $75 for a seafood dinner for two, with a couple of exotic cocktails or glasses of wine.
Open daily 11:30 a.m.-3 p.m. & 5 p.m.-10 p.m. All major cards.

Casa Italiana

2989 Haleko Rd.,
Lihue
• 245-9586
ITALIAN

9/20

The brothers Iaskolk (Anthony and Rosario) supervised the make-over that transformed this nineteenth-century estate into an Italian café. Dinner is served in three of the estate rooms that now sport red-tile floors and hanging plants, which creates an open-patio feeling. The noise level, however, matches any restaurant in Rome, New York or L.A., a blow to expectations of Island serenity. These canny brothers make their own pasta daily, and we could taste the difference in the lasagne and fettuccine Alfredo. The veal scaloppine alla Marsala was also good. All dinners include salad bar. The wine list is adequate, and, as one would expect, depends heavily upon Italian wines. Dinner for two, with Italian wine, about $80.
Open Mon.-Sat. 5 p.m.-10 p.m. Cards: MC, V.

Charo's

5-7132 Kuhio Hwy.,
Haena
• 826-6422
MEXICAN

7/20

The best thing about Charo's is its location—beachfront in Haena—but we really hate the rush. That's precisely why we came to Kauai in the first place. Go at sunset and watch the dazzling array of colors while the sun sinks behind the mountains. Occasionally, Charo herself is in the restaurant glad-handing, blowing kisses and even serving a drink or two. A beautiful woman and a gorgeous view, however, don't compensate for mediocre food at high prices. The menu features an array of Mexican food, steaks and some seafood items. There are burrito plates with beans and rice, enchiladas and other unmemorable south-of-the-border dishes. Service tends to be rushed; no lingering here. There's a lengthy wine list that might as well have come from a shopping spree at the corner-grocery store. Expect to spend $90 for dinner for two, with wine.
Open daily 11:30 a.m.-9 p.m. All major cards.

Duke's Canoe Club

Westin Kauai,
Nawiliwili,
Lihue
• 246-9599
STEAKHOUSE/SEAFOOD

11/20

Entering Duke's is like stepping into the jungle: waterfalls plummet 30 feet down, and lush tropical greenery surrounds a pathway snaking through the restaurant. The view from inside is of rolling surf against the white sands of Kalapaki Beach. All this, and tasty seafood and steaks upstairs; sandwiches and burgers await in "The Grill" downstairs. The ribs and chicken are mouth-watering, after a stint of slow cooking in the koa-smoker ovens. The chef also knows how not to ruin the fresh fish. Upstairs the dress is resort-casual; downstairs it's plain casual, which means shorts, T-shirts and beach cover-ups. The wine list will serve modest needs. Dinner for two upstairs, with wine, will set you back about $85.

Open nightly 5 p.m.-10 p.m. Grill: 4 p.m.-11 p.m. Cards: AE, MC, V.

Flamingo Cantina

2301 Nalo Rd.,
Poipu
• 742-9505
MEXICAN

11/20

Reminiscent of the chain Mexican restaurants that blanket Southern California suburbia, Flamingo Cantina owes its popularity to its family atmosphere, grande margaritas (mango, papaya, strawberry), low prices (by Hawaiian, not Cal-Mex, standards) and, of course, the undying appeal of simple, messy Mexican food. You'll get exactly what you'd expect at Flamingo: nachos, sizzling platters of fajitas, messy enchiladas, globs of beans and rice, decent chips. None of it is in any way remarkable, but it satisfies that Mexican-food itch just peachy. The young staff, which includes more than a few California transplants, helps keep the mood upbeat and fun. Kids love the huge aquarium. Dinner for two, with margaritas, costs about $32.

Open daily 3:30 p.m.-9:30 p.m. No cards.

Gaylord's Restaurant

Kilohana Plantation
Estate,
Hwy. 50,
Lihue
• 245-9593
CONTINENTAL

10/20

As any Kauai visitor who reads the local publications will discover ad nauseum, Gaylord's was written up favorably in *Gourmet* magazine in 1988. No doubt *Gourmet* or anyone else had a hard time finding *any* restaurant on Kauai offering truly gourmet dining. It's certainly a lovely and romantic place, a series of open-air dining areas wrapped around the lush back garden of the Kilohana Plantation Estate. That Gaylord's has gourmet pretensions is immediately obvious, thanks to the tuxedoes on the waiters (completely ridiculous in Kauai) and the impressive but frighteningly expensive wine list. The dinner menu is your basic Continental, with a few 1980s-cuisine touches (duck salad with raspberry vinaigrette, lamb with a raspberry-mango chutney). While perfectly edible, the cooking doesn't nearly live up to Gaylord's ambitions—or prices. French onion soup is fine but run-of-the-mill. Raspberry duck salad is a weak attempt at Californian cuisine (though, to be fair, it's only $4.95). Roast duck on a bed of three sauces (green peppercorn, port and Madeira) featured tough, tasteless duck. You're better off with the tasty prime rib, which the kitchen doesn't muck up with any gourmet fantasy. Desserts are generic upscale-restaurant offerings, with more calories than flavor. Instead of spending $100 for two to have dinner with wine, visit for lunch or Sunday brunch—you can enjoy the setting and much simpler food (omelets, waffles, burgers) for much less money.

Open Mon.-Sat. 11 a.m.-3:30 p.m. & 5 p.m.-9:30 p.m., Sun. 10 a.m.-3 p.m. & 5 p.m.-9 p.m. Cards: AE, MC, V.

Hanalei Dolphin

Hanalei
• 826-6113
STEAKHOUSE/SEAFOOD

10/20

This used to be one of our favorite restaurants on Kauai. Built on the site of a historic boat shed and located on a scenic spot with lush tropical foliage at the bend in the river, the Hanalei Dolphin was a romantic spot with excellent cuisine prepared by Roger and Barbara Ross, who spent years in the finest restaurants in starstruck Aspen, Colorado. Our return visit made us sad. The boom in tourism has not only ruined the romantic atmosphere (now the sound of traffic is the background music), but the food service is so frenzied that it makes fast-food joints look lethargic by comparison. The cooking suffers as well. For example, the fresh fish was always *kini popo* (right on the money), but lately it's invariably overcooked. The place is so popular (mainly tourists who come once) that management refuses to take reservations. It's a good place for a sunset drink, although in the summer people actually line up outside half an hour before it opens. Expect a wait to be seated, a hurried dinner and a bill of $80 for dinner and wine for two.
Open nightly 6 p.m.-10 p.m. Cards: AE, MC, V.

Hanamaulu Restaurant, Tea House, Sushi Bar & Robata

Kuhio Hwy.,
Hanamaulu
• 245-2511
JAPANESE/SUSHI

12/20

The Miyake family has owned this restaurant for three generations. Not only are they conversant with the art of cooking, but their Japanese gardens and koi ponds are exquisitely beautiful. We recommend bypassing the main dining room in the front and reserving a table in the back, which overlooks the gardens and pond. You sit on cushions Japanese-style, with room under the sunken tables for long legs. The shoji-screen-partitioned rooms are decorated with carved wood. The rambling building also houses a sushi bar, which overlooks another manicured garden and koi pond. The menu features both Chinese and Japanese food. Dishes on the Chinese side include lup cheong (Chinese sausage), kau yuk (pot-roasted pork loin) and the Hanamauli Cafe specialty—crispy-fried ginger chicken. On the Japanese side, the entrées range from beef, chicken or pork sukiyaki to fish, chicken or beef teriyaki. Best bang for the buck? Try the nine-course dinner from either side of the menu for $12.95. The catch of the day is cooked in a sweet teriyaki sauce and a very light tempura batter with just a taste of ginger. Try the robatayaki. Select from prawns, lobster, crab, steak or chicken, and your order will be grilled tableside. The wine list is small; sample the saké instead. This is one of Kauai's most popular restaurants, and it's frequently reserved for weddings and large parties. Definitely reserve a table in advance. About $50 will get you dinner and saké for two.
Open Tues.-Fri. 9 a.m.-1 p.m. & Tues.-Sun. 4:30 p.m.-9 p.m. Cards: MC, V.

House of Seafood

1941 Poipu Rd.,
Poipu
• 742-6433
SEAFOOD

8/20

There can be as many as nine different varieties of fish on the menu, and none is really remarkably prepared. In addition to the fins, there's filet mignon, New York steak and a range of seafood dishes. This second-story restaurant overlooks the tennis courts of the Poipu Kai condominiums. Large windows guarantee a free-flowing breeze. The wine list is ample; service can be inattentive. Dinner for two, with wine, costs about $100. *Open daily 4 p.m.-9:30 p.m. All major cards.*

Inn on the Cliffs

Westin Kauai,
Nawiliwili,
Lihue
• 246-5054
SEAFOOD

The Inn is an experience in elegance and fine dining. The views alone could knock the breath out of unsuspecting patrons: through the floor-to-ceiling windows both Nawiliwili Harbor and Ninini Point are visible. To catch this breathtaking panorama you have to go before dark. Arrive before your reservation to have a drink in the lounge: sink into the padded chairs in front of the fireplace and let the music from the baby grand serenade you. Dinner in this romantic setting begins with appetizers served hot (steamed clams with white wine, garlic and herbs, sautéed ginger shrimp with cilantro and onions, or broiled scallops with avocado, sour cream and spicy salsa) or cold (oysters on the half shell, a shellfish platter with lobster and shrimp, oysters and crab claws with a tangy tarragon-dill sauce, sashimi, beechwood-smoked salmon, or jumbo shrimp). The creative menu features fresh locally caught fish, but they do offer beef and chicken. The sautéed ginger shrimp with cilantro and onions are nice for starters. The pasta dishes can be ordered as appetizers or as entrées. We delighted in the spinach cheese ravioli with bay scallops, Parmesan cheese and vegetables. The wine list, which contains some 121 selections, is a bit on the pricey side, with high-end items such as Dom Perignon going for $125 and Opus One for $105. The service is attentive. Dinner reservations are a must; during the high season book two to three days in advance. Dinner and wine for two will run around $110.
Open daily 11:30 a.m.-2 p.m. & 5:30 p.m.-9:30 p.m. All major cards.

Kapa'a Fish Chowder House

1639 Kuhio Hwy.,
Kapaa
• 822-7488
SEAFOOD

10/20

You can't miss this place: a huge cargo net and half a boat drape the front of the gray-and-blue-trimmed building. The nautical theme continues inside with wooden tables and captain's chairs. Sit in the garden dining room in the back where hanging asparagus ferns add to the decor. A range of fresh fish comes out of the exhibition kitchen. The night we ate there the choice was ahi (tuna), ono (wahoo), ulua (trevally) or orange roughy. The filets can be broiled or sautéed or come à la meunière, and then finished with a simple sauce, such as the old warhorse, sauce tartare. It's that kind of a place. Just as you'd expect, a range of steaks, prime rib, chicken and steak-lobster combos are available as well. The wine list of some 50 labels is big on California whites (especially Chardonnays), with a couple of French regions (Graves, Vouvray) represented. Our favorite dessert is the "Onolicious," a Fig Newton crust, layers of chocolate, bananas and French vanilla ice cream with peanut butter between the layers, topped off with whipped cream and hot fudge. Genteel, it ain't. Expect to pay about $85 for dinner and wine for two. *Open daily 5:30 p.m.-9:30 p.m. Cards: AE, MC, V.*

Koloa Broiler

Hwy. 52,
Koloa
• 742-9122
AMERICAN

11/20

Vacationers love the Koloa Broiler. And for good reason. Not for the gourmet food—"gourmet" is a word that would be scoffed at here. Not for the posh setting—this place is as relaxed and funky as can be, where shorts and thongs are as dressy as it gets. No, the Koloa Broiler is great because, unlike so many local restaurants, it hasn't the hint of pretension, just tasty, extremely modest food at unbeatable prices. The formula is a simple one: you settle down at one of the plain wood tables (you may have to push one of the house cats off your chair), order a drink (perhaps a good fruit margarita) and, if you're really hungry, an appetizer (only three are offered; the sashimi is reliably fresh), then head for the bare-bones salad bar. Next, tell your waiter your choice of entrées: steak, beef kebab, chicken, burger, mahimahi or one of the daily fresh-fish specials. You'll then be given the raw materials—emphasis on raw—and be shown to the big, open grill in the center of the room. If you need help determining cooking times, you'll get it; otherwise, you cook it exactly the way you want it, then fill out your plate with delicious baked beans, white rice and hunks of sourdough bread. This is fresh, tasty home cooking for hardly more than you'd pay at the market: about $30 for a hefty dinner for two, with beer. *Open daily 11 a.m.-10 p.m. All major cards.*

King and I

Waipouli Plaza,
4-901 Kuhio Hwy.,
Kapaa
• 822-1642
THAI

12/20

If you're driving by the nondescript Waipouli Plaza on a Friday or Saturday night don't be surprised if there is a line of people snaking through the parking lot. The best attracts a crowd and this is Kauai's best Thai restaurant. The secret of the King and I is that the chef has a flair for unique combinations and stunning visual presentations. Inside, pink walls covered with Thai memorabilia and an abundance of green plants set the stage for the exotic food to come. Choose from the chef's suggested dinners for two, three or four diners; or roam through the multipage menu, filled with tangy dishes, such as spring roll (mushroom, carrot, long rice, onion wrapped in rice paper and served with lettuce and mint leaves), green papaya salad (island papaya, tomato and red chili in spicy sauce) and Siam coconut soup (chicken simmered in coconut milk with green onion, Thai parsley and some secret Thai spices that the chef refused to divulge—he grows his own). There is also a special vegetarian section. All dishes come in mild, medium and hot. The King and I offers a surprisingly good wine list and imported-beer list. Dinner for two, with wine, will cost about $50.

Open Mon., Tues., Thurs. & Fri. 11 a.m.-2 p.m. & nightly 5 p.m.-9 p.m. Cards: AE, MC, V.

Mangos Tropical Restaurant & Bar

Koloa
• 742-7377
SEAFOOD/AMERICAN

9/20

Mangos greets you with turquoise walls, brass-trimmed planters filled with with lush foliage and large, open windows swinging out onto a courtyard. The menu presents a variety of fish, chicken, burgers and ribs. Among curiosities are the mango chips: local yams, thinly sliced and fried, served with a honey mustard sauce. Everything else is good, but not terribly inventive. Service is so-so, the wine list adequate. Dinner for two, with wine, is around $70.

Open daily 7:30 a.m.-10 p.m. Cards: MC, V.

The Masters

Westin Kauai,
Nawiliwili,
Lihue
• 245-5050
FRENCH

Here's an island of European class on the island of Kauai. As you enter, the music of a flute-and-guitar duo envelops you. This cuisine-cathedral's "rose windows" arch 25 feet high and overlook the lagoon. Reserve one of the two tables facing them for the best view. The intimately arranged place setting includes lace with Bauscher-Weiden china, Klingenbrun glassware, pink rose buds in cut-crystal vases and small silver lamps. The menu changes regularly with the seasons; ingredients are always fresh. Two prix-fixe dinners ($60 and $75 per person), featuring four to five courses, are offered daily. For example, the lower-priced version in early winter began with pink-snapper soup with late-fall vegetables, seasoned with fennel, chervil and Chardonnay, topped with cream; the next course was Hawaiian spiny lobster on a bed of greens with a truffled vinaigrette; the entrée was twin mignons of beef with wild mushrooms, served with Cabernet Sauvignon jus; and the feast ended with a selection from the dessert menu. Entrées we've enjoyed à la carte here include a moist roasted rack of lamb with mustard, rosemary and melba crumbs, and a fine venison napped with poivrade sauce, served with carmelized pearl onions. There are also some excellent fish selections, including live Maine lobster served in a Pernod-laced cream sauce. The Masters' specializes in dessert soufflés (chocolate, Grand Marnier or macadamia nut), but don't forget about the double-chocolate mousse terrine with pistachio sauce. Service is impeccable. The expansive wine list would make any cathedral bell tower chime. Jackets required for men (ties preferred). An elegant dinner for two, with wine, is $165.

Open nightly 6 p.m.-10 p.m. All major cards.

Naniwa

Sheraton Kauai Hotel,
2440 Hoonani Rd.,
Poipu
• 742-1661
JAPANESE

11/20

Hawaii is blessed with an abundance of Japanese restaurants, thanks to the many Japanese-Hawaiian residents, the deluge of Japanese tourists and the abundance of pristine fresh seafood, the most critical component of any good Japanese restaurant. Naniwa is the South Shore's Japanese-cuisine representative, and while hardly remarkable (and quite pricey), it'll satisfy that Japanese-food craving just fine. The best bet here for sushi and sashimi fans is the Saturday evening buffet ($21 per person), an all-you-can-eat raw-fish fest. The buffet is less recommended for those who don't like sushi, since many of the cooked dishes suffer from the common buffet problems: too much deep frying, too soggy, not enough flavor. The regular menu offers your basic assortment of upscale Japanese fare, from fresh sushi-sashimi assortments to so-so tempura to good tableside-prepared teppanyaki. The atmosphere is pleasantly serene: a standard but handsome country-Japanese decor, with walls of glass looking onto soothing carp ponds. Dinner for two, with saké or Japanese beer, will run $65 to $75.
Open nightly 6 p.m.-10 p.m. All major cards.

Norberto's El Café

4-1373 Kuhio Hwy.,
Kapaa
• 822-3362
MEXICAN

11/20

The Moranz family has been turning out some of the best Mexican food west of the mainland since 1977. Housed in a tiny structure, the two-tier restaurant has plain wood tables decorated with fresh flowers and the usual Mexican items on the walls. The food is fantastico. No *faux* Mexicana here, gringo: from the bean-soup appetizer to the burrito ranchero, enchiladas grandes and rellenos (stuffed green-chile peppers) Tampico, the dishes are authentic, delicious and inexpensive. The entire family works in the restaurant. Service sometimes is slow, but friendly, and all the food is prepared to order, so cool your heels and enjoy a pitcher of margaritas. Dinner for two, with a couple of cold margaritas (the wine list isn't much), will run around $40.
Open nightly 5:30 p.m.-9 p.m. Cards: AE, MC, V.

Ono Family Restaurant

4-1292 Kuhio Hwy.,
Kapaa
• 822-1710
AMERICAN/HAWAIIAN

8/20

If you've been dying to try the latest in low-cholesterol meats, hunker on down to Ono's for a buffalo burger. That's right. This is the only restaurant on Kauai—nay, perhaps in the Pacific—to serve the burly bison (it's prepared three ways: the aforementioned burger, ribs or steaks topped with pineapple and teriyaki sauce). Buffalo has an interesting, but somewhat gamy, taste. A local favorite for Kauai residents, the Ono Family Restaurant is a dressed-up coffee shop with an expanded menu. The decor is country-kitchen with a splattering of antiques. Other menu items include beef, ribs, chicken and fish dinners, a host of sandwiches and ten different hamburgers. For dessert try the macadamia-nut pie, served either as a cream or a custard pie. Service can be slow. No alcohol served. Dinner for two, with a papaya, banana and coconut-milk smoothie, runs around $35.

Open daily 7 a.m.-9 p.m. Cards: AE, MC, V.

Plantation Gardens

Kiahuna Plantation,
Poipu Rd.,
Poipu
• 742-1695
SEAFOOD/AMERICAN

For more than twenty years, Plantation Gardens has been *the* place for a nice dinner out in the Poipu area. Happily, it is not resting on its laurels—the food is every bit as appealing as the setting and decor. Tucked into a quiet, lushly landscaped corner of the Kiahuna Plantation condo complex, Plantation Gardens lives up to its name: the plantation-style dining room, with its white beamed ceiling dotted with lazily turning fans, is open on three sides to the night breezes, beautiful grounds and tiki torches outside. The separate café (Tropical Garden Café) is even more romantic, its small tables set outside among the foliage and discreet lighting. The dining room is efficient and well run (particularly by Hawaiian standards), featuring a wait staff that knows their fish. And while there are a few good meat dishes (steak, prime rib), it'd be a shame to pass up the excellent seafood creations. Feel free, however, to pass up the taste-free bread, saving room for an appetizer. The ruby-red ahi sashimi is the best in these parts; other good starters include the generous Caesar salad, potent with anchovy, and the simple Maui onion–tomato salad. At $30 or so (price varies seasonally), the abalone entrée is a considerable splurge, but so is a trip to Hawaii, and seafood lovers owe it to themselves to revel in the rich, delicate flavor of this rare gastropod. The kitchen executes the abalone with skill and a generous hand: large slices, pounded till thin and tender, dipped in the lightest of breading, delicately sautéed and paired with a smooth lemon-butter sauce. Also worthy are any of the daily fresh fish, from ahi to opakapaka; and the camarones florés, sweet, juicy jumbo shrimp wrapped in bacon and broiled, served with a dipping pot of excellent salsa. Desserts range from the obligatory mud-pie variation ("naughty hula pie") to such specials as heavenly ice-cream-filled profiteroles with rich hot-fudge sauce. A delicious, romantic dinner for two, with wine or tropical drinks, will run $85; abalone will set you back another $10 or so per person.

Open nightly 5:30 p.m.-10 p.m. Cards: AE, MC, V.

I SELL SEA SHELLS

Among the many exotic local ingredients that are beginning to find their way into Hawaii's restaurant kitchens are *opihi*: small mollusks that come in black, red or yellow. Their chewy, briny-tasting meat is similar to abalone, and even more expensive: a gallon sells for about $160. Hawaiians traditionally have eaten them raw or in salads, and chefs are now them mixing them into dishes of fettuccine or angel-hair pasta.

Shell House

55156 Kuhio Hwy.,
Hanalei
• 826-7977
AMERICAN/SEAFOOD

11/20

This tiny place is one of our favorites when we have an itch for good seafood. The Shell House also serves hearty breakfasts, and lunches with Mexican specials. It's an old place with a funky interior. And, goodness, beware of sitting on the lanai—it leaks when it rains, and the traffic noise is just a few feet from your table. The fresh fish of the day is prepared with whatever creative sauce the kitchen has come up with. An odd specialty is Chef Mike Moore's "sweet mustard chicken," a boneless chicken breast sautéed with bacon and onions, topped with jack cheese and honey-mustard sauce. Here's a warning from the some-don't-like-it-so-hot department: the Cajun blackened fish and the Thai scallops are smokers. There's a good wine list with a large selection of wines by the glass. Sample without regret any of the homemade desserts. Reservations are a must. Dinner for two, with wine, will cost about $75.
Open daily 8 a.m.-10:30 p.m. Bar until 11 p.m. Cards: AE, MC, V.

THE *POI*-FECT STAPLE

China has its rice, India has its breads, Mexico its tortillas, Italy its pasta; in Hawaii, the ubiquitous carbohydrate staple is *poi*. Made from the starchy taro root, it is boiled and then mashed or pounded into a gray, glutinous substance reminiscent of baby mash, and is served with almost anything. Taro root is also used to make chips, biscuits, turnovers and so on, and its greens are eaten as a vegetable, boiled and seasoned with coconut milk.

Not even the snails that live in taro fields escape the cook's pot: these small creatures (called—you guessed it—taro snails) are prepared like escargots, or stir-fried with ginger and garlic. Taro snails must be soaked overnight in water before cooking, however, or they literally taste like mud.

Sirena del Lago

Westin Kauai,
Nawiliwili,
Lihue
• 245-5050
ITALIAN

Restaurateur Guido Calcaterra has left his creation and moved, we hear, to the greener pastures of Vancouver. As we go to press, Sirena del Lago is an orphan, the cooking duties being split among the various cuisiniers of the Westin. The new menu features everything from tuna carpaccio with shaved Parmesan to penne with Mascarpone, porcini mushrooms and Parma ham. Until things settle down, we'll withhold both our judgment and our rating.
Open nightly 6 p.m.-10 p.m. All major cards.

Tahiti Nui

Kuhio Hwy.,
Hanalei
• 826-6277
SEAFOOD/HAWAIIAN

9/20

More than 30 years ago "Auntie" Louise Marston came to Hawaii from Tahiti and converted a small store (which was 70-plus years old at the time) into a restaurant and bar. She did everything: shop, prepare the food, tend bar, serve the meals and entertain the guests. Word got out, and today people from around the world flock to this dilapidated old green building with the wooden porch out front—-not only for the food but for the ambience that Auntie Louise has single-handedly maintained. Truly a taste of Tahiti (the surroundings are rundown, but the people are great), the action here begins in the afternoon when people begin filing into the rattan bar. By 6 p.m., the dining room is occupied and Auntie Louise is in action, overseeing the dinners, laughing with the guests and directing the entertainers. Auntie Louise knows fish: this is the place to get a fresh catch prepared in true Polynesian fashion. She also broils a mean New York steak, guaranteed to please or she'll do it over. The wine list is small, but this is Polynesia not Bordeaux. A satisfying dinner for two, with wine, costs about $68.

Open daily 11 a.m.-2 a.m. Cards: MC, V.

G'DAY, MACADAMIA

Since almost every macadamia nut you've ever seen was probably in a jar labeled Mauna Loa, you thought they were Hawaiian nuts, right? The name "macadamia" even sounds exotic enough and sports enough vowels to be properly Hawaiian. Actually, the nut is native to Australia, and was named after Australian chemist John Macadam. The nut was brought to the Big Island from Down Under in 1882, but wasn't produced commercially until 1948. Now Hawaii's crops account for more than 65 percent of the world's production; the Islands' contribution in 1989 was 55 million pounds of in-shell nuts.

Tempura Garden
Westin Kauai,
Nawiliwili,
Lihue
• 246-5053, 245-5050
JAPANESE

It seems like practically every major Hawaiian hotel has a Japanese restaurant, and most are indistinguishable from one another (for example, Naniwa above). Tempura Garden, however, stands out from the crowd. Like everything else at the overblown Westin Kauai, Tempura Garden charges a shogun's ransom. But here, at least, you (almost) get your money's worth in exceptional sushi and sashimi, and in meticulously prepared cooked dishes. The house specialty is the $59-a-head kaiseki dinner, a parade of small delicacies (soup, salads, sashimi, sushi, broiled fish and/or meat, and so on), each one a delight. All the dinners, in fact, are fixed-price (from $25 to $39), bringing you superb miso soup; a crisp, sharp Japanese salad; a bit of sashimi; an entrée (light, heavenly tempura, tender teriyaki, lovely broiled fish); rice; tea; and dessert, usually ice cream. Sushi buffs can skip the set dinners and order to their heart's content (and wallet's distress) at the large sushi bar (the focal point of the room, where most diners are seated). In every dish we've tried, the ingredients were exceptional, the cooking and sushi artistry precise, and the flavors clear and true. The kindly service and marvelous garden setting (waterfalls, fish ponds, birds) round out a lovely dining experience. Dinner for two, with saké, ranges from $80 to $95, more if you splurge on the kaiseki dinner.

Open daily 5 p.m.-9:30 p.m. All major cards.

QUICK BITES

BARBECUE

Barbecue Inn
2982 Kress St.,
Lihue
• 245-2921

Despite its name, there are not many barbecued items at the Barbecue Inn. With a spruced-up coffeeshop-style interior (vinyl booths, cutesy yellow curtains), this renovated restaurant serves mainly local residents who want no-nonsense meat-and-rice-type meals heaped out in generous portions. The food, cooked in American, Chinese and Japanese styles, varies from burgers to lobsters and steak. Full bar, quick service, and they cater to kids. Dinner for two, with wine, comes to around $20. *Open Mon.-Sat. 7:30 a.m.-1:30 p.m. & 4:30 p.m.-8:30 p.m. No cards.*

CAFES & DINERS

Fast Freddy's Diner
4-1302 Kuhio Hwy.,
Kapaa
• 822-0488

Hawaiian-funky is the best description of Fast Freddy's interior. This hole in the wall offers great, cheap food served on Hawaiian time. The meals vary from his famous "Deuces Wild" breakfast (two eggs, two pancakes and bacon or sausage) for $2.22, to all-you-can-eat scampi dinner for $9.95. Service is very friendly but tends to be slow. Be warned: Freddy likes to go fishing, and his diner isn't always open when he says it will be. Burgers, fries and coffee for two costs $10 (no liquor, but you can bring your own). *Open Mon.-Sat. 6:30 a.m.-1 p.m. & 5:30 p.m.-8:30 p.m., Sun 7:30 a.m.-noon. No cards.*

Tip Top Motel, Café & Bakery
3173 Akahi St.,
Lihue
• 245-2333

The weather-beaten exterior is the first clue that this spartan café is not a prime place to eat, even if it's for a quick bite. Inside, the blaring television set and formica tables with stacked chairs diminishes the appetite of even the most hungry. But, never mind. The Tip Top is famous for its bakery's macadamia-nut cookies, and rightly so. A pound of cookies and two cups of coffee for $4.63 will keep you happy for a long time.
Open Mon.-Fri. 6:45 a.m.-8 p.m. & Sat.-Sun. 7 a.m.-8:30 p.m. No cards.

West of the Moon Café
Kauhale Center,
Kuhio Hwy. & Aku Rd.,
Hanalei
• 826-7640

This tiny (only six tables) café is open only for breakfast—but what a breakfast! The house specialty is deep-dish custard-style French toast. Equally scrumptious are the fresh baked goodies (Irish scones, bran muffins and more) and the specials of the day (like buttermilk pancakes topped with bananas and coconut or a three-egg omelet with cheese, avocado, salsa, beans and sour cream). The cheery decor (white walls, powder-blue trim and white lace curtains) and the sunny disposition of the staff are a great way to start the day. Breakfast for two runs about $15.
Open daily 7:30 a.m.-1 p.m. No cards.

HAMBURGERS & HOT DOGS

Brennecke's
2100 Hoone Rd.,
Poipu Beach
• 742-7588

The quintessential beach fast-food stand, Brennecke's is found downstairs from the ever-popular Brennecke's Beach Broiler and across the street from Poipu Beach Park; Brennecke's Beach, the legendary bodysurfing spot that lost its oomph in the big hurricane a few years ago, is just around the bend in the road. The food dispensed by the teenagers behind the window—shave ice, sandwiches, chili dogs—isn't nearly as satisfying as those Brennecke's waves once were, but after a morning of sand and sea, it goes down beautifully. About $8 for lunch for two.
Open daily 10:30 a.m.-4 p.m. No cards.

Camp House Grill
Kaumualii Hwy. 50,
Kalaheo
• 332-9755

For a day away from the tourist pleasures of Poipu or the East Shore, we highly recommend heading west on the Kaumualii Highway until it deadends at Polihale State Park, at the beginning of the Na Pali Coast; on the way you can stop in funked-out Hanapepe, historic Russian Fort and wherever whim takes you. And for another, more spectacular day, head in the same direction for Waimea Canyon, one of Hawaii's great natural treasures. On your way to or from both trips, don't miss fueling up at the Camp House Grill, a terrific roadhouse with honest

American food, friendly people and a scarcity of tourists. Breakfast is no-frills perfection: bacon and eggs, omelets, home fries, fresh juice. Good grilled burgers and onion rings are the call for lunch; Camp House's barbecued chicken keeps the locals returning for dinner. About $12 for breakfast for two; dinner for two, with beer, runs $25 to $30.
Open daily 6:30 a.m.-10:30 a.m. & 11 a.m.-9 p.m. Cards: MC, V.

Duane's Ono-Char Burger
Kuhio Hwy.,
Anahola
• 822-9181

No, it's not the sugar shack, Jack, it's the burger shack. Tucked away in a small shopping area next to the Anahola post office is burger heaven. This is for burger-aficionados: big burgers cooked to perfection with everything imaginable on them. Owner Duane Horka is behind the grill whipping out some of the best patties on the planet. His best-seller is the teriyaki burger (a quarter-pounder with lettuce, tomato, mayo, homemade teriyaki sauce, plus whatever else you want: cheese, avocado, sprouts). There are no indoor tables, just a quaint covered picnic area under a shady poinciana tree next door. A couple of burgers and two of his thickest shakes will run you $14.
Open daily 10 a.m.-6 p.m. No cards.

Kountry Kitchen
1485 Kuhio Hwy.,
Kapaa
• 822-3511

Sidle up to some home cooking in a quaint country atmosphere. Ruffled curtains, overstuffed booths and kitchenish wallpaper set the scene for this popular restaurant. The food is good and served in more than generous portions. Breakfast features a variety of omelets, served with homemade corn bread. Lunch has a host of burgers, luncheon-special plates and sandwiches; dinner sports fish, barbecued ribs, fried chicken and beef. Beer and wine available. Lunch for two, with a couple of beers, is about $17.
Open daily 6 a.m.-2:30 p.m. & 5 p.m.-8:30 p.m. Cards: MC, V.

Paradise Hot Dogs
Kiahuna Shopping
Village,
2360 Kiahuna
Plantation Dr.,
Poipu Beach
• 742-7667

The husband-and-wife team that runs this engaging hot-dog stand are no wiener dilletantes—they've traveled the mainland, tasting its finest dogs, and brought their expertise back to Kauai. The result is a hot dog that could cut the mustard in New York, Chicago or L.A.: thick, juicy and very savory, as simple or as complicated as you like (the chili dog is highly recommended). There's also bockwurst, Polish sausage, hot link or Portuguese sausage.
Open Mon.-Sat. 10 a.m.-9 p.m., Sun. 11 a.m.-6 p.m. No cards.

MEXICAN FAST FOOD

Tropical Taco Café & Cantina
Kuhio Hwy.,
Kapaa Shopping Center,
Kapaa
• 822-3622

This Mexican restaurant has had its ups and downs over the years with a merry-go-round of different owners. The crowded, noisy cantina's fans have weathered all the changes as long as there was abundant *cerveza fria*. The food here has been both great and terrible: dine at your own risk on tacos, burritos, tostadas, enchiladas and rellenos. Service is slow. Lunch, with beer, for two costs $20.
Open daily 11 a.m.-9:30 p.m. Cards: MC, V.

PIZZA

Brick Oven Pizza
2488-A Kaumualii Hwy.,
Kalaheo
• 332-8561

This tasty, hearty, home-style pizza is hands down the best in these parts (not that there's much competition). Unfortunately, Brick Oven doesn't deliver, but it's a fun, red-checkered-table-cloth, family-style joint. The pizza is thin of crust (whole-wheat or white) and generous of topping, with a good cheese-sauce balance. The rest of the offerings run toward the standard salad/meatball-sandwich variety. The location is ideal for a pit stop on the way to or from Waimea Canyon or Polihale State Park, and it's fifteen minutes from Poipu. Less than $25 for a pizza-and-beer dinner for two.

Pizza Bella
Kiahuna Shopping Village,
2360 Kiahuna Plantation Dr.,
Poipu Beach
• 742-9571

Steer clear of the California-style "gourmet" pizzas here; instead, opt for the good old classic pizza, or a messy, straightforward hero or meatball sandwich. The best thing about Pizza Bella is that it delivers. About $20 for pizza and beer for two.
Open daily 11:30 a.m.-10 p.m. Open Tues.-Sun. 11 a.m.-11 p.m. Cards: MC, V.

SAIMIN

Hamura Saimin Stand
2956 Kress St.,
Lihue
• 245-3271

Ready for a dose of unadulterated Kauaian charm? Then get over to Hamura Saimin Stand, a local's dive if ever there was one. And it's a great dive, specializing in all different types of bowls of saimin—that wonderful Japanese/Hawaiian meal-in-a-bowl of savory soup broth, lots of crinkled noodles and various vegetables and meats (watch out for the Spam!). Hamura's adjacent sister business, Halo Halo Shave Ice, serves some of the best shave ice on the island. Less than $10 for a saimin-and-soda meal for two.
Open Mon.-Thurs. 10 a.m.-2 a.m., Fri.-Sat. 10 a.m.-4 a.m., Sun. 10 a.m.-11 p.m. No cards.

HOTELS & CONDOMINIUMS

CONDOMINIUMS

Garden Isle Cottages
2666 Puuholo Rd., Koloa
• 742-6717
No fax

These small, charming cottages, spread out in three locations near Poipu Beach, all nestle in tropical gardens. And the price is just right. Individual cottages vary: some rooms have maid service; some have kitchens. Nearby there's golf, tennis, swimming, snorkeling and groceries. The Garden Isle will make car rental arrangements for you.
Studios: $45-$68; 1 bedroom: $75-$105; 2 bedrooms: $135.

Hanalei Bay Resort
5380 Honoiki Rd., Princeville
• 826-6522
No fax

Tucked away between holes on the Princeville Golf Course lies the sprawling Hanalei Bay Resort. Built into a steep hillside, the units range from plain hotel rooms to one-, two- and three-bedroom condos. Amenities include a restaurant on the property, tennis courts, pool, laundry, phones in each unit and, of course, the Princeville golf course right next door.
Rooms: $80-$145; 1 bedroom: $155-$195; 2 bedrooms: $210-$290; 3 bedrooms: $435; suites: $500-$1,000.

Hanalei Colony Resort Condominiums
5-7130 Kuhio Hwy., Haena
• 826-6235
No fax

Located on a spectacular beach near Charo's Restaurant (see Kauai Restaurants, page 264), these two-bedroom units each boast a fully equipped kitchen, one bath, a lanai and a wonderful ocean view. Amenities include a white-sand beach, pool, jacuzzi and five acres of lush foliage.
2 bedrooms: $100-$155.

Kaha Lani

4460 Nehe Rd.,
Lihue
• 822-9331
No fax

Off the beaten tourist path, this is for people who want to get away from it all. Located on the ocean, this area of Kapaa is nearly always windy. Another drawback: the ocean here churns angrily, making swimming impossible except in the summer. Besides that, the beach is not powder-white sand but more like a concrete reef ledge. The units have one, two or three bedrooms, all 100 yards from the ocean, with garden view, ocean view, or ocean frontage. Amenities include a pool, tennis and volleyball.
1 bedroom: $117-$145; 2 bedrooms: $149-$177; 3 bedrooms: $230.

> ### IT'S THATTA WAY
>
> **If you ask for directions, don't expect the reply to include familiar words, such as "north" or "south." Basic compass points include makai, toward the sea, and mauka, toward the mountains.**

Kiahuna Plantation

Poipu Beach
• 742-6411
Fax (415) 283-3129

So you wanted a place to relax and soak up Mother Nature? Here 'tis. The Kiahuna is a plantation-style beachfront and garden condominium resort. The foliage is lush tropical jungle with lily ponds, manicured gardens (with all the trees and plants labeled), koi ponds and huge sprawling monkey-pod trees. Amenities include an excellent restaurant, pool, tennis and golf. Units have either one or two bedrooms.
1 bedroom: $135-300; 2 bedrooms: $225-$395.

Koloa Landing Cottages

2704B Hoonani Rd.,
Koloa
• 742-1470
No fax

Modest, quiet, away from the usual tourist haunts, these excellent budget accommodations are located in a private residential garden setting, with easy access to golf, sandy beaches, restaurants, shops, and shows at the hotels. The management requires a four-night deposit.
Studios: $50; 2 bedrooms–2 baths: $70-$80.

Lanikai Condominiums

390 Papaloa Rd.,
Kapaa
• 822-7456
No fax

Lanikai sits right on the ocean but, alas, without the benefit of a white-sand beach. These two-bedroom, two-bath units are large (1,700 square feet) and beautifully decorated. All have full kitchens with microwave and wet bar. Don't forget the panoramic ocean view. Amenities include a pool and gas barbecue.
2 bedrooms: $230.

Lawai Beach Resort

5017 Lawai Rd.,
Koloa
• 742-9581
No fax

Although each of the 114 rooms has a full kitchen, this project operates more like a hotel. We found it poorly designed, *mauvais goût*, if you know what we mean. For example, in the two-bedroom units the master bedroom has no privacy and is separated from the rest of the space by thin folding doors. The kitchens are cramped and dark. And what about those aggressive sales people trying to push time-sharing contracts? On the plus side, the oceanfront units do have great views. Amenities include a nice sandy cove across the street (not as nice as Poipu down the street), tennis and a rental hut with beach supplies.
1 bedroom $120-$165; 2 bedrooms $180-$230.

Pali Ke Kua

Princeville
• 826-6262, 826-9066
No fax

Located on the grounds of the Princeville resort, the units squat on a bluff with spectacular views across Hanalei Bay. Only a few of the units are available for rental. These have either one or two bedrooms, fully electric kitchens, washer/dryer units and lanais; most have with ocean views. Amenities include a pool and restaurant (Beamreach; see Kauai Restaurants, page 263) on the property; a golf course and tennis courts are nearby.
1 bedroom $105-$140; 2 bedrooms $120-$160.

Poipu Kai Resort

Rte. 1,
Koloa
• 742-6464
No fax

Poipu Kai is a 110-acre resort sloping down to the sea at Poipu. The one-, two- and three-bedroom units have either garden or ocean views; some are located on the ocean front. All units have private lanais, full kitchens and daily maid service. Amenities include two beaches, tennis courts, five swimming pools and a restaurant (The House of Seafood) on the property.
1 bedroom: $140-$210; 2 bedrooms: $190-$265; 3 bedrooms: $240-$275.

Poipu Kapili Condominiums

2221 Kapili Rd.,
Koloa
• 742-6449
No fax

Architects arranged the handsome plantation-style Poipu Kapili around a pool and green lawns. The ocean lies just across the road, but sadly the sandy beach was washed out by a recent hurricane and is mostly rocks now. The one- and two-bedroom units are quite large, with full kitchens, television, sleeper sofas, king-sized beds and daily maid service. Nearly all of the units have ocean views. The decor varies with the owner, but count on lots of wicker/rattan. Amenities include nice tennis courts (guests can also join round-robin play at the Sheraton courts across the street). Sand beaches at Sheraton and Waiohai are a walk away. If you're looking for quiet and relaxation, check in here. There's a four-night minimum, seven nights during Christmas vacation.
1 bedroom: $140; 2 bedrooms: $260.

Whaler's Cove at Poipu

2640 Puuholo Rd., Koloa
• 742-7571
Fax 742-1185

Whaler's Cove offers large, bright two-bedroom units with fabulous views. The units have gourmet kitchens, a whirlpool bath in the master suite and ocean-front lanais. The decor is contemporary. There's a swimming pool on the property but no tennis or other sports. While there's no sandy beach, the shoreline does have a cove that is good for diving and snorkeling. The location's quiet enough, but we feel it's overpriced because of the lack of amenities. There's a minimum two-night stay, seven nights during Christmas.
2 bedrooms: $295-$345.

LUXURY

Aston Kauai Resort

3-5920 Kuhio Hwy., Kapaa
• 245-3931
Fax 822-7339

Accommodations at the Aston Kauai Resort range from spacious guest rooms and studios to one-bedroom cottages. They all have minirefrigerators, cable televisions and air conditioning, and they all overlook a large public-beach park (Lydgate Park) and the mouth of the famed Wailua River, which meanders up to the Fern Grotto. Two pools and new tennis courts keep the guests happy.
Doubles: $129-$159; studios: $179; cottages: $189.

Kauai Hilton and Beach Villas

4331 Kauai Beach Dr., Lihue
• 245-1955
Fax 246-9085

On an island blessed with beautiful beaches, the Kauai Hilton was built on a poor one that offers a strip of sand suited for little more than sunning or strolling; ocean access is poor-to-dangerous for most of the year. A modern aquatic fantasy pool graces the hotel's forefront and attracts most sunbathers and water lovers after one look at the meager, windswept beach. The hotel is well situated for quick access to a variety of visitor attractions from the romantic Fern Grotto to the adjacent eighteen-hole Wailua Golf Course, and good local restaurants in Lihue and Kapa'a. There are four tennis courts, of which two are lighted for night play. The most expensive rooms are the "two-bedroom ocean-front villas"; most expensive suites are "parlor and two rooms." The adjacent Beach Villas are luxury condominiums with access to all facilities and services, plus the simple advantage of including a kitchen and laundry facilities.
Doubles: $135-$185; suites: $300-$700; Beach Villas (condominiums): $150-$260.

LIFE'S A BEACH

Question: Okay, how many beaches are there in Hawaii?

Answer: 280. If you don't believe us, you have permission to start counting yourself.

Sheraton Kauai Hotel

R.R. 1,
Box 303,
Poipu
• 742-1661
Fax 742-9777

The Sheraton Kauai Hotel's location in Poipu, with access to one of the best white-sand beaches on Kauai, and the dependable leeward weather adds immensely to its attractiveness. Twenty acres of beautifully landscaped gardens and tranquil lagoons, plus immediate access to water sports and the championship Kiahuna golf course, as well as several fine restaurants, make this one of the better choices on Kauai.
Doubles: $160-$280; suites: $360-$1,200.

Stouffer Waiohai Beach Resort

2249 Poipu Rd.,
Poipu
• 742-9511
Fax 742-7214

Stouffer manages one of our favorite Kauai properties here on dependably sunny Poipu Beach. The resort features oversize rooms with fully stocked wet bars, refrigerators and private lanais (suites have whirlpools). Surfing, windsurfing, catamaran rentals, three pools, Robert Trent Jones, Jr.–designed Kiahuna golf course across the street, Laykold tennis courts and fitness center round out some of the options. This is a heavily landscaped, sprawling facility, well located at the center of Poipu. Front rooms/suites are terrific, large and similar to living at the beach. Breakfast on the Waiohai Terrace is highly recommended; the award-winning Tamarind Restaurant is one of the better hotel-based eateries on the island. Convention facilities for 900 can burden the place with large groups on occasion. Two meal plans available, but be adventurous: there are many great places to eat within walking distance.
Doubles: $150-$325; suites: $405-$1,285.

Westin Kauai

Nawiliwili,
Lihue
• 245-5050
Fax 245-5049

There has been a lot of media hype and hoopla about the 800-acre Kauai Lagoons development and the gorgeous Westin Kauai resort hotel that anchors the resort, fronting on lovely Kalapaki Beach. Most of the hype is deserved. The place has something for everyone—if anything it has too much for anyone: stupendous pool, windsurfing, sailing, tennis, horseback riding, two Jack Nicklaus Signature Golf Courses, twelve restaurants, Clydesdale, Belgian and Percheron horse-drawn carriage rides, complete health spa, waterway tours by Venetian launch or canoe, an array of wildlife—whew, it is amazing. On the other hand, it can honestly be said, as one of our critics noted: "ridiculously overdone, confusing, huge, ostentatious." We have been similarly unimpressed with the massive gushing fountains everywhere, garish over-decoration with Asian religious artifacts and other inappropriate antiques, ersatz architectural features, endless hallways and the high cost of many features ($50 a head to visit the famed draft horse stables!) Nonetheless we vote this a must-visit resort. You'll either love

FIRST CLASS

Coco Palms Resort
P.O. Box 631,
Lihue
• 822-4921
Fax 822-7189

Sprawled throughout Hawaii's oldest and largest coconut plantation, adjacent to the Wailua River, lies one of the most nostalgic and romantic of Kauai's resort hotels, the famed Coco Palms. The resort covers 45 luxuriant acres soothed by the sounds of palm leaves whispering in the breeze. The clear calm water of the lagoon reflects an earlier era, and continuity with the past is a hallmark of the hotel; many employees dating back to the days when Mitzi Gaynor washed that man right outta her hair in the musical *South Pacific* and Elvis crooned "Blue Hawaii" on the resort grounds. The private cottages feature lava-rock, whirlpool spas. There are nine championship tennis courts, including three clay courts, which are rare in Hawaii. Delightful, intimate and relaxing, it's one of Hawaii's older premier resorts.
Singles & doubles: $95-$145; cottages: $155-$250; suites: $155-$300.

Sheraton Coconut Beach Hotel
P.O. Box 830,
Coconut Plantation,
Kapaa
• 822-3455
Fax 822-1830

The lesser of two Sheraton properties in Kauai, the Sheraton Coconut Beach still possesses a special charm, possibly because of its location in an ancient coconut grove, adjacent to the charming town of Kapaa. One special feature of the resort is a nightly Hawaiian luau, complete with pig fresh from the imu (underground oven), traditional and modern local foods and excellent Hawaiian entertainment. The beach leaves a little to be desired; ocean access is dangerous at best; the pool is modest, though well protected from the near-constant wind that pleasantly sings through the coastal ironwood trees (casuarina) and the stately coconut palms. Bring your racquet for the tennis courts.
Singles & doubles: $110-$205; suites $325.

PRACTICAL

Kauai Sands Hotel
420 Papaloa Rd.,
Kapaa
• 822-4951
Fax 922-0052

Occasionally, you've got to have "budget" (tell that to Congress and Mr. President), and this simple budget hotel is located near the Coconut Plantation Marketplace, just seven miles from the airport and the capital town of Lihue. Twenty of the 201 rooms have kitchenettes. Good basic accommodations, particularly for someone more interested in actively exploring Kauai than languishing around the pool sipping flower-bedecked mai tais.
Rooms: $58-$75; suites: $83.

Kokee Lodge

Kokee Rd.,
Kokee State Park
• 335-6061
No fax

And you thought that Kauai was all sand and suntan lotion! Well, there's another side to the stereotype, as you will discover at this humble mountain inn. The views are smashing, and the setting inside the state park couldn't be more tranquil. *Rooms: $35-$50.*

Stouffer Poipu Beach Resort

2251 Poipu Rd.,
Poipu
• 742-1681
No fax

Associated with the Stouffer Waiohai next door, the Stouffer Poipu Beach features 138 units with kitchenettes (two-burner stove and refrigerator). Guests enjoy budget prices but can use all the amenities at the Waiohai: tennis courts, fitness center, restaurants, lounge and beach, everything except the swimming pools and Jacuzzi. This is an older hotel built in 1963, but it has been renovated recently. The rooms are comfortable with rattan furniture, cable television and air conditioning. The property has a swimming pool, shops, restaurant and lounge. *Rooms: $90-$160; suites: $305.*

NIGHTLIFE

BARS	284
DANCING	286
LUAUS	286

BARS

Collonade Lounge

Westin Kauai,
Nawiliwili,
Lihue
• 246-9599

This is an all-day poolside "lounge" that's ideal for people-watching. Go here for a morning espresso, or tropical drinks in the evening. It's a nice spot for island-inspired music at night. *Open daily 8 a.m.-11 p.m. All major cards.*

Cook's at the Beach

Westin Kauai,
Nawiliwili,
Lihue
• 246-9599

An indoor/outdoor facility that's particularly appealing during summery evenings, when the torch-lighting ceremony and entertainment by a Hawaiian trio let you know that you're in a "Fantasy Island"–style paradise. The three squares are also served here daily. *Open daily 6:30 p.m.-11 p.m. All major cards.*

Charo's

5-7132 Kulio Hwy.,
Haena
• 826-6422

The question always comes up, "Is Charo here today?" Lucky is the visitor who actually finds Charo on the premises (she spends most of her time wowing them in Waikiki). The bar, at the far end of a scenic drive along Kauai's north shore, is a perfect place to pause before the trip back to your hotel. Tropical drinks and margaritas are thirst-quenchers; try the bountiful and savory appetizer of fried zucchini.
Open daily 11:30 a.m.- 5 p.m. & 6 p.m.-9 p.m.; cocktail service at all times. All major cards.

Duke's Canoe Club

Westin Kaui,
Nawiliwili,
Lihue
• 246-9599

A tropical setting, complete with waterfall, is part of the charm here. The "Duke," specifically, is Duke Kahanamoku, the world-famous surfer, and the surfing motif aims at the beach-blonde set. Partake of the pupus with your drinks at the Kau Kau Grill, or paddle away to a full-course meal in the upstairs dining room (see Kauai Restaurants, page 264). Contemporary entertainment that varies from Hawaiian to pop runs every evening from 5 p.m. to 9 p.m.
Open nightly 4 p.m.-midnight. All major cards.

Gaylord's Restaurant

Kilohana Plantation
Estate,
Hwy. 50,
Lihue
• 245-5608

It's a bar, a lounge, a restaurant (see Kauai Restaurants, page 265), a plantation estate home; for cocktails, the courtyard setting brings back images of sugar barons of yesteryear. Cheerful cordials, attractive menus and a spectacular view of the Kilohana mountains make this a splendid spot to stop.
Open Mon.-Sat. for cocktails and pupus 3:30 p.m.-10 p.m. All major cards.

Inn On The Cliffs

Westin Kauai,
Nawiliwili,
Lihue
• 246-9599

Even if you go only for a drink, the Inn On The Cliffs is a smart stop. You'll enjoy a sweeping view of Nawiliwili and environs, and, as they say, getting there is half the fun. The lounge and the restaurant (see Kauai Restaurants, page 267) are accessible only by motor launch in the artificial canal, or by horse and carriage from the hotel's porte cochere. In the evening's there's either a pianist or a tropical-jazz quartet.
Open for lounge entertainment Tues. 7 p.m.-11 p.m., Wed.-Sun. 8 p.m.-midnight.

Keoki's Paradise

Kiahuna Shopping
Village,
Poipu
• 742-7534

The indoor-outdoor setting, amid a manmade waterfall, is a cozy gathering spot for enjoying tropical drinks. In the Seafood and Taco Bar, you may order seafood appetizers and, yes, tacos—along with margaritas. Some like it so much that they cancel their reservations in the dining room.
Open daily for bar service 4:30 p.m.-midnight. All major cards.

The Tamarind
Stouffer Waiohai Beach
Resort,
Poipu
• 742-9511

Kimo Garner provides impeccable piano stylings in the lounge, an exotic canopy accompanying an evening of fine dining. Whether you sip and enjoy a cool one near the piano, or experience the Continental and Far Eastern delicacies in the main dining room, the music is a constant delight.
Open Tues.-Sun. 6 p.m.-11:30 p.m. All major cards.

DANCING

Paddling Club
Westin Kauai,
Kalapaki Beach
• 246-9599

The music gets louder as the evening gets later, and this is easily the most popular disco on the island. You amble down a curving walkway to the lower-level dance floor and Blam!—the recorded throbbing dance rhythms are as intoxicating as the tropical drinks you may want to order.
Open Mon.-Thurs. 9 p.m.-2 a.m., Fri.-Sat. 9 p.m.-4 p.m. No cover charge. All major cards.

LUAUS

**Sheraton
Coconut Beach
Hotel**
P.O. Box 830,
Coconut Plantation,
Kapaa
• 822-3455

Our second choice for a luau is at the Sheraton Coconut Beach Hotel. The nightly luaus begin with the torch-lighting ceremony, followed by a lei greeting, cocktails and unearthing the pig from the imu (underground oven). Dinner is a lavish buffet of pig, chicken, fish, beef taro, sweet potato, poi, greens and dessert. Victor and Kuulei Punua, their children and grandchildren perform the Polynesian entertainment. The Punua Polynesian Show has been entertaining Kauai since 1961. Dinner for two (including drinks) is $86.
Open nightly 6:30 p.m.-9:30 p.m. All major cards.

Tahiti Nui
Kuhio Hwy.,
Hanalei
• 826-6277

The best luau on Kauai is the Tahiti Nui's shindig at Hanalei. Tahitian "Auntie" Louise Marston has been putting on luaus for 30 years; she knows not only what to serve but how it should be served and the best, authentic entertainment. The real spirit of luaus comes out at Tahiti Nui, where the entire staff joins in to make sure that every guest leaves happy. Only 130 people can fit around the long-tabled dining area. Drinks are served, and at 7:15 p.m. the feast is set out buffet-style: fish, chicken, kalua pig, lomi lomi salmon, poi and homemade desserts. The entertainment begins at 8:30 p.m. On Wednesdays, the show features Tahitian drums and dancing and Hawaiian hulas both ancient and modern. On Fridays, a hula show is performed by a local halau (hula school). Cost is a mere $60 for two.
Open Wed. & Fri. 6:30 p.m.-9:30 p.m. Cards: MC, V.

SHOPS

Coming to Kauai to shop is a little like visiting New Jersey to enjoy the beaches: yes, it's possible, but certainly not the best reason for the trip. Nonetheless, there are possibilities, not the least of which are the four malls we list here. Just west of Lihue on Highway 50, there's the **Kukui Grove Center** (2600 Kaumualii Hwy.) where you'll find the island's major department stores, **Sears**, **JC Penney** and **F.W. Woolworth**. This is also the biggest shopping center on the island. There's a free shuttle bus (for information, call 245-7771). On the east side, you might stop at the **Coconut Plantation Market Place** (484 Kuhio Hwy.), which is a shopping center nestled into a larger resort complex. There aren't any department stores, but you will find items of Island interest—such as the muumuu you promised to Aunt Nelli—at **Hilo Hattie Fashion Factory** (245-3404). To the north, the best bet for a quick spree is the **Princeville Center** (4280 Kuhio Hwy.), where the prices are skewed toward the well-heeled traveler. If you feel moved to ship a few dozen assorted leis back home, take a look at **Flowers Forever** (826-7420). It will handle all of the nasty details, including the agricultural inspection. Finally, in Waimea, there is the new **Waimea Canyon Plaza** on Highway 50, which features gifts ranging from fashionable to funky.

SIGHTS

BEACHES

Brennecke's Beach
East of Poipu
• 245-8821

Until Hurricane Iwa hit in 1982, this was one of the best bodysurfing beaches in the state. Unfortunately, the hurricane sucked out a lot of sand and replaced it with large rocks. Local residents and experts still bodysurf at high tide, but board-surfing outside the reef is safer.

Donkey Beach (Kumukumu Beach)
Hwy. 56, just past the 11-mile marker,
Kealia
No phone

Looking for a remote, hidden beach? This is the place. Don't let the name fool you. In the 1960s, this was a haven for hippies clad only in rays of sunshine. They mistakenly called the mules, which grazed on the grassy meadow nearby, donkeys, thus the name—Donkey Beach. This spot is off the beaten path and a quarter-mile hike down a dusty cane road to the beach, but it's worth the effort. Try hiding away here for a day. Swimming can be dangerous in the winter. Surfing can be excellent.

Haena Beach Park
Hwy. 56,
5 miles west of Haena
• 245-8821

If your idea of going to the beach is plopping down in the sand with a good book, here's your spot. It's five acres of paradise, bordered by the sea on one side and sheer cliffs on the other. A full array of county-sponsored facilities includes picnic tables, rest rooms, showers and a campground. A word of caution: Swimming here can be very tricky. During the summer, the safest place is the west end behind the reef. Through much of the year, swimming is dangerous due to the shorebreak, backwash and rip currents. Surfing is for experts only. Fishing is excellent for papio and ulua.

Hanalei
Hwy. 56
• 245-8821

This is the picture-perfect beach: white sand, crescent shape. *South Pacific* was filmed right here. Three county facilities offer a variety of services: Hanalei Beach Park, Hanalei Pavilion and Waioli Beach Park. The surfing's excellent during winter. Also, there's good swimming near the Hanalei pier.

Kalihiwai Beach
Kalihiwai Rd.,
Kalihiwai
No phone

Kalihiwai is one of our favorite scenic beaches. A sheer rock wall protects the beach on one side, the rugged coastline on the other. In between lies a rolling green glen with a waterfall. Not easy to find, mainly because there are two Kalihiwai roads off Highway 56. Take the one closest to Lihue. This washboard road leads directly to the ironwood-bordered beach, which is good for fishing, swimming, snorkeling, surfing and just plain vegetating.

Poipu Beach Park	Poipu has something for everyone: a grassy area for picnickers,

Poipu Beach Park
Hoona Rd.,
Poipu
• 742-6722

Poipu has something for everyone: a grassy area for picnickers, a white-sand beach for sun worshipers, excellent swimming, the best snorkeling and diving on the south side, and good fishing. If all this isn't to your satisfaction, try the beaches west of the park that fronts the hotels. If you still are unhappy, consider therapy.

EXCURSIONS

North Shore

Haena Beach to Kee Beach
Haena Hwy. 56

On the island's northern tip lies the verdant tropical jungle that many people associate with Hawaii. This is the Kauai of lush rain forests, tumbling waterfalls and multihued rainbows. In the mood for relaxation, lazing at the beach or gazing at the sunset? A trip to Haena-Kee is the ticket. Start at Haena: this five-acre county beach offers excellent swimming in the summer but a dangerous shorebreak and backwash in the winter. Across from the Haena Beach Park is Maniniholo Dry Cave. This cave (formerly a lava tube) burrows about 300 feet into the mountain, gradually narrowing to a small hole. Farther down the highway are the Waikapalae and Waikanaloa Wet Caves, which are filled with water. Scuba divers have explored the Waikanaloa (water of the god Kanaloa) about 100 yards inland. At the end of the road is Kee Beach, arguably the best place in Hawaii to watch the sun slowly sink into the west.

KAUAI'S BIG RAINBOW

If you thought the rainbow was invented to lead you to an Irish pot of gold, think again. Hawaiian legend has it that the rainbow came to the Islands in Kauai's Hanalei Valley. A local resident threw a piece of brightly colored *kapa* cloth into the pool at Namolokama Falls. The cloth's colors arced up in the mist of the falls, and through them Anuenue, the goddess of the rainbow, emerged. In a chant, Anuenue told the villager that she had been hidden in the water and was now free to roam the islands of Hawaii. Whenever you see a rainbow in Hawaii, it is Anuenue waving her blessing on the land.

Hanalei
Hwy. 56

Hanalei remains an unspoiled jewel, with traditional taro fields, cascading waterfalls and carved cliffs. It has been, after all, the location for numerous movies, including *South Pacific*. One of the most popular photographic view points on Kauai is the Hanalei Valley Lookout. On Highway 56, it overlooks the lush green taro fields, which appear much as they did hundreds of years ago. Continuing north along the highway, the carved landscape suggests French Polynesia: majestic peaks rising behind crescent-shaped white-sand coves. In the midst of this tropical paradise is the Hanalei Garden Farm, which raises buffalo as a beef substitute for local restaurants. (Note the eight-foot fence: buffalo may look big and awkward, but they can clear seven feet, no problem). Before the town of Hanalei, check out the Hanalei National Wildlife Refuge, an excellent spot for viewing water fowl and other birds. The town of Hanalei is a step back in time, filled with historical museums and buildings that suggest the missionary era.

Kilauea Point National Wildlife Refuge

Lighthouse Rd.,
Kilauea
• 828-1413

Kilauea Point, the northernmost point in the main Hawaiian Islands, is the site of a 167-acre wildlife refuge. Choose between the half-hour or three-hour self-guided coastal hike through this unique wilderness area, where sea birds such as the booby, albatross and frigate nest in nearby cliffs. Binoculars and information on the area are available at the small shop near the lighthouse. The 1913 lighthouse had the largest clam-shaped lens ever made, beaming up to 90 miles at sea. It was replaced in 1976 by a smaller, high-intensity light.
Open Mon.-Fri. 10 a.m-4 p.m. Fee $2.

Princeville

Hwy. 56
• 826-3040

Once the site of a coffee plantation and now a growing resort area, Princeville is 11,000 acres filled with the usual hotels, condominiums, golf courses, shops and restaurants. Let's not forget the three excellent beaches. The area was originally named Kikiula. When King Kamehameha IV and Queen Emma visited the plantation in 1860, owner R. C. Wyllie was so taken with the royal couple's two-year-old son, Prince Albert, he decided to change the name of his plantation to Princeville. The coffee plantation failed, but the name stuck.

South Shore

Barking Sands Beach

End of Hwy. 50,
U.S. Navy Pacific
Missile Range Facility
• 335-4346, 335-4356

Kauai offers many unusual natural phenomena, but Barking Sands Beach is certainly one of the strangest. The name is sometimes loosely applied to the entire coastline from Polihale to Kekaha. But the "true" Barking Sands is a half-mile-long sand dune. About 50 feet high, it's located north of Nohili Point, adjacent to the Barking Sands Beach. Believe it or not, the beach actually barks. During certain times of the year (when the sand has the right humidity and salt content), shuffle your feet in the sand and the friction produces a sound like that of a barking dog. Local residents joke that the name is not derived from the woofing sound, but from tourists getting dog-tired after repeated attempts to get the mute sand to "speak." The wide beach offers great sunbathing, swimming, surfing and fishing. It is on a military reservation, so do call in advance to make sure the main gate is open.

Hawaiian Salt Ponds
Lolokai Rd., Hanapepe

These ancient Hawaiian salt ponds are still harvested every summer by the descendants of the original managers of the ancestral plots, who use techniques first described by Captain Cook in 1778. "Hawaiian salt" is a tasty reddish-colored spice, which is a popular seasoning throughout the state. Besides, stopping by will allow you to tell your friends that you went to "the salt mines" on your vacation in Hawaii.

Kokee State Park
Hwy. 550, Kokee
• 335-5871

A few miles from the renowned, picture-perfect and better-publicized scenic spots lies Kokee. At an elevation of 4,000 feet, the Kokee State Park is a haven from the heat, the hordes and the hurly-burly of vacation resorts. Sunlight pours majestically through towering redwoods and "sugi" pines. The fragrance of sweet-smelling yellow ginger wafts through the crisp mountain air, and birds serenade the traveler with melodious songs. More than 45 miles of trails snake through the 4,345-acre park. Clearly marked, some trails traverse into cloud-shrouded, lush tropical rain forests, where the only sounds are piercing bird calls and the whispering of the wind. There is magic in Kokee. Hikers report walking in bright sunshine, while the surrounding terrain is blanketed in mist. The streams of Kokee are among the few places in the Hawaiian Islands where rainbow trout live. Eight streams, filled with these tasty, scrappy fish, are open to anglers in August and September. Facilities in this mountain park are scarce. The only restaurant, the Kokee Lodge, offers meals and a dozen extremely inexpensive cabins for visitors. Some private cabins are occasionally available. For more information, stop by the Kokee Natural History Museum.

A VISUAL MAP

The "Garden Isle" of Kauai lies north of Oahu. It is roughly divided into two distinct geographical areas. Lush tropical jungle, taro fields and thundering waterfalls envelop the north and east shores of the island, and abundant sunshine and endless white-sand beaches line the southern and western shores. Kauai holds the distinction of having the wettest spot on Earth, atop Mount Waialeale, which receives about 480 inches a year. It also boasts the 3,600-foot-deep valley called Waimea Canyon, which Mark Twain dubbed the "Grand Canyon of the Pacific."

Koloa-Poipu-Spouting Horn
Hwy. 520

Koloa (which translates as "tall cane") was originally a community of 4,000 Hawaiians who lived in grass shacks on scattered taro farms. These former home sites can still be found between Koloa and the ocean in areas not cleared for sugarcane. The Kiahuna Golf Course has dramatic, well-preserved archaeological sites. In the 1800s, Koloa was a sugar-plantation town. Today, it includes three acres of boutique shops and restaurants. Beyond Koloa, facing the ocean, is the resort area of Poipu, which has some of the best swimming and surfing beaches on the island. West of Poipu, along Shoreline Road, Mother Nature has created a natural phenomenon not to be missed: Spouting Horn. As the surf rolls into the rocky shoreline, an eerie moaning or wheezing sound emerges from the mouth of a lava tube. Depending on the weather, the lava tube can spit a funneled wave up to 50 feet in the air and emit a honk that sounds just like a fog horn.

LUAUS

The best luau on Kauai is the **Tahiti Nui's** shindig at Hanalei. Tahitian "Auntie" Louise Marston has been putting on luaus for 30 years; she knows not only what to serve but how it should be served, as well as the best, authentic entertainment. The real spirit of luaus comes out at Tahiti Nui, where the entire staff joins in to make sure that every guest leaves happy. Luaus are every Wednesday and Friday beginning at 6:30 p.m. Only 130 people can fit in the long-tabled dining area. Drinks are served and at 7:15 p.m. the feast is set out buffet style: fish, chicken, kalua pig, lomi lomi salmon, poi and homemade desserts. At 8:30, when everyone is satiated, the entertainment begins. On Wednesdays the show features Tahitian drums and dancing and Hawaiian hulas both ancient and modern. Fridays there's an entire hula show performed by a local *halau* (hula school). Cost is a mere $60 for two.

Our second choice for a luau is at the **Sheraton Coconut Beach Hotel.** The nightly luaus begin at 6:30 p.m. with a torch-lighting ceremony, followed by a lei greeting, cocktails and unearthing the pig from the imu pit. Dinner is a lavish buffet of pig, chicken, fish, beef taro, sweet potato, poi, greens and dessert. The Polynesian entertainment is done by Victor and Kuulei Punua, their children and grandchildren. The Punua Polynesian Show has been entertaining Kauai since 1961. Dinner for two (including drinks) is $85.80.

GOING WHOLE HOG

Almost every luau features what must be one of the most memorable of Hawaiian feasts: kalua pig. Kalua ("baked" or "to bake in a ground oven") pig is prepared in a lengthy, festive procedure outdoors, not unlike a New England clambake. The ceremony begins with the digging of an *imu*, a pit six feet wide and four feet deep, which is lined with wood and lava rocks. When the wood has burned down to coals, the pig (usually about 60 pounds) is sliced open, salted and stuffed with some of the sizzling rocks. The pit is lined with banana leaves and the moist pieces of a banana-tree stump, which create steam for cooking. The pig is then wrapped in leaves and wire, hoisted into the pit and covered with tea leaves, banana leaves and hot stones (and sometimes dirt, burlap or canvas). It's left to cook for about four hours, to smoky succulence.

MUSEUMS

Grove Farm Homestead Museum
Box 1631,
Lihue
• 245-3202

This fragile fragment of Hawaii's past is very hard to get into. Built in 1860, the former plantation home of George Wilcox is today a tribute to the life of a sugar baron. The family lived in the house until 1980, when Mable Wilcox endowed the eight-acre plantation to the museum. The old place isn't what it used to be—in fact it is structurally unstable, and the number of people allowed inside has to be limited. Advance reservations (up to three months ahead) are the only way to get in. If it is not raining—it is closed on rainy days—and you do manage to get in, you can wander around the house, office, wash house, teahouse and guest cottage. The museum has done an excellent job of leaving things just as George left them, even down to the paperwork of the plantation still on George's desk. The tour, given by knowledgeable docents, lasts two hours. To really get a feel for the era, read *Grove Farm Plantation*, by Bob Krauss and William Alexander, before you go.
Tours Mon., Wed., Thurs. 10 a.m. & 1 p.m. Closed rainy days and national holidays. Admission $3.

Kauai Museum
4428 Rice St.,
Lihue
• 245-6931

This was the site of the first public library built on Kauai in 1924. Today, it houses an ethnic-heritage museum, geological exhibits and an art museum featuring work from Kauai and Niihau.
Open Mon.-Fri. 9 a.m.-4:30 p.m., Sat. 9 a.m.-1 p.m. Admission $3.

Kilohana
3-2087 Kaumualii Hwy.,
Lihue
• 245-5608

This restored 1930s plantation home now houses a museum, a restaurant and boutique shops. The living room and main dining room of the old home have been converted into a museum. Other rooms are small, one-of-a-kind shops, and the courtyard is the site of the restaurant, which serves lunch and dinner. Food is so-so; shops are fabulous; the museum-home terrific. Be sure to check out the horse-driven carriage tours of the grounds.
Open Mon.-Sat. 9:30 a.m.-9:30 p.m., Sun. 9:30 a.m.-5 p.m.

Kokee Natural History Museum
Kokee State Park
• 335-9975

Located in a tiny cabin surrounded by the towering trees of Kokee Park, this minimuseum has geographic maps and exhibits of Kauai's indigenous bird and plant life. If you are planning to spend time in Kokee, this is an excellent information source on nearly everything in the park.
Open daily 10 a.m.-4 p.m. Admission free.

Waioli Mission House Museum
P.O. Box 1631,
Lihue
• 245-3202

Associated with the Grove Farm Homestead, this was the Wilcox family home in Hanalei. Built in 1837 out of coral limestone blocks by Rev. William Alexander, this was one of the first missionary homes to be placed on the National Register of Historic Places. For background material, read *Waioli Mission House*, by Barnes Riznick. No reservations needed, but call to get directions on how to get there.
Open Tues., Thurs. & Sat. 9 a.m.-3 p.m. Closed rainy days and holidays. Tours take 30 minutes. Admission free, donations accepted.

PARKS & GARDENS

Kokee State Park
Kokee
• 335-5871

Located 4,000 feet up in the clouds, the Kokee State Park is another side of the tropical climate that people associate with Kauai. Forty-five trails snake through the forests of ohia, tree ferns and koa trees in the 4,345-acre park. The temperatures are cooler, the air crisper and the flora, fauna and bird life simply magical. During August and September, fishing for rainbow trout is permitted in the Kokee's eight streams. There are also spectacular views of the Na Pali Coast.

National Tropical Botanical Gardens
Box 340,
Lawai
• 332-7361

These magical gardens are not to be missed. The former home of Queen Emma was purchased by Chicago stockyard magnate Robert Allerton in 1937 and converted into the Garden of Eden. The three-hour tour covers more than two miles of the 286-acre botanical garden, which is filled with more than 6,000 varieties of tropical plants. Elegant sculptures dot the well-manicured grounds. Tiny gazebos suggest meditation. An atmosphere of serenity permeates this verdant haven. Reservations are a must, as this is Kauai's most popular (and best!) garden tour.
Open daily. Tours 9 a.m. & 1 p.m.. Admission $15. Annual membership for 2 $35 (allows unlimited tours for a year).

Smith's Tropical Paradise
174 Wailua Rd.,
Kapaa
• 822-4654

Thirty acres of botanical gardens bordering the Wailua River, include a Japanese garden, and Filipino and Polynesian villages. A bit on the commercial-touristy side for our taste. At night, the gardens host a luau, complete with the ceremonial uncovering of the *imu* (earthen cooking pit).
Open daily 8:30 a.m.-4 p.m. Admission $4. (Luau Mon.-Fri. 6 p.m. Cost $39.50.)

Waimea Canyon State Park
Waimea
• 245-4444

When Mark Twain looked out upon the 3,600-foot-deep Waimea Canyon, he dubbed it "the Grand Canyon of the Pacific." In a lot of ways, this 1,800-acre state park does resemble the landscape of the southwest. Burnt-orange, pale-brown and mustard hues cover the gaping canyon walls. Dirt paths meander along the canyon walls. Get there early: by midday not only do the clouds roll into the canyon blocking much of the view, but hordes of buses filled with camera-clicking tourists mob the few lookout points.

HAWAII'S LITTLE PEOPLE

The most puzzling myth on Kauai refers to the *Menehunes*, believed to be the leprechauns of Hawaii, who perform superhuman feats of work only at night. This race of miniature forest people is credited with works that still perplex archaeologists today. For example, the Menehune Ditch, outside of Waimea, is an extraordinary engineering feat of stonework found nowhere else in Hawaii. Another work attributed to these people is the Menehune Fish Pond, next to Nawiliwili Harbor. Archaeologists have dated the stones in the pond to well before the Polynesians arrived in the Islands. According to legend, the gnomelike Menehunes formed a 25-mile-long chain and, passing rocks from hand to hand, built the pond in a single night.

TOURS

Kauai Mountain Tours
Box 3069,
Lihue
• 245-7224

For a spectacular four-wheel-drive adventure through the magic of Kokee State Park, don't miss this all-day tour. The pickup at your hotel includes a hot cup of coffee and a homemade roll. This is the only company with a state permit to enter the Na Pali Kona National Forest Reserve. As you venture through this enchanted forest, your guide gives a fact-filled commentary on the plants, flowers, wildlife and legends of this magical place. Tour includes catered picnic lunch.
Tours daily. Hotel pickup beginning at 7:15 a.m. Fees: $75; youths 10-13 $55, children 3-9 $40.

Na Pali Coast Cruise Line
Box 869,
Eleele
• 335-5078

See Kauai from the sea. This six-hour cruise of the southwest and Na Pali coastlines also includes a stop for snorkeling (all gear provided), meals and beverages.
Cruises daily. Fee $85.

Na Pali Coast with Captain Zodiac

Box 456,
Hanalei
• 826-9371

Clancy Greff, "Captain Zodiac," initiated the now-famous sea tours of the spectacular Na Pali Coastline. He has specially designed tours for his fleet of 23-foot inflatable boats, depending on the weather and sea conditions. In the calmer summer waters, his tours explore the sea caves and hidden waterfalls. In the winter, he offers a three-hour, thirteen-mile narrated tour (includes snorkeling) and a five-hour, fifteen-mile tour that features a beach landing, lunch, snorkeling and hiking. On the morning tour, the water is calmer, but there are more people—from other tour boats—in the water than there is sea life. *Tours daily, 3-hour tour 8:45 a.m. ($78) & 12:15 p.m. ($67.60); 5-hour tour $98.80.*

Niihau Helicopter

Box 370,
Makaweli
• 335-3500

Here's the only way to see the "Forbidden Isle" of Niihau. A cattle plantation, which has been owned by the Robinson family since 1864, Niihau is off-limits to visitors. Approximately 225 Hawaiians live on Niihau not much differently from their ancestors. Niihau Helicopter's primary purpose is to provide medical-emergency air transportation to island residents. To fund this service, Niihau Helicopters offers two-hour flights that cover the island and include two stops. To respect the residents' privacy, the tours do not go near the island's one town. *Tours Mon.-Fri. Flights leave 9 a.m., noon & 3 p.m. from the heliport located between Hanapepe and Waimea in Kaumakani. Cost $185 per person.*

North Shore Bike Cruise & Snorkel

Box 1192,
Kapaa
• 822-1582

This is an all-day experience, beginning with hotel pickup (no pickup in the Poipu area). Things get started with an easy six-mile ride into a lush area with freshwater pools and tumbling waterfalls. Afternoon activities include snorkeling in the ocean and a huge barbecue on the beach. *Daily tours. $75 per person.*

Papillon Hawaiian Helicopters

Princeville Airport
• 826-6591

Of all the helicopter tours operating out of Kauai, Papillon is our favorite. Not only is the operation professionally run, but their tours are truly awesome. Choose from a range of twirly tours: Discover, a half-hour overview of Waimea Canyon and the Na Pali Coast; Butterfly Special, a 50-minute tour of Waimea Canyon, the Na Pali Coast plus Mount Waialeale, the wettest spot on Earth; Sunset Flight, 50 minutes in the air and an hour stop at sunset on the Na Pali Coast, complete with Champagne and "hors d'oeuvres," plus a range of other choices. *Daily tours. Discover, $95 per person; Butterfly Special, $130; Sunset Flight, $165.*

SPORTS

BICYCLING

Aquatics Kauai
733 Kuhio Hwy.,
Kapaa
• 822-9213

While Aquatics Kauia offers mostly mountain bikes, some ten-speed bikes are also available.
Open daily 8:30 a.m.-5:30 p.m. Cost $17.50 for 24 hours.

Pedal & Paddle
Ching Yung Shopping Center,
Hanalei
• 826-9069

P&P offers a huge variety of bicycles for rent, ranging from mountain bikes to racing bikes.
Open daily 9 a.m.-5 p.m. Cost $4 per hour & $20 per day.

South Shore Activities
Box 982, Koloa,
located adjacent to
Sheraton Kauai,
Poipu
• 742-6873

Five-speed bikes are available for rent.
Open Mon.-Sat. 9 a.m.-5 p.m. Cost from $4 per hour to $50 per week.

DIVING & SNORKELING

Aquatics Kauai
733 Kuhio Hwy.,
Kapaa
• 822-9213, 822-9422

All diving and snorkeling gear is available for rent. *Open daily 8:30 a.m.-5:30 p.m. Cost snorkeling gear $8.50 per day; scuba equipment $30 per day.*

Bubbles Below Scuba Charters
6251 Hauaala Rd.,
Kapaa
• 822-3483

This shop specializes in educating visitors about Hawaii's bountiful sea life. It has certification classes, daily dive charters and, on occasion, special all-day dives around Niihau, the "Forbidden Island." *Daily four-hour morning and evening charters. Fee $75 for 2-tanks/2-locations, boat dive; $90 if complete rental equipment is needed. Dive computers and photography equipment provided. Monthly dive to Niihau, 5 a.m.-sunset, 3-tanks, including meals $165 ($185 if complete rental gear is needed).*

Fathom Five Adventures
3450 Poipu Rd.,
Koloa
• 742-6991

Fathom Five has two boats, so booking a dive charter is generally not a problem. A full-service shop with everything from certification classes to daily two-tank dives, they specialize in charters exploring the south shore. *Open Mon.-Sat. 7:30 a.m.-7 p.m., Sun. 7:30 a.m.-4:30 p.m. Certification classes $350 for 5.5 days of classroom and diving instruction. Daily 2-tank scuba charters $80, includes all equipment ($65 if you provide your own). Fee for rental equipment $30 per day.*

Kiahuna Beach Services
Rte. 1,
Box 73,
Poipu Rd.,
Koloa
• 742-6411

This is one of the few places that offer an introductory snorkeling tour for first-timers. Equipment rental available. *Open 8 a.m.-6 p.m. Snorkel tour $20 for 2-hour tour, plus use of gear for an additional half hour.*

Poipu Dive Co.
Kiahuna Shopping Village,
Poipu
• 742-7661

In addition to equipment rental, they also offer guided shore, boat and night dives. *Open Mon.-Sat. 8:30 a.m.-9 p.m., Sun. 8:30 a.m.-6 p.m. Cost snorkeling gear $10 per day; scuba equipment $35 per day.*

Sea Sage Diving Center
4-1378 Kuhio Hwy.,
Kapaa
• 822-3841

This complete professional diving center carries a full line of snorkeling and scuba equipment. A speedy repair facility will fix up any equipment that may have been mishandled en route to Kauai. Founder Nick Konstaninou, son of noted marine biologist and shark specialist Eugenie Clark, has established a range of programs from certification classes to both shoreline and boat dives (including a very popular night dive that is not to be missed). The company uses the largest boat on Kauai, which is 43 feet in length and has plenty of room for any nondiving friends who just want to go along for the scenic ride.

Open daily 7:30-5:30 p.m. Introductory shoreline 1-tank dive $75, includes all equipment. Introductory boat dive $90, includes equipment and lunch. Certified divers can choose from guided shoreline dives $60, or boat dives $90. Certification classes $350.

South Shore Activities
2230 Kapili Rd.,
Koloa
• 742-6873

Snorkeling gear and underwater cameras are available.
Open Mon.-Sat. 9 a.m.-5 p.m. Cost snorkeling gear $3.50 per hour, $33 per week. No scuba equipment rental.

FISHING

Bass Guides of Kauai
Box 3525,
Lihue
• 822-1405

One of the few opportunities in Hawaii to match your skill against freshwater battlers, Bass Guides offers year-round fishing with local experts who provide all the equipment you need. Full-day and half-day charters aboard a 17-foot aluminum bass boat on private reservoirs for largemouth, smallmouth and peacock bass.
Charters daily. Half-day charters from $95; full-day from $180.

Gent-Lee Fishing and Sightseeing Charters
Box 1691,
Lihue
• 245-7504

Try your luck at landing marlin, tuna, wahoo or the popular mahimahi on this 32-foot sportfishing boat. All tackle and beverages provided.
Charters daily. Half-day/share-boat rates from $93.60 per person; 6 hours $125 per person.

Sport Fishing Kauai
Box 1195,
Koloa
• 742-7013

For the angler seeking a real challenge, Sportfishing Kauai offers expeditions for big fish on light tackle.
Charters daily. Half-day/share-boat rates from $85 per person; full-day $130 per person.

GOLF

Kiahuna Golf Course
Poipu
• 742-9595

Frequently windy, this par-70, eighteen-hole course was designed by Robert Trent Jones, Jr.
Daily tee times begin 7 a.m.; last tee 4 p.m. Green fee $63, if staying in Poipu area; $70 all others, including cart.

Kukuiolono Golf Course
Kalaheo
• 332-9151

Wide fairways and few traps make for a relaxed atmosphere on this nine-hole county course. To get in eighteen holes, local residents just play the course twice from a second set of tees.
Daily tee times begin 6:30 a.m.; last tee time 4:30. Green fee $5; optional cart $5. No reservations.

Princeville Makai Golf Course
Princeville
• 826-3580

Location for the Women's LPGA Kemper Open, Princeville features three nine-hole courses (Ocean, Lake and Woods) that can be played in any eighteen-hole combination. The Robert Trent Jones, Jr.–designed course is windy in the winter and contains lots of hazards.
Daily tee times begin 7 a.m.; last tee time 4:30 p.m. Green fees $85 for non-Princeville guests; $75 for guests, including cart.

Wailua Golf Course
Wailua
• 245-2163

A municipal course that shows some wear, Wailua is still one of our favorites. It's challenging without being too difficult, with lots of sand and water hazards.
Daily tee times begin 7 a.m.; last tee time 2 p.m. Green fees $10 weekdays, $11 weekends; optional carts $12. Reservations taken up to a week in advance for 2 or more golfers.

Westin Kauai
Nawiliwili,
Lihue
• 245-5050

Take your pick from two excellent courses designed by Jack Nicklaus: for the low-handicapper, the Kauai Kiele Championship Course, an eighteen-hole course for the pros; and the Kauai Lagoons Course, eighteen holes for the recreational golfer.
Daily tee times begin 7 a.m.; last tee 2 p.m. Fees $105 (Kiele) & $70 (Lagoons) for hotel guests; $135 (Kiele) & $90 (Lagoons) for others; prices include cart.

HIKING

For information on trails, hiking and camping throughout Kauai, contact one of the following organizations: **Division of State Parks** (Box 1671, Lihue; 245-4444); **Hawaii Geographic Society** (Box 1698, Honolulu; 1-538-3952), which offers an excellent information packet for $6; the **Hawaiian Trail and Mountain Club** (Box 2238, Honolulu; 1-734-5515) which has a $1 information kit describing hiking on all of the islands; the **Kauai County Division of Parks and Recreation** (4193 Hardy St., Lihue; 245-1881); and the **Sierra Club** (Box 3412, Lihue), which schedules hikes throughout the year, open to the public. Following are some of Kauai's better trails:

> ## ONE ROCK TOO MANY
>
> **Behind the town of Kapaa is Nounou (Throwing) Mountain, also known as Sleeping Giant. A legend claims that Puni, a giant who once roamed Kauai, lay down to rest there. The village people, being of bad temper, threw rocks at him to wake him. One rock landed in his mouth, which caused him to choke to his demise. Now and for all of eternity, Puni, the giant, will sleep in the hills behind Kapaa.**

Alakai Swamp
Mohihi Rd.,
Kokee State Park
• 335-5871

This boggy seven-mile round-trip hike begins at Mohiki Road in Kokee Park. If swarms of mosquitoes, pouring rain and mud to your knees is your idea of fun, this is the hike for you. There is a reward at the end, if it is not raining or shrouded in clouds: a spectacular view from the Kilohana Lookout, high above Hanalei Bay. Bring insect repellent, rain gear and boots to slog through the rain forest and swamp.

Awaawapuhi Trail
Rte. 55,
Kokee State Park
• 335-5871

Not for the acrophobic, but those in good shape will enjoy this hike to a bird's-eye view of the Na Pali Coast. The six-mile round-trip hike begins one-and-a-half miles past the Kokee State Park Headquarters at telephone pole No. 1-4/2P/152 on the left side of the road. The trail winds through a lush forest to a breathtaking lookout over the cliff to the coast, some 2,500 feet below. The trail connects with the Nualolo Trail to extend the hike into an eight-and-a-half-mile loop.

Kailua Ridge Trail
Hwy. 580 near Keahua
Arboretum,
Wailua

A scenic four-mile round-trip walk, starting just a mile past the University of Hawaii Agricultural Experiment Station, this trail abounds in picnic areas, wild orchids and cascading waterfalls.

Kalalau Trail
Na Pali Coastline
• 245-4444

Without a doubt, this is our favorite scenic trail. An eleven-mile hike along the rugged Na Pali Coast lasts several days. Scenery includes lush rain forests; stream-filled verdant valleys and steep, jagged cliffs. Light pours through fruit-filled guava trees, and the whispering wind is the only sound as sea birds appear to hang in midair on the thermals. The trail begins at the end of Route 56, near Kee Beach. The first part is a two-mile, somewhat arduous hike to Hanakapiai Valley, where several side hikes into the valley can be taken. Then the trail gets rougher, the foliage thicker and the climb up the cliff steeper as you make your way to Hanakoa Valley. The scenery is well worth the sweat. The final destination on the trail is Kalalau Valley, where a stream bubbles through the lush valley, ending in a white-sand beach. Anyone hiking beyond Hanakapiai or camping must have a permit: contact the State Parks Division at the above phone number.

Koaie Canyon Trail
Waimea Canyon,
Waimea

Named after the Koaie tree, a hardwood that Hawaiians used to make spears, this is a very easy six-mile round-trip jaunt. Hikers can enjoy the stark beauty of the multicolored canyon that crosses Waimea River, passing by ancient Hawaiian terraces and rock walls. The trail begins at the end of Kukui Trail (see below) and ends at Lonomea Camp, a wilderness campsite with shelter and a cool, welcoming deep-water swimming hole.

Kukui Trail
Rte. 55,
Waimea Canyon,
Waimea

Here's the shortest route into Waimea Canyon, the "Grand Canyon of the Pacific." The five-mile round-trip begins at the Iliau Loop Trail and goes through a series of switchbacks, dropping some 2,000 feet to the floor of the canyon. Panoramas change constantly as the sun moves across the sky. At the canyon floor, you are rewarded with a large swimming hole near Wiliwili Camp, a wilderness campsite.

HORSEBACK RIDING

CJM Country Stables
5598 Tapa St.,
Koloa
• 245-6666, 742-6096

See the south shore of Kauai from a different perspective—on a horse. Escorted rides travel along cliffs, oceanfronts and next to beaches, including a popular three-hour Paniolo beach breakfast ride.

Open Mon.-Sat. Cost 1-hour ride $25, 2-hour ride $45 & 3-hour Paniolo beach breakfast ride $60.

Pooku Stables
Box 888,
Hanalei, located on Hwy.
56, near Princeville
• 826-6777, 826-7473

Guided trail rides along the scenic north shore include a one-hour excursion along the upper edge of Hanalei Valley; a two-hour Hawaiian Country Ride across range lands with unbelievable views; and a three-hour waterfall-picnic ride, which lets you stop and take a dip (bring a swimsuit).
Open Mon.-Sat. Cost 1-hour ride $25; 2-hour Hawaiian Country Ride $46; 3-hour waterfall-picnic ride $70, including lunch. Weight limit 230 pounds.

KAYAKING

Island Adventure
Box 3370, Lihue,
located at Nawiliwili
Boat Harbor
• 245-9662

An unforgettable two-and-a-half-hour guided tour up Huleia River into the Federal Wildlife Sanctuary, the only way the natural wildlife refuge can be explored. The tour includes not only the guided water trip but also a walk through the wildlife sanctuary.
Tours Mon.-Sat. 8:45 a.m. & 12:45 p.m. Cost $32, including snacks.

Kayak Kauai
Box 508,
Hanalei
• 826-9844

Kayak Kauai offers guided tours to the Hanalei Wildlife Refuge, Hanalei Bay, Na Pali Coast or Wailua River. For the more adventuresome, take a two-passenger kayak with maps and tips on where to go.
Open daily 8 a.m.-4:30 p.m. Guided 3-hour tour of Hanalei Wildlife Refuge and Hanalei Bay $45, 6-hour tour of Na Pali Coast $95. Equipment rental $48 for a two-passenger kayak.

Pedal & Paddle
Ching Yung Shopping
Center,
Hanalei
• 826-9069

Rentals only.
Open daily 9 a.m.-5 p.m. Inflatable kayaks and canoes $45 for 2 passengers & $55 for 3 passengers.

SAILING

Bluewater Sailing
• 335-6440 (Port Allen),
822-0525 (Anahola)

This 42-foot, ketch-rigged Pearson yacht carries up to twelve passengers on its year-round sailing charters. Half-day or full-day charters include lunch; there's also a sunset sail with snacks and soft drinks. In winter, trips commence from Port Allen in Eleele, and in summer the yacht sails from Anahola in Hanalei, along Na Pali Coast.
Daily charters. Cost $60 per half day, $100 per full day; $35 for sunset sails.

Captain Andy's Sailing Adventures
Box 1291,
Koloa
• 822-7833

Cruise along the south shore in a 40-foot trimaran, on a half-day sail-and-snorkel cruise, which includes lunch and soft drinks. During the winter months, Captain Andy's Sailing Adventures also offers a whale-watching trip. Call for departure times and prices.
Daily charters. Cost $65 per person for half day.

SURFING

Kiahuna Beach Services
Rte. 1, Box 73,
Poipu Rd.,
Koloa
• 742-6411

Margo Oberg, seven-time women's world-surfing champion, has been teaching novices how to surf for more than fifteen years. Not only does she start her pupils out on the sand before they hit the waves, but she lets them use specially designed beginners' surfboards for the first hour after their introductory lesson. She guarantees even rank beginners will learn to ride the waves. Surfboards, snorkels and boogie boards may be rented.
Open daily 8 a.m.-6 p.m. Lessons $35.

TENNIS

The Kauai County Department of Parks and Recreation (4280-A Rice St., Building B, Lihue; 245-1881) has public courts scattered across the island. Most are not maintained very well, but they are free. If you want to pay to play, below are some of Kauai's better clubs and resorts:

Coco Palms Tennis Shop
Coco Palms Resort,
Wailua
• 822-4921

Under the famous palm trees surrounding the resort are nine tennis courts open to the public: two are lit for night play, three are clay, and six are hard. There are no strict dress policies here.
Open daily 8 a.m.-noon. (Pro shop open Tues.-Sun. 8 a.m.-5 p.m. Check in at the hotel front desk at other times.) Cost $10 per court/per day.

Kiahuna Plantation Tennis Club
Koloa
• 742-9533

People staying in the Poipu area flock to these courts because of the special weekly rates that also allow use of the pool. Kiahuna has ten courts, none of which is lit for night play.
Open daily 7:30 a.m.-6 p.m. Cost $9 per person/per hour; $30 per person/per week, $40 per couple/ per week.

Princeville Tennis Club
Princeville Resort
• 826-9823

These are the best courts in the Princeville area. There are only six courts, which are frequently booked, so call in advance.
Open daily 9 a.m.-5 p.m. Cost $5 per person/per hour; $20 per person/per week, $35 per couple/per week.

Stouffer Waiohai Beach Resort
2249 Poipu Rd.,
Poipu
• 742-9511

The resort has six courts, including four that may be lit for night play. Dress code calls for no running shoes and no tank tops or cut-off jeans for men.
Open daily 7 a.m.-9 p.m. (Pro shop open daily 7 a.m.-7 p.m.; arrangements for night lighting must be made in advance.) Cost (for guests & visitors) $15 per day, $75 per week.

WINDSURFING

Westin Kauai
Nawiliwili,
Lihue
• 245-5050 ext. 5232
or ext. 5269

Glide over the clear blue water on a sailboard. Group and individual lessons instruct the novice or fine-tune the more experienced windsurfer. Located on the western end of the beach facing the hotel, the instruction includes a sailboard simulator to ease the landlubber into this oceanic rock and roll. *Open daily 7 a.m.-7 p.m. Best time for a lesson is 11 a.m. Fee: three-hour lesson $80 individual, or $60 per person for groups of three; one-hour minilesson for experienced windsurfers $35.*

HOLLYWOOD FAR WEST

Kauai could be dubbed "Hollywood West." Its super-green valleys, white-sand beaches, rugged coastlines and jungle swamps have been the location of numerous movies and television shows. Because of the island's versatility, producers have gravitated to Kauai to depict everything from paradise to a war zone.

Elvis Presley got married on the Wailua River in *Blue Hawaii*. Jack Lemmon and Ricky Nelson sailed the same river in *The Wackiest Ship in the Army*. Mitzi Gaynor belted out "I'm Gonna Wash That Man Right Outta My Hair," and "Bloody Mary" warbled "Bali Hai" on the shores of Hanalei Bay in Joshua Logan's *South Pacific*.

Steven Spielberg and George Lucas shot the opening scenes of *Raiders of the Lost Ark* on Kauai and passed it off as South America. They came back for more Kauai footage in *Indiana Jones and the Temple of Doom*. Dino DeLaurentiis' remake of *King Kong*, with Jessica Lange and Jeff Bridges, also had scenes filmed in the lush areas of Kauai. Those same areas became a Vietnam war zone in *Uncommon Valor*, starring Gene Hackman. The drier parts of Kauai suddenly became Australia in Richard Chamberlain's *The Thorn Birds*, a miniseries on TV.

Other films shot on Kauai include: *None But the Brave*, starring Frank Sinatra; John Ford's *Donovan's Reef*, starring John Wayne and Cesar Romero; and *Last Flight of Noah's Ark*, with Elliot Gould, Genevieve Bujold and Ricky Schroeder.

BASICS

GETTING AROUND

Airport

Kauai is served by the main airport in Lihue and a small commuter airport at Princeville near Hanalei. Like all so-called "neighbor islands," transportation to and from the airports is by taxi or prearranged limo, if you are not picking up a rental car.

Budget 245-9031 mustang — 299 → Miata

Cars

Kauai is small and does not have many roads. You may decide to rely on taxis and tour operators to get you where you want to go, but it is expensive. Many taxi companies also offer tours, but a rental car is probably your best best, for the freedom it gives you in exploring. Agencies: **Alamo** (246-0645), **Avis** (Lihue, 245-3512; Princeville, 926-9773), **Budget** (245-9031), **Dollar** (245-3651), **Hertz** (Lihue, 245-3356; Princeville, 826-7455), **Honolulu Rent-a-Car** (245-8726), **National Car Rental** (245-3502), **Thrifty** (Lihue, 245-7388; Hanalei, 826-6230), **Tropical** (245-6988), **United** (245-8894). Serving the Poipu area are **Budget** (742-1558) and **Westside U-Drive** (332-8644). For exotic car rentals try **Fantasy Auto** (245-3006) or **Garden Island Exoticars** (826-1138). **Sunshine Rent-a-Car** rents sports cars and jeeps (245-9541).

Sunshine → Budget

Taxis

Taxis are metered at $1 for the first one-eighth mile, 20 cents each additional mile, 25 cents per bag and $3 per surfboard or bicycle. Companies that serve Lihue include **Abba Taxi** (245-5225), **Green Island Taxi** (245-2723) and **Kauai Cab** (246-9544). In Wailua, try **ABC** (822-7641) or **Akiko's** (822-3613); in Poipu, there's **Al's** (742-1390) and **Poipu Taxi** (742-1717); and in Hanalei there's **North Shore Cab** (826-6189); . For special occasions, **Krystal Karriage Kompany** offers horse-drawn taxi and sightseeing tours (822-4485).

TELEPHONE NUMBERS

Airports
Lihue 246-1400
Princeville 826-3040
Chamber of Commerce 245-7363
Civil Defense 245-4001, 742-1373
Coast Guard .... (800) 331-6176
Directory Assistance (local) 411
(interisland) 1-555-1212
Emergency
(Ambulance, Fire, Rescue, Police) 911
Helpline 245-3411
Hospital 245-1100
Hyperbaric Center, Honolulu 1-523-9155
Library Information 245-3617
Marine Forecasts 245-3564
Poison Control Center .... (800) 362-3585
Postal Information 245-4994
Time 245-0212
Visitors Information Bureau 245-3971
Weather 245-6001

GOINGS-ON

Be sure to check the *Garden Island* newspaper and listen to KAUI-720 AM radio during the early morning for the exact times of these and other events.

February

- **Captain Cook Festival**, including a Waimea Town Party, canoe race, reenactment of Cook's landing, food, games, craft booths, cultural exhibits, fun run and a luau. Call Elizabeth Faye; 338-1625.
- **LPGA Women's Kemper Open Golf Tournament**, including Helene Curtis Pro-Am, $400,000 purse. Mirage Princeville Golf Course, Princeville Resort; 826-3580.

March

- **Prince Kuhio Festival**, Jonah Kuhio Kalanianaole, born March 26, 1871, on Kauai, might have been Hawaii's next king, except that Hawaii became part of the United States. He was elected to Congress in 1902. This is a state holiday, but Kauai makes a real show of it: pageantry, songs and dances from the era of Prince Kuhio, canoe races, and festivities in Lihue and other towns—all culminating in a royal ball; 245-3971.

April

- **Buddha Day**, celebrated on all islands, close to April 8; 245-3971.
- **Kauai Kite Festival**, mid-April; Kilohana; 822-9083.
- **Polo season** begins, through the spring and summer at the polo field; Anini Beach Park on the North Shore; 245-3971.

May

- **Fiesta Filipina**, colorful Filipino ceremonies at various places on Kauai, with Miss Kauai Filipina contest; 245-3971.
- **Ke Ola Hou Hawaiian Spring Festival**, featuring Hawaiian arts and crafts, hula, foods, games, Tahitian competition, contests and entertainment; Hanapepe; 335-5765 or 335-6466.
- **Lei Day**, Saturday closest to May 1, with lei-making contests, displays and other events; Kauai Museum; 245-6931.

June

- **Bon Season** begins, through August, with a Buddhist temple hosting a Bon Odori festival each weekend. Check newspapers or call Hawaii Visitors Bureau; 245-3971.
- **Bougainvillea Festival**, Hanapepe; 245-3971.
- **King Kamehameha Day**, (June 11) includes islandwide festivities, such as a parade and arts and crafts booths; 245-3971.

July

- **Kekaha Fourth of July Celebration**, including entertainment, food booths, festivities and fireworks; Kekaha; 337-1671 or 338-1122.
- **King Kong Ultra Triathlon**, Participants swim across Hanalei Bay and back (about two miles), bicycle to Waimea and back to Wailua (about 90 miles), and run the Powerline Trail to Princeville (about eighteen miles). A benefit for the Kauai Loves You Triathlon and the Gorilla Foundation; Hanalei; 826-9343.
- **Koloa Plantation Days**, celebrating the opening of the sugar plantations, including a historical parade, entertainment, crafts, games and a luau; 742-7444 or 742-6534.

August

- **Admission Day**, August 21, a state holiday; 245-3971.
- **Pooku Hanalei Stampede**, the biggest rodeo event of the season, drawing cowboys from all islands. Barbecue, country music and dancing; Hanalei; 826-6777.
- **Tahiti Fête**, a reenactment of the Tahitians' landing on Kauai. Held the third week in August; Kapaa; 822-3630 or 822-3441.

September

- **Aloha Week**, celebrated on all islands in September and October, includes Hawaiian pageantry, canoe races, street parties, a parade and entertainment; 245-3971.
- **Hawaii State Golf Tournament**, Wailua Golf Course; 245-2163.
- **Kauai County Fair**, exhibits, produce, flowers, livestock and entertainment. Kauai War Memorial Convention Hall; Lihue; 245-3971

- **Kauai Mokihana Festival**, a series of events focusing on Hawaiian music and dance. Includes Kauai Composer Contest and Concert, and a modern hula competition; Waimea and Lihue; 245-1955.
- **Polynesian Sailing Canoe Race**, Oahu to Kauai, ending at the Westin Kauai; Lihue; 245-5050.

October

- **Kauai Loves You Triathlon**, a 1.5-mile swim, a 54-mile bike ride and a 12.4-mile run; Hanalei ; (800) 247-9201 or 822-0902.

November

- **Annual Garden Island Triple Feature**, with visitors and residents competing in 2-, 5- and 10-kilometer runs along the Poipu coastline. Prizes provided by merchants. A Rehabilitation Unlimited fund-raiser; 245-7255.
- **Garden Island Half-Marathon and 5K Run**; 245-3971.
- **Thanksgiving Day on Kauai**, services with Hawaiian hymns; 245-3971.
- **Underwater Film Festival**, the best from around the world each year, with filmmakers on hand to talk about them; 245-3971.

December

- **Bodhi Day**, the traditional Buddhist Day of Enlightenment, celebrated by Buddhist temples on all islands in early December, Hawaii Buddhist Council; 1-522-9200.
- **Christmas in Waimea**, candlelight tour of missions and churches, caroling and displays of the Twelve Days of Christmas, Hawaiian-style; 245-3971.
- **Kauai Museum Holiday Festival**, a Christmas sale of handcrafted gifts and baked goods; Lihue; 245-6931.

LANAI

RESTAURANTS

Lodge at Koele Dining Room
Lanai City
• 565-7245
NEW AMERICAN/
HAWAIIAN

The best part of any stay at this lodge is the food. Unfortunately, it is too soon to rate the restaurant, although our initial experiences have been very good. The creative menu, designed by executive chef John Farnsworth, who has been with Rockresorts since 1976, features local island food, grown on the lodge's organic farm; beef and pork are raised at the resorts' cattle ranch. Breakfast might include a zucchini omelette made of Lanai farm eggs with fresh basil and Gruyère cheese, sweet rice waffles with lilikoi-coconut chutney and warm Vermont maple syrup, and poached eggs on Kona crabcakes with watercress-tomato hollandaise. Our favorites for lunch are: the seared ahi on a salad of field greens and vegetables with a cilantro dressing; grilled pastrami of striped marlin served on a tomato-fennel salad; seared veal sirloin with stewed leeks and straw-potato cakes. Dinners can be delightful as well. Farnsworth combines his fourteen years of experience in preparing tropical Caribbean dishes with the challenge of creating innovative ways to prepare the local fish and game of Hawaii. We loved an appetizer of marble of ahi and snapper, which is a molded ball of pink-and-white swirls on a bed of crisp radish, fennel and mustard seed; also delicious are the tiger prawns in a spicy piri-piri sauce served with a cooling side dish of melon-and-basil relish. The entrées are well suited to such a rugged destination. For example, there's a Lanai mixed grill of pheasant, quail and axis deer sausage prepared in a Pinot Noir reduction; loin of lamb with carrot dauphinoise and yellow split peas; charred mignon of pork with black-bean sauce and corn cakes. Desserts, like all of the presentations, are a feast for both eye and palate: a simple freshly made raspberry sorbet, scooped in three equal balls, rides a garland of fresh blueberries and is topped by three macaroon slices, the whole thing dusted in powdered sugar—all laid out on a black-glass plate with a sprig of wintergreen as an accent mark. Wonderful. The wine list features domestic, French, Italian and Australian labels, with more-than-ample selection: from Tedeschi Vineyards' Maui Blanc Dry Pineapple Wine (which can be purchased as a gag gift, but never taken internally), to Big-Boy French reds, Pauillac 1979. Château Yquem 1982 and Soleil David Stare (Dry Creek) 1986. Dinner for two with wine will cost $175.
Open daily 6 a.m.-9:30 p.m. All major cards.

WORTH THE WAIT

How long does it take to grow a pineapple? After all, they look big, but not that big. You'll have to wait somewhere between a year and a half and two years to enjoy the fruit, which, by the way, was brought to the Islands by the Tahitians.

HOTELS

LUXURY

Lodge at Koele
Lanai City 96763
• 565-7245
Fax 565-6477

Lanai City is a small plantation town, where the 2,000 residents not only know their neighbors, but heartily wave at the island's new spectacle—tourists. Where could these newfound visitors be headed? If they're lucky (and they probably are, since there are only three spots to stay on Lanai), it's the new Lodge at Koele. This unique Rockresorts-managed property reigns supreme at 1,700 feet, above Lanai City. The 102-room lodge is reminiscent of a fine English country estate. The architectural details are overflowing with "good-life" goodies, such as polished eucalyptus floors, beam ceilings, field-stone fireplaces, beveled-glass windows and overstuffed reading chairs. For music buffs, consider the music room, complete with antique instruments. Guests enter the massive "Great Hall" (read, "The Lobby") and are warmed by the two roaring fireplaces that comfortably offset the temperature at this altitude. More nice surprises await in the rooms: the beds are four-poster; the porches all overlook the manicured grounds. Both the wooden writing desk and the upholstered window seat are fine touches, indeed. VCRs and a well-stocked video library will intrigue videophiles. The landscaped grounds are a combination of 100-foot Cook Island pines and ancient banyan, eucalyptus and jacaranda trees and just-planted Hawaiian and Japanese botanical gardens. A nearby reservoir is stocked with fish. Lodge activities include: hunting, horseback riding, jeep rides, skeet shooting, tennis, swimming, croquet, lawn bowling, picnicking, hiking, and all beach and boating activities. A shuttle is available to Manele Bay Hotel and Hulopoe Beach. The lodge soon will have its own championship mountain golf course, designed by Greg Norman.
Singles: $275-$350; suites: $425-$900.

> ### PINEAPPLE PALACE
>
> Lanai, aptly named the "Pineapple Isle," is literally a giant pineapple plantation. The luxe new Lodge at Koele, owned by L.A. developer David Murdock, is located on the island's only accessible white-sand beach, but life on Lanai revolves around the small village of Lanai City, in the clouds at 1,620 feet.

Manele Bay Hotel
Hulopoe Bay 96763
• 565-7245
Fax 565-6477

Some 250 luxury villas and suites, housed in nineteen elegant two-story buildings, will overlook the island of Kahoolawe from high above the white-sand beach of Hulopoe Bay on the south shore of Lanai. The architecture is a unique blend of traditional

Hawaiian and Mediterranean featuring formal gardens and lavishly landscaped courtyards with waterfalls and ponds. Activities include: tennis, swimming, snorkeling, scuba diving, horseback riding, archaeological walks, boat trips. Shuttle to The Lodge at Koele.

Rates were not set at press time, but are estimated to begin at $295.

SIGHTS & SPORTS

BEACHES	314
EXCURSIONS	315
SPORTS	316

BEACHES

Hulopoe Beach
End of Rte. 441

Lanai doesn't have a lot of accessible white-sand beaches, but this one is the island's best, and one of the prettiest in the state. There's excellent snorkeling around the lava pool and near the rocks on both ends of the beach. The well-protected beach is also a good swimming area. Hulopoe is a protected marine conservation area, and fishing is forbidden in the bay.

Manele Bay
End of Rte. 441

Located adjacent to Hulopoe Bay, Manele is primarily a small-boat harbor, and a good place to "talk story" with local fishermen and visiting yachties.

Polihua Beach
11 miles north of Lanai City through pineapple fields

An isolated white-sand beach on the generally windy northwest shore of the island. On calm days, diving for lobster here is excellent. Fishing is generally good year-round, especially for papio and ulua.

Shipwreck Beach
Rte. 44

This is a beachcomber's dream come true. The series of white-sand patches are the recycling center of the sea. Glass balls, old fishing equipment, and tons of junk float up on these beaches all year long. Some local residents come here to gather everything from mismatched slippers to styrofoam ice chests.

EXCURSIONS

Munro Trail
Rte. 44,
Koele

Just outside Lanai City, a trail named after New Zealand naturalist George Munro begins. This seven-mile jeep trail climbs upward through rain forest and groves of Norfolk pines, offering spectacular views in the process. Once you reach the top, Lanaihale, the highest point on Lanai (3,370 feet), you can see Oahu, Molokai, Maui, Kahoolawe, and the peaks of the Big Island volcanoes.

Shipwreck Beach-Kahea Heiau
Eastern shoreline

At the northern end of the eastern shoreline, off a dirt road, lies Shipwreck Beach. True to its name, the coral reef outside the beach has snatched ships since the whaling days. The rusting hulk slowly eroding offshore is left over from World War II. Moving south on the bone-jarring dirt road leads to a white-paint marked path showing the way to ancient Hawaiian petroglyphs—carvings in stone depicting aspects of Hawaiian life. Ten miles south is a ghost town, Keomuku. Once a booming headquarters for the Maunalei Sugar Company, the town closed down in 1901 when the water supply mysteriously turned brackish and undrinkable. Hawaiians say ill fortune befell Keomuku because the company used sacred stones from the Kahea Heiau to build the plantation town.

THE ORIGINAL GHOSTBUSTER

According to the ancient legends, Lanai was once inhabited by evil spirits, and Hawaiians didn't live on the island for nearly 1,000 years for that very reason. The first Hawaiian to set foot on Lanai was a juvenile delinquent. Kaululaau, son of the Maui king, Kaalaneo, just loved to pull up breadfruit trees in his home town of Lahaina. The king kept trying to stop Kaululaau's breadfruit rampages, since it was a staple crop, but his young son persisted. Finally in frustration, the king sentenced his son to the spookyard of Lanai. He figured that either the evil spirits would kill the boy, or his son would grow up real fast.

Once on the island, Kaululaau hid in caves during the night and tracked down the evil ghosts during the day, killing them one by one. When the last one was killed, he returned to Maui, a reformed man. He could have been the original ghostbuster. To this day no breadfruit trees grow on Lanai, the legend goes, because Kaululaau couldn't resist pulling them all up in his exile.

SPORTS

Golf

**Lodge at Koele
Golf Course**
Lodge at Koele,
P.O. Box 774,
Lanai City
• 565-7245

Still on the drawing board as we went to press, the eighteen-hole course will be Australian Greg Norman's first in the United States. According to the proposed plan, the course will take advantage of the Norfolk and Scotch pines that have flourished in Koele for years. There will be one departure from the Hawaiian golf tradition of planting Bermuda grass: the Koele course will be sown with Bent grass. The plans call for nine holes to be situated on a high plateau overlooking the Pacific Ocean and nine holes in the mountain valley surrounded by the pines.

**Manele Bay
Hotel Golf
Course**
P.O. Box 774,
Lanai City
• 565-7245

Plans for this course-to-be are even sketchier. Proposals call for the course to hug the rugged Lanai shoreline and feature narrow fairways in the midst of native vegetation, which right now is scrub kiawe trees. Planners would like to see the course dotted with dramatic water holes, reminiscent of Pebble Beach.

THE GARDEN OF THE GODS

At the end of the Awalua Highway, beyond the pineapple fields, is a strange phenomenon that remains unexplained even today. The local residents call it the Garden of the Gods. Here, seven miles from Lanai City, lie oddly strewn boulders and bizarre-shaped lava formations. Nowhere else on Lanai are rocks and lava formations found such as those at the Garden. Local legend claims the rocks dropped from the sky—and, in fact, at night you can sometimes hear the spirits whistling as they tend to their garden.

Tennis

The **Maui County Department of Parks and Recreation**(Lanai District Office; 565-6979) has courts available free to the public on a first-come, first-served basis. The courts are also lit for night play with a simple self-serve device.

BASICS

GETTING AROUND

L anai Airport is served by **Aloha Island Air** and **Hawaiian Airlines**. Lanai Airport is four miles from Lanai City; it's really just a landing strip. If you are staying at Hotel Lanai, transportation to town is provided. If you are renting a vehicle, the garage will pick you up. Keep in mind that there are very few paved roads on Lanai! If you want to explore, you'll want a four-wheel-drive jeep or similar vehicle. Cars and jeeps may be rented from **Lanai City Service & U-Drive** (565-7227) and **Oshiro Service & U-Drive** (565-6952). Oshiro also provides tours.

TELEPHONE NUMBERS

Airport 565-6757
Camping 565-6661
Directory Assistance (local) 411
    (interisland) 1-555-1212
Emergency
    (Ambulance, Fire & Rescue) 911
Hospital 565-6411
Library Information 565-6996
Postal Information 565-6517
Weather 565-6033

MOLOKAI

HOTELS

PRACTICAL

Hotel Molokai
P.O. Box 546,
Kaunakakai
• 553-5347
No fax

Located two miles outside of Kaunakakai, the Hotel Molokai is a complex of wooden Polynesian-style, A-frame buildings housing 57 units. The best bet here is to reserve a deluxe room that has a high ceiling, a lanai, small refrigerator, and a large plate-glass window. Other amenities include a pool, restaurant and bar, and gift shop. TV rentals available. Good budget hotel. *Rooms: $55-$115.*

Kaluakoi Hotel and Golf Club
Kepuhi Beach,
• 552-2555
Fax 526-2017

Molokai's top hotel is located near a three-mile-long white-sand beach. The 292-room hotel is on the west end of the island where the beaches are grand, but the area is arid and nearly always windy. The rooms are comfortable and well furnished. Amenities include restaurant, lounge, pool, tennis courts, a golf course, and a fabulous view of Diamond Head on Oahu. *Rooms: $95-$240.*

Pau Hana Inn
P.O. Box 860,
Kaunakakai
• 553-5342
No fax

Molokai's oldest hotel has 39 rooms scattered throughout buildings and cottages spread over the lush surrounding lawn. The budget standard rooms are just that—small, with twin beds and little decor. We recommend the deluxe units, which have a lanai and fan (some have tiny kitchenettes). Amenities include a small pool, restaurant, and bar. *Rooms: $45-$85.*

Wavecrest Resort
Star Rte. 155,
Ualapue
• 558-8101
No fax

Only a few of the 126 units in this condominium complex are available for rent. The units are one or two bedrooms, all with ocean views, full kitchen and all necessary furnishings. Amenities include pool, lighted tennis courts, shuffleboard and putting green. No restaurant or lounge. Unfortunately, the beach out front is not good for swimming; however, an excellent swimming-snorkeling beach is just five miles away. *Rooms: $61-$81.*

SIGHTS & SPORTS

BEACHES

East End
Rte. 45, from the
18-mile marker on

A series of beaches lines the east end of Molokai, after the eighteen-mile marker on the road. These white-sand spots are the stuff of which dreams are made: not only are they physically beautiful, but frequently they are completely free of humanity. Who says it can't be done in Hawaii!

Halawa Park
End of Rte. 45

At the very eastern end of Molokai is the tropical paradise people visualize when they think of Hawaii—palm trees border the beach with grassy fields behind and waterfalls cascading in the distance. Although sometimes windy, this is one of the best surfing spots on the island.

Kawakiu Bay
Molokai Ranch
• 553-5115

Facing Honolulu, Kawakiu is a white-sand beach that gently slopes down into the sandy-bottomed ocean. Access to this popular camping area is through Molokai Ranch, and you must call them to get the key to open the gates. A shady grove of trees borders the beach on one side, and rocky coastline defines the outer boundaries.

Moomomi Beach (Homestead Moomomi)
Farrington Ave.
• 567-6104

For lovers of the remote, this is the place. Excellent swimming in the bay by the Hawaiian Homes pavilion. If you get a pass from the Department of Hawaiian Homes in advance, you can even spend the night in this romantic spot.

Onealii Beach Park
Rte. 45, Kaunakakai

Picture a beach park out of yesteryear: spacious grassy playing field, coconut grove, picnic area, and loads of white sand. The shallow waters and offshore reef make this an ideal swimming area for small children or novice snorkelers. One problem: the park is so popular with local residents that it is very crowded on weekends.

Papohaku Beach
Kalukoi Road

The largest white-sand beach on Molokai, over two miles long and a 100 yards wide, with a view of Oahu on the horizon. The best activity here is just relaxing. Use caution when swimming, as rip currents and strong, alongshore currents persist throughout the year. Fishing for reef fish can be productive, and surfing is occasionally good when the wind is right.

EXCURSIONS

East End
Rte. 45

Kaunakakai, the business center of the island, is a quiet two-street town with false-front buildings. Shopping here means buying staples—food and farm supplies. Before leaving town, check out the remains of King Kamehameha V's summer house next to the pier. The view alone will tell you why Hawaii's monarch chose this spot to vacation. Heading east on Route 45, this tiny two-lane road meanders through the remains of Molokai's past. Just outside town, a Hawaii Visitors' Bureau marker notes the sight of a famous battleground where Kamehameha the Great landed his canoe flotilla, which supposedly covered four miles of the shoreline. Farther down the road are ancient fish ponds, where the Hawaiians practiced aquaculture. The largest pond on the coast is Keawanui Pond, built for one of Molokai's chiefs. At the 25-mile marker are the ruins of Molokai's first sugar mill. At the end of the road lies Halawa Valley, a lush valley bordered by sheer cliffs and tumbling waterfalls on one side and crashing surf on the other. It was once home to thousands of Hawaiian people.

A SPOOKY GROVE

Near the end of the east end of Molokai, just beyond the Puu O Hoku (Hill of Stars) Ranch stands a grove of kukui trees. Even today, as people pass the gray-barked, silvery-leafed trees, there is an eerie atmosphere emanating from the grove. Molokai, at one time, was the gathering place of powerful *kahunas* (priests). In the midst of the grove lived one of the most powerful, Lanikaula. The Hawaiians refuse to go there, claiming the powerful *mana* (spirit) of the kahunas remains there.

A few years ago, a tenant on land near the grove cut down a few trees to plant pineapple. The pineapples flourished all around the grove, but those planted where the trees were cut down wilted and died. Go figure.

Molokai Forest Reserve
Main Forest Rd.

Molokai may appear flat, but it actually has a substantial upland wooded area. In fact, at one time this area was filled with giant sandalwood trees. Nine miles down Main Forest Road is a huge depression cut into the hill. Lua Moku Iliahi (Sandalwood Measuring Pit) is an area the Hawaiians cut into the earth to measure the hull size of old sailing ships, so they would know how much sandalwood was needed for a full load. Unfortunately too many of these depressions were filled and the sandalwood has all but disappeared. Farther down the road is the Waikolu Picnic Grove, a woody area complete with picnic tables, outhouse, and running water. Adjacent is the Waikolu Valley Lookout, with a view of spectacular Waikolu Valley and the ocean, some 3,000 feet below.

West End
Rtes. 46 & 47

Heading west out of Kaunakakai is a seemingly unending stand of coconut trees. Kiowea Park and Kapuaiwa Grove were planted in 1860 by Kamehameha V. Across the street from the grove is church row—seven different denominations, all filled on Sundays, a testament to the influence of missionaries in the Hawaiian Islands.

Take the side road, Route 47, up to the Kalaupapa Lookout, for a bird's-eye view of Kalaupapa National Historical Park. Designated in 1980, it is one of our newest national parks and is well worth your attention. This beautiful peninsula, cut off by the steepest cliffs in the world, was used from 1866 until just over twenty years ago as a place to which those suffering from Hansen's Disease (leprosy) were sent—a lifelong exile. It was to this hopeless community that Father Damien, a Belgian priest, came in 1873 to ease the suffering of the afflicted. Eventually succumbing to leprosy himself, Father Damien devoted his life to restoring the dignity of these unfortunates, inspiring others to follow in his footsteps after his death in 1889. (Father Damien is being considered for sainthood by the Church; but locals already consider him a saint.) With the introduction of sulfone drugs in the 1940s, Hansen's Disease was brought under control; today's Kalaupapa residents remain there through choice and frequently enjoy trips to the mainland.

PHALLIC ROCK

On the 2,000-foot cliffs overlooking the Kalaupapa Peninsula, the highest cliffs in the world, is an interesting geological formation, Ka Ule O Nanahoa. Standing in the middle of a grove of ironwood trees is an anatomically shaped, six-foot-long phallic rock, which legend says cures infertility in women.

It is possible to hike or take a mule down, or fly into the settlement, but whichever method you choose, you must contact Damien's Tours first at 567-6171. They offer the only tour of Kalaupapa, and limit the numbers visiting out of respect for the residents. (For further information, see "Tours" section, page 326.) Next to the lookout is Phallic Rock. Back on Route 46, the highway passes through former pineapple fields and by the old pineapple plantation town Maunaloa, which is now fading into oblivion. At the end of the road lies the Kaluakoi Hotel, a 292-room hotel, complete with pool, tennis courts, golf course, and restaurant.

PARKS

One of our newest national parks (designated in 1980) **Kalaupapa National Historical Park**, on the west end of Molokai, is well worth a visit (see information above and in the "Tours" section, page 326). Another beautiful spot, set in a forest away from the beach, the 34-acre **Palaau State Park** (off Route 47 in Kalae; 567-6083) offers hiking on easy trails, ancient petroglyphs, the **Phallic Rock**, **Kalaupapa Lookout** and complete park facilities.

SPORTS

Fishing

Alyce C
P.O. Box 825,
Kaunakakai
• 558-8377

Not exactly the sportfishing capital of Hawaii, Molokai does have one charter boat, captained by Joe Reich. When the customers are few and far between, he goes commercial fishing, so he always knows where the fish are biting. Charters are available daily.
Cost $200 per half day & $300 per full day.

Golf

Kaluakoi Golf Course
Kaluakoi Resort
P.O. Box 26,
Maunaloa,
Molokai
• 552-2739

Designed by Ted Robinson, this par-72, 6,618-yard golf course meanders along the ocean (six holes along the shoreline) and through the woods (where wild turkeys come out to watch the golfers). Our vote for toughest hole is the par-4, 373-yard seventh tee, which is smack into the trade winds. The most scenic hole is the sixteenth, a par 3 over a gorge.
Tee times Mon.-Fri. begin at 7:30 a.m., Sat.-Sun & holidays at 7 a.m. Last tee time 4 p.m. $45 for resort guests, $65 for others (includes cart).

Hiking

For information on trails, hiking and camping on the island of Molokai, contact the following organizations: **Hawaiian Homes** (P.O Box 198, Hoolehua, Molokai; 567-6104), which is run by the State Department of Hawaii; the **Maui County Department of Parks and Recreation** (P.O. Box 526, Kaunakakai, Molokai; 553-5141); and the **State Department of Land and Natural Resources** (Palaau Park Office, Kalae, Molokai; 567-6083).

Halawa Valley Trail
Rte. 45,
Halawa Valley

This is on the "must-do" list for active Molokai visitors. At the base of the lush Halawa Valley is a well-marked, four-mile round-trip hike to the base of Moaula Falls. It's also easy. The trail passes through fruit trees, ancient Hawaiian house sites, ferns, and swarms of mosquitoes. The reward is Moaula Falls, a 250-foot waterfall that thunders down a sheer wall into an ice-cold, deep-mountain pool, which is perfect for swimming.

A NASTY LIZARD

On the north end of the slender slipper of Molokai is the home of a giant lizard, Mo'o. He lives at the bottom of the pool at Moaula Falls, a 250-foot-long cascading waterfall in Halawa Valley. The hike up to Moaula Falls is usually a sweaty affair, and hikers are lured by the refreshment of the deep-water pool. The legend warns, however, that would-be swimmers must first ask permission from Mo'o, by throwing a ti leaf into the pool. If the ti leaf floats, then Mo' o is not at home and it's safe to swim. If it sinks, an angry Mo'o will come out of his underwater lair and drag swimmers under, pulling them down to his Neptunian cave.

Snorkeling

Molokai Fish & Dive Corp.
Kaunakakai
• 553-5926

No longer renting or filling tanks, they will rent mask, snorkel, and fins, and point out some great spots to go snorkeling. *Open Mon -Fri. 9 a.m.-6 p.m., Sat. 8 a.m.-6 p.m. & Sun. 8 a.m.-2 p.m. Rental $6.98 per day.*

Tennis

Maui County Department of Parks and Recreation
Mitchell Pauole Center,
Kaunakakai
• 553-5141

These are Molokai's only public tennis courts, all two of them, both lit for night play. The facility is operated on a first-come, first-served basis.
Open daily, lights on till 10:30 p.m. every night.

CANOE RACE

Every October, about 50 international teams compete in the Bankoh Molokai Hoe (the Bank of Hawaii Men's Molokai-to-Oahu Canoe Race). For information, call Ocean Promotion in Honolulu (842-5500). The race crosses the rough Molokai Channel and finishes in Waikiki, Oahu.

TOURS

Father Damien Tours
P.O. Box 1,
Kalaupapa
• 567-6171

This is the only tour of the former Hansen's Disease (leprosy) settlement on the Kalaupapa Peninsula. It takes all day to visit this incredibly beautiful, but sad area, where leprosy victims were sent involuntarily from 1866-1969. The tour will pick up clients either at the small airport, or at the bottom of the Kalaupapa Trail. Visitors tour the small village, which hasn't changed in 40 years (in fact, the residents still drive cars of 1950s vintage); historic sites, such as Father Damien's church and monument; and the rugged coastline. There is a stop for a picnic lunch, which you must provide as no food is available on the peninsula. Minimum age on the tour is 16. The maximum number of people allowed on the peninsula at one time is 40, to protect the privacy of the residents.
Tours daily, 10:15 a.m.-3 p.m. Cost $40.

Molokai Mule Ride
P.O. Box 200,
Kualapuu
• 567-6088

Atop a mule's back is the only way to traverse the steep, switchback trail that descends from "top side" down to the Kalaupapa Peninsula. The tour includes three hours astride a slow but sure-footed mule, an additional three-hour tour of the peninsula in a van (but not the Hansen's Disease settlement— see entry above), and an hour for lunch.
Tours daily 8:30 a.m-4 p.m. Cost $78.

BASICS

GETTING AROUND

Molokai airport is served by **Aloha Island Air** and **Hawaiian Airlines**. The airport is seven miles from Kaunakakai. For taxis, call **Molokai Taxi** (552-0041) or **TEEM Cab** (553-3433). **Gray Line** (567-6177) and **Robert's Hawaii** (552-2751) provide tours and transportation. Rentals cars and jeeps are available from **Budget** (567-6877), **Dollar** (567-6156) and **Tropical** (567-6118).

There is a small airstrip at Kalaupapa, Molokai. Aloha Island Air lands there, but each person on board must have a "sponsor." Arrangements will be made through **Damien Tours** if you are taking the Kalaupapa settlement tour.

TELEPHONE NUMBERS

Airport 567-6140
Directory Assistance (local) 411
    (interisland) 1-555-1212
Emergency
    (Ambulance, Fire & Rescue) 911
Hospital 553-5331
Library Information 553-5483
Marine Forecasts...................................552-2477
Parks 553-5141
Postal Information 553-5845
Weather 552-2477

MAPS

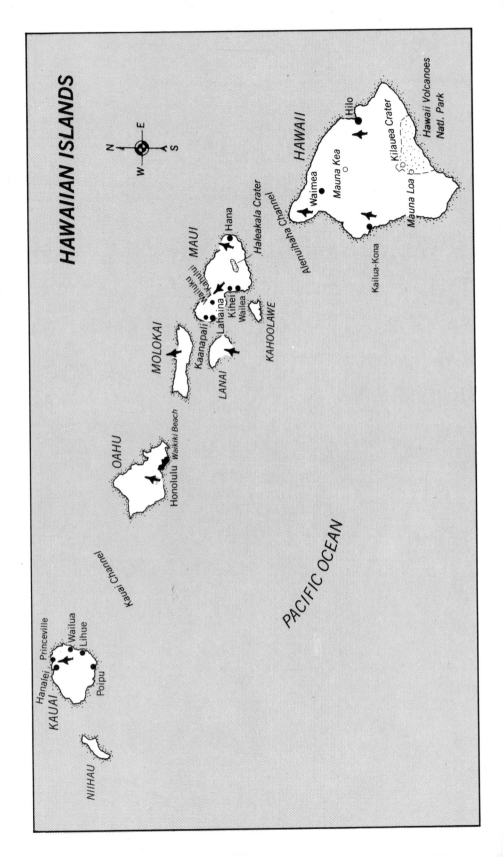

HAWAIIAN ISLANDS

PACIFIC OCEAN

NIIHAU

KAUAI
Hanalei
Princeville
Wailua
Lihue
Poipu

Kauai Channel

OAHU
Honolulu Waikiki Beach

MOLOKAI

MAUI
Kaanapali
Lahaina
Kihei
Wailea
Kahului
Wailuku
Hana
Haleakala Crater

LANAI

KAHOOLAWE

Alenuihaha Channel

HAWAII
Waimea
Hilo
Mauna Kea
Kilauea Crater
Mauna Loa
Kailua-Kona
Hawaii Volcanoes
Natl. Park

N E S W

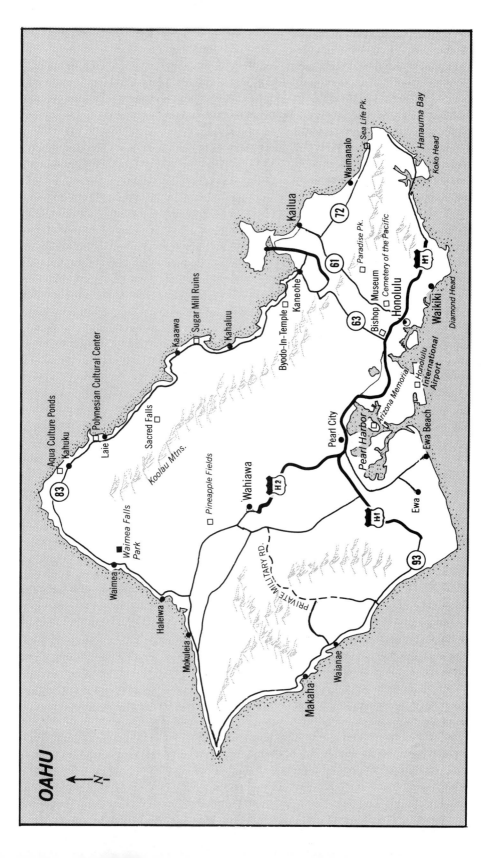

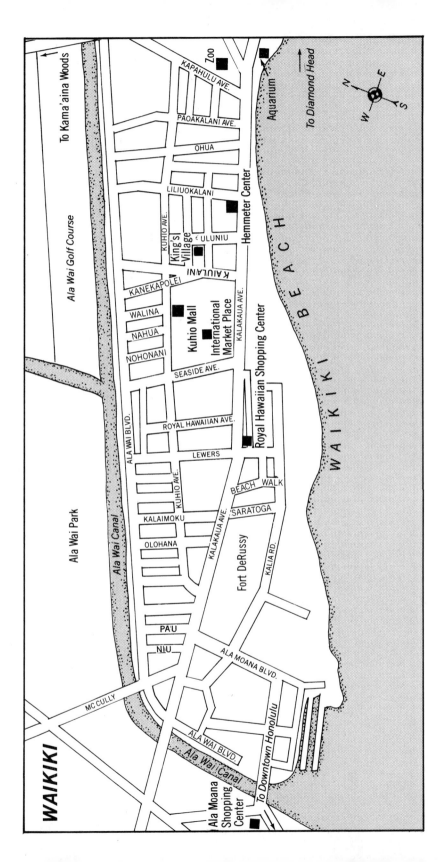

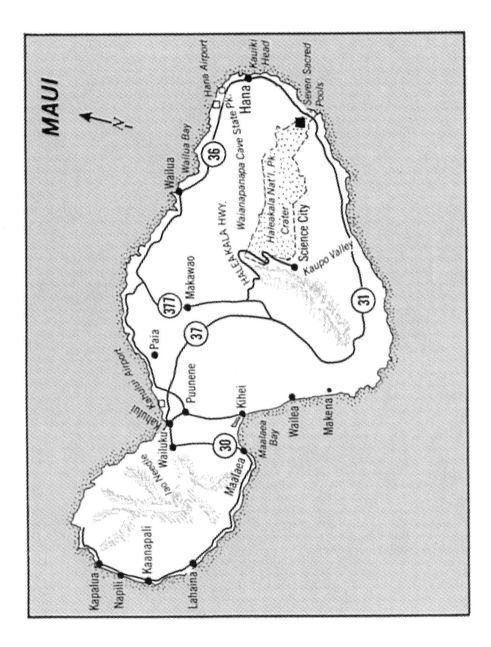

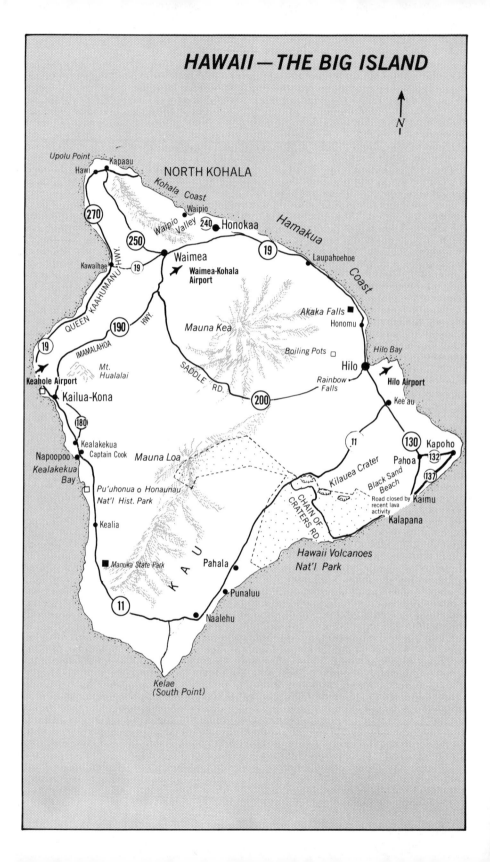

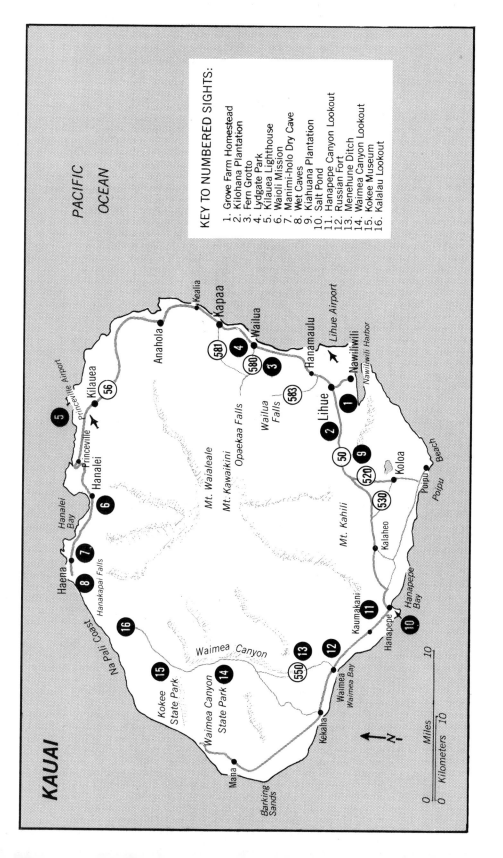

KAUAI

PACIFIC

OCEAN

KEY TO NUMBERED SIGHTS:

1. Grove Farm Homestead
2. Kilohana Plantation
3. Fern Grotto
4. Lydgate Park
5. Kilauea Lighthouse
6. Waioli Mission
7. Manimi-holo Dry Cave
8. Wet Caves
9. Kiahuana Plantation
10. Salt Pond
11. Hanapepe Canyon Lookout
12. Russian Fort
13. Menehune Ditch
14. Waimea Canyon Lookout
15. Kokee Museum
16. Kalalau Lookout

Kealia
Kapaa
Wailua
Anahola
Hanamaulu
Lihue Airport
581
580
583
Nawiliwili
Kilauea
Princeville Airport
56
Wailua Falls
Opaekaa Falls
Lihue
Nawiliwili Harbor
Princeville
Hanalei
Hanalei Bay
Mt. Waialeale
Mt. Kawaikini
50
520
Koloa
Poipu Beach
Poipu
Haena
530
Hanakapai Falls
Mt. Kahili
Kalaheo
Na Pali Coast
Kaumakani
Hanapepe
Hanapepe Bay
Waimea Canyon
550
Waimea Bay
Waimea
Kokee State Park
Waimea Canyon State Park
Kekaha
Mana
Barking Sands

N

Miles   10
Kilometers   10
0
0

INDEX

MORE *GAULT MILLAU* GUIDES TO THE BEST

Now the guidebook series known throughout Europe for its wit and savvy reveals the best of major U.S., European and Asian destinations. **Gault Millau** books include full details on the best of everything that makes these places special: the restaurants, diversions, nightlife, hotels, shops and arts. The guides offer practical information on getting around and enjoying the area—perfect for visitors and residents alike.

Please send me the books checked below:

☐ The Best of Chicago $15.95
☐ The Best of London $16.95
☐ The Best of Los Angeles $15.95
☐ The Best of New England...$16.95
☐ The Best of New York $16.95
☐ The Best of Paris $16.95
☐ The Best of San Francisco $16.95
☐ The Best of Washington, D.C. $16.95
☐ The Best of France $16.95
☐ The Best of Italy...$16.95
☐ The Best of Hong Kong $16.95

PRENTICE HALL PRESS
Order Department—Travel Books
200 Old Tappan Road
Old Tappan, NJ 07675

In the U.S., include $2 (UPS shipping charge) for the first book, and $1 for each additional book. Outside the U.S., $3 and $1 respectively. Enclosed is my check or money order made out to **Prentice Hall Press**, for $ _____

NAME _____

ADDRESS _____

CITY_____ STATE _____

ZIP _____ COUNTRY_____

André Gayot's
TASTES
with the Best of Gault Millau

THE WORLD DINING & TRAVEL CONNECTION

P.O. Box 361144, Los Angeles, CA 90036

♦ All you'll ever need to know about the beds and tables (and under the tables) of the world.
♦ The best—and other—restaurants, hotels, nightlife, shopping, fashion.
♦ What's hot, lukewarm and cold from Hollywood to Hong Kong via Paris.

☐ **YES,** please enter/renew my subscription for 6 bimonthly issues at the rate of $30. (Outside U.S. and Canada, $35.)

Name_____

Address_____

City_____State _____

Zip_____Country _____

☐ **ALSO,** please send a gift subscription to: *

Name_____

Address_____

City_____State _____

Zip_____Country _____

Gift from_____
(We will notify recipient of your gift)

* With the purchase of a gift subscription or a second subscription, you will receive, **FREE,** the **Gault Millau guidebook of your choice**—a $17 value. (See preceding order form for a complete list of Gault Millau guides.)

☐ CHECK ENCLOSED FOR $ _____.
☐ PLEASE SEND ME, **FREE,** THE GAULT MILLAU GUIDE OF MY CHOICE: _____

312/90